barbecues

and salads

barbecues
and salads

Creative ideas for outdoor eating with more than
400 sizzling barbecue recipes and succulent salads

Christine France and
Steven Wheeler

LORENZ BOOKS

This edition is published by Lorenz Books
Lorenz Books is an imprint of Anness Publishing Ltd, Hermes House, 88–89 Blackfriars Road, London SE1 8HA
tel. 020 7401 2077; fax 020 7633 9499; www.lorenzbooks.com; info@anness.com
© Anness Publishing Ltd 2002, 2006

UK agent: The Manning Partnership Ltd, 6 The Old Dairy, Melcombe Road, Bath BA2 3LR
tel. 01225 478444; fax 01225 478440; sales@manning-partnership.co.uk
UK distributor: Grantham Book Services Ltd, Isaac Newton Way, Alma Park Industrial Estate, Grantham, Lincs NG31 9SD
tel. 01476 541080; fax 01476 541061; orders@gbs.tbs-ltd.co.uk
North American agent/distributor: National Book Network, 4501 Forbes Boulevard, Suite 200, Lanham, MD 20706
tel. 301 459 3366; fax 301 429 5746; www.nbnbooks.com
Australian agent/distributor: Pan Macmillan Australia, Level 18, St Martins Tower, 31 Market St, Sydney, NSW 2000
tel. 1300 135 113; fax 1300 135 103; customer.service@macmillan.com.au
New Zealand agent/distributor: David Bateman Ltd, 30 Tarndale Grove, Off Bush Road, Albany, Auckland
tel. (09) 415 7664; fax (09) 415 8892

Publisher: Joanna Lorenz
Editorial Director: Helen Sudell
Project Editor: Valerie Ferguson
Copy Editor: Linda Doeser
Designers: Bill Mason, Nigel Partridge and Ian Sandom
Jacket Illustration and Design: Katrina Dallaware
Illustrations: Madeleine David, Lucinda Ganderton and Anna Koska
Consultant Editors: Christine France and Steven Wheeler
Photographers: William Adams-Lingwood, Karl Adamson, Edward Allwright, Steve Baxter, James Duncan, John Freeman,
Michelle Garrett, Amanda Heywood, David Jordan, Dave King, Don Last, Patrick McLeavey, Michael Michaels,
Thomas Odulate, Debbie Patterson, Juliet Piddington, Craig Robertson and Simon Smith
Recipes contributed by: Michelle Berriedale Johnson, Angela Boggiano, Janet Brinkworth, Carla Capalbo, Kit Chan, Jacqueline Clark,
Carole Clements, Roz Denny, Nicola Diggins, Matthew Drennan, Joanna Farrow, Rafi Fernandez, Christine France, Silvana Franco,
Brian Glover, Rosamund Grant, Rebekah Hassan, Deh-Ta Hsiung, Christine Ingram, Judy Jackson, Soheila Kimberley, Lucy Knox,
Elisabeth Lambert Ortiz, Ruby Le Bois, Lesley Mackley, Sue Maggs, Maggie Mayhew, Jane Milton, Sallie Morris, Annie Nichols,
Maggie Pannell, Katherine Richmond, Keith Richmond, Anne Sheasby, Liz Trigg, Hilaire Walden, Steven Wheeler, Kate Whiteman,
Elizabeth Wolf-Cohen and Jeni Wright

Previously published as *Barbecue*

1 3 5 7 9 10 8 6 4 2

NOTES
Bracketed terms are intended for American readers.
For all recipes, quantities are given in both metric and imperial measures and, where appropriate, measures are also given in
standard cups and spoons. Follow one set, but not a mixture, because they are not interchangeable.
Standard spoon and cup measures are level. 1 tsp = 5ml, 1 tbsp = 15 ml, 1 cup = 250ml/8fl oz
Australian standard tablespooons are 20ml. Australian readers should use 3 tsp in place of 1 tbsp for measuring
small quantities of gelatine, flour, salt, etc.
Medium (US large) eggs are used unless otherwise stated.

CONTENTS

· · ·

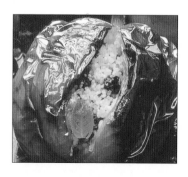

INTRODUCTION

o o o

There is something special about eating outdoors – the appetite is sharpened, the aroma is more tempting, the flavour is enhanced and it is altogether more fun. Whether you are planning an *al fresco* family lunch in the garden, a barbecue for family and friends, a picnic at the coast or a sophisticated summer evening dinner party, you will find the perfect recipe for success here.

The first part of the book focuses on barbecues, offering a huge choice, from family favourites, such as home-made burgers and kebabs, to more exotic dishes inspired by cuisines from around the world. There are recipes for all occasions and every course, including delicious vegetable accompaniments, vegetarian dishes and fabulous grilled desserts. A chapter is dedicated to salsas, dips and marinades to inspire your creativity, and there is also advice on salad accompaniments and outdoor entertaining.

The second part concentrates on salads – from simple side dishes to luxurious special occasion menus and from quick and easy accompaniments to substantial main courses. You can mix and match with the recipes in the first part of the book, pick and choose delicious and healthy side salads to go with an ordinary family meal or plan an entire menu from the appetizer to a refreshing fruit salad dessert. Forget boring sandwiches – most of the salads featured can be transported in cool bags and plastic containers for a wonderful picnic, whether in the country, on the beach or simply in the local park. Make the best of both worlds and take a portable barbecue with you as well.

Both parts of the book include a wealth of practical information about ingredients, cooking and preparation techniques, types of barbecue and fuel, and dressings, marinades and other accompaniments to ensure success every time you cook.

Planning a Barbecue

A well-run barbecue is one of the most enjoyable ways to spend a warm afternoon or evening and it is not at all difficult to make sure that everything runs smoothly. In the following pages, you will find advice, hints and tips on how to do this.

Cooking on the barbecue is always fun and you will probably have plenty of volunteers who are willing to help. However, if too many cooks can spoil the broth, think of the havoc they can wreak with hot coals. You can make use of their enthusiasm by asking them to carry bowls of salad, dishes, cutlery and so on between the kitchen and the

garden. It is also sensible to have a designated adult to watch the barbecue if you need to leave it for any reason – once lit, it should never be left unattended, especially if there are children present.

One reason why barbecues are such a good way to entertain is that much of the work can be done in advance. Marinades, which not only tenderize ingredients but also give them flavour, need time to take effect, so you can often start the preparation the evening before. Meat and fish can be cut up for kebabs, and burgers can be made and stored, covered with clear film (plastic wrap) in the refrigerator.

Safety First

It is all too easy to get carried away with enthusiasm and invite half the neighbourhood to your barbecue. Be sensible about the numbers that can be safely contained at the venue and for whom you can cook without ending up limp and exhausted with scorched food. Serving large numbers of people increases the risk of not cooking the food sufficiently. While part of the charm of a barbecue is that instead of being hidden in the kitchen, you are at the centre of things and can chat to your guests, you won't want to spend the whole time slaving over a hot grill.

Although you don't have to be totally abstemious, remember that cooking on a barbecue is thirsty work and it is very easy to underestimate how much you are drinking. Too high an alcohol intake and hot charcoal could be a lethal combination. Keep an eye on the safety of drinking guests, too. Make sure that you have a good supply of soft drinks for children, drivers and those who prefer them. In the chapter on Outdoor Entertaining, you will find some delicious recipes for both alcoholic and non-alcoholic drinks.

Selecting the Food

Offering a choice of foods is part of the pleasure, but don't be over-ambitious. Depending on how many people you

will be serving, a good selection would include two or three different main ingredients, such as fish, meat and poultry, a vegetarian option and, perhaps, child-friendly food, such as burgers. However, you may be surprised to discover a toddler happily consuming a spicy chicken satay or a plateful of stuffed squid. There is nothing like a barbecue for bringing out just everyone's sense of adventure.

The one thing no one has any control over is the weather. Even when the forecast is promising and there have been weeks of clear blue skies, a sudden downpour or gusting wind can spoil the best-laid plans. It is therefore worth making some contingency arrangements. Before inviting your guests, think about the available space indoors if they need sudden shelter.

Most of the recipes in this book are easily adapted for cooking in the kitchen. Kebabs, drumsticks, steaks, chops and chunky fish fillets can all be cooked under a conventional grill (broiler) for the same length of time. Parcels can be cooked in a moderate oven, for about the same length of time as given in the recipe. Otherwise, if you

have a barbecue with a lid, grab an umbrella, put a smile on your face and pass the plates through the nearest window into the house.

Salad for all Seasons

When the temperature soars and the evenings are long and light, no one wants to cook. Happily, this is just the time when baby vegetables are in season, salad leaves flourish and tomatoes, aubergines (eggplant) and courgettes (zucchini) ripen in the warm sunshine.

Nowadays, the range of salad ingredients is almost endless. Even the choice of salad leaves has expanded enormously. Supermarkets and other stores are packed with both familiar and exotic vegetables in a tempting array of colours, shapes and sizes.

While salads are, understandably, at their most popular in the summer, they are also a refreshing and healthy option all year round. All the chapters in the second half of this book include some winter specialities, based on seasonal produce, such as potatoes, fennel or celeriac, or on pasta and rice. However, with modern transportation, almost all vegetables are available at any time of year so that you can have greater variety of ingredients.

Side salads, whether made from raw or cooked ingredients, are versatile accompaniments to almost every main course dish, whether pasta, casseroles or grills. You can serve them as an appetizer, with the main course or, French-style, as a palate cleanser afterwards. They can range from a simple selection of salad leaves tossed in a vinaigrette to a colourful compilation of several different ingredients in a spicy or creamy dressing. You are sure to find a recipe whose flavours are the perfect complement to your chosen main course. Most can be prepared or partially prepared in advance, making entertaining easy.

Main Course Salads

It is during the summer months that main course salads reign supreme. They can be based around almost any ingredients from duck breast fillets to smoked trout and from mussels to steak. A quick and easy salad can provide an economical and filling midweek family supper, while a more elaborate and luxurious dish makes a wonderful centrepiece for a party

buffet or can play a starring role at an *al fresco* dinner. The chapter on Special Occasion Salads will be an eye-opener for those whose imagination has not stretched much beyond ham, hard-boiled eggs and lettuce. However, if these are your favourite salad

ingredients, you will be pleased to find them presented in new and ingenious ways in the chapter called Main Course Salads.

Perfect Picnics

Salads are an excellent choice for picnics and packed lunches. Make the dressing in a screw-top jar and transport it this way to your picnic site or workplace. Assemble the salad in advance or pack the separate ingredients in rigid plastic containers or plastic bags. Then all you have to do is toss it in the dressing and serve.

Use this book to plan an entire menu for a dinner party or special occasion or simply dip into it for ideas and suggestions for family meals. Whatever your taste, budget and level of culinary skill, you will find a recipe for every course and every kind of occasion to delight your family and friends.

SIZZLING
BARBECUES

o o o

Just a glance through this mouthwatering selection of recipes, from seared scallops to glazed duck and from sirloin steaks to fruit kebabs, will give you an idea of just how versatile and tasty grilled food can be.

This section of the book begins with some practical guidance about cooking on a barbecue, including safety tips, cooking times and choosing the equipment and fuel. It also offers some handy hints on the magic of marinating.

The remaining chapters cover every aspect of the barbecue menu – from appetizers and snacks to desserts – and includes some unusual and delicious vegetable accompaniments, as well as an entire chapter on salsas, dips and marinades and a special section on outdoor entertaining that will inspire you to party throughout the summer.

While steaks, chicken drumsticks, chops and burgers are traditional barbecue fare, the range of suitable ingredients is far more extensive. Firm-textured fish, such as monkfish and tuna, can be cooked directly on the grill and respond beautifully to the smoky flavour imparted by the fire, while prawns (shrimp) make fabulous and colourful kebabs. More delicate fish can be wrapped in foil parcels to protect their texture from the fierce heat. Foil parcels are an ideal way of cooking vegetables, too, and this section of the book includes a chapter of succulent vegetable recipes, many of which are wonderful, main course vegetarian dishes.

Whatever your plan, from an impromptu midweek supper on a hot summer evening to a full-scale barbecue party at the weekend, you will find the recipes you want here. Accompany cold canapés with hot snacks straight from the grill, cook an entire meal, or even choose an unusual grilled dessert to follow an *al fresco* meal.

CHOOSING A BARBECUE

There is a huge choice of ready-made barbecues on the market, and it's important to choose one that suits your needs. First decide how many people you want to cook for and where you are likely to use the barbecue. For instance, do you usually have barbecues just for the family, or are you likely to have barbecue parties for lots of friends? Once you've decided on your basic requirements, you will be able to choose between the different types more easily.

ABOVE: *Hibachi barbecue*

Hibachi Barbecues

These small cast-iron barbecues originated in Japan – the word *hibachi* translates literally as "firebox". They are inexpensive, easy to use and easily transportable. Lightweight versions are now made in steel or aluminium.

Disposable Barbecues

These will last for about an hour and are a convenient idea for picnic-style barbecues or for cooking just a few small pieces of food.

Portable Barbecues

These are usually quite light and fold away to fit into a car boot (trunk) so you can take them on picnics. Some are even small enough to fit into a rucksack.

Brazier Barbecues

These open barbecues are suitable for use on a patio or in the garden. Most have legs or wheels and it's a good idea to check that the height suits you. The grill area of a brazier barbecue varies in size and the barbecue may be round or rectangular. It's useful to choose one that has a shelf attached to the side. Other extras may include an electric, battery-powered or clockwork spit: choose one on which you can adjust the height of the spit. Many brazier barbecues have a hood, which is useful as a windbreak and gives a place to mount the spit.

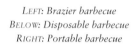

LEFT: *Brazier barbecue*
BELOW: *Disposable barbecue*
RIGHT: *Portable barbecue*

ABOVE: Gas barbecue

Kettle-grill Barbecues

These have a large, hinged lid which can be used as a windbreak; when closed, the lid allows you to use the barbecue rather like an oven. Even large pieces of meat or whole chickens cook successfully, as the heat reflected within the dome helps to brown the meat evenly. The heat is easily controlled by the use of efficient air vents. This type of barbecue can also be used for home-smoking foods.

Gas Barbecues

The main advantage of these is their convenience – the heat is instant and easily controllable. The disadvantage is that they tend to be quite expensive.

Permanent Barbecues

These are a good idea if you often have barbecues at home. They can be built simply and cheaply. Choose a sheltered site that is a little way from the house, but with easy access to the kitchen. Permanent barbecues can be built with ordinary house bricks, but it's best to line the inside with firebricks, which will withstand the heat better. Use a metal shelf for the fuel and a grid at whatever height you choose. Packs are available containing all you need to build a barbecue.

Improvised Barbecues

Barbecue cooking adds to the fun of eating outdoors on picnics and camping trips but transporting the barbecue for the rest of the day can make the idea more of a chore than a treat. Basic barbecues can be built at almost no cost and can be dismantled after use as quickly as they were put together. A pile of stones topped with chicken wire and fuelled with driftwood or kindling makes a very efficient barbecue. Or take a large metal biscuit container with you and punch a few holes in it; fill it with charcoal and place a grid on top. With just a little planning, you can turn your trip into a truly memorable event.

ABOVE: Improvised barbecue

ABOVE: Permanent barbecue

TYPES OF FUEL

. . .

If you have a gas or electric barbecue, you will not need to buy extra fuel, but other barbecues require either charcoal or wood. Choose good-quality fuel from sustainable sources, and always store it in a dry place.

Lumpwood Charcoal

Lumpwood charcoal is usually made from softwood, and comes in lumps of varying size. It is easier to ignite than briquettes, but tends to burn up faster.

Charcoal Briquettes

Briquettes are a cost-effective choice of fuel as they burn for a long time with the minimum of smell and smoke. They can take a long time to ignite, however.

ABOVE: *Charcoal briquettes*

Self-igniting Charcoal

This is simply lumpwood charcoal or briquettes, treated with a flammable substance that catches light very easily. It's important to wait until the ignition agent has burnt off before cooking food, or the smell may taint the food.

Coconut-shell Charcoal

This makes a good fuel for small barbecues. It's best used on a fire grate with small holes, as the small pieces tend to fall through the gaps.

Wood

Hardwoods, such as oak and olive, are best for barbecues, as they burn slowly with a pleasant aroma. Softwoods tend to burn too fast and give off sparks and smoke, making them unsuitable for most barbecues. Wood fires need constant attention to achieve an even, steady heat.

CONTROLLING THE HEAT

There are three basic ways to control the heat of the barbecue during cooking time.

1 Adjust the height of the grill rack. Raise it for slow cooking, or use the bottom level for searing foods. For a medium heat, the rack should be about 10cm/4in from the fire.

2 Push the burning coals apart for a lower heat; pile them closer together to increase the heat of the fire.

3 Most barbecues have air vents to allow air into the fire. Open the vents to make the fire hotter, or close them in order to lower the temperature.

LIGHTING THE FIRE

Follow these basic instructions for lighting the fire unless you are using self-igniting charcoal, in which case you should follow the manu-facturer's instructions.

1 Spread a layer of foil over the base of the barbecue, to reflect the heat and make cleaning easier.

2 Spread a layer of wood, charcoal or briquettes on the fire grate about 5cm/2in deep. Pile the fuel in a small pyramid in the centre.

3 Push one or two firelighters into the pyramid or pour over about 45ml/3 tbsp liquid firelighter and leave for 1 minute. Light with a long match or taper and leave to burn for 15 minutes. Spread the coals evenly and leave for 30–45 minutes, until they are covered with a film of grey ash, before cooking.

Woodchips and Herbs

These are designed to be added to the fire to impart a pleasant aroma to the food. They can be soaked to make them last longer. Sprinkle woodchips and herbs straight on to the coals during cooking, or place them on a metal tray under the grill rack. Packs of hickory or oak chips are easily available, or you can simply spread twigs of juniper, rosemary, thyme, sage or fennel over the fire.

BELOW: *Lumpwood charcoal*

BELOW: *Coconut shell*

SAFETY TIPS

Barbecuing is a perfectly safe method of cooking if it's done sensibly – use these simple guidelines as a basic checklist to safeguard against accidents. If you have never organized a barbecue before, keep your first few attempts as simple as possible, with just one or two types of food. When you have mastered the technique of cooking on a barbecue, you can start to become more ambitious. Soon you will progress from burgers for two to meals for large parties of family and friends.

✰ Make sure the barbecue is sited on a firm surface and is stable and level before lighting the fire. Once the barbecue is lit, do not move it.

✰ Keep the barbecue sheltered from the wind, and keep it well away from trees and shrubs.

✰ Always follow the manufacturer's instructions for your barbecue, as there are some barbecues that can use only one type of fuel.

✰ Don't try to hasten the fire – some fuels may take quite a time to build up heat. Never pour flammable liquid on to the barbecue.

✰ Keep children and pets away from the fire and make sure the cooking is always supervised by adults.

✰ Keep perishable foods cold until you're ready to cook – especially in hot weather. If you take them outdoors, place them in a cool bag until needed.

✰ Make sure meats, such as burgers, sausages and poultry, are thoroughly cooked – there should be no trace of pink in the juices. Pierce a thick part of the flesh as a test: the juices should run clear.

RIGHT: Poultry can be pre-cooked in the oven or microwave, before being finished off on the barbecue.

ABOVE: *Light the fire with a long match or taper, and leave it to burn for about 15 minutes.*

✰ Wash your hands after handling raw meat and before touching other foods. Don't use the same utensils for raw ingredients and cooked food.

✰ You may prefer to pre-cook poultry in the microwave or oven and then transfer it to the barbecue to finish off cooking and to attain the flavour of chargrilled food. Don't allow meat to cool down before transferring it to the barbecue; poultry should never be reheated once it has cooled.

✰ In case the fire should get out of control, have a bucket of sand and a water spray on hand to douse the flames.

✰ Keep a first-aid kit handy. If someone burns themselves, hold the burn under cold running water.

✰ Trim excess fat from meat and don't use too much oil in marinades. Fat can cause dangerous flare-ups if too much is allowed to drip on to the fuel.

✰ Use long-handled barbecue tools, such as forks, tongs and brushes, for turning and basting food; keep some oven gloves to hand, preferably the extra-long type, to protect your hands.

✰ Always keep the raw foods to be cooked away from foods that are ready to eat, to prevent cross-contamination.

BASIC TIMING GUIDE

⋄ ⋄ ⋄

It is almost impossible to give precise timing guides for barbecue cooking as there are so many factors to consider. The heat will depend on the type and size of barbecue, the type of fuel used, the height of the grill above the fire and, of course, the weather. Cooking times will also be affected by the thickness and type of food, the quality of the meat, and whereabouts on the grill it is placed.

Bearing this in mind, the chart below provides only a rough guide to timing. Food should always be tested to make sure it is thoroughly cooked. The times given here are total cooking times, allowing for the food to be turned. Most foods need turning only once, but smaller items, such as kebabs and sausages, need to be turned more frequently to be sure of even cooking. Foods wrapped in foil cook more slowly and will need longer on the barbecue.

Type of Food	Weight/ Thickness	Heat	Total Cooking Time
Beef			
steaks	2.5cm/1in	hot	rare: 5 minutes
			medium: 8 minutes
			well done: 12 minutes
burgers	2cm/³⁄₄in	hot	6–8 minutes
kebabs	2.5cm/1in	hot	5–8 minutes
joints	1.5kg/3¹⁄₂lb	spit	2–3 hours
Lamb			
leg steaks	2cm/³⁄₄in	medium	10–15 minutes
chops	2.5cm/1in	medium	10–15 minutes
kebabs	2.5cm/1in	medium	6–15 minutes
butterfly leg	7.5cm/3in	low	rare: 40–45 minutes
			well done: 1 hour
rolled shoulder	1.5kg/3¹⁄₂lb	spit	1¹⁄₄–1¹⁄₂ hours
Pork			
chops	2.5cm/1in	medium	15–18 minutes
kebabs	2.5cm/1in	medium	12–15 minutes
spare ribs		medium	30–40 minutes
sausages	thick	medium	8–10 minutes
joints	1.5kg/3¹⁄₂lb	spit	2–3 hours

Type of Food	Weight/ Thickness	Heat	Total Cooking Time
Chicken			
whole	1.5kg/3¹⁄₂lb	spit	1–1¹⁄₄ hours
quarters		medium	30–35 minutes
boneless breasts		medium	10–15 minutes
drumsticks		medium	25–30 minutes
kebabs		medium	6–10 minutes
poussin, whole	450g/1lb	spit	25–30 minutes
poussin, spatchcocked	450g/1lb	medium	25–30 minutes
Duckling			
whole	2.25kg/5lb	spit	1–1¹⁄₂ hours
half		medium	35–45 minutes
breasts, boneless		medium	15–20 minutes
Fish			
large, whole	2.25–4.5kg/ 5–10lb	low/ medium	allow 10 minutes per 2.5cm/1in thickness
small, whole	500–900g/ 1¹⁄₄–2lb	hot/ medium	12–20 minutes
sardines		hot/ medium	4–6 minutes
steaks or fillets	2.5cm/1in	medium	6–10 minutes
kebabs	2.5cm/1in	medium	5–8 minutes
large prawns (shrimp) in shell		medium	6–8 minutes
large prawns, (shrimp) shelled		medium	4–6 minutes
scallops/mussels in shell		medium	until open
scallops/mussels, shelled, skewered		medium	5–8 minutes
half lobster		low/ medium	15–20 minutes

MARINATING

Marinades are used to add flavour and to moisten or tenderize foods, particularly meat. Marinades can be either savoury or sweet and are as varied as you want to make them: spicy, fruity, fragrant or exotic. Particular classic combinations always work well with certain foods. Usually, it is best to choose oily marinades for dry foods, such as lean meat or white fish, and wine- or vinegar-based marinades for rich foods with a higher fat content. Most marinades don't contain salt, which can draw out the juices from meat. It's better to add salt just before, or after, cooking.

1 Place the food for marinating in a wide, non-metallic dish or bowl, preferably a dish that is large enough to allow the food to lie in a single layer.

2 Mix together the ingredients for the marinade according to the recipe. The marinade can usually be prepared in advance and stored in a jar with a screw-top lid until needed.

3 Pour the marinade over the food and turn the food to coat it evenly.

4 Cover the dish or bowl with clear film (plastic wrap) and chill in the refrigerator for anything from about 30 minutes up to several hours or even overnight, depending on the recipe. Turn the food over occasionally and spoon the marinade over it to make sure that it is well coated.

5 Remove the food with a slotted spoon, or lift it out with tongs, and drain off and reserve the marinade. If necessary, allow the food to come to room temperature before cooking.

6 Use the marinade for basting or brushing the food during cooking.

BASIC BARBECUE MARINADE

This can be used for meat or fish.

1 garlic clove, crushed
45ml/3 tbsp sunflower or olive oil
45ml/3 tbsp dry sherry
15ml/1 tbsp Worcestershire sauce
15ml/1 tbsp dark soy sauce
freshly ground black pepper

RED WINE MARINADE

This is good with red meats and game.

150ml/¼ pint/⅔ cup dry red wine
15ml/1 tbsp olive oil
15ml/1 tbsp red wine vinegar
2 garlic cloves, crushed
2 dried bay leaves, crumbled
freshly ground black pepper

BELOW: Marinating foods before cooking adds to the flavour and makes sure the food is kept tender and moist.

To keep your guests happy while they wait for the main event,

begin your barbecue with exciting appetizers that are quick to

cook and fun to eat. Here is a collection of flavoursome dishes

guaranteed to disappear from the grill rack as soon as they're

cool enough to snatch away.

APPETIZERS AND
SNACKS

ROASTED GARLIC TOASTS

Cooking garlic in its skin on the barbecue produces a soft, aromatic purée with a sweet, nutty flavour. Spread on crisp toast to make a delicious appetizer.

INGREDIENTS
2 whole garlic heads
extra virgin olive oil
fresh rosemary sprigs
ciabatta loaf or thick baguette
chopped fresh rosemary
salt and freshly ground
black pepper

SERVES 4

1 Slice the tops from the heads of garlic, using a sharp kitchen knife.

2 Brush the garlic heads with extra virgin olive oil and add a few sprigs of fresh rosemary, before wrapping in kitchen foil. Cook the foil parcels on a medium-hot barbecue for about 25–30 minutes, turning occasionally, until the garlic is soft.

3 Slice the bread and brush each slice generously with olive oil. Toast the slices on the barbecue until crisp and golden, turning once.

4 Squeeze the garlic cloves from their skins on to the toasts. Sprinkle with the chopped fresh rosemary and olive oil, and add salt and black pepper to taste.

ROASTED PEPPER ANTIPASTO

Jars of Italian mixed peppers in olive oil are a common sight in supermarkets, yet none can compete with this freshly made version, perfect as an appetizer.

INGREDIENTS

3 red (bell) peppers
2 yellow or orange (bell) peppers
2 green (bell) peppers
50g/2oz/½ cup sun-dried tomatoes
in oil, drained
1 garlic clove
30ml/2 tbsp balsamic vinegar
75ml/5 tbsp olive oil
few drops of chilli sauce
4 canned artichoke hearts, drained
and sliced
salt and freshly ground
black pepper
fresh basil leaves, to garnish

SERVES 6

1 Cook the whole peppers on a medium-hot barbecue, turning frequently, for about 10–15 minutes, until they begin to char. Cover the peppers with a clean dishtowel and leave to cool for 5 minutes.

2 Use a sharp kitchen knife to slice the sun-dried tomatoes into thin strips. Thinly slice the garlic clove.

3 Beat together the balsamic vinegar, olive oil and chilli sauce in a small bowl, then season with a little salt and freshly ground black pepper.

4 Stalk and slice the peppers. Mix with the sliced artichokes, sun-dried tomatoes and garlic. Pour over the dressing and sprinkle with basil leaves.

Cook's Tip

If you prefer your peppers to have a softer texture and sweeter flavour, peel them once they have cooled down after grilling, using a small sharp knife. They will then be very easy to slice.

HERB-STUFFED MINI VEGETABLES

∘ ∘ ∘

These little hors d'oeuvres are ideal for parties as they can be prepared in advance, and simply assembled and cooked at the last minute.

INGREDIENTS

30 mini vegetables: courgettes (zucchini), patty pan squashes and large button (white) mushrooms
30ml/2 tbsp olive oil
fresh basil or parsley, to garnish

FOR THE STUFFING
30ml/2 tbsp olive oil
1 onion, finely chopped
1 garlic clove, finely chopped
115g/4oz/1¹/2 cups finely chopped button (white) mushrooms
1 courgette (zucchini), finely chopped
1 red (bell) pepper, finely chopped
65g/2¹/2 oz/¹/3 cup orzo pasta
90ml/6 tbsp/¹/3 cup passata (bottled strained tomatoes)
2.5ml/¹/2 tsp dried thyme
120ml/4fl oz/¹/2 cup chicken stock
5–10ml/1–2 tsp chopped fresh basil
50g/2oz/¹/2 cup coarsely grated mozzarella or fontina cheese
salt and freshly ground black pepper

MAKES 30

1 For the stuffing, heat the oil over a medium heat in a pan. Add the onion and cook for 2 minutes, until tender. Stir in the garlic, mushrooms, courgette and red pepper. Season and cook for 2 minutes, until the vegetables soften.

2 Stir in the pasta, passata, thyme and chicken stock and bring to the boil, stirring. Reduce the heat and simmer for 10–12 minutes, until reduced and thickened. Remove from the heat and cool slightly. Stir in the basil and the grated cheese.

3 Drop the courgettes and squashes into a pan of boiling water and cook for 3 minutes. Drain and refresh under cold running water. Trim the bottoms so they are flat, trim a small slice off the tops and scoop out the centres with a spoon or melon baller. Remove the stems from the mushrooms. Brush all the vegetables with olive oil.

4 Using a teaspoon, fill the vegetables with the stuffing and arrange on a rack. Cook on a medium-hot barbecue for 10–15 minutes, until the filling is hot and bubbling. Garnish with the fresh basil or parsley. The vegetables can be served either warm or cool.

POLPETTES WITH MOZZARELLA AND TOMATO

These Italian-style meatballs are made with beef and topped with creamy melted mozzarella and savoury anchovies.

INGREDIENTS

*1/2 slice white bread,
crusts removed
45ml/3 tbsp milk
675g/1¹/2lb/6 cups minced
(ground) beef
1 egg, beaten
50g/2oz/²/3 cup dry breadcrumbs
olive oil for brushing
2 beefsteak tomatoes, sliced
15ml/1 tbsp chopped fresh oregano
1 mozzarella cheese, cut into
6 slices
6 drained, canned anchovy fillets,
cut in half lengthways
salt and freshly ground
black pepper*

SERVES 6

1 Put the bread and milk into a small pan and heat very gently, until the bread absorbs all the milk. Mash it to a pulp and set aside to cool.

2 Put the minced beef into a bowl with the bread mixture and the egg and season with plenty of salt and freshly ground black pepper. Mix well, then shape the mixture into six patties, using your hands. Sprinkle the breadcrumbs on to a plate and dredge the patties, coating them thoroughly.

3 Brush the polpettes with olive oil and cook them on a hot barbecue for 2–3 minutes on one side, until brown. Turn them over.

4 Without removing the polpettes from the barbecue, lay a slice of tomato on top of each polpette, sprinkle with chopped oregano and season with salt and pepper. Place a mozzarella slice on top and arrange two strips of anchovy in a cross over the cheese.

5 Cook for 4–5 minutes more until the polpettes are cooked through and the mozzarella has melted.

STUFFED KIBBEH

• • •

Kibbeh is a tasty Middle Eastern speciality of minced lamb and bulgur wheat, which can be eaten with no further cooking or shaped into patties and cooked on the barbecue.

INGREDIENTS

450g/1lb lean lamb
45ml/3 tbsp olive oil
avocado slices and fresh coriander
(cilantro) sprigs, to serve

FOR THE KIBBEH
225g/8oz/1⅓ cups bulgur wheat
1 fresh red chilli, seeded and
roughly chopped
1 onion, coarsely chopped
salt and freshly ground
black pepper

FOR THE STUFFING
1 onion, finely chopped
50g/2oz/⅔ cup pine nuts
30ml/2 tbsp olive oil
7.5ml/1½ tsp ground allspice
60ml/4 tbsp chopped fresh
coriander (cilantro)

SERVES 4–6

1 Cut the lamb into coarse chunks, using a heavy kitchen knife. Process the chunks in a blender or food processor until finely minced (ground). Divide the minced meat into two equal portions and set aside until needed.

2 To make the kibbeh, soak the bulgur wheat for 15 minutes in cold water. Drain well, then process in the blender or food processor with the chopped chilli and onion, half the meat and plenty of salt and pepper.

3 To make the stuffing, cook the onion and pine nuts in the olive oil for 5 minutes. Add the allspice and remaining minced meat and cook gently, breaking up the meat with a wooden spoon, until browned. Stir in the coriander and a little seasoning.

4 Turn the kibbeh mixture out on to a clean work surface and use your hands to shape the mixture into a cake. Divide the cake into 12 wedges.

5 Flatten one wedge in the palm of your hand and spoon a little stuffing into the centre. Bring the edges of the kibbeh over the stuffing to enclose it. Make into a firm, egg-shaped mould between the palms of your hands, checking that the filling is completely encased. Repeat with the other kibbeh.

6 To barbecue the kibbeh, lightly brush with olive oil and cook on a medium barbecue for 10–15 minutes, turning carefully, until evenly browned and cooked through. To fry the kibbeh, heat oil to a depth of 5cm/2in in a large pan until a few kibbeh crumbs sizzle on the surface. Lower half the kibbeh into the oil and fry for about 5 minutes, until golden. Drain on kitchen paper and keep hot while frying the remainder. Serve hot with avocado slices and fresh coriander sprigs.

HERB POLENTA

* * *

*Golden polenta with fresh summer herbs makes a delicious appetizer or
light snack, served with barbecue-cooked tomatoes.*

3 Remove from the heat and stir in the
butter, chopped herbs and pepper.

4 Lightly grease a wide dish and tip
the polenta into it, spreading it evenly.
Leave until cool and set.

1 Prepare the polenta in advance: place
the stock or water in a pan, with the
salt, and bring to the boil. Reduce the
heat and stir in the polenta.

2 Stir constantly over a moderate heat
for 5 minutes, until the polenta begins
to thicken and come away from the
sides of the pan.

Cook's Tip

Try using fresh basil or fresh chives
alone, for a distinctive flavour.

5 Turn out the polenta and cut into
squares or stamp out rounds with a
large biscuit (cookie) cutter. Brush with
olive oil. Lightly brush the tomatoes
with olive oil and sprinkle with salt and
pepper to taste. Cook the tomatoes and
polenta on a medium-hot barbecue for
about 5 minutes, turning once. Serve
garnished with fresh herbs.

BRIE PARCELS WITH ALMONDS

° ° °

Creamy French Brie makes a sophisticated appetizer or light meal, wrapped in vine leaves and served hot with chunks of crusty bread.

2 Cut the Brie into four chunks and place each chunk on a vine leaf.

3 Mix together the chives, ground almonds, peppercorns and olive oil, and place a spoonful on top of each piece of cheese. Sprinkle with flaked almonds.

INGREDIENTS

4 large vine (grape) leaves, preserved in brine
200g/7oz piece Brie cheese
30ml/2 tbsp chopped fresh chives
30ml/2 tbsp ground almonds
5ml/1 tsp crushed black peppercorns
15ml/1 tbsp olive oil
flaked (sliced) almonds

SERVES 4

1 Rinse the vine leaves thoroughly under cold running water and dry them well. Spread the leaves out on a clean work surface or chopping board.

4 Fold the vine leaves over tightly to enclose the cheese completely. Brush the parcels with olive oil and cook on a hot barbecue for about 3–4 minutes, until the cheese is hot and melting. Serve immediately.

TOFU STEAKS

° ° °

Vegetarians and meat-eaters alike will enjoy these grilled tofu steaks. The combination of ingredients in the marinade gives the steaks a distinctly Japanese flavour.

INGREDIENTS

1 packet fresh tofu
(10 x 8 x 3cm/4 x 3¼ x 1¼in),
300g/11oz drained weight
2 spring onions (scallions), thinly
sliced, to garnish
mixed salad leaves, to garnish

FOR THE MARINADE
45ml/3 tbsp sake
30ml/2 tbsp soy sauce
5ml/1 tsp sesame oil
1 garlic clove, crushed
15ml/1 tbsp grated fresh
root ginger
1 spring onion (scallion), chopped

SERVES 4

1 Wrap the tofu in a clean dishtowel and place it on a chopping board. Put a large plate on top and leave the beancurd for 30 minutes to remove any excess water.

2 Slice the tofu horizontally into three pieces, then cut the slices into quarters. Set aside. Combine all the ingredients for the marinade in a large bowl. Add the tofu to the bowl in a single layer and set aside to marinate for about 30 minutes. Drain the tofu steaks and reserve the marinade to use for basting while cooking.

3 Cook the steaks on the barbecue for 3 minutes on each side, basting regularly with the marinade, or fry them for 3 minutes in a large pan.

4 Arrange three tofu steaks on each plate. Any remaining marinade can be heated in a pan and then poured over the steaks. Sprinkle with the spring onions and garnish with mixed salad leaves. Serve immediately.

Cook's Tip
Firm tofu is easily obtainable from supermarkets and health food stores, and is an ideal alternative to meat.

GRILLED ASPARAGUS WITH SALT-CURED HAM

∘ ∘ ∘

Barbecue-cooked asparagus has a wonderfully intense flavour that stands up well to the wrapping of crisp, salty ham. Serve this traditional tapas dish with drinks before a meal.

INGREDIENTS

6 slices of serrano ham
12 asparagus spears
15ml/1 tbsp olive oil
sea salt and coarsely ground
black pepper

SERVES 4

1 Halve each slice of ham lengthways and wrap one half around each of the asparagus spears.

2 Brush the ham and asparagus lightly with olive oil and sprinkle with salt and pepper. Cook on a medium barbecue for about 4 minutes, turning frequently, until the asparagus is tender but still firm. Serve immediately.

Cook's Tip

If you can't find serrano ham, try using Italian prosciutto or Portuguese presunto.

POTATO SKINS WITH CAJUN DIP

As an alternative to deep-frying, cooking potato skins on the barbecue crisps them up in no time and gives them a wonderful chargrilled flavour. This spicy dip makes the perfect partner.

INGREDIENTS

4 large baking potatoes
olive oil for brushing
250ml/8fl oz/1 cup natural
(plain) yogurt
2 garlic cloves, crushed
10ml/2 tsp tomato purée (paste)
1 small fresh green chilli, chopped
2.5ml/½ tsp celery salt
salt and freshly ground
black pepper

SERVES 4

1 Bake or microwave the potatoes until tender. Cut them in half and scoop out the flesh, leaving a thin layer of potato on the skins. The scooped-out potato can be reserved in the refrigerator or freezer for another meal.

2 Cut each potato shell in half again and lightly brush the skins with olive oil. Cook on a medium-hot barbecue for 4–5 minutes, or until crisp.

3 Mix together the remaining ingredients in a bowl to make the dip. Serve the potato skins with the Cajun dip on the side.

Cook's Tip

If you don't have any fresh chillies, add 5 ml/1 tsp green chilli paste or one or two drops of hot pepper sauce to the dip instead.

SPICY CHICKEN WINGS

∘ ∘ ∘

These deliciously sticky bites will appeal to adults and children alike, although younger eaters might prefer a little less chilli.

INGREDIENTS

8 plump chicken wings
2 large garlic cloves, cut
into slivers
15ml/1 tbsp olive oil
15ml/1 tbsp paprika
5ml/1 tsp chilli powder
5ml/1 tsp dried oregano
salt and freshly ground
black pepper
lime wedges, to serve

SERVES 4

1 Using a small sharp kitchen knife, make one or two cuts in the skin of each chicken wing and slide a sliver of garlic under the skin. Brush the wings generously with the olive oil.

2 In a large bowl, stir together the paprika, chilli powder and oregano and season with plenty of salt and pepper. Add the chicken wings and toss together until very lightly coated in the mixture.

3 Cook the chicken wings on a medium barbecue for 15 minutes, until they are cooked through, with a blackened, crispy skin. Serve with fresh lime wedges to squeeze over.

32

CHICKEN WINGS TERIYAKI STYLE

This Japanese glaze is very simple to prepare and adds a unique flavour to the meat. The glaze can be used with any cut of chicken or with fish.

INGREDIENTS

1 garlic clove, crushed
45ml/3 tbsp soy sauce
30ml/2 tbsp dry sherry
10ml/2 tsp clear honey
10ml/2 tsp grated fresh root ginger
5ml/1 tsp sesame oil
12 chicken wings
15ml/1 tbsp sesame seeds, toasted

SERVES 4

1 Place the garlic, soy sauce, sherry, honey, grated ginger and sesame oil in a large bowl and beat with a fork to mix the ingredients together evenly.

2 Add the chicken wings and toss thoroughly, to coat in the marinade. Cover the bowl with clear film (plastic wrap) and chill in the refrigerator for about 30 minutes, or longer.

3 Cook the chicken wings on a fairly hot barbecue for about 20–25 minutes, turning occasionally and basting with the remaining marinade.

4 Sprinkle the chicken wings with sesame seeds. Serve the wings on their own as an appetizer or side dish, or with a crisp green salad.

SKEWERED LAMB WITH RED ONION SALSA

∘ ∘ ∘

A simple salsa makes a refreshing accompaniment to this summery dish – make sure you use a mild-flavoured red onion that is fresh and crisp, and a tomato that is ripe and full of flavour.

INGREDIENTS
225g/8oz lean lamb, cubed
2.5ml/½ tsp ground cumin
5ml/1 tsp ground paprika
15ml/1 tbsp olive oil
salt and freshly ground
black pepper

FOR THE SALSA
1 red onion, very thinly sliced
1 large tomato, seeded
and chopped
15ml/1 tbsp red wine vinegar
3–4 fresh basil or mint leaves,
roughly torn
small mint leaves, to garnish

SERVES 4

1 Place the lamb in a large bowl with the cumin, paprika and olive oil and season with plenty of salt and freshly ground black pepper. Toss well. Cover the bowl with clear film (plastic wrap) and leave in a cool place for several hours, or in the refrigerator overnight, so that the lamb absorbs the flavours.

2 Spear the lamb cubes on four small skewers. If using wooden skewers, soak them first in cold water for at least 30 minutes to prevent them from burning when placed on the barbecue.

3 To make the salsa, put the sliced onion, tomato, red wine vinegar and torn fresh basil or mint leaves in a small bowl and stir together until thoroughly blended. Season to taste with salt and garnish with mint.

4 Cook the skewered lamb on a hot barbecue for about 5–10 minutes, turning the skewers frequently, until the lamb is well browned on the outside, but still slightly pink in the centre. Serve hot, with the salsa.

SPICY MEATBALLS

• • •

These meatballs are delicious served piping hot with chilli sauce. Keep the sauce on the side so that everyone can add as much heat as they like.

2 Add the minced beef, shallots, garlic, breadcrumbs, beaten egg and parsley, with plenty of salt and pepper. Mix well, then use your hands to shape the mixture into 18 small balls.

3 Brush the meatballs with olive oil and cook on a medium barbecue, or fry them in a large pan, for 10–15 minutes, turning regularly until evenly browned and cooked through.

INGREDIENTS

115g/4oz fresh spicy sausages
115g/4oz/1 cup minced
(ground) beef
2 shallots, finely chopped
2 garlic cloves, finely chopped
75g/3oz/1½ cups fresh
white breadcrumbs
1 egg, beaten
30ml/2 tbsp chopped fresh parsley,
plus extra to garnish
15ml/1 tbsp olive oil
salt and freshly ground
black pepper
Tabasco sauce, to serve

SERVES 6

1 Use your hands to remove the skins from the spicy sausages, placing the sausagemeat in a mixing bowl and breaking it up with a fork.

4 Transfer the meatballs to a warm dish and sprinkle with chopped fresh parsley. Serve with Tabasco sauce.

FIVE-SPICE RIB-STICKERS

° ° °

*Choose the meatiest spare ribs you can find, to make these a real success, and
remember to keep a supply of paper napkins within easy reach.*

2 Mix together all the remaining
ingredients, except the spring onions,
and pour over the ribs. Toss to coat
evenly. Cover the bowl and leave to
marinate in the refrigerator overnight.

3 Cook the ribs on a medium-hot
barbecue, turning frequently, for about
30–40 minutes. Brush occasionally
with the remaining marinade.

INGREDIENTS

*1kg/2¼lb Chinese-style pork
spare ribs*
*10ml/2 tsp Chinese five-
spice powder*
2 garlic cloves, crushed
15ml/1 tbsp grated fresh root ginger
2.5ml/½ tsp chilli sauce
60ml/4 tbsp dark soy sauce
*45ml/3 tbsp dark muscovado
(molasses) sugar*
15ml/1 tbsp sunflower oil
4 spring onions (scallions)

SERVES 4

1 If the spare ribs are still attached
to each other, cut between them to
separate them (or you could ask your
butcher to do this when you buy them).
Place the spare ribs in a large bowl.

4 While the ribs are cooking, finely
slice the spring onions. Sprinkle them
over the ribs and serve immediately.

SALMON WITH SPICY PESTO

. . .

This is a great way to bone salmon steaks to give a solid piece of fish. The pesto uses sunflower seeds and chilli as its flavouring, rather than the classic basil and pine nuts.

INGREDIENTS

4 salmon steaks, about
225g/8oz each
30ml/2 tbsp sunflower oil
finely grated rind and juice
of 1 lime
salt and freshly ground
black pepper

FOR THE PESTO
6 mild fresh red chillies
2 garlic cloves
30ml/2 tbsp sunflower or
pumpkin seeds
juice and finely grated rind
of 1 lime
75ml/5 tbsp olive oil

SERVES 4

1 Insert a very sharp knife close to the top of the bone. Working closely to the bone, cut your way to the end of the steak to release one side. Repeat with the other side. Pull out any extra visible bones with a pair of tweezers.

2 Sprinkle salt on the work surface and take hold of the end of the salmon piece, skin-side down. Insert the knife between the skin and the flesh and, working away from you, remove the skin, keeping the knife as close to it as possible. Repeat for each piece of fish.

3 Curl each piece of fish into a round, with the thinner end wrapped around the fatter end. Secure the shape tightly with a length of string.

4 Rub the sunflower oil into the boneless fish rounds. Put the salmon into a large bowl or dish and add the lime juice and rind and the salt and pepper. Leave the salmon to marinate in the refrigerator for up to 2 hours.

5 For the pesto, seed the chillies and place with the garlic cloves, sunflower or pumpkin seeds, lime juice, rind and seasoning in a food processor. Process until well mixed. With the motor running, gradually pour in the olive oil until the sauce has thickened and emulsified. Drain the salmon from its marinade. Cook the fish steaks on a medium barbecue for 5 minutes each side and serve with the spicy pesto.

GRILLED KING PRAWNS WITH ROMESCO SAUCE

• • •

This sauce comes from the Catalan region of Spain and is served with fish and seafood.
Its main ingredients are sweet pepper, tomatoes, garlic and almonds.

INGREDIENTS

24 raw king prawns
(jumbo shrimp)
30–45ml/2–3 tbsp olive oil
flat leaf parsley, to garnish
lemon wedges, to serve

FOR THE SAUCE
2 well-flavoured tomatoes
60ml/4 tbsp olive oil
1 onion, chopped
4 garlic cloves, chopped
1 canned pimiento, chopped
2.5ml/½ tsp dried chilli flakes
75ml/5 tbsp fish stock
30ml/2 tbsp white wine
10 blanched almonds
15ml/1 tbsp red wine vinegar
salt

SERVES 4

1 To make the sauce, immerse the tomatoes in boiling water for about 30 seconds, then refresh them under cold running water. Peel off the skins and coarsely chop the flesh.

2 Heat 30ml/2 tbsp of the oil. Add the onion and three of the garlic cloves and cook until soft. Add the pimiento, tomatoes, chilli, fish stock and wine. Cover and simmer for 30 minutes.

3 Toast the almonds under the grill (broiler) until golden. Transfer to a blender or food processor and grind coarsely. Add the remaining oil, the vinegar and the last garlic clove and process until evenly combined. Add the tomato and pimiento sauce and process until smooth. Season with salt.

4 Remove the heads from the prawns, leaving them otherwise unpeeled and, with a sharp knife, slit each one down the back and remove the dark vein. Rinse and pat dry on kitchen paper. Toss the prawns in olive oil, then spread them out on the barbecue and cook over a medium heat for about 2–3 minutes on each side, until pink. Serve immediately, garnished with parsley and accompanied by lemon wedges and the romesco sauce.

GRILLED MUSSELS WITH PARSLEY AND PARMESAN

*Mussels release an irresistible aroma as they cook on the barbecue: don't be surprised
if they are devoured the moment they are ready.*

INGREDIENTS

450g/1lb fresh mussels
45ml/3 tbsp water
15ml/1 tbsp melted butter
15ml/1 tbsp olive oil
*45ml/3 tbsp freshly grated
Parmesan cheese*
30ml/2 tbsp chopped fresh parsley
2 garlic cloves, finely chopped
*2.5ml/1/2 tsp coarsely ground
black pepper*

SERVES 4

2 Place the mussels with the water
in a large pan. Cover with the lid and
steam for 5 minutes, or until all of the
mussels have opened.

4 In a large bowl, mix together
the melted butter, olive oil, grated
Parmesan cheese, chopped parsley,
garlic and ground black pepper.

1 Scrub the mussels, scraping off any
barnacles and pulling out the beards.
Tap any open mussels sharply with a
knife and discard any that fail to close.

3 Drain the mussels, discarding any
that remain closed. Snap the top shell
off each, leaving the mussel still
attached to the bottom shell.

5 Using a teaspoon, place a small
amount of the cheese mixture on top
of each mussel.

6 Cook the mussels in a pan on a
medium barbecue for 2–3 minutes or
until the mussels are sizzling hot. Serve
immediately, with crusty French bread.

QUICK SHELLFISH PIZZA

· ○ ○ ·

Make four mini pizzas or one large one with the same quantities of ingredients.
If you are short of time, use a pizza-base mix instead of making the dough.

INGREDIENTS

FOR THE PIZZA BASE
5ml/1 tsp easy-blend (rapid-rise)
dried yeast
450g/1lb/4 cups strong white
bread flour
15ml/1tbsp sugar
5ml/1tsp sea salt
300ml/½ pint/1¼ cups
lukewarm water
30ml/2tbsp extra virgin olive oil

FOR THE FISH TOPPING
15ml/1 tbsp olive oil
1 onion, finely chopped
800g/1¾lb canned or fresh plum
tomatoes, chopped
salt and ground black pepper
15ml/1 tbsp chopped fresh thyme
100g/4oz cherry tomatoes, halved
12 fresh anchovy fillets, or 1 can
anchovy fillets, drained
8 fresh, peeled prawns (shrimp)
fresh thyme sprigs, to garnish

SERVES 4

1 Stir the easy-blend yeast into the flour in a large bowl. Add the sugar and sea salt and mix together well.

2 Add the water and olive oil to the bowl, and stir to make a firm dough.

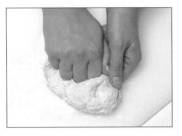

3 Knead the dough for 10 minutes. Cover and leave in a warm place until it has doubled in size.

4 Knock back (punch down) the dough and knead for 5 minutes, then cut the dough into four. Shape each of the four pieces of dough into 13m/5in rounds.

5 Cook the onions until soft. Add the canned tomatoes, seasoning and thyme and simmer for 15 minutes. Brush the pizza bases with olive oil and cook on a medium-hot barbecue, oiled-side down, for 6–8 minutes, until firm and golden underneath. Oil the uncooked side and turn the pizzas over.

6 Cut the cherry tomatoes in half. Assemble each of the pizzas with a spoonful of the sauce, a couple of anchovy fillets and prawns and the cherry tomatoes. Return the pizzas to the barbecue and cook for a further 8–10 minutes until golden and crispy. Sprinkle a few fresh sprigs of thyme on top of the pizzas to serve.

Variation
Add your favourite shellfish, such as fresh or canned mussels, to the topping.

CIABATTA WITH MOZZARELLA AND ONIONS

· · ·

Ciabatta bread is readily available and is even more delicious when made with spinach,
sun-dried tomatoes or olives: you can find these variations in most supermarkets.

INGREDIENTS

1 ciabatta loaf
60ml/4 tbsp red pesto
2 small onions
olive oil, for brushing
225g/8oz mozzarella cheese, sliced
8 black olives, halved and pitted

MAKES 4

1 Cut the bread in half horizontally and toast the cut sides lightly on the barbecue. Spread with the red pesto.

2 Peel the onions and then slice them horizontally. Brush with oil and cook on a hot barbecue for 4–5 minutes, until the edges are caramelized.

3 Arrange the cheese on the bread. Add the onion slices and sprinkle some olives over. Cut in half. Return to the barbecue to melt the cheese.

CROSTINI WITH TOMATO AND ANCHOVY

Crostini are little rounds of bread cut from a baguette and crisply toasted, then covered with a topping, such as this savoury mixture of tomato and anchovy.

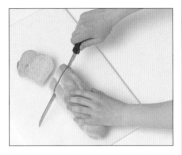

2 Cut the bread diagonally into eight slices about 1cm/½in thick and brush with the remaining oil. Toast on the barbecue until golden, turning once.

3 Spoon a little tomato mixture on to each slice of bread. Place an anchovy fillet on each one and dot with the halved olives. Serve the crostini garnished with a sprig of fresh basil.

INGREDIENTS

60ml/4 tbsp olive oil
2 garlic cloves
4 tomatoes, peeled and chopped
15ml/1 tbsp chopped fresh basil
15ml/1 tbsp tomato purée (paste)
1 small baguette (large enough to give 8 slices)
8 canned anchovy fillets
12 black olives, halved and pitted
salt and freshly ground
black pepper
fresh basil, to garnish

MAKES 8

1 Heat half the olive oil in a frying pan and cook the whole garlic cloves with the chopped tomatoes for about 4 minutes. Stir in the chopped basil, tomato purée and season with plenty of salt and freshly ground black pepper.

Variation

CROSTINI WITH ONION AND OLIVE
Cook 2 large onions, sliced, in 30ml/2 tbsp olive oil until golden. Stir in 8 chopped anchovy fillets, 12 halved, pitted black olives, some seasoning and 5ml/1 tsp dried thyme. Spread the bread with 15ml/1 tbsp black olive paste and cover with the onion mixture.

Succulent grilled cuts of meat are often the starting point when
planning a barbecue, and chargrilling gives meat a unique
flavour. The recipes in this chapter draw on cuisines from all
over the world to offer an exciting range of dishes that are easy
to prepare and deliciously succulent.

MEAT
DISHES

MIXED GRILL SKEWERS WITH HORSERADISH SAUCE

○ ○ ○

This hearty selection of meats, cooked on a skewer and drizzled with horseradish sauce, makes a
popular main course. Keep all the pieces of meat about the same thickness so they cook evenly.

INGREDIENTS
4 small lamb noisettes
4 lamb's kidneys
4 streaky (fatty) bacon
* rashers (strips)*
8 cherry tomatoes
8 chipolata sausages
12–16 bay leaves
salt and freshly ground
* black pepper*

FOR THE HORSERADISH SAUCE
30ml/2 tbsp horseradish relish
45ml/3 tbsp melted butter

SERVES 4

3 Thread the lamb noisettes, bacon-wrapped kidneys and cherry tomatoes, chipolatas and bay leaves on to four long metal skewers. Set aside while you prepare the sauce.

4 Mix the horseradish relish with the melted butter in a small bowl and stir until thoroughly mixed.

5 Brush a little of the horseradish sauce over the meat and sprinkle with salt and freshly ground black pepper.

6 Cook the skewers on a medium barbecue for 12 minutes, turning occasionally, until the meat is golden brown and thoroughly cooked. Serve hot, drizzled with the remaining sauce.

1 Trim any excess fat from the lamb noisettes with a sharp knife. Halve the kidneys and remove the cores, using kitchen scissors.

2 Cut each bacon rasher in half and wrap around the tomatoes or kidneys.

SAUSAGES WITH PRUNES AND BACON

○ ○ ○

Sausages are a perennial barbecue favourite and this is a delicious way to ring the changes.
Serve with crusty French bread or warmed ciabatta.

2 Spread the cut surface with the mustard and then place three prunes in each sausage, pressing them in firmly.

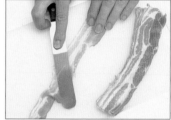

3 Stretch the bacon rashers out thinly, using a round-bladed knife.

INGREDIENTS

8 large, meaty sausages, such as
Toulouse or other good-quality
pork sausages
30ml/2 tbsp Dijon mustard, plus
extra to serve
24 ready-to-eat prunes
8 smoked streaky (fatty)
bacon rashers (strips)

SERVES 4

1 Use a sharp knife to cut a long slit down the length of each sausage, about three-quarters of the way through.

4 Wrap one bacon rasher tightly around each of the sausages, to hold them in shape. Cook on a hot barbecue for 15–18 minutes, turning occasionally, until evenly browned and thoroughly cooked. Serve immediately, with lots of fresh crusty bread and the additional mustard.

SHISH KEBAB

*Many different kinds of kebab are eaten throughout the Middle East, and they are
almost always cooked over an open wood or charcoal fire.*

INGREDIENTS

450g/1lb boned leg of lamb, cubed
1 large green (bell) pepper, seeded
and cut into squares
1 large yellow (bell) pepper, seeded
and cut into squares
8 baby (pearl) onions, halved
225g/8oz button
(white) mushrooms
4 tomatoes, halved
15ml/1 tbsp melted butter

FOR THE MARINADE
45ml/3 tbsp olive oil
juice of 1 lemon
2 garlic cloves, crushed
1 large onion, grated
15ml/1 tbsp fresh oregano
salt and freshly ground
black pepper

SERVES 4

1 First make the marinade: blend
together the olive oil, lemon juice,
crushed garlic, onion, fresh oregano
and seasoning. Place the cubed meat
in a shallow dish and pour over the
marinade. Cover with clear film (plastic
wrap) and leave to marinate for several
hours, or overnight, in the refrigerator.

2 Thread the lamb on to metal skewers,
alternating with pieces of pepper,
onions and mushrooms. Thread the
tomatoes on to separate skewers.

3 Cook the kebabs and tomatoes on a
hot barbecue for 10 minutes, turning
occasionally and basting with butter.
Serve with bulgur wheat.

BACON KOFTA KEBABS AND SALAD

. . .

Kofta kebabs can be made with any type of minced meat, but bacon is very successful, if you have a food processor.

INGREDIENTS

250g/9oz lean bacon rashers
(strips), coarsely chopped
1 small onion, coarsely chopped
1 celery stick, coarsely chopped
75ml/5 tbsp fresh wholemeal
(whole-wheat) breadcrumbs
45ml/3 tbsp chopped fresh thyme
30ml/2 tbsp Worcestershire sauce
1 egg, beaten
salt and freshly ground
black pepper
olive oil, for brushing

FOR THE SALAD
115g/4oz/³⁄4 cup bulgur wheat
60ml/4 tbsp toasted
sunflower seeds
15ml/1 tbsp olive oil
salt and freshly ground
black pepper
handful of celery leaves, chopped

SERVES 4

1 Place the bacon, onion, celery and breadcrumbs in a food processor and process until chopped. Add the thyme, Worcestershire sauce and seasoning. Bind to a firm mixture with the egg.

2 Divide the mixture into eight equal portions and use your hands to shape them around eight bamboo skewers.

3 For the salad, place the bulgur wheat in a bowl and pour over boiling water to cover. Leave to stand for 30 minutes, until the grains are tender.

4 Drain well, then stir in the sunflower seeds, olive oil, salt and pepper. Stir in the celery leaves.

5 Cook the skewers on a medium-hot barbecue for 8–10 minutes, turning occasionally, until golden brown. Serve with the salad.

PEPPERED STEAKS IN BEER AND GARLIC

The robust flavours of this dish will satisfy the heartiest appetites.
Serve the steaks with baked potatoes and a crisp mixed salad.

2 Remove the steaks from the dish and reserve the marinade. Sprinkle the peppercorns over the steaks and press them into the surface.

3 Cook the steaks on a hot barbecue, basting them occasionally with the reserved marinade during cooking. (Take care when basting, as the alcohol will tend to flare up: spoon or brush on just a small amount at a time.)

INGREDIENTS

4 beef sirloin or rump (round)
steaks, about 175g/6oz each
2 garlic cloves, crushed
120ml/4fl oz/1/2 cup stout
30ml/2 tbsp dark muscovado
(molasses) sugar
30ml/2 tbsp Worcestershire sauce
15ml/1 tbsp corn oil
15ml/1 tbsp crushed
black peppercorns

SERVES 4

1 Place the steaks in a dish and add the garlic, stout, sugar, Worcestershire sauce and oil. Turn to coat evenly, then leave to marinate in the refrigerator for 2–3 hours or overnight.

4 Turn the steaks once during cooking, and cook them for 3–6 minutes on each side, depending on whether you like them rare, medium or well done.

SIRLOIN STEAKS WITH BLOODY MARY SAUCE

This cocktail of ingredients is just as delicious as the drink that inspired it, and as the alcohol evaporates in cooking you need not worry about a hangover.

INGREDIENTS

4 sirloin steaks, about
225g/8oz each
30ml/2 tbsp dark soy sauce
60ml/4 tbsp balsamic vinegar
30ml/2 tbsp extra virgin
olive oil

FOR THE BLOODY MARY SAUCE
1kg/2¼lb very ripe tomatoes,
peeled and chopped
tomato purée (paste), if required
50g/2oz/½ cup chopped onions
2 spring onions (scallions)
5ml/1 tsp chopped fresh
coriander (cilantro)
5ml/1 tsp ground cumin
5ml/1 tsp salt
15ml/1 tbsp fresh lime juice
120ml/4fl oz/½ cup beef
consommé
60ml/4 tbsp vodka
15ml/1 tbsp Worcestershire sauce

SERVES 4

1 Lay the steaks in a shallow dish. Mix together the soy sauce, vinegar and olive oil, pour over the steaks and leave to marinate in the refrigerator for at least 2 hours, turning once or twice.

2 Place all the sauce ingredients in a food processor and blend to a fairly smooth texture. If the tomatoes are not quite ripe, add a little tomato purée. Put in a pan, bring to the boil and simmer for about 5 minutes.

3 Remove the steaks from the dish and discard the marinade. Cook the steaks on a medium-hot barbecue for about 3–6 minutes each side, depending on how rare you like them, turning once during cooking. Serve the steaks with the Bloody Mary sauce.

BEEF RIB WITH ONION SAUCE

· · ·

Rib of beef is a classic large roasting joint, but just one rib, barbecue-cooked on the bone then carved into succulent slices, makes a perfect dish for two. Serve with a mellow red onion sauce.

INGREDIENTS

1 beef rib on the bone, about
1kg/2¼lb and about 4cm/1½in
thick, well trimmed of fat
5ml/1 tsp "steak pepper" or lightly
crushed black peppercorns
15ml/1 tbsp coarse sea
salt, crushed
30–45ml/2–3 tbsp olive oil

FOR THE RED ONION SAUCE
40g/1½ oz butter
1 large red onion or
8–10 shallots, sliced
250ml/8fl oz/1 cup fruity red wine
250ml/8fl oz/1 cup beef or
chicken stock
15–30ml/1–2 tbsp redcurrant jelly
or seedless raspberry preserve
1.5ml/¼ tsp dried thyme
salt and freshly ground
black pepper

SERVES 2–4

1 Wipe the beef with damp kitchen paper. Mix the "steak pepper" or crushed peppercorns with the crushed salt and press on to both sides of the meat. Leave the meat to stand, loosely covered, for 30 minutes.

2 To make the sauce, melt the butter over a medium heat. Add the onion or shallots and cook for 3 minutes, until softened. Add the wine, stock, jelly or preserve and thyme and bring to the boil. Reduce the heat and simmer for 30–35 minutes until the liquid has evaporated and the sauce has thickened. Season and keep warm.

3 Brush the meat with olive oil and cook on a hot barbecue, or in a pan over a high heat, for 5–8 minutes each side, depending on how rare you like it. Transfer the beef to a board, cover loosely and leave to stand for about 10 minutes. Using a knife, loosen the meat from the rib bone, then carve into slices. Serve with the red onion sauce.

STILTON BURGERS

A variation on the traditional burger, this tasty recipe contains a delicious surprise:
a creamy filling of lightly melted Stilton cheese.

INGREDIENTS

450g/1lb/4 cups minced
(ground) beef
1 onion, chopped
1 celery stick, chopped
5ml/1 tsp dried mixed herbs
5ml/1 tsp prepared mustard
50g/2oz Stilton cheese
4 burger buns
salt and freshly ground
black pepper

SERVES 4

1 Mix the minced beef with the chopped onion, celery, mixed herbs and mustard. Season well with salt and pepper, and bring together with your hands to form a firm mixture.

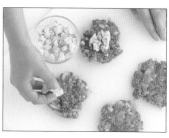

2 Divide the mixture into eight equal portions. Shape four portions into rounds and flatten each one slightly. Crumble a little of the cheese in the centre of each round.

3 Shape and flatten the remaining four portions and place on top. Use your hands to mould the rounds together, encasing the crumbled cheese, and shaping them into four burgers.

4 Cook on a medium barbecue for about 10 minutes, or until cooked through, turning once. Split the burger buns and place a burger inside each. Serve with salad and mustard pickle.

SPICED BEEF SATAY

. . .

Tender strips of steak threaded on skewers and spiced with the characteristic flavours of Indonesia are popular with everyone.

INGREDIENTS

450g/1lb rump (round) steak, cut
in 1cm/½in strips
5ml/1 tsp coriander seeds, dry-fried
and ground
2.5ml/½ tsp cumin seeds, dry-fried
and ground
5ml/1 tsp tamarind pulp
1 small onion
2 garlic cloves
15ml/1 tbsp brown sugar
15ml/1 tbsp dark soy sauce
salt

To SERVE
cucumber chunks
lemon or lime wedges
Sambal Kecap

MAKES 18 SKEWERS

1 Mix the meat and spices in a large non-metallic bowl. Soak the tamarind pulp in 5 tablespoons water.

2 Strain the tamarind and reserve the juice. Put the onion, garlic, tamarind juice, sugar and soy sauce in a food processor and blend well.

3 Pour the marinade over the meat and spices in the bowl and toss together well. Leave for at least 1 hour.

4 Meanwhile, soak some bamboo skewers in water to prevent them from burning while cooking. Thread 5 or 6 pieces of meat on to each skewer and sprinkle with salt. Cook on a medium-hot barbecue, turning the skewers frequently and basting with the marinade, until the meat is tender.

5 Serve with cucumber chunks and wedges of lemon or lime for squeezing over the meat. Sambal Kecap makes a traditional accompaniment.

SAMBAL KECAP
Mix 1 fresh red chilli, seeded and finely chopped, 2 crushed garlic cloves and 60ml/4 tbsp dark soy sauce with 20ml/4 tsp lemon juice and 30ml/2 tbsp hot water in a bowl. Leave to stand for 30 minutes before serving.

VEGETABLE-STUFFED BEEF ROLLS

. . .

These Japanese-style beef rolls are very popular for al fresco meals. You could roll up many
other vegetables in the sliced beef. Pork is also very good cooked this way.

INGREDIENTS

50g/2oz carrot
50g/2oz green (bell) pepper, seeded
bunch of spring onions (scallions)
400g/14oz beef topside (pot roast),
thinly sliced
plain (all-purpose) flour, for dusting
15ml/1 tbsp olive oil
fresh parsley sprigs, to garnish

FOR THE SAUCE
30ml/2 tbsp sugar
45ml/3 tbsp soy sauce
45ml/3 tbsp mirin

SERVES 4

1 Use a sharp knife to shred the
carrot and green pepper into 4–5cm/
1½–2in lengths. Wash and peel the
outer skins from the spring onions,
then halve them lengthways. Shred the
spring onions diagonally into
4–5cm/1½–2in lengths.

2 The beef slices should be no more
than 2mm/1/12in thick, and about
15cm/6in square. Lay a slice of beef
on a chopping board and top with
strips of the carrot, green pepper and
spring onion. Roll up quite tightly and
dust lightly with flour. Repeat with the
remaining beef and vegetables.

3 Secure the beef rolls with cocktail
sticks or toothpicks, soaked in water to
prevent them from burning, and cook
on a medium barbecue or in a pan over
a medium heat, for 10–15 minutes,
turning frequently, until golden brown
and thoroughly cooked.

4 Blend the ingredients for the sauce in
a small pan and cook to dissolve the
sugar and form a glaze. Halve the
cooked rolls, cutting at a slant, and
stand them on a plate with the sloping
cut ends facing upwards. Dress with the
sauce and garnish with fresh parsley.

LAMB STEAKS MARINATED IN MINT AND SHERRY

*The marinade in this recipe is extremely quick to prepare, and is the key
to its success: the sherry imparts a wonderful tang to the meat.*

INGREDIENTS
6 large lamb steaks or
12 smaller chops

FOR THE MARINADE
30ml/2 tbsp chopped fresh
mint leaves
15ml/1 tbsp black peppercorns
1 medium onion, chopped
120ml/4fl oz/¹/₂ cup sherry
60ml/4 tbsp extra virgin olive oil
2 garlic cloves

SERVES 6

1 Process the fresh mint leaves and
peppercorns in a food processor until
finely chopped. Add the onion and
process again until smooth. Add the
rest of the marinade ingredients and
process until completely mixed. The
marinade should be a thick consistency.

2 Add the marinade to the lamb and
cover with clear film (plastic wrap).
Marinate in the refrigerator overnight.

3 Cook the steaks on a medium
barbecue for 10–15 minutes, basting
occasionally with the marinade.

SKEWERED LAMB WITH HERB YOGURT

These Turkish kebabs are traditionally made with lamb, but lean beef or pork work equally well.
You can alternate pieces of pepper, lemon or onions with the meat for extra flavour and colour.

INGREDIENTS
900g/2lb lean boneless lamb
1 large onion, grated
3 bay leaves
5 sprigs of thyme or rosemary
grated rind and juice of 1 lemon
pinch of caster (superfine) sugar
75ml/3fl oz/¹/₃ cup olive oil
salt and freshly ground
black pepper
sprigs of fresh rosemary to garnish
lemon wedges, to serve

FOR THE HERB YOGURT
150ml/¹/₄ pint/²/₃ cup thick natural
(plain) yogurt
15ml/1 tbsp chopped fresh mint
15ml/1 tbsp chopped fresh
coriander (cilantro)
10ml/2 tsp grated onion

SERVES 4

1 To make the herb yogurt, mix together the natural yogurt, chopped fresh mint, chopped fresh coriander and grated onion. Transfer the yogurt to a serving bowl.

2 To make the kebabs, cut the lamb into 2.5cm/1in cubes and put in a bowl. Mix together the onion, herbs, lemon rind and juice, sugar and oil, then season to taste.

3 Pour the marinade over the meat and stir to ensure it is covered. Cover with clear film (plastic wrap) and leave to marinate in the refrigerator for several hours or overnight.

4 Drain the meat and thread on to metal skewers. Cook on a hot barbecue for about 10 minutes. Garnish with rosemary and lemon wedges and serve with the herb yogurt.

LAMB BURGERS WITH REDCURRANT CHUTNEY

These rather special burgers take a little extra time to prepare but are well worth it.
The redcurrant chutney is the perfect complement to the minty lamb taste.

INGREDIENTS

500g/1¼ lb/5 cups minced
(ground)lean lamb
1 small onion, finely chopped
30ml/2 tbsp finely chopped
fresh mint
30ml/2 tbsp finely chopped
fresh parsley
115g/4oz mozzarella cheese
30ml/2 tbsp oil, for basting
salt and freshly ground
black pepper

FOR THE REDCURRANT CHUTNEY
115g/4oz/1½ cups redcurrants
10ml/2 tsp clear honey
5ml/1 tsp balsamic vinegar
30ml/2 tbsp finely chopped mint

SERVES 4

1 In a large bowl, mix together the minced lamb, chopped onion, mint and parsley until evenly combined. Season well with plenty of salt and freshly ground black pepper.

Cook's Tip

If time is short, or if fresh redcurrants are not available, serve the burgers with ready-made redcurrant sauce.

2 Roughly divide the meat mixture into eight equal pieces and use your hands to press each of the pieces into flat rounds.

3 Cut the mozzarella cheese into four chunks. Place one chunk of cheese on half the lamb rounds. Top each with another round of meat mixture.

4 Press each of the two rounds of meat together firmly, making four flattish burger shapes. Use your fingers to blend the edges neatly and seal in the cheese completely.

5 Place all the ingredients for the chutney in a bowl and mash them together with a fork. Season well with salt and freshly ground black pepper.

6 Brush the lamb burgers with olive oil and cook them over a moderately hot barbecue for about 15 minutes, turning once, until golden brown. Serve with the redcurrant chutney.

BARBECUE-COOKED LAMB WITH POTATO SLICES

∘ ∘ ∘

A traditional mixture of fresh herbs adds a summery flavour to this simple lamb dish.
A leg of lamb is easier to cook evenly on the barbecue if it's boned out, or "butterflied" first.

INGREDIENTS

1 leg of lamb, about 1.75kg/4½lb
1 garlic clove, thinly sliced
handful of fresh flat leaf parsley
handful of fresh sage
handful of fresh rosemary
handful of fresh thyme
90ml/6 tbsp dry sherry
60ml/4 tbsp walnut oil
500g/1¼lb medium-size potatoes
salt and freshly ground
black pepper

SERVES 4

2 Use a sharp kitchen knife to scrape away the meat from the bone on both sides, until the bone is completely exposed. Carefully remove the bone and cut away any sinews and excess fat from the meat.

4 Place the meat in a bowl and pour over the sherry and walnut oil. Chop half the remaining herbs and sprinkle over the meat. Cover the bowl with a clean dishtowel and leave to marinate in the refrigerator for 30 minutes.

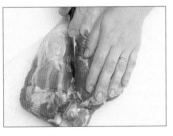

1 Place the lamb on a board, smooth-side downwards, so that you can see where the bone lies. Using a sharp heavy knife, make a long cut through the flesh down to the bone.

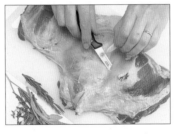

3 Cut through the thickest part of the meat so that you can open it out as flat as possible. Make several cuts in the lamb with a sharp kitchen knife, and push slivers of garlic and sprigs of fresh herbs into the cuts.

5 Remove the lamb from the marinade and season. Cook on a medium-hot barbecue for 30–35 minutes, turning occasionally and basting with the reserved marinade.

Cook's Tip

If you have a spit-roasting attachment, the lamb can be rolled and tied with herbs inside, and spit roasted for 1–1½ hours. A spit makes it much easier to cook larger pieces of lamb.

6 Scrub the potatoes, then cut them in thick slices. Brush with the marinade and place around the lamb. Cook for about 15 minutes, until golden brown.

LAMB WITH LAVENDER BALSAMIC MARINADE

• • •

Lavender is an unusual flavour to use with meat, but its heady, summery scent works well with lamb cooked on the barbecue. If you like, rosemary can take its place.

2 Sprinkle the chopped fresh lavender over the lamb in the bowl.

3 Beat together the vinegar, olive oil and lemon juice and pour them over the lamb. Season well with salt and pepper and then turn to coat evenly.

INGREDIENTS

4 racks of lamb, with
3–4 cutlets each
1 shallot, finely chopped
45ml/3 tbsp chopped
fresh lavender
15ml/1 tbsp balsamic vinegar
30ml/2 tbsp olive oil
15ml/1 tbsp lemon juice
salt and freshly ground
black pepper
handful of lavender sprigs

SERVES 4

1 Place the racks of lamb in a large mixing bowl or wide dish and sprinkle over the chopped shallot.

4 Scatter a few lavender sprigs over the grill or on the coals of a medium-hot barbecue. Cook the lamb for about 15–20 minutes, turning once and basting with any remaining marinade, until golden brown on the outside and still slightly pink in the centre.

LAMB WITH MINT AND LEMON

Use this simple and traditional marinade to make the most of fine quality lamb leg steaks.
Lemon and fresh mint combine extremely well with the flavour of lamb cooked on the barbecue.

INGREDIENTS

4 lamb steaks, about
225g/8oz each
fresh mint leaves, to garnish

FOR THE MARINADE
grated rind and juice of ½ lemon
1 garlic clove, crushed
1 spring onion (scallion), chopped
5ml/1 tsp finely chopped fresh mint
30ml/2 tbsp extra virgin olive oil
salt and freshly ground
black pepper

SERVES 4

1 Mix all the marinade ingredients and season to taste. Place the lamb steaks in a shallow dish and add the marinade. Cover with clear film (plastic wrap) and marinate in the refrigerator for several hours or overnight.

2 Drain the lamb steaks and cook on a medium-hot barbecue for about 10–15 minutes until just cooked, basting with the marinade occasionally and turning once. Garnish the lamb steaks with the fresh mint leaves.

STUFFED AUBERGINES WITH LAMB

*Minced lamb and aubergines go together beautifully. This is an attractive dish,
using different coloured peppers in the lightly spiced stuffing mixture.*

INGREDIENTS

2 medium aubergines (eggplant)
30ml/2 tbsp vegetable oil
1 medium onion, sliced
5ml/1 tsp grated fresh root ginger
5ml/1 tsp chilli powder
1 garlic clove, crushed
1.5ml/¼ tsp ground turmeric
5ml/1 tsp ground coriander
1 medium tomato, chopped
350g/12oz/3 cups minced (ground)
lean lamb
1 medium green (bell) pepper,
coarsely chopped
1 medium orange (bell) pepper,
coarsely chopped
30ml/2 tbsp chopped fresh
coriander (cilantro)

FOR THE GARNISH
½ onion, sliced
2 cherry tomatoes, quartered
fresh coriander (cilantro) sprigs

SERVES 4

1 Cut the aubergines in half lengthways
with a heavy sharp knife. Scoop out
most of the flesh and reserve it for
another dish. Brush the shells with a
little vegetable oil.

2 In a medium pan, heat 15ml/1 tbsp
oil and cook the sliced onion until
golden brown. Stir in the grated ginger,
chilli powder, garlic, turmeric and
ground coriander. Add the chopped
tomato, lower the heat and cook for
about 5 minutes, stirring constantly.

3 Add the minced lamb to the pan and
continue to cook over a medium heat
for about 7–10 minutes. Stir in the
chopped green and orange peppers
and the fresh coriander.

4 Spoon the lamb mixture into the
aubergine shells and brush the edges
of the shells with the remaining oil.
Cook on a medium-hot barbecue for
15–20 minutes, until cooked through.
Garnish with sliced onion, cherry
tomatoes and coriander and serve.

VEAL CHOPS WITH BASIL BUTTER

Veal chops from the loin are an expensive cut and are best cooked quickly and simply.
The flavour of basil goes well with veal, but other herbs can be used instead if you like.

INGREDIENTS

25g/1oz/2 tbsp butter, softened
15ml/1 tbsp Dijon mustard
15ml/1 tbsp chopped fresh basil
olive oil, for brushing
2 veal loin chops, 2.5cm/1in thick,
about 225g/8oz each
salt and freshly ground
black pepper
fresh basil sprigs, to garnish

SERVES 2

1 To make the basil butter, cream the softened butter with the Dijon mustard and chopped fresh basil in a large mixing bowl, then season with plenty of freshly ground black pepper.

2 Brush both sides of each chop with olive oil and season with a little salt.

3 Cook the chops on a hot barbecue for 7–10 minutes, basting with oil and turning once, until done to your liking. (Medium-rare meat will still be slightly soft when pressed, medium will be springy and well-done firm.) Top each chop with half the basil butter and serve immediately, garnished with basil.

PORK AND PINEAPPLE SATAY

. . .

This variation on the classic satay has added pineapple, but keeps the traditional coconut and peanut sauce.

INGREDIENTS

500g/1¼lb pork fillet (tenderloin)
1 small onion, chopped
1 garlic clove, chopped
60ml/4 tbsp soy sauce
finely grated rind of ½ lemon
5ml/1 tsp ground cumin
5ml/1 tsp ground coriander
5ml/1 tsp ground turmeric
5ml/1 tsp dark muscovado
(molasses) sugar
225g/8oz can pineapple chunks, or
1 small pineapple, peeled and diced
salt and freshly ground
black pepper

FOR THE SATAY SAUCE
175ml/6fl oz/¾ cup coconut milk
90 ml/6 tbsp crunchy peanut butter
1 garlic clove, crushed
10ml/2 tsp soy sauce
5ml/1 tsp dark muscovado
(molasses) sugar

SERVES 4

1 Using a sharp kitchen knife, trim any fat from the pork fillet and cut it in 2.5cm/1in cubes. Place the meat in a large mixing bowl and set aside.

2 Place the onion, garlic, soy sauce, lemon rind, spices and sugar in a blender or food processor. Add two pieces of pineapple and process until the mixture is almost smooth.

3 Add the paste to the pork, tossing well to coat evenly. Thread the pieces of pork on to bamboo skewers, with the remaining pineapple pieces.

4 To make the sauce, pour the coconut milk into a small pan and stir in the peanut butter. Stir in the remaining sauce ingredients and heat gently over the barbecue, stirring until smooth and hot. Cover and keep warm on the edge of the barbecue.

5 Cook the pork and pineapple skewers on a medium-hot barbecue, turning occasionally, for 10–12 minutes, until golden brown and thoroughly cooked. Serve with the satay sauce.

Cook's Tip

If you cannot buy coconut milk, use creamed coconut (coconut cream). Dissolve a 50g/2oz piece in 150ml/¼ pint/⅔ cup boiling water and use as above.

LEMON GRASS PORK CHOPS WITH MUSHROOMS

• • •

Thai flavourings are used to make an aromatic marinade and a spicy sauce. The sauce can be put together in a pan on the barbecue while the chops and mushrooms are cooking.

INGREDIENTS

*4 pork chops, about 225g/8oz each
4 large field (portabello)
mushrooms
45ml/3 tbsp vegetable oil
4 red chillies, seeded and sliced
45ml/3 tbsp Thai fish sauce
90ml/6 tbsp lime juice
4 shallots, chopped
5ml/1 tsp roasted ground rice
30ml/2 tbsp spring onions
(scallions), chopped
fresh coriander (cilantro) leaves
and 4 shredded spring onions,
to garnish*

*FOR THE MARINADE
2 garlic cloves, chopped
15ml/1 tbsp sugar
15ml/1 tbsp Thai fish sauce
30ml/2 tbsp soy sauce
15ml/1 tbsp sesame oil
15ml/1 tbsp whisky or dry sherry
2 lemon grass stalks,
finely chopped
2 spring onions (scallions), chopped*

SERVES 4

2 Place the mushrooms and marinated pork chops on a rack and brush with 15ml/1 tbsp vegetable oil. Cook the pork chops on a medium-hot barbecue for 10–15 minutes and the mushrooms for about 2 minutes, turning once. Brush both with the marinade while they are cooking.

3 Meanwhile, heat the remaining oil in a small frying pan, then remove from the heat and mix in the remaining ingredients. Put the pork chops and mushrooms on a serving plate and spoon over the sauce. Garnish with the fresh coriander leaves and shredded spring onions.

1 To make the marinade, mix all the ingredients together. Arrange the pork chops in a shallow dish. Pour over the marinade and leave for 1–2 hours.

FARMHOUSE PIZZA

• • •

Pizza is not a dish usually associated with barbecue cooking, but in fact the open fire gives the base a wonderfully crisp texture. Shape the dough to fit the grill rack of your barbecue.

INGREDIENTS

90ml/6 tbsp olive oil
225g/8oz button (white)
mushrooms, sliced
300g/11oz packet pizza-base mix
300ml/½ pint/1¼ cups tomato
sauce
300g/11oz mozzarella cheese,
thinly sliced
115g/4oz wafer-thin smoked
ham slices
6 bottled artichoke hearts in oil,
drained and sliced
50g/2oz can anchovy fillets,
drained and halved lengthways
10 pitted black olives, halved
30ml/2 tbsp chopped fresh oregano
45ml/3 tbsp freshly grated
Parmesan cheese
freshly ground black pepper

SERVES 8

1 Heat 30ml/2 tbsp oil in a pan, add the mushrooms and cook until all the juices have evaporated. Leave to cool.

2 Make up the pizza dough according to the directions on the packet. Roll it out on a lightly floured surface to a 30 x 25cm/12 x 10in rectangle. Brush with oil and place, oiled-side down, on a medium-hot barbecue. Cook for 6 minutes until firm.

3 Brush the uncooked side of the dough with oil and turn over. Spread with the tomato sauce and arrange the sliced mozzarella on top. Scrunch up the smoked ham and arrange on top with the artichoke hearts, anchovies and cooked mushrooms.

4 Dot with the halved olives, then sprinkle over the fresh oregano and Parmesan. Drizzle over the remaining olive oil and season with black pepper. Return to the barbecue and cook for a further 8–10 minutes, or until the dough is golden brown and crisp.

Chicken cooked on a barbecue is unfailingly popular with both

adults and children, and it can be as simple or sophisticated as

you choose. Don't forget other types of poultry, particularly

duck, which stays beautifully juicy and moist when prepared

in this way.

POULTRY AND
GAME

CHICKEN WITH PINEAPPLE

· · ·

The pineapple juice in this Indian recipe is used to tenderize the meat, but it also gives the chicken a deliciously tangy sweetness.

INGREDIENTS

225g/8oz can pineapple chunks
in juice
5ml/1 tsp ground cumin
5ml/1 tsp ground coriander
1 garlic clove, crushed
5ml/1 tsp chilli powder
5ml/1 tsp salt
30ml/2 tbsp natural (plain) yogurt
15ml/1 tbsp chopped fresh
coriander (cilantro)
few drops orange food
colouring (optional)
275g/10oz skinless, boneless
chicken breast and thigh meat
1/2 red (bell) pepper
1/2 yellow or green (bell) pepper
1 large onion
6 cherry tomatoes
15ml/1 tbsp vegetable oil

SERVES 6

1 Drain the canned pineapple into a bowl. Reserve twelve large chunks of pineapple. Squeeze the juice from the remaining chunks into the bowl, then discard the chunks. You should be left with about 120ml/4fl oz/1/2 cup pineapple juice.

2 In a large bowl, blend together the cumin, ground coriander, garlic, chilli powder, salt, yogurt, fresh coriander and food colouring, if using. Pour in the pineapple juice and mix together.

3 Cut the chicken into cubes, add to the yogurt and spice mixture and leave to marinate for about 1–1 1/2 hours. Cut the peppers and onion into chunks.

4 Arrange the chicken pieces, vegetables and reserved pineapple chunks alternately on six skewers.

5 Brush the kebabs with oil and cook on a medium barbecue for about 10 minutes, turning and basting the chicken pieces regularly with the marinade, until cooked through. Serve with salad or plain boiled rice.

CITRUS KEBABS
° ° °

Serve these succulent grilled chicken kebabs on a bed of lettuce leaves, garnished with sprigs of fresh mint and orange and lemon slices.

INGREDIENTS
4 skinless, boneless chicken
breast portions
fresh mint sprigs, to garnish
orange and lemon or lime slices,
to garnish

FOR THE MARINADE
finely grated rind and juice of
1/2 orange
finely grated rind and juice of
1/2 lemon or lime
30ml/2 tbsp olive oil
30ml/2 tbsp clear honey
30ml/2 tbsp chopped fresh mint
1.5ml/1/4 tsp ground cumin
salt and freshly ground
black pepper

SERVES 4

1 Use a heavy knife to cut the chicken into 2.5cm/1in cubes.

2 Combine the marinade ingredients in a large bowl, add the chicken and cover with clear film (plastic wrap). Leave to marinate for at least 2 hours, or overnight in the refrigerator.

3 Thread the chicken on to metal skewers and cook on a medium barbecue for 10 minutes, basting with the marinade and turning frequently. Garnish with mint and citrus slices.

SWEET AND SOUR KEBABS

. . .

*This marinade contains sugar and will burn very easily, so cook the kebabs slowly
and turn them often. Serve these kebabs with harlequin rice.*

INGREDIENTS

2 skinless, boneless chicken
breast portions
8 pickling (pearl) onions or
2 medium onions
4 rindless streaky (fatty) bacon
rashers (strips)
3 firm bananas
1 red (bell) pepper, diced

FOR THE MARINADE
30ml/2 tbsp soft brown sugar
15ml/1 tbsp Worcestershire sauce
30ml/2 tbsp lemon juice
salt and freshly ground
black pepper

FOR THE HARLEQUIN RICE
30ml/2 tbsp olive oil
1 small red (bell) pepper, diced
225g/8oz/1$\frac{1}{3}$ cup cooked rice
115g/4oz/1 cup cooked peas

SERVES 4

1 Combine the marinade ingredients.
Cut each chicken portion into four
pieces, add to the marinade, cover and
leave for at least 4 hours, or preferably
overnight in the refrigerator.

3 Cut each rasher of bacon in half with
a sharp knife. Peel the bananas and cut
each one into three pieces. Wrap half a
bacon rasher around each of the
banana pieces.

5 Cook on a low barbecue for about
15 minutes, turning and basting
frequently with the marinade.

6 Meanwhile, heat the oil in a
frying pan and stir-fry the diced pepper
briefly. Add the rice and peas and stir
until heated through. Serve the
harlequin rice with the kebabs.

2 Peel the pickling onions, blanch them
in boiling water for 5 minutes and
drain. If using medium onions, quarter
them after blanching.

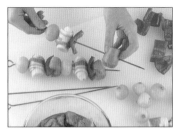

4 Thread the bacon and bananas
on to metal skewers with the chicken
pieces, onions and pepper pieces. Brush
generously with the marinade.

BLACKENED CAJUN CHICKEN AND CORN

This is a classic American Deep-South method of cooking in a spiced coating, which can be used for poultry, meat or fish. The coating should begin to char and blacken slightly at the edges.

INGREDIENTS

8 chicken joints (drumsticks, thighs or wings)
2 whole corn cobs
10ml/2 tsp garlic salt
10ml/2 tsp ground black pepper
7.5ml/1½ tsp ground cumin
7.5ml/1½ tsp paprika
5ml/1 tsp cayenne pepper
45ml/3 tbsp melted butter
chopped parsley, to garnish

SERVES 4

1 Trim any excess fat from the chicken, but leave the skin in place. Slash the thickest parts with a knife, to allow the flavours to penetrate the meat as thoroughly as possible.

2 Pull the husks and silks off the corn cobs, then rinse them under cold running water and pat them dry with kitchen paper. Cut the cobs into thick slices, using a heavy kitchen knife.

3 Mix together all the spices. Brush the chicken and corn with the melted butter and sprinkle the spices over them. Toss well to coat evenly.

4 Cook the chicken pieces on a medium-hot barbecue for about 25 minutes, turning occasionally. Add the corn after 15 minutes, and grill, turning often, until golden brown. Serve garnished with chopped parsley.

CHICKEN WITH HERB AND RICOTTA STUFFING

· · ·

These little chicken drumsticks are full of flavour and the stuffing and bacon help to keep them moist and tender.

INGREDIENTS

60ml/4 tbsp ricotta cheese
1 garlic clove, crushed
45ml/3 tbsp mixed chopped fresh mixed herbs
30ml/2 tbsp fresh brown breadcrumbs
8 chicken drumsticks
8 smoked streaky (fatty) bacon rashers (strips)
5ml/1 tsp whole-grain mustard
15ml/1 tbsp sunflower oil
salt and freshly ground black pepper

SERVES 4

1 Mix together the ricotta, garlic, herbs and breadcrumbs. Season well with plenty of salt and pepper.

2 Carefully loosen the skin from each drumstick and spoon a little of the herb stuffing under each, smoothing the skin back over firmly.

3 Wrap a bacon rasher tightly around the wide end of each drumstick, to hold the skin in place over the stuffing during the cooking time.

4 Mix together the mustard and oil and brush them over the chicken. Cook on a medium-hot barbecue for about 25 minutes, turning occasionally.

BABY CHICKENS WITH LIME AND CHILLI

Poussins are small birds which are ideal for one to two portions. The best way to prepare them is spatchcocked – flattened out – to ensure more even cooking.

INGREDIENTS

4 poussins or Cornish hens, about
450g/1lb each
45ml/3 tbsp butter
30ml/2 tbsp sun-dried
tomato paste
finely grated rind of 1 lime
10ml/2 tsp chilli sauce
juice of ½ lime
lime wedges, to serve
fresh flat leaf parsley sprigs,
to garnish

SERVES 4

1 Place each poussin on a chopping board, breast side upwards, and press down firmly with your hand, to break the breastbone.

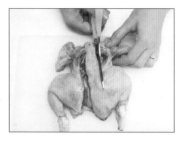

2 Turn the poussin over and, with poultry shears or strong kitchen scissors, cut down either side of the backbone. Remove it and discard.

3 Turn the poussin breast-side up and flatten it gently. Lift the breast skin carefully and gently ease your fingertips underneath, to loosen it from the flesh.

4 Mix together the butter, sun-dried tomato paste, lime rind and chilli sauce in a small bowl. Spread about three-quarters of the mixture under the skin of the poussins, smoothing it evenly over the surface of the flesh.

5 To hold the poussins flat during cooking, thread two bamboo skewers through each bird, crossing at the centre. Each skewer should pass through a drumstick and then out through a wing on the other side.

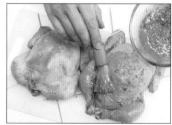

6 Mix the reserved paste with the lime juice and brush it over the skin of the poussins. Cook on a medium-hot barbecue, turning occasionally, for 25–30 minutes, or until there is no trace of pink in the juices when the flesh is pierced. Garnish with lime wedges and fresh flat leaf parsley.

CHICKEN COOKED IN SPICES AND COCONUT

This chicken dish can be prepared in advance and then placed in the refrigerator until you are ready to light the barbecue. Serve the chicken with naan bread.

INGREDIENTS

200g/7oz block creamed coconut
(coconut cream)
3 garlic cloves, chopped
2 spring onions
(scallions), chopped
1 fresh green chilli, chopped
5cm/2in piece fresh root
ginger, chopped
5ml/1 tsp fennel seeds
2.5ml/½ tsp black peppercorns
seeds from 4 cardamom pods
30ml/2 tbsp ground coriander
5ml/1 tsp ground cumin
5ml/1 tsp ground star anise
5ml/1 tsp ground nutmeg
2.5ml/½ tsp ground cloves
2.5ml/½ tsp ground turmeric
4 large, skinless, boneless chicken
breast portions
onion rings and fresh coriander
(cilantro) sprigs, to garnish

SERVES 4

2 Make several diagonal cuts across the chicken. Arrange in a shallow dish. Spoon over half the coconut mixture and toss well to coat the chicken evenly. Cover the dish and leave to marinate for at least 30 minutes, or overnight in the refrigerator.

3 Cook the chicken on a medium barbecue for about 12–15 minutes, turning once, until well browned and thoroughly cooked. Heat the remaining coconut mixture gently until boiling. Serve with the chicken, garnished with onion rings and sprigs of coriander.

1 Break up the coconut and put it in a jug (pitcher). Pour in 300ml/½ pint/ 1¼ cups boiling water and leave to dissolve. Place the chopped garlic, spring onions, chilli, ginger and all of the spices in a blender or food processor. Pour in the coconut mixture and blend to a smooth paste.

GRILLED CASHEW NUT CHICKEN

*This dish comes from the beautiful Indonesian island of Bali, where nuts are widely used as a
base for sauces and marinades. Serve it with a green salad and a hot chilli dipping sauce.*

INGREDIENTS

4 chicken legs
radishes, sliced, to garnish
1/2 cucumber, sliced, to garnish
Chinese leaves (Chinese cabbage),
to serve

FOR THE MARINADE
50g/2oz raw cashew nuts
2 shallots, or 1 small onion,
finely chopped
2 garlic cloves, crushed
2 small red chillies, chopped
5cm/2in piece lemon grass
15ml/1 tbsp tamarind sauce
30ml/2 tbsp dark soy sauce
15ml/1 tbsp Thai fish sauce
10ml/2 tsp sugar
2.5ml/1/2 tsp salt
15ml/1 tbsp rice or white
wine vinegar

SERVES 4

1 Using a sharp, heavy kitchen knife, slash the chicken legs several times through to the bone. Chop off the knuckle end and discard.

2 To make the marinade, place the cashew nuts in a food processor or pestle and mortar and grind until fine.

3 Add the chopped shallots or onion, garlic, chillies and lemon grass and process. Add the remaining marinade ingredients and process again.

4 Spread the marinade over the chicken and leave for up to 8 hours in the refrigerator. Cook the chicken on a medium barbecue for 25 minutes, basting and turning occasionally. Garnish with radishes and cucumber and serve on a bed of Chinese leaves.

THAI GRILLED CHICKEN

. . .

Thai-style chicken is especially delicious when cooked on the barbecue.
Serve it on a bed of crisp salad with lime wedges to offset its richness.

INGREDIENTS

900g/2lb chicken drumsticks
or thighs
salt and freshly ground
black pepper
1/2 cucumber, cut into strips,
to garnish
4 spring onions (scallions),
trimmed, to garnish
2 limes, quartered, to garnish
crisp lettuce leaves, to serve

FOR THE MARINADE
5ml/1 tsp black peppercorns
2.5ml/1/2 tsp caraway or
cumin seeds
20ml/4 tsp sugar
10ml/2 tsp paprika
2cm/3/4in piece fresh root ginger,
chopped
3 garlic cloves, crushed
15g/1/2oz coriander (cilantro),
white root or stem, finely chopped
45ml/3 tbsp vegetable oil

SERVES 4–6

1 Chop through the narrow end
of each drumstick with a heavy knife.
Score the chicken pieces deeply to
allow the marinade to penetrate and
arrange in a shallow bowl.

2 Grind the peppercorns, caraway
or cumin seeds and sugar in a pestle
and mortar or a food processor. Add
the paprika, ginger, garlic, coriander
and oil and grind to a paste.

3 Spread the marinade over the chicken
and set aside in the refrigerator to
marinate for 6 hours. Cook the chicken
on a medium barbecue for 20 minutes,
basting with the marinade and turning
once. Season, arrange on a bed of
lettuce and garnish before serving.

MEDITERRANEAN TURKEY SKEWERS

*These attractive kebabs can be assembled in advance and left to marinate until you are ready
to cook them. Cooking on the barbecue intensifies the Mediterranean flavours of the vegetables.*

INGREDIENTS

2 medium courgettes (zucchini)
1 long thin aubergine (eggplant)
*300g/11oz boneless turkey, cut
into 5cm/2in cubes*
12–16 pickling (pearl) onions
*1 red or yellow (bell) pepper, cut
into 5cm/2in squares*

FOR THE MARINADE
90ml/6 tbsp olive oil
45ml/3 tbsp fresh lemon juice
1 garlic clove, finely chopped
*30ml/2 tbsp chopped fresh basil
salt and freshly ground
black pepper*

SERVES 4

3 Prepare the skewers by alternating
the turkey, onions and pepper pieces.
Lay the prepared skewers on a platter
and sprinkle with the flavoured oil.
Leave to marinate for 30 minutes.

4 Cook on a medium barbecue or
under a grill for about 10 minutes,
or until the turkey is cooked and the
vegetables are tender, turning the
skewers occasionally.

1 To make the marinade, mix the olive
oil with the lemon juice, garlic and
chopped fresh basil. Season well with
plenty of salt and black pepper.

2 Slice the courgettes and aubergine
lengthways into strips 5mm/¼in thick.
Cut them crossways about two-thirds
down their length. Discard the shorter
lengths. Wrap half the turkey pieces
with the courgette slices and the other
half with the aubergine slices.

QUAIL WITH A FIVE-SPICE MARINADE

Blending and grinding your own five-spice powder for this Vietnamese dish will give the freshest-tasting results. If you are short of time, buy a ready-mixed blend from the supermarket.

INGREDIENTS

6 quails, cleaned
2 spring onions (scallions),
coarsely chopped, to garnish
mandarin orange or satsuma,
to garnish
banana leaves, to serve

FOR THE MARINADE
2 pieces star anise
10ml/2 tsp ground cinnamon
10ml/2 tsp fennel seeds
10ml/2 tsp Sichuan pepper
a pinch ground cloves
1 small onion, finely chopped
1 garlic clove, crushed
60ml/4 tbsp clear honey
30ml/2 tbsp dark soy sauce

SERVES 4–6

1 Remove the backbones from the quails by cutting down either side with a pair of strong kitchen scissors.

2 Flatten the birds with the palm of your hand and secure each bird using two bamboo skewers.

3 To make the marinade, place the five spices in a mortar or spice mill and grind to a fine powder. Add the onion, garlic, clear honey and soy sauce, and combine until thoroughly mixed.

4 Arrange the quails on a flat dish and pour over the marinade. Cover with clear film (plastic wrap) and leave in the refrigerator for 8 hours or overnight for the flavours to mingle.

5 Cook the quails on a medium barbecue for 15–20 minutes until golden brown, basting occasionally with the marinade and turning once.

6 To garnish, remove the outer rind from the mandarin orange or satsuma, using a vegetable peeler. Shred the rind finely and combine with the chopped spring onions. Arrange the quails on a bed of banana leaves and garnish with the orange rind and spring onions.

Cook's Tip

If you prefer, or if quails are not available, you could use other poultry, such as poussins, as a substitute.

PHEASANTS WITH SAGE AND LEMON

Pheasant is quick to cook and makes a really special summer meal.
This recipe can also be used for guinea fowl.

INGREDIENTS

2 pheasants, about 450g/1lb each
1 lemon
60ml/4 tbsp chopped fresh sage
3 shallots
5ml/1 tsp Dijon mustard
15ml/1 tbsp brandy or dry sherry
150ml/5fl oz/2/3 cup crème fraîche
salt and freshly ground
black pepper
lemon wedges and sage sprigs,
to garnish

SERVES 4

2 Finely grate the rind from half the lemon and slice the rest thinly. Mix together the lemon rind and half the chopped sage in a small bowl.

5 Meanwhile, cook the shallots on the barbecue for about 10–12 minutes, turning occasionally, until the skin is blackened and the inside very soft. Peel off the skins, chop the flesh roughly and mash it with the Dijon mustard and brandy or sherry.

1 Place the pheasants, breast side upwards, on a chopping board and cut them in half lengthways, using poultry shears or a sharp kitchen knife.

3 Loosen the skin on the breasts and legs of the pheasants and push a little of the sage mixture under each. Tuck the lemon slices under the skin, smoothing the skin back firmly.

6 Stir in the crème fraîche and add the reserved chopped sage. Season with plenty of salt and freshly ground black pepper. Serve the dressing with the pheasants, garnished with lemon wedges and sprigs of fresh sage.

4 Place the half-pheasants on a medium-hot barbecue and cook for about 25–30 minutes, turning once.

Cook's Tip

Try to choose pheasants with undamaged skins, so that the flavourings stay in place during cooking.

SPICED DUCK WITH PEARS

. . .

This delicious casserole can be cooked on the barbecue or stove. The browned pears are added towards the end of cooking, along with a pine nut and garlic paste to flavour and thicken.

INGREDIENTS

6 duck portions, either breast or
leg pieces
15ml/1 tbsp olive oil
1 large onion, thinly sliced
1 cinnamon stick, halved
2 sprigs of fresh thyme
475ml/16fl oz/2 cups duck or
chicken stock

To FINISH
3 firm ripe pears, peeled and cored
30ml/2 tbsp olive oil
2 garlic cloves, sliced
25g/1oz/¹/₃ cup pine nuts
2.5ml/¹/₂ tsp saffron threads
25g/1oz/2 tbsp raisins
salt and freshly ground
black pepper
thyme sprigs or parsley, to garnish

SERVES 6

1 Fry the duck portions in olive oil for 5 minutes, until golden, or brush the portions with oil and cook them on a hot barbecue for 8–10 minutes, until golden. Transfer the duck to a large flameproof dish. If frying, drain off all but 15ml/1 tbsp of fat left in the pan.

2 Cook the onion in the frying pan for 5 minutes until golden. Add the cinnamon stick, thyme and stock and bring to the boil. Pour over the duck in the dish and cook slowly on a low barbecue for about 1¼ hours.

3 Halve the pears, brush with oil and cook on the barbecue until brown, or fry them in the oil on the hob (stovetop). Pound the garlic, pine nuts and saffron with a pestle and mortar, to a paste.

4 Add the paste, raisins and pears to the flameproof dish. Cook for 15 minutes until the pears are tender.

5 Season to taste and garnish with the fresh herbs. Serve with mashed potato and a green vegetable, if you like.

Cook's Tip

A good stock is essential for this dish. Buy a large duck (plus two extra duck breasts if you want portions to be generous) and cut it up yourself, using the giblets and carcass for stock. If you buy duck portions, use a well-flavoured chicken stock.

DUCK WITH RED PEPPER JELLY GLAZE

∘ ∘ ∘

Sweet potatoes have pinkish skins and flesh varying from creamy white to deep orange.
Choose a long cylindrical tuber to make neat round slices for this Cajun dish.

INGREDIENTS

2 duck breast fillets
1 sweet potato, about 400g/14oz
30ml/2 tbsp red (bell) pepper jelly
15ml/1 tbsp sherry vinegar
50g/2oz/4 tbsp butter, melted
coarse sea salt and freshly ground
black pepper

SERVES 2

4 Meanwhile, warm the red pepper jelly and sherry vinegar together in a bowl set over a pan of hot water, stirring to mix them as the jelly melts. Brush the skin of the duck with this jelly glaze and return to the barbecue, skin-side down, for 2–3 minutes more to caramelize it.

5 Brush the sweet potato slices with melted butter and sprinkle with coarse sea salt. Cook on a hot barbecue for 8–10 minutes until soft, brushing with more butter and sprinkling with salt and pepper when you turn them. Serve the duck sliced with the sweet potatoes and accompany with a green salad.

1 Slash the skin of the duck diagonally at 2.5cm/1in intervals and rub plenty of salt and pepper over the skin and into the cuts.

2 Scrub the sweet potato and cut into 1cm/½in slices, discarding the ends.

3 Cook the duck on a medium barbecue, skin side down, for about 5 minutes. Turn them over and cook for 8–10 minutes more, according to how pink you like your duck.

DUCK WITH RED PLUMS

* * *

The rich fruity sauce for this dish combines brandy and red plums with double cream and coriander. The sauce can be made in a pan on the barbecue while the duck is cooking.

INGREDIENTS

4 duck breast fillets, 175g/6oz each
10ml/2 tsp crushed cinnamon stick
50g/2oz/¼ cup butter
15ml/1 tbsp plum brandy
250ml/8fl oz/1 cup chicken stock
250ml/8fl oz/1 cup double (heavy) cream
6 fresh red plums, stoned (pitted) and sliced
6 sprigs fresh coriander (cilantro) leaves, plus extra to garnish
salt and freshly ground black pepper

SERVES 4

1 Skin the duck fillets, score them and sprinkle with salt. Press the crushed cinnamon on to both sides of the duck breasts. Brush with butter and cook on a medium barbecue for 15–20 minutes, turning once, until the duck is tender.

2 To make the sauce, melt half the remaining butter in a pan. Add the plum brandy and set it alight. When the flames have died down, add the stock and cream and simmer gently until reduced and thick. Season to taste with salt and pepper.

3 In a pan, melt the other half of the butter and cook the plums and coriander just enough to cook the fruit through. Slice the duck fillets and pour some sauce around each one, then garnish with the plum slices and the chopped fresh coriander.

JUNIPER-SPICED VENISON CHOPS

* * *

Depending on the type of venison available, the chops will vary in size,
so you will need either one or two per person.

INGREDIENTS

4–8 venison chops
250ml/8fl oz/1 cup red wine
2 medium red onions
6 juniper berries, crushed
1 cinnamon stick, crumbled
1 dried bay leaf, crumbled
thinly pared strip of orange rind
olive oil, for brushing
salt and freshly ground black
pepper

SERVES 4

2 Add the juniper berries, cinnamon, bay leaf and orange rind. Toss well to coat evenly and then cover the bowl and leave to marinate for at least an hour, or overnight in the refrigerator.

1 Place the venison chops in a large mixing bowl and pour over the red wine. Using a sharp knife, cut the red onions in half crossways and add them to the bowl.

3 Drain the venison and onions and reserve the marinade. Brush the venison and onions generously with the olive oil and sprinkle with plenty of salt and freshly ground black pepper.

4 Cook the venison and onions on a medium-hot barbecue for about 8–10 minutes on each side, basting regularly with the marinade. The venison should still be slightly pink inside even when fully cooked.

Cook's Tip
Tender farmed venison
is now widely available from
supermarkets and good butchers
shops, but if venison is difficult
to find, beef steaks could be
used instead.

Oily fish, such as tuna, are perfectly suited to grilling and won't

dry out. Use plump prawns or shrimps or firm-textured fish,

such as monkfish, for kebabs, but marinate them first to keep

them moist. More delicate fish can be cooked wrapped in foil,

either on the rack or directly on the coals.

FISH AND
SHELLFISH

Spiced Prawns with Vegetables

• • •

This is a light and nutritious Indian dish, excellent served either on a bed of lettuce leaves,
or with plain boiled rice or chappatis.

INGREDIENTS

20 cooked king prawns (jumbo
shrimp), peeled
1 courgette (zucchini), sliced
1 medium onion, cut into 8 chunks
8 cherry tomatoes
8 baby corn cobs
mixed salad leaves, to serve

FOR THE MARINADE
30ml/2 tbsp chopped fresh
coriander (cilantro)
5ml/1 tsp salt
2 fresh green chillies, seeded
45ml/3 tbsp lemon juice
30ml/2 tbsp vegetable oil

SERVES 4

1 To make the marinade, process the coriander, salt, chillies, lemon juice and oil together in a food processor.

2 Empty the contents from the processor and transfer to a bowl.

3 Add the peeled king prawns to the mixture in the bowl and stir to make sure that all the prawns are thoroughly coated. Cover the bowl with clear film (plastic wrap) and set aside in a cool place, to marinate for 30 minutes.

4 Arrange the vegetables and prawns alternately on four long skewers. Cook on a medium barbecue for 5 minutes, turning frequently, until cooked and browned. Serve immediately, on a bed of mixed salad leaves.

TIGER PRAWN SKEWERS WITH WALNUT PESTO

This is an unusual appetizer or main course, which can be prepared in advance and kept in the refrigerator until you're ready to cook it.

INGREDIENTS

*12–16 large, raw, unpeeled tiger
    prawns (jumbo shrimp)
50g/2oz/¹/2 cup walnut pieces
60ml/4 tbsp chopped fresh flat
    leaf parsley
60ml/4 tbsp chopped fresh basil
2 garlic cloves, chopped
45ml/3 tbsp freshly grated
    Parmesan cheese
30ml/2 tbsp extra virgin olive oil
30ml/2 tbsp walnut oil
salt and freshly ground
    black pepper*

SERVES 4

3 Add half the pesto to the prawns, toss them well, then cover and chill in the refrigerator for a minimum of 1 hour, or leave them overnight.

4 Thread the prawns on to skewers and cook them on a hot barbecue for 3–4 minutes, turning once. Serve with the remaining pesto and a green salad.

1 Peel the prawns, removing the head but leaving the tail. Devein and then put the prawns in a large mixing bowl.

2 To make the pesto, place the walnuts, parsley, basil, garlic, cheese and oils in a food processor and process until finely chopped. Season to taste.

MACKEREL KEBABS WITH SWEET PEPPER SALAD

· · ·

Mackerel is an excellent fish for barbecue-cooking because its natural oils keep it moist and tasty.
This recipe combines mackerel with peppers and tomatoes in a flavoursome summer salad.

INGREDIENTS

4 medium mackerel, about
225g/8oz each, filleted
2 small red onions, cut in wedges
30ml/2 tbsp chopped
fresh marjoram
60ml/4 tbsp dry white wine
45ml/3 tbsp olive oil
juice of 1 lime

FOR THE SALAD
1 red (bell) pepper
1 yellow (bell) pepper
1 small red onion
2 large plum tomatoes
15ml/1 tbsp chopped
fresh marjoram
10ml/2 tsp balsamic vinegar
salt and freshly ground
black pepper

SERVES 4

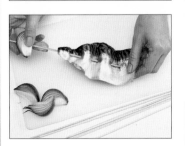

1 Thread each mackerel fillet on to a skewer, with an onion wedge on each end. Arrange the skewers in a dish.

2 Combine the marjoram, wine, oil and lime juice and spoon over the mackerel. Cover and chill in the refrigerator for at least 30 minutes, turning once.

3 To make the salad, quarter and seed both peppers and halve the onion. Place the peppers and onion, skin-side down, with the whole tomatoes, on a hot barbecue and leave until the skins are blackened and charred.

4 Remove the vegetables from the barbecue and leave until they are cool enough to handle. Use a sharp knife to peel off and discard the skins.

5 Chop the vegetables coarsely and put them in a bowl. Stir in the marjoram and balsamic vinegar and season to taste. Toss thoroughly.

6 Remove the kebabs from the refrigerator and cook on a hot barbecue for about 10–12 minutes, turning occasionally and basting with the marinade. Serve with the sweet pepper salad.

Cook's Tip
Other oily fish can be used for this dish: try fillets or cubes of herring, rainbow trout or salmon, instead.

SWORDFISH KEBABS

Swordfish has a firm meaty texture that makes it ideal for cooking on a barbecue.
Marinate the fish first to keep it moist.

INGREDIENTS

900g/2lb swordfish steaks
45ml/3 tbsp olive oil
juice of ½ lemon
1 garlic clove, crushed
5ml/1 tsp paprika
3 tomatoes, quartered
2 onions, cut into wedges
salt and freshly ground
black pepper
salad and pitta bread, to serve

SERVES 4–6

1 Use a large kitchen knife to cut the swordfish steaks into large cubes. Arrange the cubes in a single layer in a large shallow dish.

2 Blend together the olive oil, lemon juice, garlic, paprika and seasoning in a bowl, and pour over the fish. Cover the dish loosely with clear film (plastic wrap) and leave to marinate in a cool place for up to 2 hours.

3 Thread the fish cubes on to metal skewers, alternating them with the pieces of tomato and onion wedges.

4 Cook the kebabs on a hot barbecue for about 5–10 minutes, basting frequently with the remaining marinade and turning occasionally. Serve with salad and pitta bread.

HERBED CHARGRILLED SHARK STEAKS

*Shark is very low in fat, with dense, well-flavoured flesh. Other close-textured fish such as tuna,
bonito and marlin work equally well in this recipe, which is ideal for a barbecue.*

INGREDIENTS

45ml/3 tbsp olive oil
2 fresh bay leaves, chopped
15ml/1 tbsp chopped fresh basil
15ml/1 tbsp chopped fresh oregano
30ml/2 tbsp chopped fresh parsley
*5ml/1 tsp finely chopped
fresh rosemary*
5ml/1 tsp fresh thyme leaves
2 garlic cloves, crushed
*4 pieces drained sun-dried
tomatoes in oil, chopped*
*4 shark steaks, about 200g/
7oz each*
juice of 1 lemon
*15ml/1 tbsp drained small capers
in vinegar (optional)*
salt and ground black pepper
grilled tomatoes, to serve

SERVES 4

1 Mix together the oil, herbs, garlic
and sun-dried tomatoes in a bowl, then
pour the mixture into a shallow dish
that is large enough to hold the shark
steaks in a single layer.

2 Season the shark steaks with salt and
pepper and brush the lemon juice over
both sides. Lay the fish in the dish,
turning the steaks to coat them all
over. Cover with clear film (plastic
wrap) and leave in the refrigerator to
marinate for 1–2 hours to allow the
flavours to develop.

3 Drain the shark steaks, reserving the
marinade, and pat dry with kitchen
paper. Cook on a hot barbecue or
ridged griddle pan for about 5 minutes
on each side, until cooked through.

4 Meanwhile, pour the marinade into a
small pan and bring to the boil either
on the barbecue or on the hob
(stovetop). Stir in the capers, if using.
Spoon the sauce over the grilled shark
steaks and serve immediately with
grilled tomatoes.

MOROCCAN SPICED MACKEREL

* * *

Mackerel is extremely good for you, but some people find its healthy oiliness too much to take. The Moroccan spices in this recipe counteract the richness of the fish.

INGREDIENTS

150ml/¼ pint/⅔ cup sunflower oil
15ml/1 tbsp paprika
5–10ml/1–2 tsp harissa or
chilli powder
10ml/2 tsp ground cumin
10ml/2 tsp ground coriander
2 garlic cloves, crushed
juice of 2 lemons
30ml/2 tbsp chopped fresh
mint leaves
30ml/2 tbsp chopped fresh
coriander (cilantro)
4 mackerel, cleaned
salt and ground black pepper
fresh mint sprigs, to garnish
couscous or rice, and lemon
wedges, to serve

SERVES 4

1 Whisk the sunflower oil with the spices, crushed garlic and lemon juice in a bowl. Season with salt and ground black pepper, then stir in the mint and fresh coriander (cilantro).

2 With a sharp knife, make five or six evenly-spaced diagonal slashes on either side of each fish.

Cook's Tip

If you have one, arrange the mackerel on a large hinged rack before placing on the barbecue to make turning easier. It will also produce an attractive striped effect on the skin.

3 Place the mackerel in a single layer in a shallow dish and pour the marinade evenly over them. Cover with clear film (plastic wrap) and leave to marinate in the refrigerator for a minimum of 3 hours.

4 Drain the mackerel, reserving the marinade. Grill the fish on a medium-hot barbecue or under a preheated grill (broiler), basting them several times with the marinade, for 5–7 minutes on each side, until just cooked. Serve hot or cold, with couscous or rice, lemon wedges and garnished with mint.

Variations

Trout, bonito, trevally and bluefish are also good cooked this way.

CALAMARI WITH TWO-TOMATO STUFFING

Calamari, or baby squid, are quick to cook, but do turn and baste them often and take care not to overcook them.

INGREDIENTS

500g/1¼ lb baby squid, cleaned
1 garlic clove, crushed
3 plum tomatoes, peeled
and chopped
8 sun-dried tomatoes in oil,
drained and chopped
60ml/4 tbsp chopped fresh basil,
plus extra, to serve
60ml/4 tbsp fresh white
breadcrumbs
45ml/3 tbsp olive oil
15ml/1 tbsp red wine vinegar
salt and freshly ground
black pepper
lemon juice, to serve

SERVES 4

1 Remove the tentacles from the squid and coarsely chop them; leave the main part of the squid whole.

2 Mix together the crushed garlic, plum tomatoes, sun-dried tomatoes, chopped fresh basil, breadcrumbs and chopped squid tentacles. Stir in 15ml/1 tbsp of the olive oil and the red wine vinegar. Season well with plenty of salt and black pepper. Soak some wooden cocktail sticks or toothpicks in water for 10 minutes before use, to prevent them from burning on the barbecue.

3 Using a teaspoon, fill the squid with the stuffing mixture. Secure the open ends with the cocktail sticks to hold the stuffing mixture in place.

4 Brush the squid with the remaining olive oil and cook on a medium-hot barbecue for 4–5 minutes, turning often. Sprinkle with lemon juice and extra chopped fresh basil to serve.

SCALLOPS WITH LIME BUTTER

• • •

Fresh scallops are quick to cook and ideal for barbecues. This recipe combines them simply with lime and fennel.

INGREDIENTS

1 fennel bulb
2 limes
12 large prepared scallops
1 egg yolk
90ml/6 tbsp melted butter
olive oil for brushing
salt and freshly ground
black pepper

SERVES 4

3 Place the egg yolk and remaining lime rind and juice in a small bowl and whisk until pale and smooth.

5 Brush the fennel wedges with olive oil and cook them on a hot barbecue for 3–4 minutes, turning once.

1 Trim any feathery leaves from the fennel and reserve them. Slice the bulb lengthways into thin wedges.

4 Gradually whisk in the melted butter and continue whisking until thick and smooth. Finely chop the reserved fennel leaves and stir them in, with salt and pepper to taste.

6 Add the scallops and cook for 3–4 minutes more, turning once. Serve immediately with the lime and fennel butter and the lime wedges.

2 Cut one lime into wedges. Finely grate the rind and squeeze the juice of the other lime and toss half the juice and rind on to the scallops. Season well with salt and pepper.

Cook's Tip
If the scallops are small, you may wish to thread them on to flat skewers to make turning them easier.

SARDINES WITH WARM HERB SALSA

· · ·

Plain grilling is the very best way to cook fresh sardines. If they are served with this luscious herb salsa, the only other essential item is fresh, crusty bread, to mop up the tasty juices.

INGREDIENTS

12–16 fresh sardines
oil for brushing
juice of 1 lemon

FOR THE SALSA
15ml/1 tbsp butter
4 spring onions
(scallions), chopped
1 garlic clove, finely chopped
rind of 1 lemon, shredded
30ml/2 tbsp finely chopped
fresh parsley
30ml/2 tbsp chopped fresh chives
30ml/2 tbsp finely chopped
fresh basil
30ml/2 tbsp green olive paste
10ml/2 tsp balsamic vinegar
salt and freshly ground
black pepper

SERVES 4

1 To clean the sardines, slit the fish along the belly with kitchen scissors and pull out the innards. Wipe the fish with kitchen paper and then arrange on a hinged rack.

2 To make the salsa, melt the butter in a small pan and gently sauté the spring onions and garlic for about 2 minutes, shaking the pan occasionally, until softened but not browned.

3 Add the lemon rind and remaining salsa ingredients to the onions and garlic in the pan and keep warm on the edge of the barbecue, stirring occasionally. Do not allow to boil.

4 Brush the sardines lightly with oil and sprinkle with lemon juice, salt and pepper. Cook on a medium barbecue for about 2 minutes on each side. Serve with the warm salsa and crusty bread.

STUFFED SARDINES

*This Middle Eastern-inspired dish doesn't take much preparation and is a meal in itself.
Just serve with a crisp green salad tossed in a fresh lemon vinaigrette to make it complete.*

INGREDIENTS

10g/¹/4 oz/¹/4 cup fresh parsley
3–4 garlic cloves, crushed
8–12 fresh or frozen
sardines, cleaned
30ml/2 tbsp lemon juice
50g/2oz/¹/2 cup plain (all-
purpose) flour
2.5ml/¹/2 tsp ground cumin
olive oil, for brushing
salt and freshly ground
black pepper
naan bread and green salad,
to serve

SERVES 4

1 Finely chop the parsley and mix
in a small bowl with the garlic. Pat the
parsley and garlic mixture all over the
outsides and insides of the prepared
sardines. Sprinkle the sardines with
lemon juice, then place them in a dish,
cover and set aside in a cool place for
up to 2 hours, to absorb the flavours.

2 Place the flour on a large plate and
season with the cumin, salt and pepper.
Roll the sardines in the flour.

3 Brush the sardines with olive oil and
cook on a medium-hot barbecue for
about 3 minutes each side. Serve with
naan bread and a green salad.

MONKFISH WITH PEPPERED CITRUS MARINADE

• • •

Monkfish is a firm, meaty fish that cooks well on the barbecue and keeps its shape.
Serve with a green salad.

INGREDIENTS
2 monkfish tails, about
350g/12oz each
1 lime
1 lemon
2 oranges
handful of fresh thyme sprigs
30ml/2 tbsp olive oil
15ml/1 tbsp mixed peppercorns,
coarsely crushed
salt and freshly ground
black pepper

SERVES 4

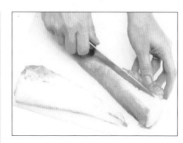

1 Using a sharp kitchen knife, remove any skin from the monkfish tails. Cut carefully down one side of the backbone, sliding the knife between the bone and flesh, to remove the fillet on one side.

2 Turn the fish and repeat on the other side, to remove the second fillet. Repeat on the second tail. (If you prefer, you can ask your fishmonger to do this for you.) Lay the four fillets out flat on a chopping board.

3 Cut two slices from each of the citrus fruits and arrange them over two of the fillets. Add a few sprigs of fresh thyme and sprinkle with plenty of salt and freshly ground black pepper. Finely grate the rind from the remaining fruit and sprinkle it over the fish.

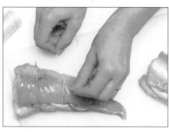

4 Lay the other two fillets on top and tie them firmly at intervals.

5 Squeeze the juice from the citrus fruits and mix it with the olive oil and more salt and pepper. Spoon over the fish. Cover with clear film (plastic wrap) and leave to marinate in the refrigerator for about 1 hour, turning the fish occasionally.

6 Drain the monkfish, reserving the marinade, and sprinkle evenly with the crushed peppercorns. Cook the fish on a medium-hot barbecue for about 15–20 minutes, turning occasionally and basting with the marinade, until the fish is evenly cooked.

SMOKED MACKEREL WITH BLUEBERRIES

Fresh blueberries burst with flavour when cooked, and their sharpness complements the rich flesh of mackerel very well.

INGREDIENTS

30 ml/2 tbsp plain (all-purpose) flour
4 hot-smoked mackerel fillets
50g/2oz/4 tbsp butter
juice of ½ lemon
salt and freshly ground
black pepper

FOR THE BLUEBERRY SAUCE
450g/1lb/4 cups blueberries
30ml/2 tbsp caster (superfine) sugar
15g/½oz/1 tbsp unsalted
(sweet) butter
SERVES 4

1 Season the flour with salt and freshly ground black pepper. Coat each fish fillet in the flour, covering it well.

2 Brush the fillets with butter and cook on a medium barbecue for a few minutes until heated through with a crisp coating.

3 To make the sauce, place the blueberries, sugar, butter and salt and pepper in a small roasting pan and cook on the barbecue, stirring occasionally, for about 10 minutes. Serve immediately, drizzling the lemon juice over the mackerel and with the blueberries on the side.

MACKEREL WITH TOMATOES, PESTO AND ONION

*Rich oily fish like mackerel needs a sharp, fresh-tasting sauce to go with it,
and this aromatic pesto is excellent drizzled over the top.*

INGREDIENTS

4 mackerel, cleaned and gutted
30ml/2 tbsp olive oil
115g/4oz onion, coarsely chopped
450g/1lb tomatoes,
coarsely chopped
salt and freshly ground
black pepper

FOR THE PESTO
50g/2oz/¹/₂ cup pine nuts
30ml/2 tbsp fresh basil leaves
2 garlic cloves, crushed
30ml/2 tbsp freshly grated
Parmesan cheese
150ml/¹/₄ pint/²/₃ cup extra virgin
olive oil

SERVES 4

1 To make the pesto, place the pine nuts, fresh basil leaves and garlic in a food processor and blend to a coarse paste. Add the Parmesan and, with the motor running, gradually add the oil.

2 Season the mackerel well with plenty of salt and freshly ground black pepper and cook on a medium-hot barbecue for about 12–15 minutes, turning the fish once.

3 Meanwhile, heat the olive oil in a large, heavy pan. Add the chopped onions and sauté, stirring occasionally, until soft and golden brown.

4 Stir the chopped tomatoes into the contents of the pan and cook for about 5 minutes. Serve the fish on top of the tomato mixture and top with a generous spoonful of the pesto.

CHARGRILLED TUNA WITH FIERY PEPPER PURÉE

· · ·

Tuna is an oily fish that barbecues well and is meaty enough to combine successfully with strong
flavours – even hot chilli, as in this red pepper purée, which is excellent served with crusty bread.

INGREDIENTS

4 tuna steaks, about 175g/6oz each
finely grated rind and juice of 1 lime
30ml/2 tbsp olive oil
salt and freshly ground black pepper
lime wedges, to serve

FOR THE PEPPER PURÉE
2 red (bell) peppers, halved
45ml/3 tbsp olive oil, plus extra
for brushing
1 small onion
2 garlic cloves, crushed
2 red chillies
1 slice white bread without
crusts, diced
salt

SERVES 4

2 To make the pepper purée, brush the pepper halves with a little olive oil and cook them, skin-side down, on a hot barbecue, until the skin is charred and blackened. Place the onion in its skin on the barbecue and cook until browned, turning it occasionally.

4 Place the cooked peppers and onion with the garlic, chillies, bread and olive oil in a food processor. Process until smooth. Add salt to taste.

5 Drain the tuna steaks from the marinade and cook them on a hot barbecue for 8–10 minutes, turning once, until golden brown. Serve with the pepper purée and lime wedges, with crusty bread if you like.

3 Leave the peppers and onion until cool enough to handle, then remove the skins, using a sharp kitchen knife.

1 Trim any skin from the tuna and place the steaks in a single layer in a dish. Sprinkle over the lime rind and juice, olive oil, salt and pepper. Cover with clear film (plastic wrap) and chill in the refrigerator until required.

Cook's Tip

The (bell) pepper purée can be made in advance, cooking the peppers and onion under a hot grill (broiler); chill until required.

TROUT WITH BACON
. . .

The smoky, savoury flavour of crispy grilled bacon perfectly complements
the delicate flesh of the trout in this simple dish.

INGREDIENTS
4 trout, cleaned and gutted
15ml/1 tbsp plain (all-purpose) flour
4 rashers (strips) smoked bacon
30ml/2 tbsp olive oil
juice of 1/2 lemon
salt and freshly ground
black pepper

SERVES 4

1 Place the trout on a chopping board
and pat them dry with kitchen paper.
Season the flour with the salt and
freshly ground black pepper. Stretch
the bacon rashers out thinly using the
back of a heavy kitchen knife.

2 Roll the fish in the seasoned flour
mixture and wrap them tightly in the
bacon. Brush with olive oil and cook
on a medium-hot barbecue for
10–15 minutes, turning once. Serve at
once, drizzled with the lemon juice.

RED MULLET WITH BASIL AND CITRUS

This Italian recipe is full of the warm, distinctive flavours of the Mediterranean.
Serve the dish with plain boiled rice and a green salad, or with lots of fresh crusty bread.

INGREDIENTS

4 red mullet or snapper, about
225g/8oz each, filleted
60ml/4 tbsp olive oil
10 peppercorns, crushed
2 oranges, one peeled and sliced
and one squeezed
1 lemon
15g/½ oz/1 tbsp butter
2 drained canned anchovy
fillets, chopped
60ml/4 tbsp shredded fresh basil
salt and freshly ground
black pepper

SERVES 4

2 Halve the lemon. Remove the skin and pith from one half using a small, sharp knife, and slice the flesh thinly. Squeeze the juice from the other half.

3 Drain the fish, reserving the marinade and orange slices, and cook on a medium-hot barbecue for about 10–12 minutes, turning once and basting with the marinade.

4 Melt the butter in a pan with any remaining marinade. Add the chopped anchovy fillets and cook until they are completely soft. Stir in the orange and lemon juice and allow to simmer on the edge of the barbecue until slightly reduced. Stir in the basil and check the seasoning. Pour over the fish and garnish with the reserved orange slices and the lemon slices.

1 Place the fish fillets in a shallow dish in a single layer. Pour over the olive oil and sprinkle with the crushed peppercorns. Lay the orange slices on top of the fish. Cover the dish with clear film (plastic wrap), and leave to marinate in the refrigerator for 4 hours.

FISH PARCELS

∘ ∘ ∘

*Sea bass is good for this recipe, but you could also use small whole trout
or a white fish fillet, such as cod or haddock.*

2 Place a piece of fish in the centre
of each piece of baking foil and season
well with plenty of salt and pepper.

3 Sprinkle over the shallots, chopped
garlic, capers, tomatoes, sliced olives
and grated lemon rind. Sprinkle with
the lemon juice and paprika.

4 Fold over the baking foil to enclose
the fish loosely, sealing the edges firmly
so that none of the juices can escape
during cooking. Place the parcels on a
moderately hot barbecue and cook for
about 8–10 minutes. To serve, place
each of the parcels on a plate and
loosen the tops to open.

Cook's Tip

These parcels can also be
baked in the oven: place them
on a baking sheet and cook at
200°C/400°F/Gas 6 for
about 15–20 minutes.

1 Clean the fish if whole. Cut four
squares of double-thickness baking foil,
large enough to enclose the fish; brush
lightly with a little olive oil.

SPICED FISH BAKED THAI STYLE

Banana leaves make a perfect, natural wrapping for barbecue-cooked foods, but if they are not available you can use baking foil instead.

INGREDIENTS

4 red snapper or mullet, about
350g/12oz each
banana leaves
1 lime
1 garlic clove, thinly sliced
2 spring onions (scallions), sliced
30ml/2 tbsp Thai red
curry paste
60ml/4 tbsp coconut milk

SERVES 4

1 Clean the fish, removing the scales, and make several deep slashes in the side of each with a sharp knife. Place each fish on a layer of banana leaves.

2 Thinly slice half the lime and tuck the slices into the slashes in the fish, with the slivers of garlic. Sprinkle the sliced spring onions over the fish.

3 Grate the rind and squeeze the juice from the remaining half-lime and mix with the curry paste and coconut milk. Spoon over the fish.

4 Wrap the leaves over the fish, to enclose them completely. Tie firmly with string and cook on a medium-hot barbecue for 15–20 minutes, turning occasionally. To serve, open up the parcels by cutting along the top edge with a knife and fanning out the leaves.

SEA BREAM WITH ORANGE BUTTER SAUCE

*Sea bream is a revelation to anyone unfamiliar with its creamy rich flavour.
The fish has a firm white flesh that goes well with this rich butter sauce, sharpened with orange.*

INGREDIENTS

2 sea bream, about 350g/12oz
each, scaled and gutted
10ml/2 tsp Dijon mustard
5ml/1 tsp fennel seeds
30ml/2 tbsp olive oil
50g/2oz watercress
175g/6oz mixed lettuce leaves,
such as escarole and frisée

FOR THE ORANGE BUTTER SAUCE
30ml/2 tbsp frozen orange
juice concentrate
175g/6oz/3/4 cup unsalted (sweet)
butter, diced
salt and cayenne pepper

SERVES 2

1 Slash the sea bream four times on
either side. Combine the mustard and
fennel seeds, then spread over both
sides of the fish. Brush with olive oil
and cook on a medium-hot barbecue
for 10–12 minutes, turning once.

2 Place the orange juice concentrate in
a bowl and heat over a pan of
simmering water. Remove the pan from
the heat and gradually whisk in the
butter until creamy. Season well.

3 Dress the watercress and lettuce
leaves with the remaining olive oil,
and arrange with the fish on two plates.
Spoon the sauce over the fish and serve
with baked potatoes, if you like.

HALIBUT WITH FRESH TOMATO AND BASIL SALSA

Take care when cooking this dish as halibut has a tendency to break easily, especially when the skin has been removed. Season well to bring out the flavour of the fish and the taste of the sauce.

INGREDIENTS

4 halibut fillets, about 175g/
6oz each
45ml/3 tbsp olive oil

FOR THE SALSA
1 medium tomato,
coarsely chopped
1/4 red onion, finely chopped
1 small jalapeño chilli
30ml/2 tbsp balsamic vinegar
10 large fresh basil leaves
15ml/1 tbsp olive oil
salt and freshly ground
black pepper

SERVES 4

1 To make the salsa, mix together the chopped tomato, red onion, jalapeño chilli and balsamic vinegar in a bowl. Slice the fresh basil leaves finely, using a sharp kitchen knife.

2 Stir the basil and the olive oil into the tomato mixture. Season to taste. Cover the bowl with clear film (plastic wrap) and leave to marinate for 3 hours.

3 Rub the halibut fillets with oil and season. Cook on a medium barbecue for 8 minutes, basting with oil and turning once. Serve with the salsa.

COD FILLET WITH FRESH MIXED-HERB CRUST

Use fresh herbs and wholemeal breadcrumbs to make a delicious crisp crust for the fish.
Season the fish well and serve with large lemon wedges.

INGREDIENTS

25g/1oz/2 tbsp butter
15ml/1 tbsp fresh chervil
15ml/1 tbsp fresh parsley, plus
extra sprigs to garnish
15ml/1 tbsp fresh chives
175g/6oz/3 cups breadcrumbs
4 thick pieces of cod fillet, about
225g/8oz each, skinned
15ml/1 tbsp olive oil
lemon wedges, to garnish
salt and freshly ground
black pepper

SERVES 4

1 Melt the butter and chop all the herbs finely, using a sharp knife. Brush the cod fillets with melted butter and mix any remaining butter with the breadcrumbs, fresh herbs and plenty of salt and freshly ground black pepper.

2 Press a quarter of the mixture on to each fillet, spreading evenly, and lightly sprinkle with olive oil. Cook on a medium barbecue for 10 minutes, turning once. Serve the fish garnished with lemon wedges and the sprigs of fresh parsley.

GRILLED SNAPPER WITH HOT MANGO SALSA

. . .

A ripe mango provides the basis for a deliciously rich fruity salsa. The dressing needs no oil and features the tropical flavours of coriander, ginger and chilli.

INGREDIENTS

350g/12oz new potatoes
3 eggs
115g/4oz green beans, trimmed
and halved
4 red snapper, about 350g/12oz
each, cleaned, scaled and gutted
30ml/2 tbsp olive oil
175g/6oz mixed lettuce leaves,
such as frisée or Webb's
2 cherry tomatoes
salt and freshly ground
black pepper

FOR THE SALSA

45ml/3 tbsp chopped fresh
coriander (cilantro)
1 medium-size ripe mango, peeled,
stoned (pitted) and diced
1/2 red chilli, seeded and chopped
2.5cm/1in fresh root ginger, grated
juice of 2 limes
generous pinch of celery salt

SERVES 4

1 Bring the potatoes to the boil in a large pan of salted water and simmer for 15–20 minutes. Drain.

2 Bring a second large pan of salted water to the boil. Put in the eggs and boil for 4 minutes, then add the beans and cook for a further 6 minutes, so that the eggs have had a total of 10 minutes. Drain and refresh the beans. Remove the eggs from the pan. Cool, then shell and cut into quarters.

3 Using a sharp knife, slash each snapper three times on either side. Brush with olive oil and cook on a medium-hot barbecue for 12 minutes, basting occasionally and turning once.

4 To make the salsa, place the chopped fresh coriander in a food processor. Add the mango chunks, chilli, grated ginger, lime juice and celery salt and process until smooth.

5 Dress the lettuce leaves with olive oil and distribute them evenly among four large plates.

6 Arrange the snapper on the lettuce and season. Halve the new potatoes and distribute them with the beans, tomatoes and quartered hard-boiled eggs over the salad. Serve immediately, with the salsa.

Variation

If fresh mangoes are unavailable, use canned ones, draining well. Sea bream are also good served with this hot mango salsa.

SMOKED HADDOCK WITH QUICK PARSLEY SAUCE

• • •

Make any herb sauce by this method, making sure it is thickened and seasoned well to complement the smoky flavour of the fish.

INGREDIENTS

*4 smoked haddock fillets, about
225g/8oz each
75g/3oz/6 tbsp butter, softened
15ml/2 tbsp plain (all-purpose) flour
300ml/½ pint/1¼ cups milk
60ml/4 tbsp chopped fresh parsley
salt and freshly ground
black pepper*

SERVES 4

1 Smear the fish fillets on both sides with 50g/2oz/4 tbsp of the butter.

2 Beat the remaining butter and flour together to make a paste.

3 Cook the fish on a medium-hot barbecue for about 10 minutes, turning once. Meanwhile, to make the sauce, heat the milk in a pan to just below boiling point. Add the flour mixture in small spoonfuls, whisking constantly over the heat. Continue whisking until the sauce is smooth and thick.

4 Add the seasoning and chopped fresh parsley to the pan and stir well. Pour the parsley sauce over the haddock fillets to serve.

SALMON WITH RED ONION MARMALADE

. . .

Salmon barbecues well but is most successful when it is at least 2.5cm/1in thick. The red onion marmalade is rich and delicious. Puréed blackcurrants work as well as crème de cassis.

INGREDIENTS

*4 salmon steaks, about 175g/
6oz each
30ml/2 tbsp olive oil
salt and freshly ground
black pepper*

FOR THE RED ONION MARMALADE
*5 medium red onions, peeled and
finely sliced
50g/2oz/4 tbsp butter
175ml/6fl oz/³/₄ cup red wine vinegar
50ml/2fl oz/¹/₄ cup crème de cassis
50ml/2fl oz/¹/₄ cup grenadine
50ml/2fl oz/¹/₄ cup red wine*

SERVES 4

1 Use your hands to rub the olive oil into the salmon flesh and season well with plenty of salt and freshly ground black pepper.

2 Melt the butter in a large heavy pan and add the sliced onions. Sauté the onions gently for 5 minutes. until golden brown.

3 Stir in the vinegar, crème de cassis, grenadine and wine and continue to cook for about 10 minutes, until the liquid has almost entirely evaporated and the onions are glazed. Season well.

4 Brush the fish with a little more oil, and cook on a medium barbecue for about 6–8 minutes, turning once.

GRILLED SEA BASS WITH CITRUS FRUIT

∘ ∘ ∘

Sea bass is a beautiful fish with a soft, dense texture and a delicate flavour. In this recipe it is complemented by citrus fruits and fruity olive oil.

INGREDIENTS

1 small grapefruit
1 orange
1 lemon
1 sea bass, about 1.5kg/
3–3¹/₂ lb, cleaned
and scaled
6 fresh basil sprigs
45ml/3 tbsp olive oil
4–6 shallots, halved
60ml/4 tbsp dry white wine
15g/¹/₂ oz/1 tbsp butter
salt and freshly ground
black pepper
fresh dill, to garnish

SERVES 6

1 Using a vegetable peeler, remove the rind from the grapefruit, orange and lemon. Cut into thin julienne strips. Peel the pith from the fruits and, working over a bowl to catch the juices, cut out the segments from the grapefruit and the orange and set aside for the garnish. Slice the lemon thickly.

2 Season the cavity of the fish with salt and pepper and slash the flesh three times on each side. Reserving a few basil sprigs for the garnish, fill the cavity with the remaining basil, the lemon slices and half the julienne strips of citrus rind. Brush with olive oil and cook on a low–medium barbecue for about 20 minutes, basting occasionally and turning once.

3 Meanwhile, heat 15ml/1 tbsp of the olive oil in a pan and cook the shallots gently until soft. Add the wine and 30–45ml/2–3 tbsp of the fruit juice to the pan. Bring to the boil over a high heat, stirring. Stir in the remaining julienne strips of rind and boil for 2–3 minutes, then whisk in the butter.

4 When the fish is cooked, transfer it to a serving dish. Remove and discard the cavity stuffing. Spoon the shallots and sauce around the fish and garnish with fresh dill sprigs, the reserved basil and segments of grapefruit and orange.

GRILLED SEA BASS WITH FENNEL

The classic combination of sea bass and fennel works particularly well when the fish is cooked over charcoal. Traditionally fennel twigs are used but this version of the recipe uses fennel seeds.

INGREDIENTS

1 sea bass, about 1.5kg/3–3½ lb,
cleaned and scaled
60ml/4 tbsp olive oil
10ml/2 tsp fennel seeds
2 large fennel bulbs
60ml/4 tbsp Pernod
salt and freshly ground
black pepper

SERVES 6

1 Make four deep slashes in each side of the fish. Brush the fish with olive oil and season well with salt and freshly ground black pepper. Sprinkle the fennel seeds in the cavity and slashes of the fish. Cook on a low barbecue for 20 minutes, basting occasionally and turning once.

2 Meanwhile, trim and slice the fennel bulbs thinly, reserving any leafy fronds to use as a garnish. Brush the slices with olive oil and barbecue for about 8–10 minutes, turning occasionally, until tender.

3 Arrange the fennel slices on a serving plate. Lay the fish on top and garnish with the reserved fennel fronds.

4 When ready for eating, heat the Pernod in a small pan on the side of the barbecue, light it and pour it, flaming, over the fish. Serve at once.

MEXICAN SALMON

. . .

The sauce for this dish is vibrant with hot, sweet and sour flavours
that permeate the fish before and during cooking.

INGREDIENTS

1 small red onion
1 garlic clove
6 plum tomatoes
25g/1oz/2 tbsp butter
45ml/3 tbsp tomato ketchup
30ml/2 tbsp Dijon mustard
30ml/2 tbsp dark brown sugar
15ml/1 tbsp clear honey
5ml/1 tsp cayenne pepper
15ml/1 tbsp ancho chilli powder
15ml/1 tbsp paprika
15ml/1 tbsp Worcestershire sauce
4 salmon fillets, about 175g/
6oz each

SERVES 4

3 Melt the butter in a large, heavy pan and gently cook the onion and garlic until translucent.

4 Add the tomatoes to the pan and simmer for 15 minutes.

5 Add the remaining ingredients, excluding the salmon, and simmer for a further 20 minutes. Pour the mixture into a food processor and blend until smooth. Leave to cool.

1 Using a sharp knife, finely chop the red onion and finely dice the garlic.

2 Next, dice the plum tomatoes finely and set them aside.

6 Brush the salmon with the sauce, and chill for at least 2 hours. Cook on a hot barbecue for 6 minutes, basting with the sauce and turning once.

SALMON WITH TROPICAL FRUIT SALSA

· · ·

*Fresh salmon really needs little adornment, but it does combine very well
with the exotic flavours in this colourful salsa.*

INGREDIENTS

*4 salmon steaks or fillets, about
175g/6oz each
finely grated rind and juice of
1 lime
1 small, ripe mango
1 small, ripe papaya
1 red chilli
45ml/3 tbsp chopped fresh
coriander (cilantro)
salt and freshly ground
black pepper*

SERVES 4

3 Halve the papaya, scoop out
the seeds with a spoon and remove the
peel. Finely chop the flesh and add it
to the mango chunks in the bowl.

5 Combine the mango, papaya, chilli
and coriander in a bowl and stir in the
remaining lime rind and juice. Season
to taste with plenty of salt and freshly
ground black pepper.

1 Place the salmon in a wide dish
and sprinkle over half the lime rind
and juice. Season with salt and pepper.

4 Cut the chilli in half lengthways.
Leave the seeds in to make the salsa hot
and spicy, or remove them for a milder
flavour. Finely chop the chilli.

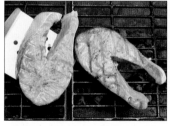

6 Cook the salmon on a medium
barbecue for about 5–8 minutes,
turning once. Serve with the fruit salsa.

2 Cut the mango in half, cutting either
side of the stone (pit), and remove
the stone. Finely chop the mango flesh
and place the pieces in a bowl.

There are lots of ideas here for vegetable accompaniments to meat and fish dishes, as well as for substantial main dishes that everyone, vegetarian or not, will love. All vegetables can be cooked in foil parcels, but many are ideally suited to direct grilling on the barbecue.

VEGETARIAN
DISHES AND
VEGETABLES

~

RED BEAN AND MUSHROOM BURGERS

. . .

Vegetarians, vegans and meat-eaters alike will enjoy these healthy, low-fat veggie burgers.
With salad, pitta bread and Greek-style yogurt, they make a substantial meal.

INGREDIENTS

15ml/1 tbsp olive oil
1 small onion, finely chopped
1 garlic clove, crushed
5ml/1 tsp ground cumin
5ml/1 tsp ground coriander
2.5ml/¹/₂ tsp ground turmeric
115g/4oz/1¹/₂ cups finely
chopped mushrooms
400g/14oz can red kidney beans
30ml/2 tbsp chopped fresh
coriander (cilantro)
wholemeal (whole-wheat) flour
olive oil, for brushing
salt and freshly ground
black pepper
Greek (US strained plain) yogurt

SERVES 4

1 Heat the olive oil in a frying pan and cook the chopped onion and garlic over a moderate heat, stirring, until softened. Add the spices and cook for a further minute, stirring constantly.

Cook's Tip

These burgers are not quite so firm as meat burgers, and will need careful handling on the barbecue.

2 Add the chopped mushrooms and cook, stirring, until softened and dry. Remove the pan from the heat and empty the contents into a large bowl.

3 Drain the beans thoroughly, place them in a bowl and mash with a fork.

4 Stir the kidney beans into the frying pan, with the chopped fresh coriander, and mix thoroughly. Season the mixture well with plenty of salt and freshly ground black pepper.

5 Using floured hands, form the mixture into four flat burger shapes. If the mixture is too sticky to handle, mix in a little wholemeal flour.

6 Lightly brush the burgers with olive oil and cook on a hot barbecue for 8–10 minutes, turning once, until golden brown. Serve with a spoonful of yogurt and a green salad, if you like.

GOAT'S CHEESE PIZZA

* * *

*Pizzas cooked on the barbecue have a beautifully crisp and golden base. The combination
of goat's cheese and red onion in this recipe makes for a flavoursome main course dish.*

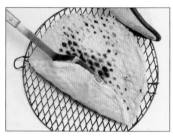

2 Brush the dough round with olive oil
and place, oiled side down, on a
medium barbecue. Cook for about
6–8 minutes until firm and golden
underneath. Brush the uncooked side
with olive oil and turn the pizza over.

3 Mix together the passata and
red pesto and quickly spread over
the cooked side of the pizza, to within
about 1cm/½in of the edge. Arrange
the onion, tomatoes and cheese on top
and sprinkle with salt and pepper.

4 Cook the pizza for 10 minutes more,
until golden brown and crisp. Sprinkle
with fresh basil and serve.

INGREDIENTS

150g/5oz packet pizza-base mix
olive oil, for brushing
150ml/¼ pint/⅔ cup passata
(bottled strained tomatoes)
30ml/2 tbsp red pesto
1 small red onion, thinly sliced
8 cherry tomatoes, halved
115g/4oz firm goat's cheese, sliced
handful shredded fresh basil leaves
salt and freshly ground black
pepper

SERVES 4

1 Make up the pizza dough according
to the directions on the packet. Roll
out the dough on a lightly floured
surface to a round of about 25cm/
10in diameter.

RED ONION GALETTES

If non-vegetarians are to eat these pretty puff pastry tarts, you can sprinkle some chopped anchovies over them before cooking them on the barbecue to add extra piquancy.

INGREDIENTS

60–75ml/4–5 tbsp olive oil
500g/1¼ lb red onions, sliced
1 garlic clove, crushed
30ml/2 tbsp chopped fresh mixed herbs, such as thyme, parsley and basil
225g/8oz ready-made puff pastry
15ml/1 tbsp sun-dried tomato paste
freshly ground black pepper
fresh thyme sprigs, to garnish

SERVES 4

1 Heat 30ml/2 tbsp oil in a frying pan and add the onions and garlic. Cover and cook gently for 15–20 minutes, stirring occasionally, until soft but not browned. Stir in the herbs.

2 Divide the pastry into four and roll out each piece to a 15cm/6in round. Flute the edges, prick all over with a fork and place on baking sheets.

3 Chill the rounds, on the baking sheets, in the refrigerator for about 10 minutes. Mix 15ml/1 tbsp of the remaining oil with the tomato paste and spread over the pastry rounds, to within about 1cm/½in of the edge.

4 Spread the onion mixture over the pastry and season with pepper. Drizzle over a little oil, then place the baking sheets on a medium barbecue for 15 minutes, until the pastry is crisp. Serve hot, garnished with thyme sprigs.

TOFU SATAY

. . .

Grill cubes of tofu until crispy then serve with a Thai-style peanut sauce. Soak the satay sticks
before use to prevent them from burning while on the barbecue.

INGREDIENTS

2 x 200g/7oz packs smoked tofu
45ml/3 tbsp light soy sauce
10ml/2 tsp sesame oil
1 garlic clove, crushed
1 yellow and 1 red (bell) pepper,
cut into squares
8–12 fresh bay leaves
sunflower oil, for brushing

FOR THE PEANUT SAUCE
2 spring onions (scallions), chopped
2 garlic cloves, crushed
good pinch of chilli powder, or a
few drops hot chilli sauce
5ml/1 tsp sugar
15ml/1 tbsp white wine vinegar
30ml/2 tbsp light soy sauce
45ml/3 tbsp crunchy peanut butter

SERVES 4–6

1 Cut the tofu into bitesize cubes and
place in a large bowl. Add the soy
sauce, sesame oil and crushed garlic
and mix well. Cover and set aside to
marinate for at least 20 minutes.

2 Beat all the peanut sauce ingredients
together in a large bowl, using a
wooden spoon, until well blended.
Avoid using a food processor to blend
the ingredients, as the texture should be
slightly chunky.

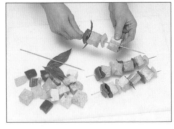

3 Drain the tofu and thread
the cubes on to 8–12 satay sticks,
alternating with the pepper squares and
bay leaves. Larger bay leaves may need
to be halved before threading.

4 Brush the satays with sunflower
oil and cook on a hot barbecue or grill
(broiler), turning occasionally, until the
tofu and peppers are browned and
crisp. Serve hot with the peanut sauce.

SWEET AND SOUR VEGETABLES WITH PANEER

The Indian cheese used in this recipe, called paneer, can be bought from Asian stores, or you can use beancurd in its place. Paneer has a good firm texture and cooks very well on the barbecue.

INGREDIENTS

1 green and 1 yellow (bell) pepper,
cut into squares
8 cherry, or 4 medium, tomatoes
8 cauliflower florets
8 fresh or canned pineapple chunks
8 cubes paneer

FOR THE SEASONED OIL
15ml/1 tbsp soya oil
30ml/2 tbsp lemon juice
5ml/1 tsp salt
5ml/1 tsp freshly ground
black pepper
15ml/1 tbsp clear honey
30ml/2 tbsp chilli sauce

SERVES 4

1 Thread the prepared vegetables, pineapple and paneer cubes on to four skewers, alternating the ingredients.

2 Mix together all the ingredients for the seasoned oil. If the mixture is a little too thick, add 15ml/1 tbsp water to loosen it. Brush the vegetables with the seasoned oil, ready for cooking.

3 Cook on a hot barbecue or grill (broiler) for 10 minutes, until the vegetables begin to char slightly, turning the skewers often and basting with the seasoned oil.

143

VEGETABLE KEBABS WITH PEPPERCORN SAUCE

. . .

Vegetables invariably taste good when cooked on the barbecue. You can include other
vegetables in these kebabs, depending on what is available at the time.

INGREDIENTS

24 mushrooms
16 cherry tomatoes
16 large fresh basil leaves
2 courgettes (zucchini), cut into
16 thick slices
16 large fresh mint leaves
1 large red (bell) pepper, cut into
16 squares

TO BASTE
120ml/4fl oz/^{1}/$_2$ cup melted butter
1 garlic clove, crushed
15ml/1 tbsp crushed
green peppercorns

FOR THE GREEN PEPPERCORN SAUCE
50g/2oz/^{1}/$_4$ cup butter
45ml/3 tbsp brandy
250ml/8fl oz/1 cup double
(heavy) cream
5ml/1 tsp crushed green
peppercorns

SERVES 4

1 Thread the vegetables on to
eight bamboo skewers that you have
soaked in water to prevent them from
burning. Place the fresh basil leaves
immediately next to the tomatoes,
and wrap the mint leaves around
the courgette slices.

2 Mix the basting ingredients in a bowl
and baste the kebabs thoroughly. Cook
the skewers on a medium-hot barbecue,
turning and basting regularly until the
vegetables are just cooked – this should
take about 5–7 minutes.

3 Heat the butter for the green
peppercorn sauce in a frying pan,
then add the brandy and light it. When
the flames have died down, stir in the
cream and the peppercorns. Cook for
2 minutes, stirring constantly. Serve the
sauce with the kebabs.

CASSAVA AND VEGETABLE KEBABS

∘ ∘ ∘

This is an attractive and delicious assortment of African vegetables, marinated in a spicy garlic
sauce, then roasted over hot coals. If cassava is unavailable, use sweet potato or yam instead.

INGREDIENTS

175g/6oz cassava
1 onion, cut into wedges
1 aubergine (eggplant), cut into
bitesize pieces
1 courgette (zucchini), sliced
1 ripe plantain, sliced
1/2 red and 1/2 green (bell)
pepper, sliced
16 cherry tomatoes
rice or couscous, to serve

FOR THE MARINADE
60ml/4 tbsp lemon juice
60ml/4 tbsp olive oil
45–60ml/3–4 tbsp soy sauce
15ml/1 tbsp tomato purée (paste)
1 green chilli, seeded and
finely chopped
1/2 onion, grated
2 garlic cloves, crushed
5ml/1 tsp mixed (apple pie) spice
pinch of dried thyme

SERVES 4

1 Peel the cassava and cut into bitesize
pieces. Place in a large bowl, cover with
boiling water and leave to blanch for
about 5 minutes. Drain well.

2 Place all the prepared vegetables,
including the cassava, in a large bowl
and mix with your hands so that all
the vegetables are evenly distributed.

3 Blend the marinade ingredients and
pour over the vegetables. Cover and
leave to marinate for 1–2 hours.

4 Thread the vegetables, with the
cherry tomatoes, on to eight skewers
and cook on a hot barbecue for about
15 minutes until tender and browned.
Turn the skewers frequently and baste
them occasionally with the marinade.

5 Meanwhile, pour the remaining
marinade into a small pan and simmer
for about 10 minutes to reduce. Strain
the reduced marinade into a jug
(pitcher). Serve the kebabs on a bed of
rice or couscous, with the sauce.

BAKED SQUASH WITH PARMESAN

. . .

*Almost all types of squash are suitable for barbecue cooking, and they are extremely easy to deal
with: simply wrap them in baking foil and place them in the hot embers until they soften.*

INGREDIENTS

*2 acorn or butternut squashes,
about 450g/1lb each
15ml/1 tbsp olive oil
50g/2oz/4 tbsp butter, melted
75g/3oz/1 cup freshly grated
Parmesan cheese
60ml/4 tbsp pine nuts, toasted
2.5ml/1/2 tsp freshly grated nutmeg
salt and freshly ground
black pepper*

SERVES 4

2 Brush the cut surfaces with oil and
sprinkle with salt and black pepper.

5 Dice the flesh, then stir in the melted
butter. Add the Parmesan, pine nuts,
salt and pepper. Toss well to mix.

1 Cut the squashes in half and scoop
out the seeds with a spoon.

3 Wrap each squash in baking foil and
place in the embers of the fire. Cook
for 25–30 minutes, until tender. Turn
the parcels occasionally so that the
squash cook evenly.

6 Spoon the mixture back into the
shells. Sprinkle with nutmeg and serve.

4 Leave the squash until cool enough to
handle. Unwrap the squashes from the
foil parcels and scoop out the flesh,
leaving the skins intact.

Cook's Tip
Spaghetti squash can also be
cooked in this way. Just scoop out
the spaghetti-like strands and toss
with butter and Parmesan cheese.

POTATO AND CHEESE POLPETTES

* * *

These little morsels of potato and Greek feta cheese, flavoured with dill and lemon juice, are excellent when grilled on the barbecue, or they can be tossed in flour and fried in olive oil.

INGREDIENTS

500g/1¼ lb potatoes
115g/4oz feta cheese
4 spring onions (scallions), chopped
45ml/3 tbsp chopped fresh dill
1 egg, beaten
15ml/1 tbsp lemon juice
30ml/2 tbsp olive oil
salt and freshly ground black pepper

SERVES 4

1 Boil the potatoes in their skins in salted water until soft. Drain, then peel while still warm. Place in a bowl and mash. Crumble the feta cheese into the potatoes and add the spring onions, dill, egg and lemon juice and season with pepper and a little salt. Stir well.

2 Cover the mixture and chill until firm. Divide the mixture into walnut-size balls, then flatten them slightly. Brush lightly with olive oil. Arrange the polpettes on a grill rack and cook on a medium barbecue, turning once, until golden brown. Serve immediately.

LOOFAH AND AUBERGINE RATATOUILLE

* * *

*Loofahs are edible gourds with spongy, creamy-white flesh. Like aubergine, their flavour is
intensified by roasting. Cooking the vegetables in a pan over the barbecue will retain their juices.*

INGREDIENTS

1 large aubergine (eggplant)
450g/1lb young loofahs or
sponge gourds
1 large red (bell) pepper, cut into
large chunks
225g/8oz cherry tomatoes
225g/8oz shallots
10ml/2 tsp ground coriander
60ml/4 tbsp olive oil
2 garlic cloves, finely chopped
fresh coriander (cilantro) sprigs
salt and freshly ground
black pepper

SERVES 4

1 Cut the aubergine into thick chunks
and sprinkle the pieces liberally with
salt to draw out the bitter juices. Leave
to drain for about 45 minutes, then
rinse under cold running water and pat
dry with kitchen paper.

2 Slice the loofahs into 2cm/¾in
pieces. Place the aubergines, loofah
and pepper pieces, together with the
cherry tomatoes and shallots, in a
roasting pan large enough to take
all the vegetables in a single layer.

3 Sprinkle the vegetables with the
ground coriander and oil. Sprinkle the
chopped garlic and fresh coriander
leaves on top and season to taste.

4 Cook on the barbecue for about
25 minutes, stirring the vegetables
occasionally, until the loofah is golden
and the peppers are beginning to char.
As an alternative, you could thread the
vegetables on skewers and grill them.

BAKED STUFFED COURGETTES

· · ·

The tangy goat's cheese stuffing contrasts well with the very delicate flavour of the courgettes in this recipe. Wrap the courgettes and bake them in the embers of the fire.

2 Insert pieces of goat's cheese in the slits. Add a little chopped mint and sprinkle over the oil and black pepper.

3 Wrap each courgette in foil, place in the embers of the fire and bake for about 25 minutes, until tender.

INGREDIENTS

8 small courgettes (zucchini), about 450g/1lb total weight
15ml/1 tbsp olive oil, plus extra for brushing
75–115g/3–4oz goat's cheese, cut into thin strips
a few sprigs of fresh mint, finely chopped, plus extra to garnish
freshly ground black pepper

SERVES 4

1 Cut eight pieces of baking foil large enough to encase each courgette, and lightly brush each piece with olive oil. Trim the courgettes and cut a thin slit along the length of each.

Cook's Tip
While almost any cheese can be used, mild cheeses such as Cheddar or mozzarella, will best allow the flavour of the courgettes (zucchini) to be appreciated.

VEGETABLE PARCELS WITH FLOWERY BUTTER

Nasturtium leaves and flowers are edible and have a distinctive peppery flavour.
They make a pretty addition to summer barbecue dishes.

INGREDIENTS
200g/7oz baby carrots
250g/9oz yellow patty-pan
squashes or courgettes (zucchini)
115g/4oz baby corn cobs
1 onion, thinly sliced
50g/2oz/4 tbsp butter, plus extra
for greasing
finely grated rind of ¹/₂ lemon
6 young nasturtium leaves
4–8 nasturtium flowers
salt and freshly ground
black pepper

SERVES 4

1 Trim the vegetables with a sharp knife, leaving them whole unless they are very large – if necessary, cut them into even-size pieces.

2 Divide the vegetables among four double-thickness squares of buttered baking foil and season well.

3 Mix the butter with the lemon rind in a small bowl. Coarsely chop the nasturtium leaves and add them to the butter. Place a generous spoonful of the butter on each pile of vegetables in the squares of baking foil.

4 Fold over the foil and seal the edges to make a neat parcel. Cook on a medium-hot barbecue for 30 minutes until the vegetables are tender. Open the parcels and top each with one or two nasturtium flowers. Serve at once.

GRILLED AUBERGINE PARCELS

. . .

*These little Italian bundles of tomatoes, mozzarella cheese and basil,
wrapped in slices of aubergine, taste delicious cooked on the barbecue.*

INGREDIENTS

2 large, long aubergines (eggplant)
225g/8oz mozzarella cheese
2 plum tomatoes
16 large fresh basil leaves
30ml/2 tbsp olive oil
salt and freshly ground
black pepper

FOR THE DRESSING
60ml/4 tbsp olive oil
5ml/1 tsp balsamic vinegar
15ml/1 tbsp sun-dried
tomato paste
15ml/1 tbsp lemon juice

FOR THE GARNISH
30ml/2 tbsp toasted pine nuts
torn fresh basil leaves

SERVES 4

1 Remove the stalks from the
aubergines and cut them lengthways
into thin slices using a mandolin or
long-bladed knife – aim to get 16 slices
in total, each about 5mm/¼in thick,
disregarding the first and last slices.

2 Bring a large pan of salted water to
the boil and cook the aubergine slices
for about 2 minutes, until just softened.
Drain the slices, then pat them dry on
kitchen paper.

3 Cut the mozzarella cheese into eight
slices. Cut each tomato into eight slices,
not counting the first and last slices.
Take two aubergine slices and arrange
in a cross. Place a slice of tomato in the
centre, season, then add a basil leaf,
followed by a slice of mozzarella,
another basil leaf, another slice of
tomato and more seasoning.

4 Fold the ends of the aubergine slices
around the filling to make a neat
parcel. Repeat with the rest of the
assembled ingredients to make eight
parcels. Chill the parcels in the
refrigerator for about 20 minutes.

5 To make the tomato dressing, whisk
together the olive oil, vinegar, sun-dried
tomato paste and lemon juice. Season
to taste with plenty of salt and freshly
ground black pepper.

6 Brush the parcels with olive oil and
cook on a hot barbecue for about
10 minutes, turning once, until golden.
Serve hot, with the dressing, sprinkled
with pine nuts and basil.

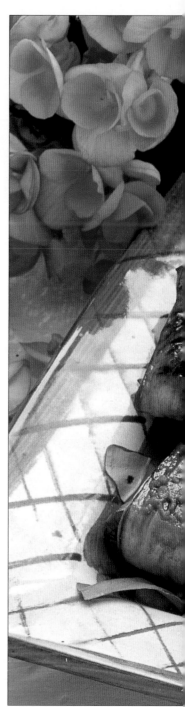

STUFFED TOMATOES AND PEPPERS

Colourful peppers and tomatoes make perfect containers for meat and vegetable stuffings. The smoky flavours in this dish are simply superb.

INGREDIENTS

2 large ripe tomatoes
1 green (bell) pepper
1 yellow or orange (bell) pepper
60ml/4 tbsp olive oil, plus extra
for sprinkling
2 onions, chopped
2 garlic cloves, crushed
50g/2oz/½ cup blanched
almonds, chopped
75g/3oz/scant ½ cup long grain
rice, boiled and drained
30ml/2 tbsp fresh mint,
coarsely chopped
30ml/2 tbsp fresh parsley,
coarsely chopped
30ml/2 tbsp sultanas (golden raisins)
45ml/3 tbsp ground almonds
salt and freshly ground
black pepper
chopped mixed fresh herbs,
to garnish

SERVES 4

2 Halve the peppers, leaving the cores intact. Scoop out the seeds. Brush the peppers with 15ml/1 tbsp olive oil and cook on a medium barbecue for 15 minutes. Place the peppers and tomatoes on a grill rack and season well with salt and pepper.

3 Cook the onions in the remaining olive oil for 5 minutes. Add the crushed garlic and chopped almonds to the pan and cook for a further minute.

4 Remove the pan from the heat and stir in the rice, chopped tomatoes, mint, parsley and sultanas. Season well with salt and pepper and spoon the mixture into the tomatoes and peppers.

1 Cut the tomatoes in half and scoop out the pulp and seeds, using a teaspoon. Leave the tomatoes to drain on kitchen paper with the cut sides facing down. Roughly chop the tomato pulp and set it aside.

5 Sprinkle with the ground almonds and drizzle with a little extra olive oil. Cook on a medium barbecue for about 15 minutes. Garnish with fresh herbs.

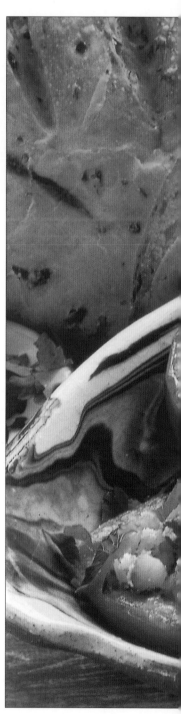

COUSCOUS STUFFED PEPPERS

Couscous makes a good basis for a stuffing, and in this recipe it is studded with raisins and flavoured with fresh mint. Charred peppers make the combination of flavours truly special.

2 To cook the couscous, bring 250ml/8fl oz/1 cup water to the boil. Add the oil and salt, then remove from the heat and add the couscous. Stir and leave to stand, covered, for 5 minutes. Stir in the onion, raisins and mint. Season well and stir in the egg yolk.

3 Use a teaspoon to fill the peppers with the couscous mixture to about three-quarters full (the couscous will swell while cooking). Wrap each pepper in a piece of oiled baking foil.

4 Cook on a medium barbecue for 20 minutes, until tender. Serve hot or cold, garnished with fresh mint leaves.

1 Carefully slit each pepper with a sharp knife and remove the cores and seeds. Melt the butter in a small pan and add the chopped onion. Cook until soft but not browned.

CORN COBS IN A GARLIC BUTTER CRUST

∘ ∘ ∘

Whether you are catering for vegetarians or serving this with meat dishes, it will disappear in a flash. The charred garlic butter crust adds a new dimension to the corn cobs.

INGREDIENTS

6 ripe corn cobs
225g/8oz/1 cup butter
30ml/2 tbsp olive oil
2 garlic cloves, crushed
115g/4oz/1 cup wholemeal (whole-wheat) breadcrumbs
15ml/1 tbsp chopped fresh parsley
salt and freshly ground black pepper

SERVES 6

1 Pull off the husks and silks and boil the corn cobs in a large pan of salted water until tender. Drain the corn cobs and leave to cool.

2 Melt the butter in a pan and add the olive oil, crushed garlic, salt and freshly ground black pepper, and stir to blend. Pour the mixture into a shallow dish. In another shallow dish blend the breadcrumbs and chopped fresh parsley. Roll the corn cobs in the melted butter mixture and then in the breadcrumbs until they are well coated.

3 Cook the corn cobs on a hot barbecue for about 10 minutes, turning frequently, until the breadcrumbs are golden brown.

STUFFED PARSLEYED ONIONS

These stuffed onions are a popular vegetarian dish served with fresh crusty bread and a crisp salad. They also make a very good accompaniment to meat dishes.

INGREDIENTS

4 large onions
60ml/4 tbsp cooked rice
20ml/4 tsp finely chopped fresh parsley, plus extra to garnish
60ml/4 tbsp strong Cheddar cheese, finely grated
30ml/2 tbsp olive oil
15ml/1 tbsp white wine
salt and freshly ground black pepper

SERVES 4

1 Cut a slice from the top of each onion and scoop out the centre to leave a fairly thick shell. Combine all the remaining ingredients in a large bowl and stir to mix, moistening with enough white wine to bind the ingredients together well.

2 Use a spoon to fill the onions, then wrap each one in a piece of oiled baking foil. Bake in the embers of the fire for 30–40 minutes, until tender, turning the parcels often so they cook evenly. Serve the onions garnished with chopped fresh parsley.

STUFFED ARTICHOKE BOTTOMS

The distinctive flavour of chargrilled globe artichokes is matched in this dish by an intensely savoury stuffing of mushrooms, cheese and walnuts.

INGREDIENTS

225g/8oz button (white)
mushrooms
15g/¹/2 oz/1 tbsp butter
2 shallots, finely chopped
50g/2oz/¹/4 cup soft cheese
30ml/2 tbsp chopped walnuts
45ml/3 tbsp grated Gruyère cheese
4 large or 6 small artichoke
bottoms (from cooked artichokes,
leaves and choke removed, or
cooked frozen or canned
artichoke hearts)
salt and freshly ground
black pepper
fresh parsley sprigs, to garnish

SERVES 4

1 To make the duxelles for the stuffing, put the mushrooms in a food processor or blender and pulse until they are finely chopped.

2 Melt the butter in a frying pan and cook the shallots over a medium heat for about 2–3 minutes until just softened. Add the mushrooms, raise the heat slightly, and cook for 5–7 minutes more, stirring frequently, until all the liquid from the mushrooms has been driven off and they are almost dry. Season with plenty of salt and freshly ground black pepper.

3 In a large bowl, combine the soft cheese and cooked mushrooms. Add the chopped walnuts and half the grated Gruyère cheese, and stir well to combine the mixture.

4 Divide the mixture among the artichoke bottoms in an oiled baking tin (pan). Sprinkle over the remaining cheese. Cook on the barbecue for 12 minutes, garnish and serve.

SPINACH WITH RAISINS AND PINE NUTS

Raisins and pine nuts are frequent partners in Spanish recipes. In this recipe they are tossed with wilted spinach and croûtons, and can be cooked quickly in a flameproof pan on the barbecue.

INGREDIENTS

50g/2oz/⅓ cup raisins
1 thick slice crusty white bread
45ml/3 tbsp olive oil
25g/1oz/¼ cup pine nuts
500g/1¼lb young spinach leaves,
stalks removed
2 garlic cloves, crushed
salt and freshly ground
black pepper

SERVES 4

1 Put the raisins in a bowl, cover with boiling water and leave to soak for 10 minutes. Drain and set aside.

2 Cut the bread into cubes and discard the crusts. Heat 30ml/2 tbsp of the olive oil in a large frying pan and fry the bread until golden brown.

3 Heat the remaining oil and fry the pine nuts, on the barbecue or hob, until beginning to colour. Add the spinach and garlic and cook quickly, turning the spinach until it has just wilted. Toss in the raisins and season lightly with salt and pepper. Transfer to a serving dish. Sprinkle with croûtons and serve.

GRILLED VEGETABLE TERRINE

* * *

A colourful terrine, using all the vegetables associated with the Mediterranean, makes an elegant dish for outdoor eating. Cooking them on the barbecue adds to the flavour.

INGREDIENTS

2 large red (bell) peppers, quartered, cored and seeded
2 large yellow (bell) peppers, quartered, cored and seeded
1 large aubergine (eggplant), sliced lengthways
2 large courgettes (zucchini), sliced lengthways
90ml/6 tbsp olive oil
1 large red onion, thinly sliced
75g/3oz/1/2 cup raisins
15ml/1 tbsp tomato purée (paste)
15ml/1 tbsp red wine vinegar
400ml/14fl oz/1 2/3 cups tomato juice
15g/1/2oz/2 tbsp powdered gelatine
fresh basil leaves, to garnish

FOR THE DRESSING
90ml/6 tbsp extra virgin olive oil
30ml/2 tbsp red wine vinegar
salt and freshly ground black pepper

SERVES 6

1 Grill the peppers, skin-side down, on a hot barbecue or grill (broiler), until the skins are beginning to blacken. Using tongs, transfer to a bowl, cover and leave to cool.

2 Brush the aubergine and courgette slices with oil and cook until tender and golden, turning occasionally.

3 Heat the remaining oil in a pan and add the onion, raisins, tomato purée and red wine vinegar. Cook until soft and syrupy. Leave to cool in the pan.

4 Pour half the tomato juice into a pan and sprinkle with the gelatine. Dissolve gently over a very low heat, stirring.

5 Line an oiled 1.75 litre/3 pint/ 7 1/2 cup terrine with clear film (plastic wrap), leaving a little hanging over the sides. Place a layer of red peppers in the base and pour in enough of the tomato juice with gelatine to cover. Repeat with the aubergines, courgettes, yellow peppers and onion mixture, ending with another layer of red peppers and covering each layer with tomato juice and gelatine.

6 Add the remaining tomato juice to any left in the pan and pour into the terrine. Give it a sharp tap to eliminate air bubbles. Cover the terrine with clear film and chill until set.

7 To make the dressing, whisk the oil and vinegar, and season with salt and black pepper. Turn out the terrine and serve in thick slices, drizzled with the dressing. Garnish with the basil leaves.

SUMMER VEGETABLES WITH YOGURT PESTO

• • •

*Chargrilled vegetables make a meal on their own, or are delicious served as a
Mediterranean-style accompaniment to grilled meats and fish.*

INGREDIENTS

2 small aubergines (eggplant)
2 large courgettes (zucchini)
1 red (bell) pepper
1 yellow (bell) pepper
1 fennel bulb
1 red onion
olive oil, for brushing
salt and freshly ground
black pepper

FOR THE YOGURT PESTO
150ml/¼ pint/⅔ cup Greek
(US plain strained) yogurt
45ml/3 tbsp pesto

SERVES 4

1 Cut the aubergines into 1cm/½in
slices. Sprinkle with salt and leave to
drain for about 30 minutes. Rinse well
in cold running water and pat dry.

2 Use a sharp kitchen knife to cut
the courgettes in half lengthways. Cut
the peppers in half, removing the seeds
but leaving the stalks in place.

3 Slice the fennel bulb and the red
onion into thick wedges, using a sharp
kitchen knife.

4 Stir the yogurt and pesto lightly
together in a bowl, to make a marbled
sauce. Spoon the yogurt pesto into a
serving bowl and set aside.

5 Arrange the vegetables on the hot
barbecue, brush generously with olive
oil and sprinkle with plenty of salt and
freshly ground black pepper.

6 Cook the vegetables until golden
brown and tender, turning occasionally.
The aubergines and peppers will take
6–8 minutes to cook, the courgettes,
onion and fennel 4–5 minutes. Serve
the vegetables as soon as they are
cooked, with the yogurt pesto.

Cook's Tip
Baby vegetables make
excellent candidates for grilling
whole, so look out for baby
aubergines and peppers, in
particular. There's no need to
salt the aubergines if they're small.

WILD RICE WITH VEGETABLES

Wild rice makes a special accompaniment to grilled vegetables in a simple vinaigrette dressing.
This recipe can be served as a side dish, but it also makes a tasty meal on its own.

INGREDIENTS
225g/8oz/1 cup wild and long
grain rice mixture
1 aubergine (eggplant), sliced
1 red, 1 yellow and 1 green (bell)
pepper, quartered, cored and seeded
2 red onions, sliced
225g/8oz shiitake mushrooms
2 small courgettes (zucchini), cut in
half lengthways
olive oil, for brushing
30ml/2 tbsp chopped fresh thyme

FOR THE DRESSING
90ml/6 tbsp extra virgin olive oil
30ml/2 tbsp balsamic vinegar
2 garlic cloves, crushed
salt and freshly ground
black pepper

SERVES 4

1 Put the wild and long grain rice
mixture in a pan of cold salted water.
Bring to the boil, then reduce the heat,
cover and simmer for 30–40 minutes
until the grains are tender (or follow
the cooking instructions on the packet,
if appropriate).

2 To make the dressing, mix together
the olive oil, vinegar, crushed garlic and
seasoning in a bowl or screw-topped
jar until well blended.

3 Place the vegetables on a rack. Brush
with oil and cook on a hot barbecue or
grill (broiler) for 8–10 minutes, until
tender and browned, turning them
occasionally and basting with oil.

4 Drain the rice and toss in half the
dressing. Tip into a serving dish and
arrange the grilled vegetables on top.
Pour over the remaining dressing and
sprinkle over the chopped fresh thyme.

POTATO SKEWERS WITH MUSTARD DIP

*Potatoes cooked on the barbecue have a tasty flavour and crisp skin.
These skewers are served with a thick, garlic-rich dip.*

INGREDIENTS
*1kg/2¼lb small new potatoes
200g/7oz/2 cups shallots, halved
30ml/2 tbsp olive oil
15ml/1 tbsp sea salt*

*FOR THE MUSTARD DIP
4 garlic cloves, crushed
2 egg yolks
30ml/2 tbsp lemon juice
300ml/½ pint/1¼ cups extra
virgin olive oil
10ml/2 tsp wholegrain mustard
salt and freshly ground
black pepper*

SERVES 4

1 To make the mustard dip, place
the garlic, egg yolks and lemon juice
in a blender or food processor and
process for a few seconds until smooth.

2 With the motor running, add the oil,
until the mixture forms a thick cream.
Add the mustard and season.

3 Par-boil the potatoes in salted boiling
water for about 5 minutes. Drain
thoroughly and then thread them on
to metal skewers with the shallots.

4 Brush with olive oil and sprinkle with
sea salt. Cook for 10–12 minutes over
a hot barbecue, turning often, until
tender. Serve with the mustard dip.

POTATO WEDGES WITH GARLIC AND ROSEMARY

Toss the potato wedges in fragrant, garlicky olive oil with chopped fresh rosemary before cooking them over the coals.

INGREDIENTS

675g/1½ lb medium old potatoes
15ml/1 tbsp olive oil
2 garlic cloves, thinly sliced
60ml/4 tbsp chopped
fresh rosemary
salt and freshly ground
black pepper

SERVES 4

1 Cut each potato into four wedges and par-boil in boiling salted water for 5 minutes. Drain well.

2 Toss the potatoes in the olive oil with the garlic, rosemary and black pepper. Arrange on a grill rack.

3 Cook the potatoes on a hot barbecue for about 15 minutes, turning occasionally, until the wedges are crisp and golden brown.

SPANISH POTATOES

. . .

This is an adaptation of a traditional recipe for peppery fried potatoes. Cook the potatoes in a flameproof dish on the barbecue or in a pan on the hob, and serve them with grilled meats.

INGREDIENTS
675g/1½ lb small new potatoes
75ml/5 tbsp olive oil
2 garlic cloves, sliced
2.5ml/½ tsp crushed chillies
2.5ml/½ tsp ground cumin
10ml/2 tsp paprika
30ml/2 tbsp red or white wine vinegar
1 red or green (bell) pepper, sliced
coarse sea salt, to serve (optional)

SERVES 4

1 Cook the potatoes in a pan of boiling salted water until almost tender. Drain and cut into chunks.

2 Heat the olive oil in a large frying pan or sauté pan and fry the potatoes, turning them frequently, until golden.

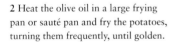

3 Meanwhile, crush together the garlic, chillies and cumin using a mortar and pestle. Mix with the paprika and wine vinegar to form a thick paste.

4 Add the garlic mixture to the potatoes with the sliced pepper and cook, stirring, for 2 minutes. Serve warm, or leave until cold. Sprinkle with coarse sea salt, if you like, to serve.

The powerful flavours of food cooked on the barbecue call for
chunky salsas and tangy barbecue sauces. This chapter also
includes some appetizing dips to go with bread sticks and
crudités, and a selection of delicious marinades suitable for a
wide variety of meat and fish.

SALSAS, DIPS
AND MARINADES

CLASSIC TOMATO SALSA

This is the traditional tomato-based salsa that most people associate with spicy Mexican-inspired food. There are innumerable recipes for it, but the basics of onion, tomato, chilli and coriander are common to every one of them. Serve this salsa as a condiment with a wide variety of dishes.

INGREDIENTS

3–6 fresh Serrano chillies
1 large white onion
grated rind and juice of 2 limes,
plus strips of lime rind, to garnish
8 ripe, firm tomatoes
large bunch of fresh
coriander (cilantro)
1.5ml/¼ tsp caster
(superfine) sugar
salt

SERVES 6

1 Use three chillies for a salsa of medium heat; up to six if you like it hot. To peel the chillies, spear them on a long-handled metal skewer and roast them over the flame of a gas burner until the skins blister and darken. Do not let the flesh burn. Alternatively, dry-fry them in a griddle pan until the skins are scorched.

Variations

Use spring onions (scallions) or mild red onions instead of the white onion. For a smoky flavour, use chipotle chillies instead of fresh Serrano chillies.

2 Place the roasted chillies in a strong plastic bag and tie the top of the bag to keep the steam in. Set aside for about 20 minutes.

3 Meanwhile, chop the onion finely and put it in a bowl with the strips of lime rind and juice. The lime juice will soften the onion.

4 Remove the chillies from the bag and peel off the skins wearing rubber gloves. Cut off the stalks, slit the chillies and scrape out the seeds with a knife. Chop the flesh coarsely and set aside.

5 Cut a small cross in the base of each tomato. Place the tomatoes in a heatproof bowl and pour in boiling water to cover.

6 Leave the tomatoes in the water for 30 seconds, then lift them out using a slotted spoon and plunge them into a bowl of cold water. Drain. The skins will have begun to peel back from the crosses. Remove the skins completely.

7 Dice the peeled tomatoes and put them in a bowl. Add the chopped onion and lime mixture. Chop the fresh coriander finely.

8 Add the coriander to the salsa, with the chillies, sugar and salt. Mix gently until the sugar has dissolved and all the ingredients are coated in lime juice. Cover and chill for 2–3 hours to allow the flavours to blend. The salsa will keep for 3–4 days in the refrigerator. Garnish with the strips of lime rind just before serving.

CHUNKY CHERRY TOMATO SALSA
· · ·

Succulent cherry tomatoes and refreshing cucumber form the base of this delicious dill-seasoned salsa. Prepare up to 1 day in advance and store in the refrigerator until needed.

INGREDIENTS

1 ridge cucumber
5ml/1 tsp sea salt
500g/1¼ lb cherry tomatoes
grated rind and juice of 1 lemon
45ml/3 tbsp chilli oil
2.5ml/½ tsp dried chilli flakes
30ml/2 tbsp chopped fresh dill
1 garlic clove, finely chopped
salt and freshly ground
black pepper

SERVES 4

1 Trim the ends off the cucumber and cut it into 2.5cm/1in lengths, then cut each piece lengthways into thin slices. Place in a colander and sprinkle with sea salt. Leave for 5 minutes.

2 Rinse the cucumber slices under cold water and dry with kitchen paper.

3 Quarter the cherry tomatoes and place in a bowl with the cucumber.

4 Whisk together the lemon rind and juice, chilli oil, chilli flakes, dill and garlic. Season, then pour over the tomato and cucumber and toss well. Marinate for 2 hours before serving.

Cook's Tip
Try flavouring the salsa with other herbs, such as tarragon or mint.

SALSA VERDE

° ° °

There are many versions of this classic green salsa. Try this one sprinkled over chargrilled squid, or with baked potatoes.

INGREDIENTS

2–4 green chillies, halved
8 spring onions (scallions)
2 garlic cloves
50g/2oz salted capers
sprig of fresh tarragon
bunch of fresh parsley
grated rind and juice of 1 lime
juice of 1 lemon
90ml/6 tbsp olive oil
about 15ml/1 tbsp green Tabasco
sauce, to taste
freshly ground black pepper

SERVES 4

1 Seed the chillies and trim the spring onions. Halve the garlic cloves. Place in a food processor and pulse briefly.

2 Use your fingers to rub the excess salt off the capers. Add them, with the tarragon and parsley, to the food processor and pulse again until the ingredients are quite finely chopped.

3 Transfer the mixture to a large bowl. Mix in the lime rind and juice, lemon juice and olive oil, stirring lightly so the citrus juice and oil do not emulsify.

4 Add green Tabasco sauce, a little at a time, and black pepper to taste. Chill the salsa in the refrigerator until ready to serve, but do not prepare it more than 8 hours in advance.

FIERY CITRUS SALSA

° ° °

*This unusual salsa makes a fantastic marinade for shellfish and it is also
delicious drizzled over meat that has been cooked on the barbecue.*

INGREDIENTS

1 orange
1 green apple
2 fresh red chillies
1 garlic clove
8 fresh mint leaves
juice of 1 lemon
salt and freshly ground
black pepper

SERVES 4

1 Using a sharp knife, remove the peel
and pith from the orange and, working
over a bowl to catch the juices, cut out
the segments. Squeeze any remaining
juice into the bowl.

2 Use a sharp kitchen knife to peel the
apple and slice it into wedges. Remove
and discard the apple core.

3 Halve the chillies and remove
the seeds, then place them in a blender
or food processor with the orange
segments and juice, apple wedges,
garlic and mint.

4 Process until smooth. With the motor
running, gradually pour in the lemon
juice. Season to taste with salt and
freshly ground black pepper and serve
the salsa immediately.

BARBECUE-COOKED CORN SALSA

Serve this succulent salsa with grilled gammon or pork, or with smoked meats. The chargrilled corn cob makes the salsa particularly flavoursome.

INGREDIENTS

2 corn cobs
30ml/2 tbsp melted butter
4 tomatoes
6 spring onions (scallions), chopped
1 garlic clove, finely chopped
30ml/2 tbsp lemon juice
30ml/2 tbsp olive oil
red Tabasco sauce, to taste
salt and freshly ground
black pepper

SERVES 4

3 Skewer the tomatoes and hold over the barbecue or grill for about 2 minutes, turning, until the skin splits and wrinkles. Slip off the skins and dice the flesh. Add to the corn with the spring onions and chopped garlic.

4 Stir the lemon juice and olive oil together, adding Tabasco, salt and black pepper to taste. Pour over the salsa, stir well, cover and leave to marinate at room temperature for 1–2 hours before serving.

1 Remove the husks and silks from the corn cobs. Brush with the melted butter and gently cook on the barbecue or grill (broiler) for 20 minutes, turning occasionally, until tender and charred.

2 To remove the kernels, stand each cob upright on a chopping board and use a large, heavy knife to slice down the length of the cob. Put the kernels in a mixing bowl.

MANGO SALSA

* * *

This has a fresh, fruity taste and is perfect with chargrilled fish. The bright colours make it an attractive addition to any barbecue party.

INGREDIENTS
2 fresh red Fresno chillies
2 ripe mangoes
½ white onion
small bunch of fresh
coriander (cilantro)
grated rind and juice of 1 lime

SERVES 4

1 To peel the chillies, spear them on a long-handled metal skewer and roast them over the flame of a gas burner until the skins blister and darken. Do not let the flesh burn. Alternatively, dry-fry them in a griddle pan until the skins are scorched.

2 Place the roasted chillies in a strong plastic bag and tie the top of the bag to keep the steam in. Leave for 20 minutes.

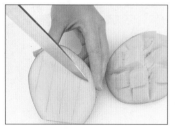

3 Meanwhile, put one of the mangoes on a board and cut off a thick slice close to the flat side of the stone (pit). Turn the mango around and repeat on the other side. Score the flesh on each thick slice with criss-cross lines at 1cm/½in intervals, taking care not to cut through the skin. Repeat with the second mango.

4 Fold the mango halves inside out so that the mango flesh stands proud of the skin, in neat dice. Carefully slice these off the skin and into a bowl. Cut off the flesh adhering to each stone, dice it and add it to the bowl.

5 Remove the roasted chillies from the bag and carefully peel off the skins. Cut off the stalks, then slit the chillies and scrape out the seeds.

Cook's Tip
Mangoes, in season, are readily available nowadays, but are usually sold unripe. Keep in a warm room for 24 hours or until they are just soft to the touch. Do not allow them to ripen beyond this point.

6 Chop the white onion and the coriander finely and add them to the diced mango. Chop the chilli flesh finely and add it to the mixture in the bowl, together with the lime rind and juice. Stir well to mix, cover and chill in the refrigerator for at least 1 hour before serving. The salsa will keep for 2–3 days in the refrigerator.

ROASTED TOMATO AND CORIANDER SALSA

• • •

Roasting the tomatoes gives a greater depth to the taste of this salsa, which also benefits from the warm, rounded flavour of roasted chillies.

INGREDIENTS
500g/1¼lb tomatoes
2 fresh Serrano chillies
1 onion
juice of 1 lime
large bunch of fresh coriander (cilantro)
salt

SERVES 6

1 Preheat the oven to 200°C/400°F/ Gas 6. Cut the tomatoes into quarters and place them in a roasting pan. Add the chillies. Roast for 45–60 minutes, until the tomatoes and chillies are charred and softened.

2 Place the chillies in a plastic bag. Tie the top of the bag to keep the steam in and set aside for 20 minutes. Leave the tomatoes to cool slightly, then remove the skins and dice the flesh.

3 Chop the onion finely, then place in a bowl and add the lime juice and the chopped tomatoes.

4 Remove the chillies from the bag and peel off the skins. Cut off the stalks, then slit the chillies and scrape out the seeds with a sharp knife. Chop chillies coarsely and add them to the onion mixture. Mix well.

5 Chop the coriander and add most of it to the salsa. Season with salt, cover and chill in the refrigerator for at least 1 hour before serving, sprinkled with the remaining coriander. This salsa will keep in the refrigerator for 1 week.

BARBECUE SAUCE

Brush this sauce liberally over chicken drumsticks, chops or kebabs before cooking on the barbecue, or serve as a hot or cold accompaniment to hot dogs and burgers.

INGREDIENTS
30ml/2 tbsp vegetable oil
1 large onion, chopped
2 garlic cloves, crushed
400g/14oz can tomatoes
30ml/2 tbsp Worcestershire sauce
15ml/1 tbsp white wine vinegar
45ml/3 tbsp clear honey
5ml/1 tsp mustard powder
2.5ml/½ tsp chilli seasoning or
mild chilli powder
salt and freshly ground
black pepper

SERVES 4

3 Pour into a food processor or blender and process until smooth.

4 Press through a sieve if you like. Adjust the seasoning to taste.

1 Heat the vegetable oil in a large pan and cook the onions and garlic until soft and golden.

2 Stir in the remaining ingredients and simmer gently, uncovered, for about 15–20 minutes, stirring occasionally. Remove the pan from the heat and leave to cool slightly.

GUACAMOLE

Nachos or tortilla chips are the classic accompaniments for this classic Mexican dip, but it also tastes great served on the side with burgers or kebabs.

INGREDIENTS

2 ripe avocados
2 red chillies, seeded
1 garlic clove
1 shallot
30ml/2 tbsp olive oil, plus
extra to serve
juice of 1 lemon
salt
fresh flat leaf parsley, to garnish

SERVES 4

1 Halve the avocados, flick out the stones (pits), using the point of a sharp knife, and use a dessert spoon to scoop the flesh into a large bowl.

2 Mash the flesh well, using a potato masher or a large fork, so that the avocado is a fairly smooth consistency.

3 Finely chop the chillies, garlic clove and shallot, then stir into the mashed avocado with the olive oil and lemon juice. Add salt to taste and mix well.

4 Spoon the mixture into a serving bowl. Drizzle over a little more olive oil and sprinkle with flat leaf parsley leaves. Serve immediately. Guacamole can be prepared up to 8 hours in advance and stored in the refrigerator, sprinkled with lemon juice and covered with clear film (plastic wrap).

TOFFEE ONION RELISH

○ ○ ○

Slow, gentle cooking reduces the onions to a soft, caramelized relish.
It makes a tasty addition to many barbecue menus.

2 Heat the butter and oil together in a large pan. Add the onions and sugar and cook very gently for 30 minutes over a low heat, stirring occasionally, until reduced to a soft rich brown toffeed mixture.

3 Coarsely chop the capers and stir them into the toffee onions. Leave to cool completely.

4 Stir in the chopped fresh parsley and add salt and ground black pepper to taste. Cover with clear film (plastic wrap) and chill in the refrigerator until ready to serve.

INGREDIENTS

3 large onions
50g/2oz/4 tbsp butter
30ml/2 tbsp olive oil
30ml/2 tbsp light muscovado
(brown) sugar
30ml/2 tbsp pickled capers
30ml/2 tbsp chopped fresh parsley
salt and freshly ground black pepper
SERVES 4

1 Peel the onions and halve them vertically, through the core, using a sharp knife. Slice them thinly.

PARSLEY BUTTER

. . .

This butter, or one of the variations below, makes a subtle accompaniment to
barbecued food, particularly fish with a delicate flavour.

INGREDIENTS
115g/4oz/½ cup softened butter
30ml/2 tbsp chopped fresh parsley
2.5ml/½ tsp lemon juice
cayenne pepper
salt and freshly ground black pepper
SERVES 4

1 Beat the butter until creamy, then beat in the parsley, lemon juice and cayenne pepper, and season lightly.

2 Spread the butter 5mm/¼in thick on to foil and chill, then cut into shapes with a knife or fancy cutter.

3 Alternatively, form the butter into a roll, wrap in clear film (plastic wrap) or foil and chill. Cut off slices as required.

Variations
LEMON OR LIME BUTTER
Add 15ml/1 tbsp finely grated lemon or lime rind and 15ml/1 tbsp juice to the butter.

HERB BUTTER
Replace the parsley with 30ml/2 tbsp chopped fresh mint, chives or tarragon.

GARLIC BUTTER
Add 2 crushed garlic cloves to the butter with 15–30ml/1–2 tbsp chopped fresh parsley.

ANCHOVY BUTTER
Add 6 anchovy fillets, drained of oil and mashed with a fork, to the butter. Season with pepper only.

MUSTARD BUTTER
Add 10ml/2 tsp English (hot) mustard and 30ml/2 tbsp chopped chives to the butter.

These butters will keep in the refrigerator for several days, and will also freeze, wrapped in clear film (plastic wrap) or foil to avoid any loss of flavour.

THOUSAND ISLAND DIP

• ◦ •

This creamy dip can be served with grilled prawns or shrimps laced on to bamboo skewers for dipping or with a simple mixed seafood salad.

INGREDIENTS

4 sun-dried tomatoes in oil
4 tomatoes
150ml/¼ pint/⅔ cup soft
white (farmer's) cheese
60ml/4 tbsp mayonnaise
30ml/2 tbsp tomato purée (paste)
30ml/2 tbsp chopped fresh parsley
grated rind and juice of 1 lemon
red Tabasco sauce, to taste
5ml/1 tsp Worcestershire or
soy sauce
salt and freshly ground black pepper

SERVES 4

1 Drain the sun-dried tomatoes on kitchen paper to remove excess oil, then finely chop.

2 Skewer each fresh tomato in turn on a metal fork and hold in a gas flame for 1–2 minutes, until the skin wrinkles and splits. Slip off and discard the skins, then halve the tomatoes and scoop out the seeds with a teaspoon. Finely chop the tomato flesh.

3 Beat the soft cheese, then gradually beat in the mayonnaise and tomato purée until blended.

4 Stir in the chopped parsley and sun-dried tomatoes, then add the chopped tomatoes and their seeds, and mix well.

5 Add the lemon rind and juice and Tabasco to taste. Stir in Worcestershire or soy sauce, and salt and pepper. Transfer the dip to a bowl, cover and chill until ready to serve.

MELLOW GARLIC DIP

. . .

Two whole heads of garlic may seem too much but, once cooked, the taste is sweet and mellow.
Serve with crunchy bread sticks and potato snacks.

2 When cool enough to handle, separate the garlic cloves and peel. Place on a chopping board and sprinkle with salt. Mash the garlic with a fork until puréed.

3 Place the garlic in a large bowl and stir in the mayonnaise, yogurt and wholegrain mustard. Mix well.

INGREDIENTS

2 whole garlic heads
15ml/1 tbsp olive oil
60ml/4 tbsp mayonnaise
75ml/5 tbsp Greek (US strained plain) yogurt
5ml/1 tsp wholegrain mustard
salt and freshly ground black pepper

SERVES 4

1 Slice the tops from the heads of garlic, using a sharp knife. Brush with olive oil and wrap in foil. Cook on a medium-hot barbecue for 25 minutes, turning occasionally.

4 Check the seasoning, adding more salt and pepper to taste, then spoon the dip into a serving bowl. Cover and chill in the refrigerator until ready to serve.

183

CREAMY AUBERGINE DIP

• • •

*Spread this velvet-textured dip thickly on to slices of French bread toasted on the barbecue,
then top with slivers of sun-dried tomato to make wonderful Italian-style crostini.*

INGREDIENTS

1 large aubergine (eggplant)
30ml/2 tbsp olive oil
1 small onion, finely chopped
2 garlic cloves, finely chopped
60ml/4 tbsp chopped fresh parsley
75ml/5 tbsp crème fraîche
red Tabasco sauce, to taste
juice of 1 lemon, to taste
salt and freshly ground
black pepper

SERVES 4

3 Peel the aubergine and mash the flesh with a large fork or potato masher to make a pulpy purée.

4 Stir in the onion and garlic, parsley and crème fraîche. Add Tabasco, lemon juice, and season to taste. Serve warm.

1 Cook the whole aubergine on a medium barbecue or grill (broiler) for about 20 minutes, turning occasionally, until the skin is blackened and the aubergine soft. Cover the aubergine with a clean dishtowel and set aside to cool for about 5–6 minutes.

2 Heat the oil in a frying pan and cook the chopped onion and garlic for about 5 minutes, until soft but not browned.

FAT-FREE SAFFRON DIP

• • •

Serve this mild dip with fresh vegetable crudités – it is particularly good with
florets of cauliflower, asparagus tips and baby carrots and corn.

INGREDIENTS

15ml/1 tbsp boiling water
small pinch of saffron threads
200g/7oz/scant 1 cup fat-free
fromage frais or farmer's cheese
10 fresh chives
10 fresh basil leaves
salt and freshly ground
black pepper

SERVES 4

1 Pour the boiling water into a bowl
and add the saffron threads. Leave to
infuse (steep) for 3 minutes.

2 Beat the fromage frais in a large bowl
until smooth. Stir in the saffron liquid
with a wooden spoon.

Cook's Tip

If you don't have any saffron, add
a squeeze of lemon or lime juice.

3 Snip the chives into the dip. Tear the
basil leaves into small pieces and stir
them in. Mix thoroughly.

4 Add salt and freshly ground black
pepper to taste. Serve the dip with fresh
vegetable crudités, if you like.

SALSAS, DIPS AND MARINADES

SPICY YOGURT MARINADE

° ° °

Use this marinade for chicken, lamb or pork, and marinate the meat, covered and chilled,
for 24–36 hours to develop a mellow spicy flavour.

INGREDIENTS

5ml/1 tsp coriander seeds
10ml/2 tsp cumin seeds
6 cloves
2 bay leaves
1 onion, quartered
2 garlic cloves
5ml/2in piece of fresh root ginger,
coarsely chopped
2.5ml/½ tsp chilli powder
5ml/1 tsp ground turmeric
150ml/¼ pint/⅔ cup natural
(plain) yogurt
juice of 1 lemon

SERVES 6

1 Spread the coriander and cumin
seeds, cloves and bay leaves over the
base of a large frying pan and dry-fry
over a moderate heat until the bay
leaves are crisp.

2 Leave the spices to cool, then grind
coarsely with a mortar and pestle.

3 Finely chop the onion, garlic and
ginger in a blender or food processor.
Add the ground spices, chilli, turmeric,
yogurt and lemon juice.

Cook's Tip
Garnish the finished dish with
fresh coriander (cilantro) leaves
and slices of lemon or lime.

4 If you are marinating cuts of chicken
or large pieces of meat, make several
deep slashes to allow the flavours to
penetrate. Arrange the pieces in a single
layer and pour over the marinade.
Cover and leave in the refrigerator to
marinate for at least 24 hours.

ORANGE AND GREEN PEPPERCORN MARINADE

○ ○ ○

This is an excellent light marinade for delicately flavoured whole fish, such as sea trout,
bass or bream. The beauty of the fish is perfectly set off by the softly coloured marinade.

INGREDIENTS

1 red onion
2 small oranges
90ml/6 tbsp light olive oil
30ml/2 tbsp cider vinegar
30ml/2 tbsp green peppercorns in
brine, drained
30ml/2 tbsp chopped fresh parsley
salt and sugar

FOR 1 MEDIUM-SIZE FISH

1 With a sharp knife, slash the fish
3–4 times on each side.

2 Cut a piece of foil big enough to
wrap the fish and use to line a large
dish. Peel and slice the onion and
oranges. Lay half the slices on the foil,
place the fish on top and cover with
the remaining onion and orange.

3 Mix the remaining marinade
ingredients and pour over the fish.
Cover and leave to marinate for
4 hours, occasionally spooning the
marinade over the fish.

4 Fold the foil loosely over the fish and
seal the edges securely. Bake on a
medium barbecue for 15 minutes for
450g/1lb, plus 15 minutes over.

187

GINGER AND LIME MARINADE

• • •

This fragrant marinade will guarantee a mouth-watering aroma from the barbecue. Shown here on prawn and monkfish kebabs, it is just as delicious with chicken or pork.

INGREDIENTS

3 limes
15ml/1 tbsp green cardamom pods
1 onion, finely chopped
2.5cm/1in piece of fresh root
ginger, grated
1 large garlic clove, crushed
45ml/3 tbsp olive oil

SERVES 4–6

3 Mix all the marinade ingredients together and pour over the meat or fish. Stir in gently, cover and leave in a cool place to marinate for 2–3 hours.

4 Drain the meat or fish when you are ready to cook it on the barbecue. Baste the meat occasionally with the marinade, while cooking.

1 Finely grate the rind from one lime and squeeze the juice from all of them.

2 Split the cardamom pods and remove the seeds. Crush the seeds with a mortar and pestle or the back of a heavy-bladed knife.

SUMMER HERB MARINADE

• • •

Make the best use of summer herbs in this marinade. Try any combination of herbs, depending
on what you have to hand, and use with veal, chicken, pork, lamb or salmon.

INGREDIENTS

large handful of fresh herb sprigs,
e.g. chervil, thyme, parsley, sage,
chives, rosemary, oregano
90ml/6 tbsp olive oil
45ml/3 tbsp tarragon vinegar
1 garlic clove, crushed
2 spring onions (scallions), chopped
salt and freshly ground
black pepper

SERVES 4

3 Place the meat or fish in a bowl and
pour over the marinade. Cover
and leave to marinate in a cool place
for 4–6 hours.

4 Drain the meat or fish when you are
ready to cook it on the barbecue. Use
the marinade to baste the meat
occasionally while cooking.

1 Discard any coarse stalks or damaged
leaves from the herbs, then chop them
very finely.

2 Add the chopped herbs to the
remaining marinade ingredients in a
large bowl. Stir to mix thoroughly.

  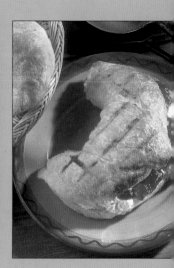

At the end of a barbecue, it's a lovely idea to use the lingering

fire to make a delicious fruity dessert. Even those who thought

they couldn't eat another bite will be beguiled. Accompany

grilled fruit with a spicy sauce, crisp toasted brioche or freshly

made griddle cakes.

DESSERTS

CHARGRILLED APPLES ON CINNAMON TOASTS

· · ·

This simple, scrumptious dessert is best made with an enriched bread such as brioche,
but any light sweet bread will do.

INGREDIENTS

4 sweet, eating apples
juice of ½ lemon
4 individual brioches or muffins
60ml/4 tbsp melted butter
30ml/2 tbsp golden caster
(superfine) sugar
5ml/1 tsp ground cinnamon
whipped cream, to serve

SERVES 4

2 Cut the brioches or muffins into thick slices. Brush the slices with melted butter on both sides.

4 Place the apple and brioche slices on a medium-hot barbecue and cook them for about 3–4 minutes, turning once, until they are beginning to turn golden brown. Do not allow to burn.

1 Core the apples and use a sharp knife to cut them into 3–4 thick slices. Sprinkle the apple slices with lemon juice and set them aside.

3 Mix together the caster sugar and ground cinnamon in a small bowl to make the cinnamon sugar. Set aside.

5 Sprinkle half the cinnamon sugar over the apple slices and brioche toasts and cook for a further minute on the barbecue, until the sugar is sizzling and the toasts are a rich golden brown.

6 To serve, arrange the apple slices over the toasts and sprinkle them with the remaining cinnamon sugar. Serve hot, with whipped cream.

PINEAPPLE WEDGES WITH RUM BUTTER GLAZE

Fresh pineapple is even more full of flavour when barbecued, and this spiced rum glaze makes it into a very special dessert.

INGREDIENTS
1 medium pineapple
30ml/2 tbsp dark brown sugar
5ml/1 tsp ground ginger
60ml/4 tbsp melted butter
30ml/2 tbsp dark rum

SERVES 4

3 Soak 4 bamboo skewers in water for 15 minutes to prevent them from scorching on the barbecue. Push a skewer through each wedge, into the stalk, to hold the chunks in place.

4 Mix together the sugar, ginger, butter and rum and brush over the pineapple. Cook the wedges on the barbecue for 4 minutes; pour the remaining glaze over the top and serve.

1 With a large, sharp knife, cut the pineapple lengthways into four wedges. Cut out and discard the central core.

2 Cut between the flesh and skin, to release the skin, but leave the flesh in place. Slice the flesh across and lengthways to make thick chunks.

Cook's Tip
For an easier version, simply remove the skin and then cut the whole pineapple into thick slices and cook as above.

BAKED BANANAS WITH SPICY VANILLA FILLING

Bananas are ideal for barbecue cooking as they bake in their skins and need no preparation at all. This flavoured butter adds richness; children may prefer melted chocolate, jam or honey.

INGREDIENTS

4 bananas
6 green cardamom pods
1 vanilla pod (bean)
finely grated rind of 1 small orange
30ml/2 tbsp brandy or orange juice
60ml/4 tbsp light muscovado
(brown) sugar
45ml/3 tbsp butter
crème fraîche, to serve

SERVES 4

1 Place the bananas, in their skins, on a hot barbecue and leave for about 6–8 minutes, turning occasionally, until they are turning brownish-black.

2 Meanwhile, split the cardamom pods and remove the seeds. Crush lightly with a mortar and pestle.

3 Split the vanilla pod lengthways and scrape out the tiny seeds. Mix them with the cardamom seeds, orange rind, brandy or juice, muscovado sugar and butter into a thick paste.

4 Using a sharp knife, slit the skin of each banana, then open out the skin and spoon in a little of the paste. Serve the bananas immediately with a spoonful of crème fraîche.

ORANGES IN MAPLE AND COINTREAU SYRUP

. . .

*This is one of the most delicious ways to eat an orange, and a luxurious way to round off
a barbecue. For a children's or alcohol-free version, omit the liqueur.*

INGREDIENTS

*20ml/4 tsp butter, plus extra,
melted, for brushing
4 medium oranges
30 ml/2 tbsp maple syrup
30ml/2 tbsp Cointreau or Grand
Marnier liqueur
crème fraîche, fromage frais or
mascarpone cheese, to serve*

SERVES 4

2 Remove some shreds of orange rind,
to decorate. Blanch these, dry them and
set them aside. Peel the oranges,
removing all the white pith and
catching the juice in a bowl.

4 Tuck the baking foil up securely
around the oranges to keep them in
shape, leaving the foil open at the top.

1 Cut four double-thickness squares of
baking foil, large enough to wrap each
of the oranges. Brush the centre
of each square of foil with plenty of
melted butter.

3 Slice the oranges crossways into thick
slices. Reassemble them and place each
orange on a square of baking foil.

5 Mix together the reserved orange
juice, maple syrup and liqueur and
spoon the mixture over the oranges.

6 Add a knob (pat) of butter to each
parcel and close the foil at the top to
seal in the juices. Place the parcels on
a hot barbecue for 10–12 minutes,
until hot. Serve with crème fraîche,
fromage frais or mascarpone cheese,
topped with the shreds of orange rind.

NECTARINES WITH MARZIPAN AND MASCARPONE

A luscious dessert that no one can resist – dieters may prefer to use low-fat soft cheese or ricotta instead of mascarpone.

INGREDIENTS

4 firm, ripe nectarines or peaches
75g/3oz/½ cup marzipan
75g/3oz/5 tbsp mascarpone cheese
3 macaroons, crushed

SERVES 4

1 Cut the nectarines or peaches in half and remove the stones (pits).

2 Divide the marzipan into eight pieces, roll into balls, using your fingers, and press one piece of marzipan into the stone cavity of each nectarine half.

Cook's Tip

Either nectarines or peaches can be used for this recipe. If the stone (pit) does not pull out easily when you halve the fruit, use a small, sharp knife to cut around it.

3 Spoon the mascarpone cheese on top of the fruit halves. Sprinkle the crushed macaroon biscuits (cookies) over the mascarpone cheese.

4 Place the half-fruits on a hot barbecue for 3–5 minutes, until they are hot and the mascarpone starts to melt. Serve immediately.

GRILLED STRAWBERRY CROISSANTS

The combination of crisp croissants, ricotta cheese and sweet strawberry conserve makes for a deliciously simple, sinful dessert, which is like eating warm cream cakes!

INGREDIENTS

4 croissants
115g/4oz/1/2 cup ricotta cheese
115g/4oz/1/2 cup strawberry
conserve or jam

SERVES 4

3 Top the ricotta with a generous spoonful of strawberry conserve and replace the top half of the croissant.

4 Place the filled croissants on a hot barbecue and cook for 2–3 minutes, turning once. Serve immediately.

1 On a chopping board, split the croissants in half and open them out.

2 Spread the bottom half of each croissant with a generous layer of the ricotta cheese.

Cook's Tip

As an alternative to croissants, try scones (biscuits), brioches or muffins, toasted on the barbecue.

GRIDDLE CAKES WITH MULLED PLUMS
• • •

*These delectably light little pancakes are fun to make on the barbecue. They are served with
a rich, spicy plum sauce, and you could offer cream or yogurt, too.*

INGREDIENTS
500g/1¼lb red plums
*90ml/6 tbsp light muscovado
(brown) sugar*
1 cinnamon stick
2 whole cloves
1 piece star anise
90ml/6 tbsp apple juice

FOR THE GRIDDLE CAKES
*50g/2oz/½ cup plain (all-
purpose) flour*
10ml/2 tsp baking powder
pinch of salt
50g/2oz/½ cup fine cornmeal
30ml/2 tbsp light muscovado sugar
1 egg, beaten
300ml/½ pint/1¼ cups milk
30ml/2 tbsp corn oil

SERVES 6

1 Halve, stone (pit) and quarter the
plums. Place them in a flameproof pan,
with the sugar, spices and apple juice.

Cook's Tip
If you prefer, make the griddle
cakes in advance, on the hob
(stovetop), and then simply heat
them for a few seconds on the
barbecue to serve with the plums.

2 Bring to the boil, then reduce the
heat, cover the pan and simmer gently
for 8–10 minutes, stirring occasionally,
until the plums are soft. Remove the
spices and keep the plums warm on
the side of the barbecue.

3 For the griddle cakes, sift the
plain flour, baking powder and salt
into a large mixing bowl and stir in
the cornmeal and muscovado sugar.

4 Make a well in the centre of
the ingredients and add the egg, then
beat in the milk. Beat thoroughly with
a whisk or wooden spoon to form a
smooth batter. Beat in half the oil.

5 Heat a griddle or a heavy frying pan
on a hot barbecue. Brush with the
remaining oil, then drop tablespoons
of batter on to it, allowing them to
spread. Cook the griddle cakes for
about a minute, until bubbles start
to appear on the surface and the
underside is golden brown.

6 Turn the cakes over and cook the
other side for a further minute, or until
golden. Serve the cakes hot from the
griddle with a spoonful of mulled
plums and cream or yogurt, if you like.

FRUIT KEBABS WITH CHOCOLATE FONDUE
. . .

*Fondues are always lots of fun, and the delicious ingredients used here – fresh fruit, chocolate
and marshmallow – mean that this recipe will be a popular choice with children and adults alike.*

2 Mix together the butter, lemon juice
and ground cinnamon and brush the
mixture generously over the fruits.

3 For the fondue, place the chocolate,
cream and marshmallows in a small
pan and heat gently, without boiling,
stirring constantly until the mixture has
melted and is smooth.

INGREDIENTS

*2 bananas and 2 kiwi fruit
12 strawberries
15ml/1 tbsp melted butter
15ml/1 tbsp lemon juice
5ml/1 tsp ground cinnamon
225g/8oz plain
(semisweet) chocolate
120ml/4fl oz/¹/₂ cup single
(light) cream
8 marshmallows
2.5ml/¹/₂ tsp vanilla
essence (extract)*

SERVES 4

1 Peel the bananas and cut into thick
chunks. Peel the kiwi fruit and quarter
them. Thread the bananas, kiwi fruit
and strawberries on to four wooden
skewers. (Soak the skewers in water
for 15 minutes beforehand to prevent
them from scorching on the barbecue.)

4 Cook the kebabs on a medium-
hot barbecue for about 2–3 minutes,
turning once, or until the fruit is
golden. Stir the vanilla essence into the
fondue. Empty the fondue into a small
bowl and serve immediately, with the
fruit kebabs.

SPICED PEAR AND BLUEBERRY PARCELS

. . .

This fruity combination makes a delicious dessert for a hot summer's evening.
You could substitute other berry fruits for the blueberries if you like.

INGREDIENTS

4 firm, ripe pears
30ml/2 tbsp lemon juice
15ml/1 tbsp melted butter
150g/5oz/1¼ cups blueberries
60ml/4 tbsp light brown sugar
freshly ground black pepper

SERVES 4

3 Cut four squares of double-thickness foil, large enough to wrap the pears, and brush them with melted butter. Place two pear halves on each, cut sides upwards. Gather the foil up around them, to hold them level.

4 Mix the blueberries and sugar together and spoon them over the pears. Sprinkle with black pepper. Seal the edges of the foil over the pears and cook on a fairly hot barbecue for 20–25 minutes.

1 Peel the pears thinly. Cut them in half lengthways. Scoop out the core from each half, using a teaspoon and a sharp kitchen knife.

2 Brush the pears with lemon juice, to prevent them from discolouring.

Cook's Tip

To assemble in advance, line with a layer of greaseproof (waxed) paper, as the acid in the juice may react with the foil and taint the flavour.

PUMPKIN IN BROWN SUGAR

· · ·

Rich, sticky and sweet, this warming dessert looks very attractive, tastes wonderful and is not at all difficult to prepare.

1 Cut six large, double thickness squares of foil and lightly grease with butter. Using a sharp knife, halve the pumpkin, cut into wedges and remove the seeds and fibres. Divide the wedges among the foil squares, placing them in a single layer skin-side down. Fill the hollows with the sugar.

2 Carefully sprinkle the water over the wedges, taking care not to wash all the sugar out of the hollows. Sprinkle on the ground cloves and add two cinnamon sticks to each parcel. Fold up the sides of the foil, then tuck in and fold over the edges to make loosely wrapped, but secure, parcels.

3 Cook the parcels on a low barbecue turning them occasionally, for about 30 minutes, or until the pumpkin is tender and the sugar and water have formed a syrup.

4 Carefully unwrap the foil parcels and transfer the pumpkin to a warm platter and pour the hot syrup over. Decorate each portion with mint and the cinnamon sticks and serve with thick yogurt or crème fraîche.

BAKED APPLES IN HONEY AND LEMON

o o o

Tender baked apples with a classic flavouring of lemon and honey make a simple dessert.
Serve with custard or a spoonful of whipped cream, if you like.

INGREDIENTS
4 medium cooking apples
15ml/1 tbsp clear honey
grated rind and juice of 1 lemon
15ml/1 tbsp butter, melted

SERVES 4

1 Remove the cores from the apples, leaving them whole. Cut four squares of double-thickness baking foil, to wrap the apples, and brush with butter.

2 With a cannelle or sharp knife, cut lines through the apple skin at regular intervals.

3 Mix together the honey, lemon rind, juice and butter in a small bowl.

4 Spoon the mixture into the apples and wrap in foil, sealing the edges securely. Cook on a hot barbecue for 20 minutes, until the apples are tender.

POACHED PEARS IN MAPLE AND YOGURT SAUCE

° ° °

This elegant dessert is easier to make than it looks – poach the pears on the hob or barbecue
when you cook the main course, and have the cooled syrup ready to add just before serving.

INGREDIENTS

6 firm pears
15ml/1 tbsp lemon juice
250ml/8fl oz/1 cup sweet white
wine or cider
thinly pared rind of 1 lemon
1 cinnamon stick
30ml/2 tbsp maple syrup
2.5ml/½ tsp arrowroot
150ml/¼ pint/⅔ cup Greek
(US plain strained) yogurt

SERVES 6

1 Peel the pears, leaving them whole and with stalks. Brush with lemon juice to prevent them from discolouring. Use a potato peeler or small knife to scoop out the core from the base of each pear.

2 Place the pears in a wide, heavy pan and pour over the wine, with enough cold water almost to cover the fruit. Add the lemon rind and cinnamon stick, and bring to the boil on the hob (stovetop) or, using a flameproof pan, on the barbecue. Reduce the heat, cover and simmer for 30 minutes, or until tender. Lift out the pears carefully.

3 Boil the remaining liquid, uncovered, until reduced to about 120ml/4 fl oz/ ½ cup. Strain and add the maple syrup. Blend a little of the liquid with the arrowroot. Return to the pan and cook, stirring, until thick and clear. Leave to cool.

4 Slice each pear, leaving the slices attached at the stem end, and fan out on serving plates. Stir 30ml/2 tbsp of the cooled syrup into the yogurt and spoon around the pears. Drizzle the pears with the remaining syrup and serve immediately.

CHOCOLATE MINT TRUFFLE FILO PARCELS

* * *

These exquisite little parcels are utterly irresistible: there will be no leftovers. The use of fresh mint in the recipe gives a wonderfully refreshing flavour.

2 Cut the filo pastry sheets into 7.5cm/3in squares and cover with a damp cloth to prevent them drying out.

3 Brush a square of filo with melted butter, lay on a second sheet, brush again and place a spoonful of filling in the middle of the top sheet. Bring in all four corners and twist to form a purse shape. Repeat to make 18 parcels.

4 Place the filo parcels on a griddle or baking sheet, well brushed with melted butter. Cook on a medium-hot barbecue for about 10 minutes, until the filo pastry is crisp. Leave to cool, then dust lightly with sifted icing sugar and then with sifted cocoa powder.

INGREDIENTS

15ml/1 tbsp chopped fresh mint
75g/3oz/³/₄ cup ground almonds
50g/2oz plain (semisweet)
chocolate, grated
115g/4oz/¹/₂ cup crème fraîche
2 eating apples, peeled and grated
9 large sheets filo pastry
75g/3oz/¹/₃ cup butter, melted
icing (confectioners') sugar, to dust
(unsweetened) cocoa powder,
to dust

MAKES 18 PARCELS

1 Mix the chopped fresh mint, almonds, grated chocolate, crème fraîche and grated apple in a large mixing bowl. Set aside.

Al fresco meals – whether in the garden, on the beach or in a grassy meadow – are a great pleasure both to organize and to take part in. This section offers inspirations for special summer meals and garden parties, including some original and delicious ideas for party drinks.

OUTDOOR
ENTERTAINING

~

VEGETABLES WITH TAPENADE AND HERB AIOLI

A beautiful platter of summer vegetables served with one or two interesting sauces makes a really delicious and informal appetizer, which is perfect for picnics as it can all be prepared in advance.

INGREDIENTS

2 red (bell) peppers, cut into strips
30ml/2 tbsp olive oil
225g/8oz new potatoes
115g/4oz green beans
225g/8oz baby carrots
225g/8oz young asparagus
12 quail's eggs
fresh herbs, to garnish
coarse salt, for sprinkling

FOR THE TAPENADE
175g/6oz/1½ cups pitted
black olives
50g/2oz can anchovy
fillets, drained
30ml/2 tbsp capers
120ml/4fl oz/½ cup olive oil
finely grated rind of 1 lemon
15ml/1 tbsp brandy (optional)
freshly ground black pepper

FOR THE HERB AIOLI
5 garlic cloves, crushed
2 egg yolks
5ml/1 tsp Dijon mustard
10ml/2 tsp white wine vinegar
250ml/8fl oz/1 cup light olive oil
45ml/3 tbsp chopped mixed fresh
herbs, such as chervil, parsley
and tarragon
30ml/2 tbsp chopped watercress
salt and freshly ground
black pepper

SERVES 6

1 To make the tapenade, finely chop the olives, anchovies and capers and beat together with the oil, lemon rind and brandy, if using. (Alternatively, lightly process the ingredients in a blender or food processor.)

2 Season with pepper and blend in a little more oil if the mixture seems very dry. Transfer to a serving dish.

3 To make the aioli, beat together the garlic, egg yolks, mustard and vinegar. Gradually blend in the olive oil, a drop at a time, whisking well until thick and smooth.

4 Stir in the mixed herbs and chopped watercress. Season with salt and pepper to taste, adding a little more vinegar if necessary. Cover with clear film (plastic wrap) and chill until ready to serve.

Cook's Tip
Any leftover tapenade is delicious tossed with pasta or spread on to warm toast. If you are making this dish as part of a picnic, leave the vegetables to cool before packing in an airtight container. Pack the quails' eggs in their original box.

5 Brush the peppers with oil and cook on a hot barbecue or under a hot grill (broiler) until just beginning to char.

6 Cook the potatoes in a large pan of boiling, salted water until tender. Add the beans and carrots and blanch for 1 minute. Add the asparagus and cook for a further 30 seconds. Drain the vegetables. Cook the quails' eggs in boiling water for 2 minutes.

7 Arrange all the vegetables, eggs and sauces on a serving platter. Garnish with fresh herbs and serve with coarse salt, for sprinkling.

FALAFEL

These North African fritters are traditionally made using dried broad beans, but chickpeas are more easily available. Serve in warmed pitta bread, with salad and garlicky yogurt.

INGREDIENTS

150g/5oz/³⁄₄ cup dried chickpeas
1 large onion, coarsely chopped
2 garlic cloves, coarsely chopped
60ml/4 tbsp coarsely chopped
fresh parsley
5ml/1 tsp cumin seeds, crushed
5ml/1 tsp coriander seeds, crushed
2.5ml/¹⁄₂ tsp baking powder
oil, for deep-frying
salt and freshly ground
black pepper

SERVES 4

1 Put the chickpeas in a large bowl and cover with plenty of cold water. Leave to soak overnight.

2 Drain the chickpeas and cover with fresh water in a pan. Bring the chickpeas to the boil, reduce the heat and simmer for about 1¹⁄₂-2 hours, or until soft. Drain thoroughly.

3 Place in a food processor with the onion, garlic, parsley, cumin, coriander and baking powder. Season to taste. Process to form a firm paste.

4 Shape the mixture into walnut-size balls, using your hands, and flatten them slightly. In a deep pan, heat 5cm/2in oil until a little of the mixture sizzles on the surface. Fry the falafel in batches until golden. Drain on kitchen paper and serve.

Cook's Tip

Although they can be fried in advance, falafel are at their best served warm. Wrap them in foil or pack them in an insulated container to take them on picnics, or keep them warm on the edge of the barbecue until needed.

HUMMUS BI TAHINA

*Blending chickpeas with garlic, lemon and oil makes a deliciously creamy purée to serve
as a dip with crudités or warmed pitta bread.*

INGREDIENTS

*150g/5oz/³/4 cup dried chickpeas
juice of 2 lemons
2 garlic cloves, sliced
30ml/2 tbsp olive oil, plus extra
to serve
150ml/¹/4 pint/²/3 cup tahini paste
salt and freshly ground
black pepper
flat leaf parsley, to garnish
cayenne pepper, to serve*

SERVES 4–6

1 Put the chickpeas in a large bowl and cover with plenty of cold water. Leave to soak overnight.

2 Drain the chickpeas and cover with fresh water in a pan. Bring the chickpeas to the boil, then reduce the heat and simmer for about 1¹/2-2 hours or until soft. Drain thoroughly.

3 Process the chickpeas to a purée in a food processor. Add the lemon juice, garlic, oil, cayenne pepper and tahini and blend until creamy.

4 Season the chickpea purée with plenty of salt and freshly ground black pepper and transfer to a serving dish. Drizzle the purée with olive oil and sprinkle lightly with cayenne pepper. Serve the dip garnished with a few flat leaf parsley sprigs.

Cook's Tip
If you do not have time to soak dried chickpeas, canned chickpeas can be used instead. Allow two 400g/14oz cans and drain them thoroughly.

TOMATO AND CHEESE TARTS

*These crisp little tartlets look impressive but are actually very easy to make.
They are best eaten fresh from the oven.*

INGREDIENTS

*3 sheets filo pastry
1 egg white
175g/6oz/³/4 cup cream cheese
handful fresh basil leaves
4 small tomatoes, sliced
salt and freshly ground
black pepper*

MAKES 12

1 Preheat the oven to 200°C/400°F/
Gas 6. Brush the sheets of filo pastry
lightly with egg white and cut into
24 x 10cm/4in squares.

2 Layer the squares in twos, in 12 bun
tins (muffin pans). Spoon the cream
cheese into the pastry cases. Season
with ground black pepper and top with
fresh basil leaves.

3 Arrange the tomatoes on the tarts,
season and bake for 10–12 minutes,
until the pastry is golden. Serve warm.

Cook's Tip
Use halved cherry tomatoes
for the tarts, if you like.

TANDOORI CHICKEN STICKS

These aromatic chicken pieces are traditionally baked in the special clay oven known as a tandoor. They are equally delicious served hot or cold, and make irresistible barbecue food.

INGREDIENTS

450g/1lb boneless, skinless chicken breast portions

FOR THE HERB YOGURT
250ml/8fl oz/1 cup natural (plain) yogurt
30ml/2 tbsp whipping cream
1/2 cucumber, peeled, seeded and finely chopped
15–30ml/1–2 tbsp fresh chopped coriander (cilantro) or mint
salt and freshly ground black pepper

FOR THE MARINADE
175ml/6fl oz/3/4 cup natural (plain) yogurt
5ml/1 tsp garam masala
1.5ml/1/4 tsp ground cumin
1.5ml/1/4 tsp ground coriander
1.5ml/1/4 tsp cayenne pepper
5ml/1 tsp tomato purée (paste)
1–2 garlic cloves, finely chopped
2.5cm/1in piece of fresh root ginger, finely chopped
grated rind and juice of 1/2 lemon
15–30ml/1–2 tbsp chopped fresh coriander (cilantro) or mint

MAKES ABOUT 25

2 To prepare the marinade, place all the ingredients in a food processor and process until smooth. Pour into a shallow dish.

3 Freeze the chicken for 5 minutes to firm them. Slice in half horizontally. Cut the slices into 2cm/3/4in strips and add to the marinade. Toss to coat well. Cover with clear film (plastic wrap) and chill for 6–8 hours or overnight.

4 Drain the chicken pieces and arrange on a rack, scrunching up the chicken slightly to make wavy shapes. Cook on a hot barbecue for 4–5 minutes until brown and cooked through, turning once. Alternatively, arrange on a foil-lined baking sheet and cook under a hot grill (broiler). Serve hot, threaded on cocktail sticks or short skewers, with the herb yogurt dip. For a picnic, cool and pack into a box.

1 For the herb yogurt, combine all the ingredients in a bowl. Season, cover and chill until ready to serve.

HAM PIZZETTAS WITH MELTED BRIE AND MANGO

These individual little pizzas are topped with an unusual but very successful combination of smoked ham, Brie and juicy chunks of fresh mango.

INGREDIENTS

225g/8oz/2 cups white bread flour
10g/¼ oz sachet easy-blend (rapid-rise) dried yeast
150ml/¼ pint/⅔ cup warm water
60ml/4 tbsp olive oil

FOR THE TOPPING
1 ripe mango
150g/5oz smoked ham, sliced wafer-thin
150g/5oz Brie cheese, diced
12 yellow cherry tomatoes, halved
salt and freshly ground black pepper

SERVES 6

1 In a large bowl, stir together the flour and yeast, with a pinch of salt. Make a well in the centre and stir in the water and 45ml/3 tbsp of the olive oil. Stir until thoroughly mixed.

Cook's Tip

It's important to flatten out the dough rounds quite thinly and to cook them fairly slowly, or they will not cook evenly. To save time, you could use a 300g/11oz packet of pizza dough mix.

2 Turn the dough out on to a lightly floured surface and knead it for about 5 minutes, or until smooth.

3 Return the dough to the bowl and cover it with a damp cloth or oiled clear film (plastic wrap). Leave the dough to rise in a warm place for about 30 minutes or until it is doubled in size and springy to the touch.

4 Divide the dough into six and roll each piece into a ball. Flatten out with your hand and use your knuckles to press each piece of dough to a round of about 15cm/6in diameter, with a raised lip around the edge.

5 Halve, stone (pit) and peel the mango and cut it into small dice. Arrange with the ham on top of the pizzettas. Top with cheese and tomatoes and sprinkle with salt and ground black pepper.

6 Drizzle the remaining oil over the pizzettas. Place them on a medium-hot barbecue and cook for 8 minutes, until golden brown and crisp underneath.

OYSTER AND BACON BROCHETTES

. . .

*Six oysters per person make a good appetizer, served with the seasoned oyster liquor to trickle
over the skewers. Alternatively, serve nine per person as a main course, accompanied by a salad.*

INGREDIENTS

36 oysters
18 thin-cut rashers (strips) rindless
streaky (fatty) bacon
15ml/1 tbsp paprika
5ml/1 tsp cayenne pepper
freshly ground black pepper
celery leaves and fresh red chillies,
to garnish

FOR THE SAUCE
1/2 fresh red chilli, seeded and very
finely chopped
1 garlic clove, crushed
2 spring onions (scallions), very
finely chopped
30ml/2 tbsp finely chopped
fresh parsley
liquor from the oysters
juice of 1/4–1/2 lemon, to taste
salt and freshly ground
black pepper

SERVES 4–6

2 Push the knife in and cut the muscle,
holding the shell closed. Tip the liquor
into the bowl. Cut the oyster free.
Discard the drained shells.

3 For the sauce, mix the chilli, garlic,
spring onions and parsley into the
oyster liquor and sharpen to taste
with lemon juice. Season with salt and
pepper and transfer to a serving dish.

4 Cut each bacon rasher across the
middle. Season the oysters lightly with
paprika, cayenne and freshly ground
black pepper and wrap each one in half
a bacon rasher, then thread them on to
skewers. Cook on a hot barbecue for
about 5 minutes, turning frequently,
until the bacon is crisp and brown.
Garnish with celery leaves and red
chillies and serve with the sauce.

1 Open the oysters over a bowl to
catch their liquor for the sauce. Wrap
your left hand (if you are right-handed)
in a clean dishtowel and cup the deep
shell of each oyster in your wrapped
hand. Work the point of a strong,
short-bladed knife into the hinge
between the shells and twist firmly.

TURKEY ROLLS WITH GAZPACHO SAUCE

This Spanish-style recipe uses quick-cooking turkey steaks, but you could also cook veal escalopes in the same way.

INGREDIENTS

4 turkey breast steaks
15ml/1 tbsp red pesto
4 chorizo sausages
15ml/1 tbsp olive oil
salt and freshly ground
black pepper

FOR THE GAZPACHO SAUCE
1 green (bell) pepper, chopped
1 red (bell) pepper, chopped
7.5cm/3in piece cucumber
1 medium tomato
1 garlic clove
45ml/3 tbsp olive oil
15ml/1 tbsp red wine vinegar

SERVES 4

1 To make the gazpacho sauce, place the peppers, cucumber, tomato, garlic, 30ml/2 tbsp of the olive oil and the vinegar in a food processor and process until almost smooth. Season to taste with salt and ground black pepper.

2 If the turkey breast steaks are quite thick, place them between two sheets of clear film (plastic wrap) and beat them with the side of a rolling pin or a meat mallet, to flatten them slightly.

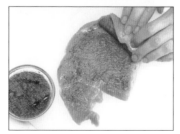

3 Spread the red pesto over the turkey, place a chorizo sausage on each piece and roll up firmly.

4 Slice the rolls thickly and thread them on to skewers. Brush with olive oil and cook on a medium barbecue for about 10–12 minutes, turning once. Serve with the gazpacho sauce.

CHICKEN, MUSHROOM AND CORIANDER PIZZA

Shiitake mushrooms add an earthy flavour to this colourful pizza, while fresh chilli and chilli-flavoured olive oil give it a hint of spiciness. Cook the pizza on the barbecue or in the oven.

INGREDIENTS

45ml/3 tbsp olive oil
350g/12oz skinless chicken breast fillets, cut into thin strips
8 spring onions (scallions), sliced
1 fresh red chilli, seeded and chopped
1 red (bell) pepper, cut into strips
75g/3oz fresh shiitake mushrooms, sliced
45–60ml/3–4 tbsp chopped fresh coriander (cilantro)
1 pizza base, about 25–30cm/10–12in diameter
15ml/1 tbsp chilli oil
150g/5oz mozzarella cheese
salt and freshly ground black pepper

SERVES 3–4

2 Pour off any excess oil, then set aside to let the chicken mixture cool.

4 Brush all over the pizza base with the chilli oil.

3 Stir the fresh coriander into the cooled chicken mixture in the wok.

5 Spoon over the chicken mixture and drizzle over the remaining olive oil.

1 Heat 30ml/2 tbsp olive oil in a wok or large frying pan. Add the chicken, spring onions, chilli, red pepper and mushrooms and stir-fry over a high heat for 2–3 minutes until the chicken is firm but still slightly pink inside. Season to taste.

6 Grate the mozzarella cheese and sprinkle it over the pizza base. Cook the pizza on a medium-hot barbecue for 15–20 minutes, until the base is crisp and golden and the cheese is bubbling. Serve the pizza immediately.

MEDITERRANEAN QUICHE

• • •

*This quiche forms the ideal base for a hearty picnic feast. The strong Mediterranean flavours of
tomatoes, peppers and anchovies complement the cheese pastry beautifully.*

INGREDIENTS

FOR THE PASTRY
225g/8oz/2 cups plain (all-
purpose) flour
pinch of salt
pinch of dry mustard
115g/4oz/¹/2 cup butter, chilled
and diced
50g/2oz/¹/2 cup grated
Gruyère cheese
salt

FOR THE FILLING
50g/2oz can anchovy fillets, drained
50ml/2fl oz/¹/4 cup milk
30ml/2 tbsp French mustard
45ml/3 tbsp olive oil
2 large Spanish onions, sliced
1 red (bell) pepper, very finely sliced
3 egg yolks
350ml/12fl oz/1¹/2 cups double
(heavy) cream
1 garlic clove, crushed
175g/6oz/1¹/2 cups grated mature
(sharp) Cheddar cheese
2 large tomatoes, thickly sliced
30ml/2 tbsp chopped fresh basil,
to garnish

SERVES 6–8

1 To make the pastry, place the flour,
salt and mustard in a food processor,
add the butter and process the mixture
until it resembles fine breadcrumbs.

2 Add the Gruyère cheese and process
again briefly. Add enough iced water to
make a stiff dough: the dough will be
ready when it forms a ball. Wrap the
dough in clear film (plastic wrap) and
chill in the refrigerator for 30 minutes.

3 Meanwhile, make the filling.
Soak the anchovies in the milk for
about 20 minutes to make them less
salty. Pour off the milk. Heat the olive
oil in a frying pan and cook the onions
and red pepper until they soften.

4 In a bowl, beat the egg yolks, double
cream, garlic and grated Cheddar
cheese together.

5 Preheat the oven to 200°C/400°F/
Gas 6. Roll out the chilled pastry and
line a 23cm/9in loose-based quiche tin
(pan). Spread the mustard over and
chill for a further 15 minutes.

6 Arrange the tomatoes in a layer in the
pastry crust. Top with the onion and
pepper mixture and the anchovy fillets.
Pour over the egg mixture. Bake for
30 minutes. Serve warm or at room
temperature, sprinkled with fresh basil.

Cook's Tip
Leave the quiche in its tin (pan) if
you are packing it for a picnic.

CHICKEN AND APRICOT FILO PIE

* * *

The filling for this pie has a Middle Eastern flavour – minced chicken combined with apricots, bulgur wheat, nuts and spices. It both looks and tastes spectacular.

INGREDIENTS

75g/3oz/1/2 cup bulgur wheat
75g/3oz/6 tbsp butter
1 onion, chopped
450g/1lb minced (ground) chicken
50g/2oz/1/4 cup ready-to-eat dried
apricots, finely chopped
25g/1oz/1/4 cup blanched
almonds, chopped
5ml/1 tsp ground cinnamon
2.5ml/1/2 tsp ground allspice
50ml/2fl oz/1/4 cup Greek
(US strained plain) yogurt
30ml/2 tbsp chopped fresh chives
30ml/2 tbsp chopped fresh parsley
6 large sheets filo pastry
salt and freshly ground
black pepper

SERVES 6

1 Preheat the oven to 200°C/400°F/ Gas 6. Put the bulgur wheat in a large bowl with 120ml/4fl oz/1/2 cup boiling water. leave the wheat to soak for 5 minutes, until the water is absorbed.

2 Heat 25g/1oz/2 tbsp of the butter in a pan and cook the onion and chicken until pale golden. Stir in the apricots, almonds and bulgur wheat and cook for a further 2 minutes. Remove from the heat and stir in the cinnamon, allspice, yogurt, half the chives and the parsley. Season to taste.

3 Melt the remaining butter. Unroll the filo pastry and cut into 25cm/10in rounds. Keep the pastry rounds covered with a clean, damp dishtowel to prevent them from drying out.

4 Line a 23cm/9in loose-based flan tin (quiche pan) with three pastry rounds, brushing each with melted butter as you layer them. Spoon in the chicken mixture and cover with three more pastry rounds, brushed with melted butter as before.

5 Crumple the remaining rounds and place on top of the pie. Brush with any remaining butter. Bake the pie for 30 minutes, until the pastry is golden brown and crisp. Serve hot or cold, garnished with the remaining chives.

CHICKEN WITH FRESH HERBS AND GARLIC

A whole chicken can be roasted on a spit on the barbecue. This marinade keeps the flesh moist and delicious and the fresh herbs add summery flavours.

INGREDIENTS

1.75kg/4½ lb free-range chicken
finely grated rind and juice of
1 lemon
1 garlic clove, crushed
30ml/2 tbsp olive oil
2 fresh thyme sprigs
2 fresh sage sprigs
90ml/6 tbsp unsalted (sweet)
butter, softened
salt and freshly ground
black pepper

SERVES 4

1 Season the chicken well. Mix the lemon rind and juice, crushed garlic and olive oil together and pour them over the chicken. Leave to marinate in the refrigerator for at least 2 hours.

Cook's Tip

If roasting the chicken in the oven, preheat the oven to 230°C/450°F/ Gas 8 and reduce the heat to 190°C/375°F/Gas 5 after 10 minutes. If you are roasting a chicken to serve cold, cooking it in foil helps to keep it succulent – open the foil for the last 20 minutes to brown the skin, then close it as the chicken cools.

2 Place the herbs in the cavity of the bird and smear the butter over the skin. Season well. Cook the chicken on a spit on the barbecue for 1½–1¾ hours, basting with the marinade, until the juices run clear when the thigh is pierced with a skewer. Leave the bird to rest for 15 minutes before carving.

PEPPER STEAK

· · ·

This easy, rather indulgent, bistro classic can be put together in a matter of minutes for an intimate summer supper in the garden. The creamy sauce helps to balance the heat of the pepper.

INGREDIENTS

30ml/2 tbsp black peppercorns
2 fillet or sirloin steaks, about
225g/8oz each
15g/½ oz/1 tbsp butter
10ml/2 tsp olive oil
45ml/3 tbsp brandy
150ml/1/4 pint/²⁄₃ cup
whipping cream
1 garlic clove, finely chopped
salt

SERVES 2

1 Place the black peppercorns in a sturdy plastic bag. Crush the peppercorns with a rolling pin or meat mallet until they are crushed to medium-coarse pepper.

2 Put the steaks on a chopping board and trim away any excess fat, using a sharp kitchen knife. Press the pepper firmly on to both sides of the meat, to coat it completely.

3 Melt the butter with the olive oil in a heavy frying pan over a medium-high heat. Add the meat and cook for 6–7 minutes, turning once, until cooked to your liking. Transfer the steaks to a warmed platter or plates and cover to keep warm.

4 Pour in the brandy to deglaze the frying pan. Bring the brandy to the boil and cook until it has reduced by half, scraping the base of the frying pan, then add the whipping cream and garlic. Bubble gently over a low-medium heat for about 4 minutes or until the cream has reduced by about one-third. Stir any accumulated juices from the meat into the sauce, taste and add salt to taste. Serve the steaks hot, with the sauce.

PORK WITH MARSALA AND JUNIPER

* * *

Sicilian marsala wine gives savoury dishes a rich, fruity and alcoholic tang. The pork is fully complemented by the flavour of the sauce in this quick and luxurious dish.

INGREDIENTS

*25g/1oz dried cep or porcini
mushrooms*
4 pork escalopes (scallops)
10ml/2 tsp balsamic vinegar
8 garlic cloves
15g/1/2 oz/1 tbsp butter
45ml/3 tbsp marsala
several rosemary sprigs
10 juniper berries, crushed
*salt and freshly ground
black pepper*

SERVES 4

1 Put the dried mushrooms in a large bowl and just cover with hot water. Leave to stand for 20 minutes to allow the mushrooms to soak.

2 Brush the pork with 5ml/1 tsp of the vinegar and season with salt and pepper. Put the garlic cloves in a pan of boiling water and cook for 10 minutes until soft. Drain and set aside.

3 Melt the butter in a large frying pan. Add the pork and cook quickly until browned on the underside. Turn the meat over and cook for 1 minute more.

4 Add the marsala, rosemary sprigs, drained mushrooms, 60ml/4 tbsp of the mushroom water, the garlic cloves, juniper berries and the remaining balsamic vinegar.

5 Simmer gently for 3–5 minutes until the pork is cooked through. Season lightly and serve hot.

STUFFED ROAST LOIN OF PORK

° ° °

This recipe uses fruit and nuts as a stuffing for roast pork in the Catalan style. It is full of flavour and is very good served cold, making an excellent centrepiece for a summer buffet or a picnic.

INGREDIENTS

60ml/4 tbsp olive oil
1 onion, finely chopped
2 garlic cloves, chopped
50g/2oz/1 cup fresh breadcrumbs
4 ready-to-eat dried figs, chopped
8 pitted green olives, chopped
60ml/4 tbsp flaked (sliced) almonds
15ml/1 tbsp lemon juice
15ml/1 tbsp chopped fresh parsley
1 egg yolk
900g/2lb boned loin of pork
salt and freshly ground
black pepper

SERVES 4

1 Preheat the oven to 200°C/400°F/
Gas 6, or prepare the barbecue. Heat
45ml/3 tbsp of the oil in a pan, add the
onion and garlic, and cook gently until
softened. Remove the pan from the
heat and stir in the breadcrumbs, figs,
olives, almonds, lemon juice, chopped
fresh parsley and egg yolk. Season to
taste with salt and ground black pepper.

2 Remove any string from the pork and
unroll the belly flap, cutting away any
excess fat or meat to enable you to do
so. Spread the stuffing over the flat
piece and roll it up, starting from the
thick side. Tie at intervals with string.

3 Pour the remaining olive oil into
a roasting pan and put in the pork, or
arrange on the spit of the barbecue.
Roast for 1 hour and 15 minutes, or
until the juices run clear from the meat.

4 Remove the pork from the oven or
the spit and, if serving hot, let it rest for
10 minutes before carving into thick
slices. If serving cold, wrap the meat in
foil to keep it moist until you carve it.

LAMB CASSEROLE WITH GARLIC AND BEANS

This recipe has a Spanish influence and makes a substantial meal, served with potatoes.
Broad beans add colour and texture to the dish.

INGREDIENTS

45ml/3 tbsp olive oil
1.5kg/3–3½ lb lamb fillet, cut
into 5cm/2in cubes
1 large onion, chopped
6 large garlic cloves, unpeeled
1 bay leaf
5ml/1 tsp paprika
120ml/4fl oz/½ cup dry sherry
115g/4oz shelled fresh or frozen
broad (fava) beans
30ml/2 tbsp chopped fresh parsley
salt and freshly ground
black pepper

SERVES 6

3 Add the garlic, bay leaf, paprika and sherry. Season to taste and bring to the boil. Cover and simmer gently for 1½ hours, until tender.

4 Add the broad beans to the casserole and simmer for a further 10 minutes. Stir in the chopped fresh parsley just before serving.

1 Heat 30ml/2 tbsp olive oil in a large flameproof casserole. Add half the meat and brown well on all sides. Transfer to a plate. Brown the rest of the meat in the same way and remove from the casserole.

2 Heat the remaining oil in the pan, add the onion and cook for about 5 minutes until soft. Return the meat to the casserole.

RED MULLET WITH LAVENDER

Cook a fish dish with a difference by adding lavender to red mullet for a wonderful aromatic flavour. Sprinkle some lavender flowers on the coals too, to give a delightful perfumed ambience.

INGREDIENTS

4 red mullet or snapper, scaled, gutted and cleaned
30ml/2 tbsp olive oil

FOR THE MARINADE
45ml/3 tbsp fresh lavender flowers or 15ml/1 tbsp dried lavender leaves, coarsely chopped
coarsely chopped rind of 1 lemon
4 spring onions (scallions), chopped
salt and freshly ground black pepper

SERVES 4

1 Place the fish in a shallow dish. Mix the ingredients for the marinade and pour over the fish. Cover with clear film (plastic wrap) and leave in the refrigerator to marinate for 3 hours.

2 Remove the fish from the marinade and brush it with olive oil. Cook the fish on a hot barbecue for about 10–15 minutes, turning once and basting with olive oil as it cooks.

SALMON STEAKS WITH OREGANO SALSA

• • •

This combination of salmon with piquant tomato works incredibly well. The barbecue gives the salmon an exquisite flavour. Served hot or cold, this is an ideal dish for a summer lunch.

INGREDIENTS
15ml/1 tbsp butter
4 salmon steaks, about 225g/
8oz each
120ml/4fl oz/½ cup white wine
freshly ground black pepper

FOR THE SALSA
10ml/2 tsp chopped fresh oregano,
plus sprigs to garnish
4 spring onions (scallions)
225g/8oz ripe tomatoes, peeled
30ml/2 tbsp extra virgin olive oil
2.5ml/½ tsp caster (superfine) sugar
15ml/1 tbsp tomato purée (paste)

SERVES 4

1 Butter four squares of double-thickness baking foil. Put a salmon steak on each and add a little wine and a grinding of black pepper. Wrap the salmon steaks loosely in the squares, sealing the edges securely. Cook on a medium-hot barbecue for 10 minutes, until just tender. If serving the steaks hot, keep them warm.

2 Put the chopped fresh oregano in a food processor and chop it very finely. Add the spring onions, tomatoes and remaining salsa ingredients. Pulse until chopped but not a smooth purée.

3 Serve the salmon hot or cold with the salsa, garnished with a few fresh sprigs of oregano.

HERBAL PUNCH

. . .

This refreshing party drink will have people coming back for more, and it is an original
non-alcoholic choice for drivers and children.

INGREDIENTS

450ml/³⁄4 pint/2 cups clear honey
4 litres/7 pints water
450ml/³⁄4 pint/2 cups freshly
squeezed lemon juice
45ml/3 tbsp fresh rosemary leaves,
plus extra to decorate
1.5kg/3¹⁄2lb/8 cups
sliced strawberries
450ml/³⁄4 pint/2 cups freshly
squeezed lime juice
1.75 litres/3 pints/7¹⁄2 cups
sparkling mineral water
ice cubes
3–4 scented geranium leaves

SERVES 30 PLUS

1 Combine the honey, 1 litre/1³⁄4 pints/
4 cups water, one-eighth of the lemon
juice and the fresh rosemary leaves in a
pan. Bring to the boil, stirring, until the
honey is dissolved. Remove from the
heat and leave to stand for about
5 minutes. Strain into a large punch
bowl and set aside to cool.

2 Press the strawberries through
a fine sieve into the punch bowl, add
the rest of the water and lemon juice,
and the lime juice and sparkling
mineral water. Stir gently to combine
the ingredients. Add the ice cubes just
5 minutes before serving, and float
the geranium and rosemary leaves
on the surface.

MINT CUP

Mint is a perennially popular flavouring and this delicate cup is a wonderful mixture with an intriguing taste. It is the perfect summer drink to serve with meals outdoors.

INGREDIENTS

handful fresh mint leaves
15ml/1 tbsp sugar
crushed ice
15ml/1 tbsp lemon juice
175ml/6fl oz/³/4 cup
grapefruit juice
600ml/1 pint/2¹/2 cups chilled
tonic water
mint sprigs and lemon slices,
to decorate

SERVES 4–6

1 Crush the mint leaves with the sugar and put into a jug (pitcher). Fill the jug to the top with crushed ice.

2 Add the lemon juice, grapefruit juice and tonic water. Stir gently to combine the ingredients and decorate with mint sprigs and slices of lemon.

STRAWBERRY AND MINT CHAMPAGNE

*This is a simple concoction that makes a bottle of champagne or sparkling white wine
go much further. It tastes very special on a hot summer's evening.*

INGREDIENTS
500g/1¼lb strawberries
6–8 fresh mint leaves
*1 bottle champagne or sparkling
white wine*
fresh mint sprigs, to decorate

SERVES 4–6

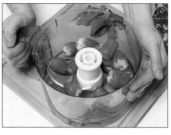

1 Purée the strawberries and fresh mint
leaves in a food processor.

2 Strain through a fine sieve into
a large bowl. Half fill a glass with the
mixture and top up with champagne
or sparkling wine. Decorate with a
sprig of fresh mint.

MELON, GINGER AND BORAGE CUP

*Melon and ginger complement each other magnificently. If you prefer, you can leave out the
powdered ginger – the result is milder but equally delicious.*

INGREDIENTS
½ large honeydew melon
1 litre/1¾ pints/4 cups ginger beer
powdered ginger, to taste
*borage sprigs with flowers,
to decorate*

SERVES 6–8

1 Discard the seeds from the half melon
and scoop the flesh into a food
processor. Blend the melon to a purée.

2 Pour the purée into a large jug
(pitcher) and top up with ginger beer.
Add powdered ginger to taste. Pour
into glasses and decorate with borage.

SENSATIONAL
SALADS

o o o

In these health-conscious days and with the increasing
availability of exotic vegetables and produce from around the
world, salads have become the fashion item in restaurants and
on dining tables everywhere. This second part of the book is
devoted to a mouthwatering selection of salads – from the
subtle flavour combination of goat's cheese and figs to the
flamboyant luxury of fresh lobster and from the charming
simplicity of salad leaves combined with fresh herbs to the
carnival colours of brown rice and tropical fruit.

This section starts with a detailed guide to ingredients –
vegetables, fruit, salad leaves, herbs, spices, vinegars, oils and
flavourings. The introductory pages also include step-by-step
recipes for the most popular salad dressings and a time-saving
selection of instant dressings and dips.

The recipes that follow cover all courses, occasions and
seasons, from light meals and appetizers to glamorous dishes
for special occasions and from raw and cooked side salads to
main meals for a midweek family supper. The final chapter
features fruit salads, and you may be surprised to discover how
many different ways this popular dessert can be prepared.

Salads add a refreshing flavour and texture to any meal, as well
as an appetizing splash of colour, but they are also a valuable
source of vitamins, minerals and other nutrients – all year
round. Nothing could make it easier to eat the five portions of
vegetables and fruit a day that are recommended by
nutritionists than this mouthwatering collection of recipes.

SALAD VEGETABLES

The salad vegetable is any type of vegetable that earns its keep in a salad by virtue of freshness and flavour. Vegetables for a salad can be raw or lightly cooked. If cooked, they are best served at room temperature to bring out their full flavour. Here is a selection of the most commonly used and popular salad vegetables.

Avocado

This has a smooth, buttery flesh when ripe and is an asset to many salads, of which Guacamole is perhaps the best known. Avocados can also be served on their own as an appetizer, with a simple, light vinaigrette dressing or a spoonful of lemon mayonnaise, or even just a squeeze of lemon juice and salt.

Carrots

These should be young, slender and sweet to taste. Either cooked or raw, they bring flavour and colour to a salad.

Celery

A useful salad vegetable, celery is grown year round for its robust, earthy flavour. The crisp stems should be neither stringy nor tough. Celery partners well with cooked ham, apple and walnut in Waldorf Salad and is also used as a crudité with dips.

Courgettes (Zucchini)

These can be bitter to the taste and are usually cooked before being combined with other young vegetables. Smooth in texture when cooked, they blend very well with tomatoes, aubergines (eggplant), (bell) peppers and different kinds of onions. Use baby courgettes for a sweeter flavour if you want to serve raw courgettes as a crudité.

Cucumbers

A common salad ingredient that turns up, invited or not, in salad bowls everywhere. The quality of this vegetable is best appreciated in strongly flavoured salads.

Fennel

The bulb (or Florence) variety has a strong, aniseed flavour and looks like a squat head of celery. Because the flavour can be dominant, it may be blanched in boiling water for 6 minutes before use in a salad.

Garlic

Strong to taste, garlic is essential to the robust cooking of South America, the Mediterranean and Asia. It should be used carefully as it can mask other flavours, but it is a vital part of salad preparation. To impart a very gentle hint of garlic rub around the inside of your salad bowl with a cut clove. Another way to moderate the strength of fresh garlic is to store a few crushed cloves in a bottle of olive oil, and use the oil sparingly in dressings.

Green Beans

The varieties are too numerous to mention here, but they all have their merits as salad vegetables. To appreciate the sweet flavour of young tender green beans, cook them for 6 minutes and then refresh immediately under cold running water so that the crispness and colour are retained. An essential ingredient of Salade Niçoise, green beans are an ideal crudité and also partner well with a spicy tomato sauce.

Mushrooms

These provide a rich tone to many salads and are eaten both raw and cooked. The oyster mushroom, which grows wild but is also cultivated, has a fine flavour and texture. White mushrooms are widely available and are often used raw, thinly sliced, in a mixed salad. Chestnut mushrooms are similar to white mushrooms but have slightly more flavour.

Onions

Several varieties are suited to salads. The strongest is the small, brown onion, which should be chopped finely and used sparingly. Less strong are the large, white Spanish and Bermuda onions, which have a sweeter, milder flavour and may be used coarsely chopped. Red onions are also sweet and mild in flavour and add a colourful touch to salads.

Potatoes

A staple carbohydrate ingredient to add bulk to a salad or provide a main element. Waxy varieties are the most suitable for potato salads and some types have been specially developed as salad potatoes.

Spring Onions (Scallions)

These have a milder flavour than the common onion and give a gentle bite to many popular salads.

Baby Corn Cobs

Baby corn cobs can be eaten whole, may be lightly cooked or raw, and should be served warm or at room temperature for maximum flavour.

Tomatoes

Technically a fruit rather than a vegetable, tomatoes are valued for their flavour and colour. Dwarf varieties usually ripen more quickly than large ones, have a better flavour and texture and are often less watery.

SALAD FRUIT

• • •

The contents of the fruit bowl offer endless possibilities for sweet and savoury salads.

Apples
This versatile fruit offers a unique flavour and crunchy texture to both sweet and savoury salads.

Apricots
You can use apricots raw, dried or lightly poached.

Bananas
These bring a special richness to fruit salads, although their flavour can often interfere with more delicate fruit.

Blackberries
With a very short season, wild blackberries have more flavour than cultivated.

Blueberries
These tight-skinned berries combine well with the sharpness of fresh oranges.

Cherries
Cherries should be firm and glossy and are a deliciously sweet and colourful ingredient in many kinds of fruit salad.

Cranberries
Too sharp to eat raw but very good for cooking.

Dates
Fresh dates are sweet and juicy, dried ones have a more intense flavour. Both kinds work well in fresh fruit salads.

Figs
Green or purple skinned fruit, with sweet, pinkish-red flesh. Eat whole or peeled.

Gooseberries
Dessert types can be eaten raw, but cooking varieties are rather more widely available.

Grapefruit
These can have yellow, green or pink flesh; the pink-fleshed or ruby varieties are the sweetest.

Grapes
Large Muscat varieties, whose season runs from late summer to autumn, are the most coveted and also the most expensive.

Kiwi Fruit
Available all the year round.

Kumquats
Tiny relatives of the orange, they can be eaten raw or cooked.

Lemons and Limes
Both these indispensable citrus fruits are used for flavour, and to prevent fruit, such as apples, pears and avocados, from turning brown.

Lychees
A small fruit with a hard pink skin and sweet, juicy flesh.

Mangoes
Tropical fruit with an exotic flavour and golden-orange flesh that is wonderful in sweet or savoury salads.

Melons
These grow in abundance from mid to late summer and provide a resource of freshness and flavour. Melon is at its most delicious served icy cold.

Nectarines
A relative of the peach with a smoother skin.

Oranges
At their best during winter, they can be segmented and added to sweet and savoury salads.

Papaya
These fruits of the tropics have a distinctive, sweet flavour. When ripe they are yellow–green.

Peaches
Choose white peaches for the sweetest flavour, and yellow for a more aromatic taste.

Pears
Perfect for savoury salads, and with strong blue cheese and toasted pecan nuts.

Physalis
These small, fragrant, pleasantly tart orange berries, wrapped in a paper cape.

Pineapples
Ripe pineapples resist firm pressure in the hand and have a sweet smell.

Plums
There are many dessert and cooking varieties.

Raspberries
Much-coveted soft fruits that partner well with ripe mango, passion fruit and strawberries.

Rhubarb
Technically a vegetable, it is too tart to eat raw.

Star Fruit
When sliced, this makes a pretty shape perfect for garnishes.

Strawberries
A popular summer fruit, especially served with cream.

LETTUCES AND LEAVES

• • •

One particular aspect of lettuce
that sets it apart from any other
vegetable is that you can buy it in
only one form – fresh.

Lettuce has been cultivated for
thousands of years. In Egyptian
times it was sacred to the fertility
god Min. It was then considered a
powerful aphrodisiac, yet for the
Greeks and the Romans it was
thought to have quite the opposite
effect, making one sleepy and
generally soporific. Chemists today
confirm that lettuce contains a
hypnotic similar to opium, and in
herbal remedies lettuce is
recommended for insomniacs.

There are hundreds of different
varieties of lettuce. Today, an
increasing choice is available in
stores so that the salad bowl can
become a riot of colour, taste and
texture with no other ingredient
than a selection of leaves.

Butterhead

These are the classic round lettuces.
They have a pale heart and floppy,
loosely packed leaves. They have a
pleasant flavour as long as they are
fresh. Choose the lettuce with the
best heart by picking it up at the
bottom and gently squeezing to
check there is a firm centre. Many
more varieties are now available.

Lollo Rosso

Both lollo rosso and lollo biondo
are similar in shape but a paler
green without any purple edges and
are non-hearting lettuces. Although
they do not have a lot of flavour,
they look superb and are often used
to form a nest of leaves on which to
place the rest of a salad. They hold
a lot of dressing.

Cos

The cos lettuce would have been
known in antiquity. It has two
names, cos, derived from the Greek
island where it was found; and
romaine, the name used by the
French. Cos is considered to have
the best flavour and is the correct
lettuce for use in the famous
American Caesar Salad.

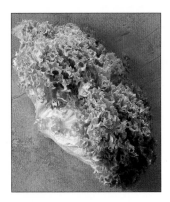

Escarole

This is one of the more robust
lettuces in terms of flavour and
texture. Like the closely related
frisée, escarole has a distinctive
bitter flavour. Served with a
judicious mixture of other leaves
and a well-flavoured dressing,
escarole and frisée will give your
salad a pleasant "bite".

Oak Leaf Lettuce

Also known as feuille de chêne and
salad bowl, oak leaf lettuce,
together with lollo rosso and lollo
biondo, is another member of the
loosehead lettuce group. Oak leaf
lettuce has a very gentle flavour. It
is an extremely decorative leaf and
makes a beautiful addition to any
salad, and a lovely garnish.

Little Gem (Bibb)
These attractive little lettuces look
like something between a baby cos
and a tightly-furled butterhead.
They have firm hearts and quite a
distinct flavour. Their tight centres
mean that they can be sliced whole
and the quarters used for carrying
slivers of smoked fish or anchovy
as a simple appetizer.

Chinese Leaves (Chinese Cabbage)
This has pale green, crinkly leaves
with long, wide, white ribs. Its
shape is a little like a very fat head
of celery, which gives rise to
another of its names, celery
cabbage. It has a crunchy texture,
and since it is available all year
round, it makes a useful winter
salad component.

Radicchio
This is a variety developed from
wild chicory (Belgian endive). It
looks like a lettuce with deep wine-
red leaves and cream ribs and owes
its splendid foliage to careful
shading from the light. If it is
grown in the dark, the leaves are
marbled pink. Its bitter flavour
contrasts well with green salads.

Lamb's Lettuce
Also known as corn salad this is a
popular winter leaf that does not
actually belong to the lettuce
family, but is terrific in salads.
Called mâche in France, lamb's
lettuce has small, attractive, dark
green, delicate leaves and grows in
pretty little sprigs. Its flavour is
mild and nutty.

Watercress
Perhaps the most robustly
flavoured of all the salad
ingredients, a handful of watercress
is all you need to perk up a dull or
boring salad. It has a distinctive
"raw" flavour, peppery and slightly
pungent, and this, together with its
shiny leaves, make it a popular and
attractive garnish.

Rocket (Arugula)
This has a wonderful peppery
flavour and is excellent in a mixed
green salad. It was eaten by the
Greeks and Romans as an
aphrodisiac. Since it has such a
striking flavour a little goes a long
way; just a few leaves will
transform a green salad and liven
up a sandwich.

HERBS

• • •

For as long as salads have drawn on the qualities of fresh produce, sweet herbs have played an important part in providing individual character and flavour. When herbs are used in a salad, they should be as full of life as the salad leaves they accompany. Dried herbs are no substitute for fresh ones and should be kept for cooked dishes, such as casseroles. Salad herbs are distinguished by their ability to release flavour without lengthy cooking.

Most salad herbs belong finely chopped in salad dressings and marinades, while the robust flavours of rosemary, thyme and fennel branches can be used on the barbecue to impart a smoky herb flavour. Ideally salad herbs should be picked just before use, but if you cannot use them immediately keep them in water to retain their freshness. Parsley, mint and coriander (cilantro) will keep for up to a week in this way if also covered with a plastic bag and placed in the refrigerator.

Basil
Remarkable for its fresh, pungent flavour unlike that of any other herb, basil is widely used in Mediterranean salads, especially Italian recipes. It has a special affinity with tomatoes. Basil leaves are tender and delicate and should be gently torn or snipped with scissors, rather than chopped with a knife, which will bruise them.

Chives
These belong to the onion family and have a mild onion flavour. The slender, green stems and soft mauve flowers are both edible. Chives are an indispensable flavouring for potato salads.

Coriander (Cilantro)
The chopped leaves of this pungent, distinctively flavoured herb are popular in Middle Eastern and Eastern salads.

Lavender
This soothingly fragrant herb is edible and may be used in both sweet and savoury salads as it combines well with thyme, garlic, honey and orange.

Mint
This much-loved, easy-to-grow herb is widely used in Greek and Middle Eastern salads, such as Tzatziki and Tabbouleh. It is also a popular addition to fruit salads. Garden mint is the most common variety; others include spearmint, pineapple mint and the round-leafed apple mint.

Above: Clockwise from top left; thyme, coriander, parsley, chives, lavender, rose, mint and basil.

Parsley
Flat leaf and curly parsley are both used for their fresh, green flavour. Flat leaf parsley is said to have a stronger taste. Freshly chopped parsley is used by the handful in salads and dressings.

Rose
Although it is not technically a herb, the sweet-scented rose can be used to flavour fresh fruit salads. It combines well with blackberries and raspberries.

Thyme
An asset to salads featuring rich, earthy flavours, this herb has a penetrating flavour.

SPICES

• • •

Spices are the aromatic seasonings found in the seed, bark, fruit and sometimes flowers of certain plants and trees. Spices are highly valued for their warm, inviting flavours, and thankfully their price is relatively low. The flavour of a spice is contained in the volatile oils of the seed, bark or fruit; so, like herbs, spices should be used as fresh as possible. Whole spices keep better than ground ones, which tend to lose their freshness within 3–4 months.

Not all spices are suitable for salad making, although many allow us to explore the flavours of other cultures. Some of the recipes in this book use curry spices, but only in moderation so as not to spoil the delicate salad flavours.

Above: Flavoursome additions to salads include (clockwise from top left) celery salt, caraway seeds, curry paste, saffron threads, peppercorns and cayenne pepper.

Caraway

These savoury-sweet-tasting seeds are widely used in German and Austrian cooking and feature strongly in many Jewish dishes. The small ribbed seeds are similar in appearance and taste to cumin. The flavour combines especially well with German mustard in a dressing for frankfurter salad.

Cayenne pepper

A type of chilli powder, this is the dried and finely ground fruit of a very hot chilli pepper. It is an important seasoning in South American cooking and is often used when seasoning fish and seafood. Cayenne pepper can be blended with paprika if it is too hot and should be used with care.

Celery salt

A combination of ground celery seed and salt, this is used for seasoning vegetables and has an especial affinity with carrots.

Cumin seeds

Often associated with Asian and North African cooking, cumin can be bought ground or as small, slender seeds. It combines well with coriander seeds.

Curry paste

Prepared curry paste consists of a blend of Indian spices preserved in oil. It may be added to dressings, and is particularly useful in this respect for showing off the sweet qualities of fish and shellfish.

Paprika

This spice is made from a variety of sweet red pepper. It is mild in flavour, and adds colour.

Pepper

Undoubtedly the most popular spice used in the West, pepper features in the cooking of almost every nation. Peppercorns can be

white, black, green or red and should always be freshly milled rather than bought already ground. Red or pink peppercorns are not actually a pepper, but a South American berry.

Saffron

The world's most expensive spice, made from the dried stigma of a crocus, real saffron has a tobacco-rich smell and gives a sweet yellow tint to liquids used for cooking. It can be used in creamy dressings and brings out the richness of fish and shellfish dishes. There are many powdered imitations which provide colour without the flavour of the real thing.

OILS, VINEGARS AND FLAVOURINGS

Oils

Oil is the main ingredient of most dressings and provides an important richness to salads. Neutral oils, such as sunflower, safflower or groundnut (peanut), are ideally used as a background for stronger oils. Sesame, walnut and hazelnut oils are the strongest and should be used sparingly. Olive oil is prized for its clarity of flavour and clean richness. The most significant producers of olive oil are Italy, France, Spain and Greece. These and other countries produce two main grades of olive oil: estate-grown extra-virgin olive oil; and semi-fine olive oil, which is of a good, basic standard.

Olive oils
Oils from different countries have distinctive characteristics.
   French olive oils are subtly flavoured and provide a well-balanced lightness to dressings.
   Greek olive oils are typically strong in character. They are often green with a thick texture and are unsuitable for mayonnaise.
   Italian olive oils are noted for their vigorous Mediterranean flavours. Tuscan oils are noted for their well-rounded, spicy flavour. Sicilian oils tend to be lighter in texture, although they are often stronger in flavour.
   Spanish olive oils are typically fruity and often have a nutty quality with a slight bitterness.

Nut oils
Hazelnut and walnut oils are valued for their strong, nutty flavour. Tasting richly of the nuts from which they are pressed, both are usually blended with neutral oils for salad dressings.

Seed oils
Groundnut oil, safflower and sunflower oil are valued for their clean, neutral flavour.

Salad Flavourings

Capers
These are the pickled flower buds of a bush native to the Mediterranean. Their strong, sharp flavour is well suited to richly flavoured salads.

Lemon and Lime Juice
The juice of lemons and limes is used to impart a clean acidity to oil dressings. They should be used in moderation.

Mustard
Mustard has a tendency to bring out the flavour of other ingredients. It also acts as an emulsifier in dressings and allows oil and vinegar to merge for a short period of time. The most popular mustards for use in salads are French, especially Dijon, German, English (hot) and wholegrain.

Above: Top left to right; Italian virgin olive oil, Spanish olive oil, Italian olive oil, safflower oil, hazelnut oil, walnut oil, groundnut oil, French olive oil, Italian olive oil, white wine vinegar. Left to right bottom; lemon, olives, limes, capers and mustard.

Olives
Black and green olives belong in salads with a Mediterranean flavour. Black olives are generally sweeter and juicier than green ones.

Vinegars

White wine vinegar
This should be used in moderation to balance the richness of an oil. A good-quality white wine vinegar will serve most purposes.

Balsamic vinegar
Sweeter than other vinegars, only a few drops of balsamic vinegar are necessary to enhance a salad or dressing. It is also a good substitute for lemon juice. The best types are more than 12 years old.

MAKING HERBED OILS AND VINEGARS

· · ·

Many herbed oils and vinegars are available commercially, but you can very easily make your own. Pour the oil or vinegar into a sterilized jar and add your flavouring. Allow to steep for 2 weeks, then strain and decant into an attractive bottle which has also been sterilized properly. Add a seal and an identifying label.

Flavoured vinegars should be used within 3 months, and herb-flavoured oils within 10 days. Fresh herbs for flavouring oils and vinegars should be rinsed clean and patted completely dry with kitchen paper before you use them.

Tarragon Vinegar

Steep tarragon in cider vinegar, then decant. Insert 2 or 3 long sprigs of tarragon into the bottle.

Rosemary Vinegar

Steep a sprig of fresh rosemary in red wine vinegar, then decant. Pour the vinegar into a sterilized, dry bottle and add a few long stems of rosemary as decoration.

Lemon and Lime Vinegar

Steep strips of lemon and lime rind in white wine vinegar, then decant. Pour into a sterilized, clean bottle and add fresh strips of rind for colour.

Raspberry Vinegar

Pour vinegar into a pan with 1 tablespoon of pickling spices and heat gently for 5 minutes. Pour the hot mixture over the raspberries in a bowl and then add 2 fresh sprigs of lemon thyme. Cover and leave the mixture to steep for two days in a cool, dark place. Strain the liquid and pour the flavoured vinegar into a sterilized bottle and seal.

Dill and Lemon Oil

Steep a handful of fresh dill and a large strip of lemon rind in virgin olive oil, then decant. Use for salads containing fish or shellfish.

Mediterranean Herb Oil

Steep fresh rosemary, thyme and marjoram in virgin or extra virgin olive oil, then decant.

Basil and Chilli Oil

Steep basil and 3 chillies in virgin olive oil, then decant. Add to tomato and mozzarella salads.

Warning

There is some evidence that oils containing fresh herbs and spices can grow harmful moulds, especially once the bottle has been opened and the contents are not fully covered by the oil. To protect against this, it is recommended that the herbs and spices are removed once their flavour has passed into the oil.

From left: Tarragon Vinegar, Rosemary Vinegar, Raspberry Vinegar, Lemon and Lime Vinegar.

VEGETABLE PREPARATION

∘ ∘ ∘

Shredding Cabbage

Cabbage features in many salad recipes, such as coleslaw, and this method for shredding can be used for all varieties.

1 Use a large knife to cut the cabbage into quarters.

2 Cut the hard core from each quarter and discard; this part is not really edible when raw.

3 Slice each quarter to form fine shreds. Shredded cabbage will keep for several hours in the refrigerator, but do not dress it until you are ready to serve.

Chopping an Onion

Chopped onions are used in many recipes and, whether they are very finely or coarsely chopped, the method is the same; just vary the gap between cuts.

1 Cut off the stalk end of the onion and cut in half through the root, leaving the root intact. Remove the skin and place the halved onion, cut-side down, on the board. Make lengthways vertical cuts into the onion, taking care not to cut right through to the root.

2 Make two or three horizontal cuts from the stalk end through to the root, but without cutting all the way through. Space the cuts at about 5mm/¼in intervals.

3 Turn the onion on to its side. Cut the onion across from the stalk end to the root, again at about 5mm/¼in intervals. The onion will fall away in small squares. Cut further apart for larger squares.

Preparing Garlic

Don't worry if you don't have a garlic press: instead, try this method, which gives wonderful, juicy results.

1 Break off the clove of garlic, place the flat side of a large knife on top and strike with your fist. Remove all the papery outer skin. Begin by finely chopping the clove.

2 Sprinkle over a little table salt and, using the flat side of a large knife blade, work the salt into the garlic, until the clove softens and releases its juices. Use the garlic pulp as required.

Preparing Chillies

Chillies add a distinct flavour, but remove the fiery-hot seeds.

1 Always protect your hands, as chillies can irritate the skin; wear rubber gloves and never rub your eyes after handling chillies. Halve the chilli lengthways and remove and discard the seeds.

2 Slice, finely chop and use as required. Wash the knife and board thoroughly in hot, soapy water. Always wash your hands thoroughly after preparing chillies.

Peeling Tomatoes

If you have the time, peel tomatoes before adding them to dressings. This avoids including rolled-up, tough pieces of tomato skin.

1 Make a cross in each tomato with a sharp knife and place in a bowl.

2 Pour over enough boiling water to cover and leave to stand for about 30 seconds. The skins should start to come away. Slightly unripe tomatoes may take a little longer.

3 Drain the tomatoes and peel off the skin with a sharp knife. Don't leave the tomatoes in the boiling water for too long.

Chopping Herbs

Chop fresh herbs just before you use them.

1 Remove the leaves and place on a clean, dry board.

2 Chop the herbs, as finely or as coarsely as required, by holding the tip of the blade of a large, sharp knife on the board and rocking the handle up and down.

Cutting Julienne Strips

Julienne strips of carrots, celery, cucumber and other vegetables make attractive garnishes and salad ingredients.

1 Peel the vegetable and use a large knife to cut it into 5cm/2in lengths. Cut a thin sliver from one side of the first piece so that it sits flat on the board.

2 Cut each piece into thin slices lengthways. Stack the slices of vegetable and then cut through them again to make fine strips.

Preparing Spring Onions (Scallions)

Spring onions make such a crisp and tasty addition to salads that they are worth the bother.

1 Trim off the root of the spring onion with a sharp knife. Peel away any damaged or tough leaves.

2 For an intense flavour and an attractive green colour cut the dark green part into thin sticks.

3 For a milder flavour just use the white part of the spring onion, discard the root and slice thinly on a slight diagonal.

FRUIT PREPARATION

• • •

Citrus Fruit

1 To peel, cut a slice from the top and from the base. Set the fruit base down on a work surface.

2 Cut off the peel lengthways in thick strips. Remove the coloured rind and all the white pith (which has a bitter taste). Cut following the curve of the fruit.

1 To remove the thin, coloured rind, use a vegetable peeler to shave off the rind in wide strips, taking none of the white pith. Use these strips whole or cut them into fine shreds with a sharp knife.

2 Alternatively, rub the fruit against the fine holes of a metal grater, turning the fruit so that you take just the rind and not the white pith. Or use a special tool, called a citrus zester, to take fine threads of rind. The shallow angle of the blade cuts into the outer surface of the rind only. Finely chop the threads for tiny pieces.

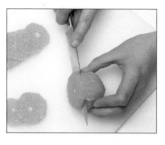

1 For slices, cut across the fruit in slices with a serrated knife.

1 For segments, hold the fruit over a bowl to catch the juice. Working from the side of the fruit to the centre, slide the knife down first one side of a separating membrane and then the other. Continue cutting out all the segments.

Fresh Currants

1 Pull small bunches of fruit through the tines of a fork to remove red, black or white currants from the stalks. This prevents squashing them.

Apples and Pears

1 For whole fruit, use an apple corer to stamp out the whole core from stalk end to base.

1 For halves, use a melon baller to scoop out the core. Cut out the stalk and base with a sharp knife.

2 For rings, remove the core and seeds. Set the fruit on its side and cut across into rings, as required.

1 For slices, cut the fruit in half and remove the core and seeds. Set one half, cut side down, and cut it across into neat slices. Repeat with the other half.

Fresh Dates

1 Halve the fruit lengthways and lift out the stone (pit).

Papayas and Melons

1 Halve the fruit. Scoop out the seeds from the central hollow, then scrape away any fibres. For slices, follow the pear technique.

Kiwi Fruit, Star Fruit (Carambola)

1 Cut the fruit across into neat slices; discard the ends.

Pineapples

1 To peel the pineapple, set the pineapple on its base, hold it at the top and cut thick slices of skin from top to bottom. Dig out any "eyes" that remain with the point of the knife.

2 For chunks, halve the peeled fruit lengthways and then cut into quarters. Cut each quarter into spears and cut out the core.Cut each spear into chunks.

3 For rings, cut the peeled fruit across into slices and cut or stamp out the core.

Keeping Fresh Colour

If exposed to the air for long, the cut flesh of fruits such as apples, bananas and avocados starts to turn brown. So if cut fruit has to wait before being served, sprinkle the cut surfaces with lemon juice, or immerse hard fruits in water and lemon juice, but do not soak or the fruit may become soggy.

Mangoes

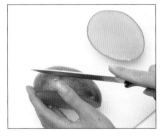

1 Cut lengthways on either side of the stone (pit). Then cut from the two thin ends of the stone.

2 Remove the skin and cut the flesh into slices or cubes.

Peaches, Nectarines, Apricots and Plums

1 Cut the fruit in half, cutting around the indentation. Twist the halves apart. Lift out the stone (pit), or lever it out with the tip of a knife. Or cut the unpeeled fruit into wedges, removing the stone. Set each wedge peel side down and slide the knife down to peel.

SALAD DRESSINGS

· · ·

Although the ingredients of a salad are important, the true secret of a perfect salad is a good dressing.

A French dressing made from the very best olive oil and vinegar can rescue even the dullest selection of lettuce leaves, while a home-made mayonnaise is impressive.

If you are a confident and experienced salad dresser you might feel able simply to add olive oil and vinegar directly to your salad just before serving, but the safest way of creating a perfect dressing is to prepare it in advance. Home-made dressings can be stored in the refrigerator for up to a week and will improve in flavour. Here is a selection of favourites.

Thousand Islands Dressing

This creamy dressing is great with green salads and grated carrot, hot potato, pasta and rice salads.

INGREDIENTS
60ml/4 tbsp sunflower oil
15ml/1 tbsp orange juice
15ml/1 tbsp lemon juice
10ml/2 tsp grated lemon rind
15ml/1 tbsp finely chopped onion
5ml/1 tsp paprika
5ml/1 tsp Worcestershire sauce
15ml/1 tbsp finely chopped fresh parsley
salt and ground black pepper

MAKES ABOUT
120ML/4FL OZ/½ CUP

Put all the ingredients into a screw-top jar and season to taste with salt and pepper. Replace the lid and shake well.

French Dressing

This is the most popular dressing.

INGREDIENTS
90ml/6 tbsp extra virgin olive oil
15ml/1 tbsp white wine vinegar
5ml/1 tsp French mustard
pinch of caster (superfine) sugar

MAKES ABOUT 120ML/
4FL OZ/½ CUP

1 Place the extra virgin olive oil and white wine vinegar in a clean screw-top jar.

2 Add the French mustard and caster sugar.

3 Replace the lid and shake the jar well to mix.

French Herb Dressing

The delicate scents and flavours of fresh herbs combine especially well in a French dressing. Use just one herb or a selection.

INGREDIENTS
60ml/4 tbsp extra virgin olive oil
30ml/2 tbsp sunflower oil
15ml/1 tbsp lemon juice
60ml/4 tbsp finely chopped fresh herbs (parsley, chives, tarragon and marjoram)
pinch of caster (superfine) sugar

MAKES ABOUT 120ML/
4FL OZ/½ CUP

1 Place the extra virgin olive oil and sunflower oil in a clean screw-top jar.

2 Add the lemon juice, chopped herbs and sugar.

3 Replace the lid and shake the jar well to mix.

Mayonnaise

For consistent results, make sure that both egg yolks and oil are at room temperature before combining. Home-made mayonnaise is made with raw egg yolks and may therefore be considered unsuitable for young children, pregnant mothers and the elderly.

INGREDIENTS
2 egg yolks
5ml/1 tsp French mustard
150ml/¼ pint/⅔ cup extra virgin olive oil
150 ml/¼ pint/⅔ cup groundnut or sunflower oil
10ml/2 tsp white wine vinegar
salt and ground black pepper

MAKES ABOUT 300ML/
½ PINT/1 ¼ CUPS

1 Place the egg yolks and mustard in a food processor and process until smoothly blended.

2 Add the olive oil through the feeder tube, a little at a time, while the processor is still running. When the mixture is thick, add the groundnut or sunflower oil in a slow, steady stream.

3 Add the vinegar and season to taste with salt and pepper.

Yogurt Dressing

This is a less rich version of a classic mayonnaise and is much easier to make. It can be used as a low-fat substitute. Change the herbs as you wish, or leave them out.

INGREDIENTS
150ml/¼ pint/⅔ cup natural (plain) yogurt
30ml/2 tbsp mayonnaise
30ml/2 tbsp milk
15ml/1 tbsp chopped fresh parsley
15ml/1 tbsp chopped fresh chives

MAKES ABOUT 200ML/
7FL OZ/SCANT 1 CUP

Put all the ingredients in a bowl. Season to taste and mix well.

Blue Cheese and Chive Dressing

Blue cheese dressings have a strong, robust flavour and are well suited to winter salad leaves such as escarole, chicory (Belgian endive) and radicchio.

INGREDIENTS
75 g/3 oz blue cheese (Stilton, Bleu d'Auvergne or Gorgonzola)
150 ml/¼ pint/⅔ cup medium-fat natural (plain) yogurt
45 ml/3 tbsp olive oil
30 ml/2 tbsp lemon juice
15 ml/1 tbsp chopped fresh chives
ground black pepper

MAKES ABOUT 350ML/
12FL OZ/1 ½ CUPS

1 Remove the rind from the cheese and combine the cheese with a third of the yogurt in a bowl.

2 Add the remainder of the yogurt, the olive oil and the lemon juice and mix well.

3 Stir in the chopped chives and season the dressing to taste with ground black pepper.

Basil and Lemon Mayonnaise

This luxurious dressing is flavoured with lemon juice and two types of fresh basil. It can be served with all kinds of leafy salads, crudités or coleslaws. The dressing will keep in an airtight jar for up to a week in the refrigerator.

INGREDIENTS

2 large (US extra large) egg yolks
15ml/1 tbsp lemon juice
150ml/¼ pint/²/₃ cup extra virgin olive oil
150 ml/¼ pint/²/₃ cup sunflower oil
4 garlic cloves
handful of fresh green basil
handful of fresh opal basil
salt and ground black pepper

MAKES ABOUT 300ML/
½ PINT/1¼ CUPS

1 Place the egg yolks and lemon juice in a blender or food processor and process briefly.

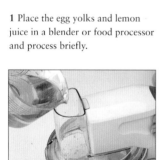

2 In a jug (pitcher), stir together both oils. With the machine running, pour in the oil very slowly, a little at a time.

3 Once half of the oil mixture has been added and the dressing has successfully emulsified, the remaining oil can be incorporated more quickly in a continuous steady stream. Continue processing until a thick, creamy mayonnaise has formed.

4 Peel and crush the garlic cloves and add to the mayonnaise. Alternatively, place the cloves on a chopping board and sprinkle with salt, then flatten them with the heel of a heavy-bladed knife and chop the flesh. Flatten the garlic again to make a coarse purée, then add to the mayonnaise.

5 Remove the basil stalks and tear both types of leaves into small pieces. Stir into the mayonnaise.

6 Add salt and pepper to taste, then transfer the mayonnaise to a serving dish. Cover and chill until ready to serve.

INSTANT DRESSINGS AND DIPS

If you need an instant dressing or dip, try one of these quick recipes. Most of them use pantry ingredients.

Creamy Black Olive Dip

Stir a little black olive paste into a carton of extra-thick double (heavy) cream until smooth and well blended. Add salt, ground black pepper and a squeeze of lemon juice to taste. Serve chilled.

Crème Fraîche Dressing with Spring Onions

Finely chop a bunch of spring onions (scallions) and stir into a carton of crème fraîche. Add a dash of chilli sauce and a squeeze of lime juice and season with salt and ground black pepper.

Yogurt and Mustard Dip

Mix a small carton of creamy, Greek (US strained plain) yogurt with 5–10ml/1–2 tsp wholegrain mustard. Serve with crudités.

Herb Mayonnaise

Liven up ready-made French-style mayonnaise with a handful of chopped fresh herbs.

Passata and Horseradish Dip

Bring a little tang to a small carton or bottle of passata (bottled strained tomatoes) by adding some horseradish sauce or 5–10 ml/ 1–2 tsp creamed horseradish and salt and pepper to taste.

Pesto Dip

Stir 15ml/1 tbsp ready-made red or green pesto into a carton of soured cream. Serve with crisp crudités or wedges of oven-roasted Mediterranean vegetables.

Spiced Yogurt Dressing

Stir a little curry paste and chutney into a carton of yogurt.

Sun-dried Tomato Dip

Stir 15–30ml/1–2 tbsp sun-dried tomato paste into a carton of Greek (US strained plain) yogurt. Season with salt and black pepper.

Above: Top row; Creamy Black Olive Dip, Crème Fraîche Dressing with Spring Onions. Second row; Herb Mayonnaise, Sun-dried Tomato Dip. Third row; Yogurt and Mustard dip, Soft Cheese and Chive Dip, Spiced Yogurt Dressing. Fourth row; Pesto Dip, Passata and Horseradish Dip.

Soft Cheese and Chive Dip

Mix a tub of soft cheese with 30–45 ml/2–3 tbsp chopped fresh chives and season to taste with salt and ground black pepper. If the dip is too thick, stir in a little milk. Use as a dressing for all kinds of salads, especially winter coleslaws.

Salads are the most versatile accompaniments to hot and cold

dishes – in both summer and winter – and are ideal for serving

at a barbecue. They are perfect for picnics and make effortless

appetizers when you are entertaining.

LIGHT AND SIDE
SALADS

CRUDITÉS

A colourful selection of raw vegetables, or crudités, may be served with drinks or as small appetizers. The term "crudités" is used both for small pieces of vegetables served with a tasty dip and for a selection of vegetable salads presented in separate dishes. By choosing contrasting colours, you can make a beautiful presentation of raw or lightly cooked vegetables, attractively arranged on a platter or in baskets and served with a tangy dip, such as aioli (garlic mayonnaise) or tapenade (olive paste). Allow 75–115g/3–4oz of each vegetable per person.

Aioli

Put four crushed garlic cloves (or more or less, to taste) in a small bowl with a pinch of salt and crush with the back of a spoon. Add two egg yolks and beat for 30 seconds with an electric mixer until creamy. Beat in 250ml/8fl oz/1 cup extra virgin olive oil, one drop at a time, until the mixture thickens. As it begins to thicken, the oil can be added in a thin, steady stream until the mixture is thick. Thin the sauce with a little lemon juice and season to taste with salt and pepper. Chill for up to 2 days; bring to room temperature and stir before serving.

Tapenade

Put 200g/7oz pitted black olives, 6 canned anchovy fillets, 30ml/ 2 tbsp rinsed capers, 1–2 garlic cloves, 5ml/1 tsp fresh thyme leaves, 15ml/1 tbsp Dijon mustard, the juice of ½ lemon, freshly ground black pepper and, if you like, 15ml/1 tbsp brandy in a food processor fitted with the metal blade. Process for 15–30 seconds until smooth, then scrape down the sides of the bowl. With the machine running, slowly add 60–90ml/4–6 tbsp extra virgin olive oil to make a smooth, firm paste. Store in an airtight container.

Raw Vegetable Platter

INGREDIENTS

2 red and 2 yellow (bell) peppers, seeded and sliced lengthways
225g/8oz fresh baby corn cobs, blanched
1 chicory (Belgian endive) head (red or white), trimmed and leaves separated
175–225g/6–8oz thin asparagus, trimmed and blanched
1 small bunch radishes with small leaves
175g/6oz cherry tomatoes
12 quail's eggs, boiled for 3 minutes, drained, refreshed and peeled
aioli or tapenade, to serve

SERVES 6–8

Arrange the prepared vegetables on a large serving plate together with the quail's eggs. Cover with a damp dishtowel until ready to serve. Serve with aioli or tapenade for dipping.

Tomato and Cucumber Salad

INGREDIENTS

1 medium cucumber, peeled and thinly sliced
5–6 ice cubes
30ml/2 tbsp white wine vinegar
90ml/6 tbsp crème fraîche or sour cream
30ml/2 tbsp chopped fresh mint
4 or 5 ripe tomatoes, sliced
salt and freshly ground black pepper

SERVES 4–6

Place the cucumber in a bowl, sprinkle with a little salt and 15ml/ 1 tbsp of the vinegar and toss with the ice cubes. Chill for 1 hour to crisp, then rinse, drain and pat dry. Return to the bowl, add the cream, pepper and mint and stir to mix well. Arrange the tomato slices on a serving plate, sprinkle with the remaining vinegar and spoon the cucumber slices into the centre.

Carrot and Parsley Salad

INGREDIENTS

1 garlic clove, crushed
grated rind and juice of 1 orange
30–45ml/2–3 tbsp groundnut (peanut) oil
450 g/1lb carrots, cut into very fine julienne strips
30–45ml/2–3 tbsp chopped fresh parsley
salt and freshly ground black pepper

SERVES 4–6

Rub a bowl with the garlic and leave in the bowl. Add the orange rind and juice and season. Whisk in the oil until blended, then remove the garlic. Add the carrots and half of the parsley and toss well. Garnish with the remaining parsley.

LETTUCE AND HERB SALAD

• • •

Stores now sell many different types of lettuce leaves all year, so try to use a mixture.

INGREDIENTS

½ cucumber
mixed lettuce leaves
1 bunch watercress, about 115g/4oz
1 chicory (Belgian endive)
head, sliced
45ml/3 tbsp chopped fresh herbs

FOR THE DRESSING
15ml/1 tbsp white wine vinegar
5ml/1 tsp prepared mustard
75ml/5 tbsp olive oil
salt and freshly ground
black pepper

SERVES 4

3 Either toss the cucumber, lettuce, watercress, chicory and herbs together in a bowl, or arrange them in the bowl in layers.

4 Stir the dressing, then pour over the salad and toss lightly to coat the salad vegetables and leaves. Serve immediately.

1 To make the dressing, mix the vinegar and mustard together, then whisk in the oil and seasoning.

2 Peel the cucumber, if you like, then halve it lengthways and scoop out the seeds. Thinly slice the flesh. Tear the lettuce leaves by hand into bitesize pieces.

MINTED MELON AND GRAPEFRUIT COCKTAIL

。 。 。

Melon is always a popular and refreshing appetizer.

INGREDIENTS

1 small Galia or charentais melon, about 1kg/2¼lb
2 pink grapefruit
1 yellow grapefruit
5ml/1 tsp Dijon mustard
5ml/1 tsp raspberry or sherry vinegar
5ml/1 tsp clear honey
15ml/1 tbsp chopped fresh mint
fresh mint sprigs, to garnish

SERVES 4

1 Halve the melon and remove the seeds with a teaspoon. With a melon baller, carefully scoop the flesh into balls.

2 With a sharp knife, peel the pink and yellow grapefruit and cut away all the white pith. Carefully remove the segments by cutting between the membranes, holding the fruit over a bowl to catch any juice.

3 Whisk the Dijon mustard, raspberry or sherry vinegar, honey, chopped mint and reserved grapefruit juice together in a mixing bowl. Add the melon balls and grapefruit segments and mix well. Cover and chill in the refrigerator for 30 minutes.

4 Ladle into four serving dishes, garnish each one with a sprig of fresh mint and serve.

BLACK AND ORANGE SALAD

. . .

This dramatically colourful salad, with its piquant, spicy dressing, is very unusual. It is a feast for the eyes as well as for the taste buds.

INGREDIENTS

3 oranges
115g/4oz/1 cup pitted black olives
15ml/1 tbsp chopped fresh
coriander (cilantro)
15ml/1 tbsp chopped fresh parsley

FOR THE DRESSING
30ml/2 tbsp olive oil
15ml/1 tbsp lemon juice
2.5ml/½ tsp paprika
2.5ml/½ tsp ground cumin

SERVES 4

1 With a sharp knife, cut away the peel and pith from the oranges and divide the fruit into segments.

2 Place the oranges in a salad bowl and add the black olives, coriander and parsley.

3 Blend together the olive oil, lemon juice, paprika and cumin. Pour the dressing over the salad and toss gently. Chill for about 30 minutes and serve.

ROCKET AND CORIANDER SALAD

. . .

Unless you have a plentiful supply of rocket, you may well have to use extra spinach or another green leaf.

INGREDIENTS

115g/4oz or more rocket
(arugula) leaves
115g/4oz young spinach leaves
1 large bunch fresh coriander
(cilantro), about 25g/1oz
2–3 fresh parsley sprigs

FOR THE DRESSING
1 garlic clove, crushed
45ml/3 tbsp olive oil
10ml/2 tsp white wine vinegar
pinch of paprika
cayenne pepper
salt

SERVES 4

1 Place the rocket and spinach leaves in a salad bowl. Chop the coriander and parsley and sprinkle them over the top.

2 In a small jug (pitcher), blend together the garlic, olive oil, vinegar, paprika, cayenne pepper and salt to taste.

3 Pour the dressing over the salad and serve immediately.

CAESAR SALAD

° ° °

There are many stories about this salad's origin. The most likely is that it was invented by Caesar Cardini in his Mexican restaurant in the 1920s.

INGREDIENTS

3 slices day-old bread, 1cm/
¹/₂in thick
60ml/4 tbsp garlic oil
50g/2oz piece Parmesan cheese
1 cos or romaine lettuce
salt and freshly ground
black pepper

FOR THE DRESSING

2 egg yolks, as fresh as possible
25g/1oz canned anchovy fillets,
drained and coarsely chopped
2.5ml/¹/₂ tsp French mustard
120ml/4fl oz/¹/₂ cup olive oil
15ml/1 tbsp white wine vinegar

SERVES 4

1 To make the dressing, combine the egg yolks, anchovies, mustard, oil and vinegar in a screw-top jar and shake well.

2 Remove the crusts from the bread with a serrated knife and cut into 2.5cm/1in fingers.

3 Heat the garlic oil in a large frying-pan, add the pieces of bread and fry until golden brown all over. Remove from the pan, sprinkle with salt and leave to drain on kitchen paper.

4 Cut thin shavings from the Parmesan cheese with a swivel-bade vegetable peeler.

5 Wash the lettuce leaves and spin dry or pat dry with kitchen paper or a clean dishtowel. Place in a salad bowl or on individual plates, smother with the dressing, and sprinkle with the garlic croûtons and Parmesan cheese shavings. Season to taste with salt and pepper and serve immediately.

Cook's Tip

The classic dressing for Caesar Salad is made with raw egg yolks. Make sure that you use only the freshest eggs, bought from a reputable supplier. Expectant mothers, young children and the elderly are not advised to eat raw egg yolks. You could omit them from the salad dressing and grate hard-boiled yolks on top of the salad instead.

TURKISH SALAD

This is a perfect combination of textures and flavours.

INGREDIENTS

1 cos or romaine lettuce heart
1 green (bell) pepper
1 red (bell) pepper
¹/₂ cucumber
4 tomatoes
1 red onion
225g/8oz feta cheese, crumbled
black olives, to garnish

FOR THE DRESSING

45ml/3 tbsp olive oil
45ml/3 tbsp lemon juice
1 garlic clove, crushed
15ml/1 tbsp chopped fresh parsley
15ml/1 tbsp chopped fresh mint
salt and freshly ground
black pepper

SERVES 4

1 Chop the lettuce into bitesize pieces. Seed the peppers, remove and discard the cores and cut the flesh into thin strips. Chop the cucumber and slice or chop the tomatoes. Cut the onion in half, then slice finely.

2 Place the chopped lettuce, peppers, cucumber, tomatoes and onion in a large salad bowl. Sprinkle the crumbled feta over the top and toss together lightly.

3 To make the dressing, blend together the olive oil, lemon juice and garlic in a small bowl. Stir in the chopped parsley and mint and season with salt and black pepper to taste. Alternatively, put all the ingredients in a screw-top jar and shake well.

4 Pour the dressing over the salad and toss lightly. Garnish with a handful of black olives and serve the salad immediately.

PERSIAN SALAD

This very simple salad can be served with almost any dish. Don't add the dressing until just before you are ready to serve.

INGREDIENTS

4 tomatoes
¹/₂ cucumber
1 onion
1 cos or romaine lettuce heart

FOR THE DRESSING

30ml/2 tbsp olive oil
juice of 1 lemon
1 garlic clove, crushed
salt and freshly ground
black pepper

SERVES 4

1 Cut the tomatoes and cucumber into small cubes. Finely chop the onion and tear the lettuce heart into pieces.

2 Place the prepared tomatoes, cucumber, onion and lettuce in a large salad bowl and mix them lightly together.

3 To make the dressing, pour the olive oil into a small bowl. Add the lemon juice, garlic and seasoning and blend together well.

4 Pour the dressing over the salad and toss lightly to mix. Sprinkle with extra black pepper to taste and serve immediately.

SPINACH AND MUSHROOM SALAD

⚬ ⚬ ⚬

This nutritious salad goes well with strongly flavoured dishes. If served alone as a light lunch, it could be dressed with a French vinaigrette and served with warm French bread.

INGREDIENTS

*10 baby corn cobs
2 medium tomatoes
115g/4oz/1½ cups mushrooms
1 medium onion cut into rings
20 small spinach leaves
25g/1oz salad cress (optional)
salt and freshly ground
black pepper*

SERVES 4

1 Halve the baby corn cobs lengthways and slice the tomatoes.

2 Trim the mushrooms and cut them into thin slices.

3 Arrange the corn cobs, tomatoes, mushrooms, onions, spinach and cress, if using, attractively in a large bowl. Season with salt and pepper to taste and serve.

NUTTY SALAD

⚬ ⚬ ⚬

A delicious salad with a tangy bite to it that can be served as an accompaniment to a main meal, or as an appetizer.

INGREDIENTS

*1 medium onion, cut into 12 rings
115g/4oz/¾ cup canned red kidney
beans, drained
1 medium green courgette
(zucchini), sliced
1 medium yellow courgette
(zucchini), sliced
50g/2oz pasta shells, cooked
50g/2oz/½ cup cashew nuts
25g/1oz/¼ cup peanuts
lime wedges and fresh coriander
(cilantro) sprigs, to garnish*

FOR THE DRESSING
*120ml/4fl oz/½ cup fromage frais
or farmer's cheese
30ml/2 tbsp natural (plain) yogurt
1 fresh green chilli, chopped*

*15ml/1 tbsp chopped fresh
coriander (cilantro)
2.5ml/½ tsp crushed
black peppercorns
2.5ml/½ tsp crushed dried
red chillies
15ml/1 tbsp lemon juice
2.5ml/½ tsp salt*

SERVES 4

1 Arrange the onion rings, red kidney beans, green and yellow courgette slices and pasta shells in a salad dish, ready for serving. Sprinkle the cashew nuts and peanuts over the top.

2 In a separate bowl, blend together the fromage frais, yogurt, green chilli, coriander and salt and beat well using a fork.

3 Sprinkle the crushed black pepper, red chillies and lemon juice over the dressing. Garnish the salad with the lime wedges and coriander sprigs and serve with the dressing in a separate bowl or poured over the salad.

FRESH CEPS SALAD

. . .

To capture the just-picked flavour of a cep, this delicious salad is enriched with an egg yolk and walnut oil dressing.

INGREDIENTS
350g/12oz fresh ceps
175g/6oz mixed salad leaves,
including batavia, young spinach
and frisée
50g/2oz/½ cup broken walnut
pieces, toasted
50g/2oz piece Parmesan cheese
salt and freshly ground
black pepper

FOR THE DRESSING
2 egg yolks
2.5ml/½ tsp French mustard
75ml/5 tbsp groundnut (peanut) oil
45ml/3 tbsp walnut oil
30ml/2 tbsp lemon juice
30ml/2 tbsp chopped fresh parsley
pinch of caster (superfine) sugar

SERVES 4

2 Trim the ceps and cut them into thin slices.

3 Place the ceps in a large salad bowl and combine with the dressing. Leave for 10–15 minutes for the flavours to mingle.

4 Wash and dry the salad leaves, then add them to the salad bowl and toss them with the ceps.

5 Turn the ceps out on to four large serving plates. Season well with salt and pepper, sprinkle with the toasted walnuts and shavings of Parmesan cheese, then serve.

1 To make the dressing, place the egg yolks in a screw-top jar with the mustard, groundnut and walnut oils, lemon juice, parsley and sugar. Shake well.

CLASSIC GREEK SALAD

. . .

If you have ever visited Greece, you'll know that this salad makes a delicious first course.

INGREDIENTS
1 cos or romaine lettuce
½ cucumber, halved lengthways
4 tomatoes
8 spring onions (scallions), sliced
black olives
115g/4oz feta cheese

FOR THE DRESSING
90ml/6 tbsp white wine vinegar
150ml/¼ pint/⅔ cup extra virgin
olive oil
salt and freshly ground
black pepper

SERVES 4

1 Tear the lettuce leaves into pieces and place in a large bowl. Slice the cucumber and add to the bowl.

2 Cut the tomatoes into wedges and put them into the bowl.

Cook's Tip
The salad can be assembled in advance and chilled, but should be dressed only just before serving. Keep the dressing at room temperature as chilling deadens the flavour.

3 Add the spring onions to the bowl together with the black olives, and toss well.

4 Cut the feta cheese into cubes and add to the salad.

5 Put the vinegar, olive oil and seasoning into a small bowl and whisk well. Pour the dressing over the salad and toss to combine. Serve with extra black olives and chunks of bread, if you like.

ORANGE AND RED ONION SALAD WITH CUMIN

. . .

Cumin and fresh mint give this refreshing salad a very Middle Eastern flavour. Small, seedless oranges are the most suitable type, if available.

INGREDIENTS

6 oranges
2 red onions
15ml/1 tbsp cumin seeds
5ml/1 tsp coarsely ground black pepper
15ml/1 tbsp chopped fresh mint
90ml/6 tbsp olive oil
salt
fresh mint sprigs and black olives, to serve

SERVES 6

1 Slice the oranges thinly, working over a bowl to catch any juice. Then, holding each orange slice in turn over the bowl, cut around with kitchen scissors to remove the peel and pith. Reserve the juice. Slice the onions thinly and separate out into rings.

2 Arrange the orange and onion slices in layers in a shallow dish, sprinkling each layer with cumin seeds, black pepper, chopped mint, olive oil and salt to taste. Pour over the reserved orange juice.

3 Leave the salad to marinate in a cool place for about 2 hours. Sprinkle over the mint sprigs and black olives and serve.

SPANISH SALAD WITH CAPERS AND OLIVES

. . .

Make this refreshing salad in the summer when tomatoes are at their sweetest.

INGREDIENTS

4 tomatoes
1/2 cucumber
1 bunch spring onions (scallions), trimmed and chopped
1 bunch watercress
8 stuffed olives
30ml/2 tbsp drained capers

FOR THE DRESSING
30ml/2 tbsp red wine vinegar
5ml/1 tsp paprika
2.5ml/1/2 tsp ground cumin
1 garlic clove, crushed
75ml/5 tbsp olive oil
salt and freshly ground black pepper

SERVES 4

1 Peel the skin from the tomatoes and finely dice the flesh. Put them in a salad bowl.

2 Peel the cucumber, dice the flesh finely and add it to the tomatoes. Add half the chopped spring onions to the salad bowl and mix lightly. Break the watercress into small sprigs. Add to the tomato mixture, with the stuffed olives and capers.

3 To make the dressing, mix the wine vinegar, paprika, cumin and garlic in a bowl. Whisk in the olive oil and season with salt and pepper to taste. Pour the dressing over the salad and toss lightly to combine. Serve the salad immediately with the remaining spring onions.

CARROT AND ORANGE SALAD

• • •

The ingredients of this fresh-tasting salad could have been made for each other.

INGREDIENTS

450g/1lb carrots
2 large oranges
15ml/1 tbsp olive oil
30ml/2 tbsp lemon juice
pinch of sugar (optional)
30ml/2 tbsp toasted pine nuts
salt and freshly ground
black pepper

SERVES 4

1 Peel the carrots and grate them into a large bowl.

2 Peel the oranges with a sharp knife and cut into segments, catching the juice in a small bowl.

Variation

Substitute shelled chopped pistachio nuts for the toasted pine nuts, if you like.

3 Blend together the olive oil, lemon juice and orange juice. Season with a little salt and pepper to taste and stir in a pinch of sugar if you like.

4 Toss the orange segments together with the carrots and pour the dressing over them. Sprinkle the salad with the pine nuts just before serving.

SPINACH AND ROAST GARLIC SALAD

Don't worry about the amount of garlic in this salad. During roasting, the garlic becomes sweet and subtle and loses its pungent taste.

INGREDIENTS

12 garlic cloves, unpeeled
60ml/4 tbsp extra virgin olive oil
450g/1lb baby spinach leaves
50g/2oz/¹/₂ cup pine nuts,
lightly toasted
juice of ¹/₂ lemon
salt and freshly ground
black pepper

SERVES 4

1 Preheat the oven to 190°C/ 375°F/Gas 5. Place the garlic cloves separately in a small roasting pan, add 30ml/2 tbsp of the olive oil and toss thoroughly to coat. Roast for about 15 minutes, until the garlic cloves are slightly charred around the edges.

2 While still warm, tip the garlic into a salad bowl. Add the spinach, pine nuts, lemon juice, remaining olive oil and a little salt. Toss well and add black pepper to taste. Serve immediately, inviting guests to squeeze the softened garlic purée out of the skin to eat.

MIXED GREEN SALAD

° ° °

*A good combination of leaves
for this salad would be rocket,
radicchio, lamb's lettuce and
frisée, with herbs such as
chervil, basil and parsley.*

INGREDIENTS
*1 garlic clove, peeled
30ml/2 tbsp red wine vinegar
5ml/1 tsp Dijon mustard (optional)
75–120ml/5–8 tbsp extra virgin
olive oil
200–225 g/7–8oz mixed salad
leaves and herbs
salt and freshly ground
black pepper*

SERVES 4–6

1 Rub a large salad bowl with the
garlic clove. Leave the garlic clove
in the bowl.

2 Add the vinegar, salt and pepper
to taste and mustard, if using. Stir
to mix the ingredients and dissolve
the salt, then gradually whisk in
the olive oil.

3 Remove the garlic clove and stir
the vinaigrette to combine.

4 Add the salad leaves to the bowl
and toss well. Serve the salad
immediately before it starts to wilt.

Variation
Try young dandelion leaves
when they are in season, but be
sure to pick them well away
from traffic routes and
agricultural crop spraying.

APPLE AND CELERIAC SALAD

° ° °

*Celeriac, despite its coarse
appearance, has a sweet and
subtle flavour. In this salad it is
served raw, allowing its unique
taste and texture to emerge.*

INGREDIENTS
*675g/1½ lb celeriac, peeled
10–15ml/2–3 tsp lemon juice
5ml/1 tsp walnut oil (optional)
1 eating apple
45ml/3 tbsp mayonnaise
10ml/2 tsp Dijon mustard
15ml/1 tbsp chopped fresh parsley
salt and freshly ground
black pepper*

SERVES 3–4

1 Using a food processor or coarse
cheese grater, shred the celeriac.
Alternatively, cut it into very thin
julienne strips.

2 Place the prepared celeriac in a
bowl and sprinkle with the lemon
juice and the walnut oil, if using.
Stir well to mix.

3 Peel the apple if you like. Cut the
apple into quarters and remove the
core. Slice the apple quarters thinly
crossways and toss together with
the celeriac.

4 Mix together the mayonnaise,
mustard and parsley and season
with salt and pepper to taste. Add
the dressing to the celeriac mixture
and stir well. Chill for several
hours until ready to serve.

Cook's Tip
The knobbly skin of celeriac is
too tough for a vegetable
peeler. Use a sharp knife.

CHICORY, FRUIT AND NUT SALAD

· · ·

The mildly bitter taste of the chicory combines well with the sweetness of the fruit and the creamy curry sauce.

INGREDIENTS

45ml/3 tbsp mayonnaise
15ml/1 tbsp Greek (US strained plain) yogurt
15ml/1 tbsp mild curry paste
90ml/6 tbsp single (light) cream
½ iceberg lettuce
2 chicory (Belgian endive) heads
50g/2oz/½ cup cashew nuts
50g/2oz/1¼ cups flaked coconut
2 red eating apples
75g/3oz/⅓ cup currants

SERVES 4

1 Mix the mayonnaise, yogurt, curry paste and single cream in a small bowl. Cover with clear film (plastic wrap) and chill in the refrigerator until required.

2 Tear the lettuce into pieces and put into a mixing bowl.

3 Cut the root end off each head of chicory, separate the leaves and add them to the lettuce. Preheat the grill (broiler).

4 Spread out the cashew nuts on a baking sheet and grill (broil) for 2 minutes, until golden. Tip into a bowl and set aside. Spread out the coconut on a baking sheet. Grill for 1 minute, until golden.

5 Quarter the apples and cut out the cores. Thinly slice the apples and add them to the lettuce with the toasted coconut and cashew nuts and the currants.

6 Spoon the dressing over the salad, toss lightly and serve.

Variation

For an even more colourful salad, use 1 head chicory (Belgian endive) and 1 head radicchio, and substitute 1 green eating apple for 1 of the red ones.

Cook's Tip

Watch the coconut flakes and cashew nuts with great care when they are under the grill (broiler), as they brown very fast and can burn easily.

FENNEL, ORANGE AND ROCKET SALAD

. . .

This light and refreshing salad is an ideal accompaniment to serve with spicy or rich foods.

INGREDIENTS

2 oranges
1 fennel bulb
115g/4oz rocket (arugula) leaves
50g/2oz/½ cup black olives

FOR THE DRESSING
30ml/2 tbsp extra virgin olive oil
15ml/1 tbsp balsamic vinegar
1 small garlic clove, crushed
salt and freshly ground
black pepper

SERVES 4

1 With a vegetable peeler, cut thin strips of rind from the oranges, making sure that you leave the pith behind. Cut the rind into thin julienne strips. Cook in a small pan of boiling water for a few minutes, then drain.

2 Peel the oranges, removing all the white pith. Slice them into thin rounds and discard any seeds.

3 Cut the fennel bulb in half lengthways with a sharp knife. Slice across the bulb as thinly as possible, using a food processor fitted with a slicing disc. Alternatively, use a mandolin.

4 Combine the oranges and fennel in a serving bowl and toss with the rocket leaves. Mix together the oil, vinegar and garlic and season to taste with salt and pepper. Pour over the salad, toss well and leave to stand for a few minutes. Sprinkle with the olives and strips of orange and serve.

AUBERGINE, LEMON AND CAPER SALAD

. . .

This cooked vegetable relish is delicious served as an accompaniment to cold meats, with pasta, or simply on its own with some good, crusty bread. Make sure the aubergine is well cooked until it is meltingly soft.

INGREDIENTS

1 large aubergine (eggplant), about
675g/1½lb
60ml/4 tbsp olive oil
grated rind and juice of 1 lemon
30ml/2 tbsp capers, rinsed
12 pitted green olives
30ml/2 tbsp chopped fresh
flat leaf parsley
salt and freshly ground
black pepper

SERVES 4

1 Cut the aubergine into 2.5cm/ 1in cubes. Heat the olive oil in a large, heavy frying pan and cook the aubergine cubes over a medium heat for about 10 minutes, tossing regularly, until golden and softened. You may need to do this in two batches. Drain on kitchen paper and sprinkle with a little salt.

2 Place the aubergine cubes in a large serving bowl. Toss with the lemon rind and juice, capers, olives and chopped parsley, and season well with salt and pepper. Serve at room temperature.

Cook's Tip

This will taste even better when made the day before. It will store, covered, in the refrigerator for up to 4 days.

APPLE COLESLAW

• • •

There are many variations of this Dutch salad; this recipe combines the sweet flavours of apple and carrot with celery salt. Coleslaw is traditionally served with ham.

INGREDIENTS
450g/1lb white cabbage
1 medium onion
2 eating apples, peeled and cored
175g/6oz carrots, peeled
150ml/¼ pint/⅔ cup mayonnaise
5ml/1 tsp celery salt
freshly ground black pepper

SERVES 4

1 Discard the outside leaves of the white cabbage if they are dirty or damaged. Cut the cabbage into 5cm/2in wedges, then remove the stem sections.

2 Feed the cabbage wedges and the onion through a food processor fitted with a slicing blade. Change to a grating blade and grate the apples and carrots. Alternatively use a vegetable slicer and a hand grater for the apples and carrots.

3 Combine all the salad ingredients in a large serving bowl. Fold in the mayonnaise and season with the celery salt and black pepper.

> ### Variation
> For a richer coleslaw, add 115g/4oz/½ cup grated Cheddar cheese. You may find you will need smaller portions, as the cheese makes a more filling dish.

CARROT, RAISIN AND APRICOT COLESLAW

. . .

*This colourful salad combines
cabbage, carrots and dried fruit.*

INGREDIENTS

*350g/12oz white cabbage,
finely shredded
225g/8oz carrots, grated
1 red onion, thinly sliced
3 celery sticks, sliced
175g/6oz/generous 1 cup raisins
75g/3oz/³⁄₄ cup dried apricots,
chopped*

FOR THE DRESSING

*120ml/4fl oz/¹⁄₂ cup mayonnaise
90ml/6 tbsp natural (plain) yogurt
30ml/2 tbsp chopped fresh herbs
salt and freshly ground
black pepper*

SERVES 6

1 Put the cabbage and carrots in a
large bowl.

2 Add the sliced onion, sliced
celery, raisins and chopped apricots
and mix well.

3 In a small bowl, mix together the
mayonnaise, yogurt and chopped
herbs and season to taste with salt
and black pepper.

4 Add the mayonnaise dressing to
the coleslaw ingredients and toss
together to mix. Cover with clear
film (plastic wrap) and chill in the
refrigerator before serving.

Variation

Substitute other dried fruit,
such as sultanas (golden
raisins) and ready-to-eat dried
pears or peaches.

FENNEL COLESLAW

* * *

The flavour of fennel plays a major role in this coleslaw.

INGREDIENTS

175g/6oz fennel
2 spring onions (scallions), plus
extra to garnish
175g/6oz white cabbage
115g/4oz celery
175g/6oz carrots
50g/2oz/scant ½ cup sultanas
(golden raisins)
2.5ml/½ tsp caraway seeds
15ml/1 tbsp chopped fresh parsley
45ml/3 tbsp extra virgin olive oil
5ml/1 tsp lemon juice

SERVES 4

3 Stir in the chopped parsley, olive oil and lemon juice and mix all the ingredients very thoroughly. Cover and chill for 3 hours to allow the flavours to mingle. Shred the spring onion for the garnish and sprinkle it over the coleslaw before serving.

1 Using a sharp knife, cut the fennel bulb and spring onions into thin slices.

2 Slice the cabbage and celery thinly and cut the carrots into fine strips. Place them in a serving bowl together with the sliced fennel and spring onions. Add the sultanas and caraway seeds and toss lightly to mix.

BEANSPROUT AND MOOLI SALAD

Ribbon-thin slices of fresh, crisp vegetables and beansprouts are served with an Asian dressing.

INGREDIENTS
225g/8oz/1 cup beansprouts
1 cucumber
2 carrots
1 small mooli (daikon)
1 small red onion, thinly sliced
2.5cm/1in fresh root ginger, cut into thin matchsticks
1 red chilli, seeded and thinly sliced
1 bunch fresh coriander (cilantro)

FOR THE ASIAN DRESSING
15ml/1 tbsp rice wine vinegar
15ml/1 tbsp light soy sauce
15ml/1 tbsp Thai fish sauce
1 garlic clove, finely chopped
15ml/1 tbsp sesame oil
45ml/3 tbsp groundnut (peanut) oil
30ml/2 tbsp sesame seeds, lightly toasted

SERVES 4

1 First make the dressing. Place all the dressing ingredients in a bottle or screw-top jar and shake well.

Cook's Tip
The dressing may be made in advance and will keep well for a couple of days if stored in the refrigerator or a cool place.

2 Wash the beansprouts and drain thoroughly in a colander. If you like, blanch them in boiling water for 1 minute, drain refresh under cold water and drain again.

3 Peel the cucumber, cut in half lengthways and scoop out the seeds. Peel the cucumber flesh into long ribbon strips using a vegetable peeler or mandolin.

4 Peel the carrots and mooli into long strips in the same way as for the cucumber.

5 Place the carrots, radish and cucumber in a large, shallow serving dish, add the onion, ginger, chilli and coriander and toss to mix. Pour the dressing over the salad just before serving and toss lightly again.

TZATZIKI

· · ·

Tzatziki is a Greek cucumber salad dressed with yogurt, mint and garlic. It is typically served with grilled lamb and chicken, but is also good with salmon and trout.

INGREDIENTS

1 cucumber
5ml/1 tsp salt
45ml/3 tbsp finely chopped fresh mint, plus a few sprigs to garnish
1 garlic clove, crushed
5ml/1 tsp caster (superfine) sugar
200ml/7fl oz/scant 1 cup Greek (US strained plain) yogurt
paprika, to garnish (optional)

SERVES 4

1 Peel the cucumber. Reserve a little to use as a garnish, if you like, and cut the remainder in half, lengthways. Remove the seeds with a teaspoon and discard. Slice the cucumber thinly and combine with the salt. Set aside for about 15–20 minutes. The salt will soften the cucumber and draw out any bitter juices.

2 Place the chopped mint, garlic, sugar and yogurt in a bowl. Stir well to combine.

3 Rinse the cucumber in a sieve under cold running water to wash away the salt. Drain well and combine with the yogurt mixture in a serving bowl. Decorate with sprigs of mint. Garnish with paprika, if you like.

Cook's Tip
If preparing tzatziki in a hurry, do not salt the cucumber. The cucumber will have a more crunchy texture, and will be slightly less sweet.

MARINATED CUCUMBER SALAD

A lovely cooling salad, with the distinctive flavour of fresh dill.

INGREDIENTS

2 medium cucumbers
15ml/1 tbsp salt
90g/3½oz/½ cup sugar
175ml/6fl oz/¾ cup dry (hard) cider
15ml/1 tbsp cider vinegar
45ml/3 tbsp chopped fresh dill
freshly ground black pepper

SERVES 4–6

1 Slice the cucumbers thinly and place them in a colander, sprinkling salt between each layer. Put the colander over a bowl and leave to drain for 1 hour.

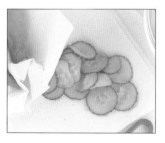

2 Thoroughly rinse the cucumber under cold running water to remove excess salt, then pat dry with kitchen paper.

3 Gently heat the sugar, cider and vinegar in a pan, until the sugar has dissolved. Remove from the heat and leave to cool. Put the cucumber slices in a bowl, pour over the cider mixture and leave to marinate for 2 hours.

Cook's Tip
The salad would be a perfect accompaniment for poached fresh salmon.

4 Drain the cucumber well and discard the marinade. Sprinkle the cucumber with the dill and pepper to taste. Mix well and transfer to a serving dish. Cover with clear film (plastic wrap) and chill in the refrigerator until ready to serve.

FLOWER GARDEN SALAD

· · ·

*Dress a colourful mixture of
salad leaves with olive oil and
lemon juice, then top it with
crispy bread crostini.*

INGREDIENTS

*3 thick slices day-old bread
120ml/4fl oz/¹/₂ cup extra virgin
olive oil
1 garlic clove, halved
¹/₂ small cos or romaine lettuce
¹/₂ small oak-leaf lettuce
25g/1oz rocket (arugula) leaves
25g/1oz fresh flat leaf parsley
a small handful of young
dandelion leaves
juice of 1 lemon
a few nasturtium leaves
and flowers
pansy and pot marigold flowers
sea salt flakes and freshly ground
black pepper*

SERVES 4–6

3 Tear all the salad leaves into
bitesize pieces and pile them into
the bowl with the oil. Season to
taste with salt and pepper. Cover
and keep chilled until you are
ready to serve the salad.

4 To serve, toss the leaves in the oil
in the base of the bowl, then
sprinkle with the lemon juice and
toss again. Scatter the crostini and
the leaves and flowers over the top
and serve immediately.

1 Cut the slices of bread into
1cm/¹/₂in cubes. Heat half the olive
oil in a heavy frying pan and fry
the bread cubes over a medium-low
heat, tossing and turning them
until they are well coated and
lightly browned. Remove and cool.

2 Rub the inside of a large salad
bowl with the cut sides of the garlic
clove, then discard the clove. Pour
the remaining olive oil into the
base of the bowl.

FRESH SPINACH AND AVOCADO SALAD

Young spinach leaves make a change from lettuce. They are delicious served with avocado, cherry tomatoes and radishes in an unusual tofu sauce.

INGREDIENTS

1 large avocado
juice of 1 lime
225g/8oz baby spinach leaves
115g/4oz cherry tomatoes
4 spring onions (scallions), sliced
1/2 cucumber
50g/2oz radishes, sliced

FOR THE DRESSING
115g/4oz soft silken tofu
45ml/3 tbsp milk
10ml/2 tsp mustard
2.5ml/1/2 tsp white wine vinegar
cayenne pepper
salt and freshly ground
black pepper
radish roses and fresh herb sprigs,
to garnish

SERVES 2–3

1 Cut the avocado in half, remove the stone (pit) and peel. Cut the flesh into slices. Transfer to a plate, and drizzle over the lime juice.

2 Wash and dry the baby spinach leaves. Put them in a mixing bowl.

3 Cut the larger cherry tomatoes in half and add all the tomatoes to the mixing bowl with the spring onions. Cut the cucumber into chunks and add to the bowl with the sliced radishes.

Cook's Tip
Use soft silken tofu rather than the firm block variety. It can be found in most supermarkets in small long-life cartons.

4 To make the dressing, put the tofu, milk, mustard, white wine vinegar and a pinch of cayenne pepper in a blender or food processor. Season with salt and pepper to taste. Process for 30 seconds, until smooth.

5 Scrape the dressing into a bowl and add a little extra milk if you like a thinner dressing. Sprinkle with a little extra cayenne, garnish with radish roses and herb sprigs and serve separately. Place the avocado slices with the spinach salad on a serving dish and serve with the tofu dressing.

289

Radish, Mango and Apple Salad

• • •

*Radish is a year-round
vegetable and this salad, with
its clean, crisp tastes and
mellow flavours, can be served
at any time of year.*

INGREDIENTS
10–15 radishes
1 apple, peeled, cored and
thinly sliced
2 celery sticks, thinly sliced
1 small ripe mango
fresh dill sprigs, to garnish

FOR THE DRESSING
120ml/4fl oz/¹/2 cup sour cream
10ml/2 tsp creamed horseradish
15ml/1 tbsp chopped fresh dill
salt and freshly ground
black pepper

SERVES 4

1 To prepare the dressing, blend
together the sour cream, creamed
horseradish and dill in a small
bowl and season to taste with a
little salt and pepper.

2 Trim the radishes and slice them
thinly. Put in a medium serving
bowl together with the apple and
celery slices.

3 Halve the mango lengthways,
cutting either side of the stone (pit).
Make even, criss-cross cuts through
the flesh of each side section,
without cutting through the skin,
and bend it back to separate the
cubes. Remove the cubes with a
small knife and add to the bowl.

4 Pour the dressing over the
vegetables and fruit and stir gently
so that all the ingredients are well
coated. Garnish with dill sprigs
and serve immediately.

MANGO, TOMATO AND RED ONION SALAD

This salad makes a flavoursome appetizer or accompaniment.

INGREDIENTS

1 firm under-ripe mango
½ cucumber
2 large tomatoes, sliced
½ red onion, sliced into rings

FOR THE DRESSING

30ml/2 tbsp sunflower oil
15ml/1 tbsp lemon juice
1 garlic clove, crushed
2.5ml/½ tsp hot pepper sauce
salt and freshly ground
black pepper
chopped chives, to garnish

SERVES 4

1 Halve the mango lengthways, cutting either side of the stone (pit). Cut the flesh into slices and peel off the skin.

2 Peel and slice the cucumber very thinly with a sharp knife. Arrange the slices of mango, tomato, red onion and cucumber decoratively on a large serving plate.

3 Blend the sunflower oil, lemon juice, garlic and pepper sauce in a blender or food processor, or place in a small screw-top jar and shake vigorously. Season to taste with salt and pepper.

4 Pour the dressing over the salad and serve immediately garnished with chopped chives.

ORANGE AND WATER CHESTNUT SALAD

· · ·

Crunchy water chestnuts combine with radicchio and oranges in this unusual salad.

INGREDIENTS

1 red onion, thinly sliced into rings
2 oranges, peeled and cut
into segments
1 can drained water chestnuts,
peeled and cut into strips
2 radicchio heads, cored
45ml/3 tbsp chopped fresh parsley
45ml/3 tbsp chopped fresh basil
15ml/1 tbsp white wine vinegar
50ml/2fl oz/¼ cup walnut oil
salt and freshly ground
black pepper
1 fresh basil sprig, to garnish

SERVES 4

1 Put the onion in a colander and sprinkle with 5ml/1 tsp salt. Leave to drain for 15 minutes.

2 In a large mixing bowl combine the oranges and water chestnuts.

3 Spread out the radicchio leaves in a large, shallow bowl or on a serving platter to make a bed for the salad.

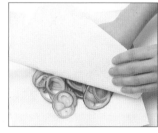

4 Rinse the onion to remove excess salt and dry on kitchen paper. Add to the mixing bowl and toss it with the water chestnuts and oranges.

5 Arrange the water chestnut, orange and onion mixture on top of the radicchio leaves. Sprinkle with the chopped parsley and basil.

6 Put the white wine vinegar, walnut oil and salt and pepper to taste in a screw-top jar and shake vigorously to combine. Pour the dressing over the salad and serve immediately, garnished with a sprig of basil.

COLESLAW WITH PESTO MAYONNAISE

Both the pesto and the mayonnaise can be made for this dish, but if time is short, buy them ready-prepared.

INGREDIENTS
1 small white cabbage
3–4 carrots, grated
4 spring onions (scallions), sliced
25–40 g/1–1½oz/¼–⅓ cup
pine nuts
15ml/1 tbsp chopped fresh mixed
herbs such as parsley, basil, chervil

FOR THE PESTO MAYONNAISE
1 egg yolk
about 10ml/2 tsp lemon juice
200ml/7fl oz/scant 1 cup
sunflower oil
10ml/2 tsp pesto
60ml/4 tbsp natural (plain) yogurt
salt and freshly ground
black pepper

SERVES 4–6

1 To make the mayonnaise, place the egg yolk in a blender or food processor and process with the lemon juice. With the machine running, gradually add the oil. As the mayonnaise emulsifies, add it more quickly in a steady stream.

2 Season to taste with salt and pepper and a little more lemon juice if necessary. Alternatively, make the mayonnaise by hand using a balloon whisk and adding the oil drop by drop.

3 Spoon 75ml/5 tbsp of the mayonnaise into a bowl and stir in the pesto and yogurt, beating well until thoroughly combined into a fairly thin dressing.

4 Remove the outer leaves of the cabbage and discard. Using a food processor or a sharp knife, thinly slice the cabbage and place in a large salad bowl.

5 Add the carrots and spring onions, together with the pine nuts and herbs, mixing thoroughly with your hands. Stir the pesto dressing into the salad or serve separately in a small dish.

> ### Variation
> You can also make the dressing with sun-dried tomato pesto.

PEPPER AND CUCUMBER SALAD

INGREDIENTS
1 yellow or red (bell) pepper
1 large cucumber
4–5 tomatoes
1 bunch spring
onions (scallions)
30ml/2 tbsp fresh parsley
30ml/2 tbsp fresh mint
30ml/2 tbsp fresh
coriander (cilantro)
2 pitta breads, to serve

FOR THE DRESSING
2 garlic cloves, crushed
75ml/5 tbsp olive oil
juice of 2 lemons
salt and freshly ground
black pepper

SERVES 4

1 Slice the pepper and discard the seeds and core. Coarsely chop the cucumber and tomatoes. Place in a large salad bowl.

2 Trim and slice the spring onions. Add to the cucumber, tomatoes and pepper. Finely chop the parsley, mint and coriander and add to the bowl. If you have plenty of herbs, you can add as much as you like.

3 To make the dressing, blend the garlic with the olive oil and lemon juice in a jug (pitcher), then season to taste with salt and pepper. Pour the dressing over the salad and toss lightly to mix.

4 Toast the pitta breads in a toaster or under a hot grill (broiler) until crisp and serve them with the pepper and cucumber salad.

Variation
If you like, make this eastern salad in the traditional way. After toasting the pitta breads, crush them in your hand and then sprinkle over the salad before serving.

GUACAMOLE SALSA IN RED LEAVES

∘ ∘ ∘

This is a lovely, light, summery and attractive appetizer.

INGREDIENTS

2 tomatoes
15ml/1 tbsp grated onion
1 garlic clove, crushed
1 fresh green chilli, halved, seeded
and chopped
2 ripe avocados
30ml/2 tbsp olive oil
2.5ml/½ tsp ground cumin
30ml/2 tbsp chopped fresh
coriander (cilantro) or parsley
juice of 1 lime
radicchio leaves
salt and freshly ground
black pepper
fresh coriander (cilantro) sprigs,
to garnish
crusty garlic bread and lime
wedges, to serve

SERVES 4

1 Using a sharp knife, slash a small cross on the top of the tomatoes, then place them in a bowl of boiling water for 30 seconds. The skins will slip off easily. Remove the core of each tomato and roughly chop the flesh.

2 Put the tomato flesh into a bowl together with the onion, garlic and chilli. Halve the avocados, remove the stones (pits), then scoop the flesh into the bowl, mashing it coarsely with a fork.

3 Add the oil, cumin, coriander or parsley and lime juice. Mix well and season to taste.

4 Lay the radicchio leaves on a platter and spoon in the salsa. Serve garnished with coriander sprigs and accompanied by garlic bread and lime wedges.

THAI FRUIT AND VEGETABLE SALAD

. . .

*A cooling, refreshing salad
served with a coconut dipping
sauce that has a slight kick.*

INGREDIENTS
*1 small pineapple
1 small mango, peeled and sliced
1 green apple, cored and sliced
6 lychees, peeled and
stoned (pitted)
115g/4oz green beans, trimmed
and halved
1 medium red onion, sliced
1 small cucumber, cut into
short fingers
115g/4oz/1/2 cup beansprouts
2 spring onions (scallions), sliced
1 ripe tomato, quartered
225g/8oz cos, romaine or iceberg
lettuce leaves*

FOR THE COCONUT DIPPING SAUCE
*30ml/2 tbsp coconut cream
30ml/2 tbsp sugar
75ml/5 tbsp/1/3 cup boiling water
1.5ml/1/4 tsp chilli sauce
15ml/1 tbsp Thai fish sauce
juice of 1 lime*

SERVES 4–6

1 To make the coconut dipping
sauce, put the coconut cream,
sugar and boiling water in a screw-
top jar. Add the chilli and fish
sauces and lime juice and shake.

2 Trim both ends of the pineapple
with a serrated knife, then cut
away the outer skin. Remove the

central core with an apple corer.
Alternatively, cut the pineapple
into quarters down the middle and
remove the core with a knife.
Roughly chop the pineapple and
set aside with the other fruits.

3 Bring a small pan of salted water
to the boil and cook the beans for
3–4 minutes. Refresh under cold
running water and set aside. To
serve, arrange the fruits and
vegetables in small heaps in a wide,
shallow bowl. Serve the coconut
sauce separately as a dip.

SWEET CUCUMBER COOLER

. . .

*Sweet dipping sauces such as
this bring instant relief to the
hot chilli flavours of Thai food.*

INGREDIENTS
*5 tbsp water
2 tbsp sugar
1/2 tsp salt
1 tbsp rice or white wine vinegar
1/4 small cucumber
2 shallots, or 1 small red onion*

MAKES 120ML/4FL OZ/1/2 CUP

1 With a small sharp knife, thinly
slice the cucumber and cut into
quarters. Thinly slice the shallots
or red onion.

2 Measure the water, sugar, salt
and vinegar into a stainless steel or
enamel pan, bring to the boil and
simmer, stirring constantly, until
the sugar has dissolved, for less
than 1 minute.

3 Remove the pan from the heat
and set aside to cool. Add the
cucumber and shallots or onion
and serve at room temperature.

TRICOLOUR SALAD

• • •

This can be a simple appetizer if
served on individual salad
plates, or part of a light buffet
meal laid out on a platter.

INGREDIENTS

1 small red onion, thinly sliced
6 large full-flavoured tomatoes
extra virgin olive oil, to sprinkle
50g/2oz rocket (arugula) or
watercress leaves,
coarsely chopped
175g/6oz mozzarella cheese, thinly
sliced or grated
30ml/2 tbsp pine nuts (optional)
salt and freshly ground
black pepper

SERVES 4–6

1 Soak the onion slices in a bowl
of cold water for 30 minutes, then
drain well and pat thoroughly dry
with kitchen paper.

2 Peel the tomatoes by cutting a
cross in the skin and plunging into
boiling water for 30 seconds: the
skins can then be easily slipped off.

3 Slice the tomatoes and arrange
half on a large platter, or divide
them among small plates.

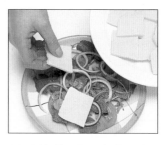

4 Sprinkle liberally with olive oil,
then layer with the chopped rocket
or watercress, onion slices and
cheese, sprinkling over more olive
oil and seasoning well with salt
and pepper between the layers.

5 Season well with more salt and
pepper to finish and complete
with a drizzle of oil and a good
sprinkling of pine nuts, if you like.
Cover the salad with clear film
(plastic wrap) and chill in the
refrigerator for at least 2 hours
before serving.

TUSCAN TUNA AND BEAN SALAD

A great pantry dish which can be put together in very little time. Served with fresh bread, it is a meal in itself.

INGREDIENTS
1 red onion
30ml/2 tbsp French mustard
300ml/½ pint/1¼ cups olive oil
60ml/4 tbsp white wine vinegar
30ml/2 tbsp chopped fresh parsley
30ml/2 tbsp chopped fresh chives
30ml/2 tbsp chopped fresh
tarragon or chervil
400g/14oz can haricot (navy) beans
400g/14oz can kidney beans
225g/8oz canned tuna in oil,
drained and lightly flaked
fresh chives and tarragon sprigs,
to garnish

SERVES 4

1 Chop the red onion finely, using a sharp knife.

2 To make the dressing, whisk together the mustard, olive oil, wine vinegar, parsley, chives and tarragon or chervil.

3 Drain the canned haricot and kidney beans through a colander, then rinse well under cold running water and drain again.

4 Mix the chopped onion, beans and dressing together thoroughly, then carefully fold in the flaked tuna. Garnish with chives and tarragon and serve immediately.

ROCKET, PEAR AND PARMESAN SALAD

For a sophisticated start to an elaborate meal, try this simple, but delicious salad.

INGREDIENTS

3 ripe pears
10ml/2 tsp lemon juice
45ml/3 tbsp hazelnut or walnut oil
115g/4oz rocket (arugula) leaves
75g/3oz piece Parmesan cheese
freshly ground black pepper

SERVES 4

1 Peel and core the pears and slice thickly. Brush all over with lemon juice to keep the flesh white.

2 Combine the hazelnut or walnut oil with the pears in a large bowl. Add the rocket leaves and toss lightly to mix.

3 Turn the salad out on to four individual plates and top with shavings of Parmesan cheese. Season to taste with black pepper and serve immediately.

Cook's Tip

Parmesan cheese is a delicious main ingredient in a salad. Buy a chunk of fresh Parmesan and shave strips off the side, using a vegetable peeler. The distinctive flavour is quite strong. Store the rest of the Parmesan uncovered in the refrigerator.

TOMATO AND FETA CHEESE SALAD

• • •

Sweet, sun-ripened tomatoes are rarely more delicious than when served with feta cheese.

INGREDIENTS
900g/2lb tomatoes
200g/7oz feta cheese
120ml/4fl oz/¹/₂ cup olive oil
12 black olives
4 fresh basil sprigs
freshly ground black pepper

SERVES 4

2 Slice the tomatoes thickly and arrange them attractively in a shallow serving dish.

3 Crumble the feta over the tomatoes, sprinkle with oil, then strew with the olives and basil sprigs. Season to taste with pepper and serve at room temperature.

1 Carefully remove the tough cores from the tomatoes, using a small, sharp knife.

Cook's Tip
Feta cheese has a strong flavour and can be salty. The least salty variety is imported from Greece and Turkey, and is available from specialist delicatessens.

301

Using cooked ingredients, such as roasted peppers, grilled cheese, hard-boiled eggs or crispy bacon vastly increases your repertoire of side salads. This chapter is packed with delicious accompaniments to serve at dinner parties, barbecues, picnics and family suppers.

COOKED SIDE
SALADS

SIMPLE COOKED SALAD

• • •

This is a version of a popular Mediterranean recipe.

INGREDIENTS

2 tomatoes, quartered
2 onions, chopped
½ cucumber, halved lengthways,
seeded and sliced
1 green (bell) pepper, halved,
seeded and chopped

FOR THE DRESSING
30ml/2 tbsp lemon juice
45ml/3 tbsp olive oil
2 garlic cloves, crushed
30ml/2 tbsp chopped fresh
coriander (cilantro)
salt and freshly ground
black pepper

SERVES 4

1 Put the tomato quarters, onions, cucumber and green pepper into a large pan, add 60ml/4 tbsp water and bring to the boil. Lower the heat and simmer for 5 minutes. Remove the pan from the heat and leave to cool.

2 For the dressing, mix together the lemon juice, olive oil and garlic.

3 Strain the cooled vegetables, then transfer them to a serving bowl. Pour over the dressing, season to taste with salt and pepper and stir in the chopped coriander. Serve the salad immediately, garnished with coriander sprigs.

SWEET-AND-SOUR ARTICHOKE SALAD

. . .

A sweet-and-sour sauce is poured over lightly cooked summer vegetables.

INGREDIENTS

6 small globe artichokes
juice of 1 lemon
30ml/2 tbsp olive oil
2 medium onions, chopped
175g/6oz/1½ cups fresh or frozen broad (fava) beans (shelled weight)
175g/6oz/1½ cups fresh or frozen peas (shelled weight)
salt and freshly ground black pepper
fresh mint leaves, to garnish

FOR THE SWEET-AND-SOUR SAUCE
120ml/4fl oz/½ cup white wine vinegar
15ml/1 tbsp sugar
a handful of fresh mint leaves, roughly torn

SERVES 4

1 Cut off the outer leaves of the artichokes. Cut the artichokes into quarters and place them in a bowl of water with the lemon juice.

2 Heat the olive oil in a large, heavy pan and add the onions. Cook, stirring occasionally, for 10 minutes until the onions are golden. Add the beans and stir, then drain the artichokes and add to the pan. Pour in 300ml/½ pint/ 1¼ cups water and cook, covered, for a further 10–15 minutes.

3 Add the peas, season to taste with salt and pepper and cook, stirring occasionally, for a further 5 minutes, until the vegetables are tender. Strain through a sieve or colander and place all the vegetables in a bowl. Leave to cool, then cover with clear film (plastic wrap) and chill.

4 To make the sweet-and-sour sauce, mix all the ingredients in a small pan. Heat gently for about 2–3 minutes, until the sugar has dissolved. Simmer gently for about 5 minutes, stirring occasionally. Leave to cool. To serve, drizzle the sauce over the vegetables and garnish with mint leaves.

TOMATO, SAVORY AND FRENCH BEAN SALAD

• • •

Savory and beans could have been invented for each other. This salad mixes them with ripe tomatoes, making a superb accompaniment for cold meats.

INGREDIENTS

450g/1lb green beans
1kg/2¼lb ripe tomatoes
3 spring onions (scallions), sliced
15ml/1 tbsp pine nuts
4 fresh savory sprigs

FOR THE DRESSING
30ml/2 tbsp extra virgin olive oil
juice of 1 lime
75g/3oz Dolcelatte cheese
1 garlic clove, crushed
salt and freshly ground black pepper

SERVES 4

1 Prepare the dressing first so that it can stand for a while before use. Place all the dressing ingredients in the bowl of a food processor, season to taste and blend until the cheese is finely chopped and you have a smooth dressing. Pour it into a jug (pitcher).

2 Trim the beans, and cook in lightly salted boiling water until they are just cooked.

3 Drain the beans and refresh under cold running water over them until they have completely cooled. Slice the tomatoes, or, if they are fairly small, quarter them.

4 Place the beans, tomatoes and spring onions in a large bowl and toss well to mix. Pour on the dressing, sprinkle the pine nuts and savory sprigs over the top and serve immediately.

SQUASH À LA GRECQUE

This recipe, usually made with small mushrooms, also works exceptionally well with patty-pan squash.

INGREDIENTS

175g/6oz patty-pan squash
250ml/8fl oz/1 cup white wine
juice of 2 lemons
1 fresh thyme sprig
1 bay leaf
small bunch of fresh chervil,
coarsely chopped
1.5ml/¼ tsp crushed
coriander seeds
1.5ml/¼ tsp crushed
black peppercorns
75ml/5 tbsp olive oil
bay leaves, to garnish

SERVES 4

1 Blanch the patty-pan squash in boiling water for 3 minutes, then refresh them in cold water.

Variation

Try using other summer squash, such as yellow courgettes (zucchini), in this recipe.

2 Place the wine, lemon juice, thyme, bay leaf, chervil, coriander and peppercorns in a pan, add 150ml/¼ pint/⅔ cup water and simmer for 10 minutes, covered. Add the squash and cook for 10 minutes, until they are tender. Remove with a slotted spoon.

3 Reduce the liquid in the pan by boiling hard for 10 minutes. Strain and pour it over the squash. Leave until cool for the flavours to be absorbed. Serve cold, garnished with bay leaves.

WARM BROAD BEAN AND FETA SALAD

This medley of fresh-tasting salad ingredients is lovely warm or cold as an appetizer or as an accompaniment to a main course fish dish.

INGREDIENTS
900g/2lb broad (fava) beans, shelled
60ml/4 tbsp olive oil
175g/6oz fresh plum tomatoes, halved, or quartered if large
4 garlic cloves, crushed
115g/4oz firm feta cheese, cut into chunks
45ml/3 tbsp chopped fresh dill
12 black olives
salt and freshly ground black pepper
chopped fresh dill, to garnish

SERVES 4–6

1 Cook the broad beans in salted boiling water until just tender. Drain and set aside.

2 Meanwhile, heat the olive oil in a large, heavy frying pan and add the tomatoes and garlic. Cook over a low heat, gently shaking the pan and turning occasionally, until the tomatoes are just beginning to change colour.

3 Add the chunks of feta to the pan and toss the ingredients together for 1 minute. Mix with the drained beans, dill and olives and season to taste with salt and pepper. Serve warm or cold, garnished with chopped dill.

> #### Cook's Tip
> Plum tomatoes are now widely available in supermarkets fresh as well as canned. Their deep red, oval shapes are very attractive in salads and they have a sweet, rich flavour.

HALLOUMI AND GRAPE SALAD

Firm, salty halloumi cheese is fried and tossed with sweet grapes which really complement its distinctive flavour.

INGREDIENTS
150g/5oz mixed green salad leaves
75g/3oz seedless green grapes
75g/3oz seedless black grapes
250g/9oz halloumi cheese
45ml/3 tbsp olive oil
fresh young thyme leaves or fresh dill, to garnish

FOR THE DRESSING
60ml/4 tbsp olive oil
15ml/1 tbsp lemon juice
2.5ml/1/2 tsp caster (superfine) sugar
15ml/1 tbsp chopped fresh thyme
salt and freshly ground black pepper

SERVES 4

1 To make the dressing, mix together the olive oil, lemon juice and sugar. Season to taste with salt and pepper. Stir in the chopped thyme and set aside.

2 Lightly toss together the salad leaves and the green and black grapes in a large bowl, then transfer to a large serving plate.

3 Thinly slice the cheese. Heat the oil in a large, heavy frying pan. Add the cheese and fry briefly until golden on the underside. Turn the cheese with a fish slice (metal spatula) and cook the other side.

4 Arrange the cheese over the salad. Pour over the dressing and garnish with sprigs of fresh thyme or dill. Serve while the cheese is still warm, as it becomes inedibly rubbery when cold.

ROCKET AND GRILLED GOAT'S CHEESE SALAD

For this recipe, look for a cylinder-shaped cheese or for small rolls that can be cut into halves, weighing about 50g/2oz.

INGREDIENTS
15ml/1 tbsp olive oil
15ml/1 tbsp vegetable oil
4 slices French bread

FOR THE DRESSING
45ml/3 tbsp walnut oil
15ml/1 tbsp lemon juice
225g/8oz cylinder-shaped goat's cheese
generous handfuls of rocket (arugula) leaves
115g/4oz frisée lettuce leaves
salt and freshly ground black pepper

FOR THE SAUCE
45ml/3 tbsp apricot jam
60ml/4 tbsp white wine
5ml/1 tsp Dijon mustard

SERVES 4

1 Heat the oils in a frying pan and fry the bread on one side only, until lightly golden. Transfer to a plate lined with kitchen paper.

2 To make the sauce, heat the jam in a small pan until it is warm and runny, but not boiling. Push it through a sieve into a clean pan, to remove the pieces of fruit, then stir in the white wine and mustard. Heat gently and keep warm until ready to serve.

3 Blend the walnut oil and lemon juice and season to taste with a little salt and pepper.

4 Preheat the grill (broiler) a few minutes before serving the salad. Cut the goat's cheese in 50g/2oz rounds and place each piece on a piece of French bread, untoasted side up. Place under the grill and cook for 3–4 minutes, until the cheese melts.

5 Toss the rocket and frisée lettuce leaves in the walnut oil dressing and arrange attractively on four individual serving plates. When the cheese croûtons are ready, arrange one each plate, pour over a little of the apricot sauce and serve.

RUSSIAN SALAD

Russian salad became fashionable in the hotel dining rooms of the 1920s and 1930s. Originally it consisted of lightly-cooked vegetables, egg, shellfish and mayonnaise. Today we find it diced in plastic pots in supermarkets. This version recalls better days and plays on the theme of the Fabergé egg.

INGREDIENTS
115g/4oz large button
(white) mushrooms
120ml/4fl oz/1/2 cup mayonnaise
15ml/1 tbsp lemon juice
350g/12oz peeled cooked
prawns (shrimp)
1 large gherkin, chopped, or
30ml/2 tbsp capers
115g/4oz broad (fava) beans
(shelled weight)
115g/4oz small new potatoes,
scrubbed or scraped
115g/4oz young carrots, trimmed
and peeled
115g/4oz baby corn cobs
115g/4oz baby
turnips, trimmed
15ml/1 tbsp olive oil
4 eggs, hard-boiled and shelled
25g/1oz canned anchovy
fillets, drained and cut into
fine strips
ground paprika
salt and freshly ground
black pepper

SERVES 4

1 Slice the mushrooms thinly, then cut into matchsticks and place in a large bowl. Combine the mayonnaise and lemon juice. Fold the mayonnaise into the mushrooms, then add the prawns and gherkin or capers and season to taste with salt and pepper.

2 Bring a large pan of lightly salted water to the boil, add the broad beans and cook for 3 minutes. Drain and refresh under cold running water, then pinch the beans between your thumb and forefinger to release them from their tough skins.

3 Boil the potatoes for about 15 minutes, and the remaining vegetables for 6 minutes. Drain and cool under running water. Moisten the vegetables with oil and divide among four shallow bowls.

4 Spoon on the prawn mixture and place a hard-boiled egg in the centre. Decorate the egg with strips of anchovy, sprinkle with paprika and serve.

311

POACHED EGG SALAD WITH CROÛTONS

∘ ∘ ∘

*Soft poached eggs, hot croûtons
and cool, crisp salad leaves
make a great combination.*

INGREDIENTS
½ small loaf white bread
75ml/5 tbsp/⅓ cup olive oil
2 eggs
115g/4oz mixed salad leaves
2 garlic cloves, crushed
7.5ml/½ tbsp white wine vinegar
25g/1oz piece Parmesan cheese
freshly ground black pepper

SERVES 2

1 Remove the crust from the loaf
of bread. Cut the bread into 2.5cm/
1in cubes.

2 Heat 30ml/2 tbsp of the oil in a
large, heavy frying pan. Cook the
bread for about 5 minutes, tossing
the cubes occasionally, until they
are golden brown.

3 Meanwhile, bring a pan of water
to the boil. Carefully slide in the
eggs, one at a time. Gently poach
the eggs for 4 minutes until lightly
cooked and the white is just set.

4 Divide the salad leaves among
two individual plates. Remove the
croûtons from the frying pan and
arrange them over the leaves. Wipe
out the frying pan clean with
kitchen paper.

5 Heat the remaining oil in the
pan, add the garlic and vinegar and
cook over a high heat for 1 minute.
Divide the warm dressing among
the two salads.

Variation
To make garlic croûtons, heat
the oil as in step 2, then add
one chopped large garlic clove
and fry for 2 minutes, without
browning. Remove and discard
the garlic and cook the bread
cubes in the flavoured oil.

6 Place a poached egg on each
plate of salad. Sprinkle with thin
shavings of Parmesan and a little
black pepper.

Cook's Tip
Add a dash of vinegar to the
water before poaching the eggs.
This helps to keep the
whites together.

To make sure that a poached egg
has a good shape, swirl the
water with a spoon, whirlpool-
fashion, before sliding in the
egg.

Before serving, trim the edges of
the egg for a neat finish.

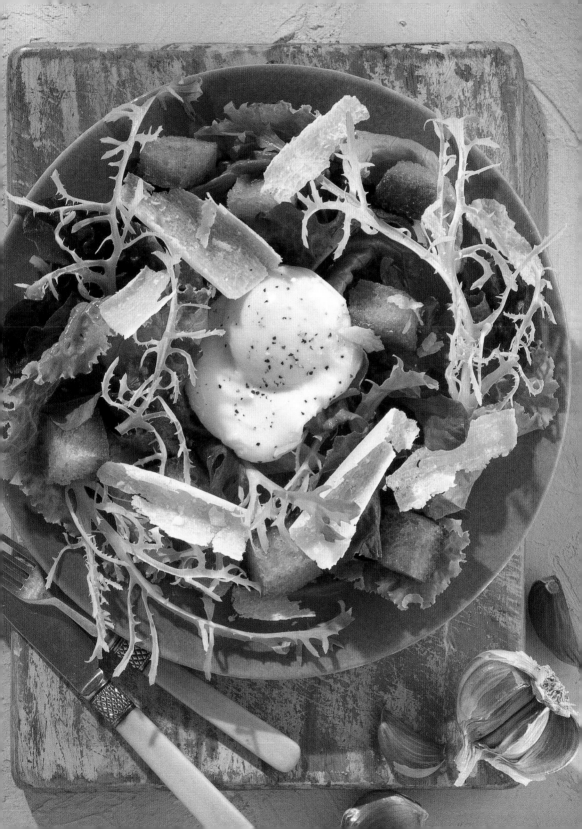

PEPPERS WITH TOMATOES AND ANCHOVIES

This is a Sicilian-style salad full of warm Mediterranean flavours. The salad improves if it is made and dressed an hour or two before serving.

INGREDIENTS

1 red (bell) pepper
1 yellow (bell) pepper
4 ripe plum tomatoes, sliced
2 canned anchovies, drained
and chopped
4 sun-dried tomatoes in oil,
drained and sliced
15ml/1 tbsp capers, drained
15ml/1 tbsp pine nuts
1 garlic clove, very finely sliced

FOR THE DRESSING
75ml/5 tbsp extra virgin olive oil
15ml/1 tbsp balsamic vinegar
5ml/1 tsp lemon juice
chopped fresh mixed herbs
salt and freshly ground
black pepper

SERVES 4

1 Preheat the grill (broiler). Cut the peppers in half and remove the seeds and stalks. Cut into quarters and grill (broil), skin-side up, until the skin chars. Transfer to a bowl, cover with kitchen paper and leave to cool. Peel the peppers and cut into strips.

2 Arrange the peppers and fresh tomatoes on a serving dish. Sprinkle over the anchovies, sun-dried tomatoes, capers, pine nuts and garlic.

3 To make the dressing, mix together the olive oil, vinegar, lemon juice and chopped fresh herbs and season with plenty of salt and pepper. Pour the dressing over the salad before serving.

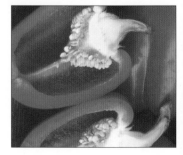

SWEET AND SOUR ONION SALAD

° ° °

This recipe for tangy, glazed onions in the Provençal style makes an unusual and flavourful accompaniment to steaks cooked on the barbecue.

INGREDIENTS

450g/1lb baby (pearl) onions
50ml/2fl oz/¼ cup wine vinegar
45ml/3 tbsp olive oil
45ml/3 tbsp caster (superfine) sugar
45ml/3 tbsp tomato purée (paste)
1 bay leaf
2 fresh parsley sprigs
65g/2½ oz/½ cup raisins
salt and freshly ground black pepper

SERVES 6

1 Put all the ingredients in a pan with 300ml/½ pint/1¼ cups water. Bring to the boil and simmer gently, uncovered, for 45 minutes, or until the onions are tender and the liquid has evaporated.

2 Remove the bay leaf and parsley, from the pan and check the seasoning. Transfer the contents of the pan to a large serving dish. Serve the salad at room temperature.

SPICED AUBERGINE SALAD

Serve this Middle-Eastern influenced salad with warm pitta bread as an appetizer, or as an accompaniment to any number of main course dishes.

INGREDIENTS

*2 small aubergines
(eggplant), sliced
75ml/5 tbsp olive oil
50ml/2fl oz/¼ cup red
wine vinegar
2 garlic cloves, crushed
15ml/1 tbsp lemon juice
2.5ml/½ tsp ground cumin
2.5ml/½ tsp ground coriander
½ cucumber, thinly sliced
2 tomatoes, thinly sliced
30ml/2 tbsp natural (plain) yogurt
salt and freshly ground
black pepper
chopped flat leaf parsley, to garnish*

SERVES 4

1 Preheat the grill (broiler). Brush the aubergine slices lightly with some of the olive oil and grill (broil) or cook over a hot barbecue until golden and tender, turning once to cook evenly. Allow the slices to cool slightly, then cut them into quarters.

2 Mix the remaining olive oil with the vinegar, crushed garlic, lemon juice, cumin and ground coriander. Season with plenty of salt and pepper and mix thoroughly. Add the warm aubergines, stir well and chill for at least 2 hours. Add the cucumber and tomatoes. Transfer the salad to a serving dish and spoon the yogurt on top. Garnish with chopped parsley to serve.

BABY AUBERGINES WITH RAISINS AND PINE NUTS

*This is a recipe with an Italian influence, in a style that would have been familiar in Renaissance
times. If possible, make it a day in advance, to allow the sweet and sour flavours to develop.*

INGREDIENTS

12 baby aubergines
(eggplant), halved
250ml/8fl oz/1 cup olive oil
juice of 1 lemon
30ml/2 tbsp balsamic vinegar
3 cloves
25g/1oz/⅓ cup pine nuts
25g/1oz/2 tbsp raisins
15ml/1 tbsp sugar
1 bay leaf
large pinch of dried chilli flakes
salt and freshly ground
black pepper

SERVES 4

1 Preheat the grill (broiler). Brush the
aubergines with olive oil and grill
(broil), turning once, for 10 minutes.

2 To make the dressing, combine
the remaining olive oil with the lemon
juice, vinegar, cloves, pine nuts, raisins,
sugar and bay leaf. Add the chilli flakes
and salt and pepper and mix well.

3 Place the hot aubergines in an
earthenware or glass bowl, and pour
over the dressing. Leave to cool,
turning the aubergines once or twice.
Serve the salad cold.

ROASTED PEPPER AND TOMATO SALAD

A lovely, colourful recipe that perfectly combines several red ingredients. Eat this dish at room temperature.

INGREDIENTS

3 red (bell) peppers
6 large plum tomatoes
2.5ml/¹/₂ tsp dried red chilli flakes
1 red onion, thinly sliced
3 garlic cloves, finely chopped
grated rind and juice of 1 lemon
45ml/3 tbsp chopped fresh flat leaf parsley
30ml/2 tbsp extra virgin olive oil
salt and freshly ground black pepper
black and green olives and extra chopped flat leaf parsley, to garnish

SERVES 4

1 Preheat the oven to 220°C/ 425°F/Gas 7. Place the peppers on a baking sheet and roast, turning occasionally, for 10 minutes or until the skins are charred and almost blackened. Add the plum tomatoes to the baking sheet and bake for 5 minutes more.

2 Place the peppers in a strong plastic bag, close the top loosely, trapping in the steam. Set aside, with the tomatoes, until cool enough to handle.

3 Carefully pull the skin off the peppers. Remove the core and seeds, then chop the peppers and tomatoes coarsely and place in a mixing bowl.

4 Add the chilli flakes, onion, garlic, lemon rind and juice. Sprinkle over the parsley. Mix well, then transfer to a serving dish. Season with salt and pepper, drizzle over the olive oil and sprinkle the olives and extra parsley over the top. Serve at room temperature.

MARINATED COURGETTES

This is a simple vegetable dish that uses the best of the season's courgettes. It can be eaten either hot or cold.

INGREDIENTS

4 courgettes (zucchini)
60ml/4 tbsp extra virgin olive oil
30ml/2 tbsp chopped fresh mint
30ml/2 tbsp white wine vinegar
salt and freshly ground black pepper
fresh mint leaves, to garnish
wholemeal (whole-wheat) Italian bread and green olives, to serve

SERVES 4

1 Cut the courgettes into thin slices. Heat 30ml/2 tbsp of the olive oil in a wide, heavy pan. Add the courgette slices in batches, and cook, stirring and turning occasionally, for 4–6 minutes, until tender and brown around the edges. Transfer the courgettes to a bowl. Season to taste with salt and black pepper.

2 Heat the remaining oil in the pan, then add the chopped mint and vinegar and let it bubble for a few seconds.

3 Pour the mint dressing over the courgettes. Cover and marinate for 1 hour, then serve garnished with mint leaves and accompanied by bread and olives.

GREEN BEAN AND SWEET RED PEPPER SALAD

· · ·

INGREDIENTS

*350g/12oz cooked green
beans, quartered
2 red (bell) peppers, seeded
and chopped
2 spring onions (scallions), both
white and green parts chopped
1 or more drained pickled serrano
chillies, well rinsed, seeded
and chopped
1 iceberg lettuce, shredded, or
mixed salad leaves
green olives, to garnish*

FOR THE DRESSING
*45ml/3 tbsp red wine vinegar
135ml/9 tbsp olive oil
salt and freshly ground
black pepper*

SERVES 4

1 Place the cooked green beans, peppers, spring onions and pickled chilli(es) in a salad bowl and toss lightly to mix.

2 To make the dressing, pour the vinegar into a bowl or jug (pitcher). Add salt and pepper to taste, then gradually whisk in the olive oil until well combined.

3 Pour the dressing over the prepared vegetables and toss lightly together to mix well and coat them all thoroughly.

4 Line a large serving platter with the shredded lettuce or mixed salad leaves and arrange the vegetable mixture attractively on top. Garnish with the olives and serve.

GREEN GREEN SALAD

. . .

Even with frozen vegetables you would still get a pretty salad.

INGREDIENTS
175g/6oz shelled broad (fava) beans
115g/4oz green beans, quartered
115 g/4oz mangetouts (snow peas)
8–10 small fresh mint leaves
3 spring onions (scallions), chopped

FOR THE DRESSING
60ml/4 tbsp green olive oil
15ml/1 tbsp cider vinegar
15ml/1 tbsp chopped fresh mint
1 garlic clove, crushed
salt and freshly ground
black pepper

SERVES 4

1 Plunge the broad beans into a pan of boiling water and bring back to the boil. Remove from the heat immediately and plunge into cold water. Drain. Repeat with the green beans.

Cook's Tip
Frozen broad (fava) beans are a good stand-by, but for this salad it is worth shelling fresh beans for the extra flavour.

2 In a large bowl, combine the blanched broad beans and green beans with the raw mangetouts, mint leaves and spring onions.

3 In another bowl, mix together the olive oil, cider vinegar, chopped or dried mint, garlic and seasoning. Pour over the salad and toss well. Cover with clear film (plastic wrap) and chill until ready to serve.

LEEK AND EGG SALAD

• • •

Smooth-textured leeks are especially delicious warm when partnered with an earthy sauce of parsley, olive oil and walnuts.

INGREDIENTS
*675g/1½ lb young leeks
1 egg
fresh parsley sprigs, to garnish*

FOR THE DRESSING
*25g/1oz/1 cup fresh parsley
30ml/2 tbsp olive oil
juice of ½ lemon
50g/2oz/½ cup broken
walnuts, toasted
5ml/1 tsp caster (superfine) sugar
salt and freshly ground
black pepper*

SERVES 4

1 Bring a pan of salted water to the boil. Cut the leeks into 10cm/4in lengths and rinse well to flush out any grit or soil. Cook the leeks for 8 minutes. Drain and partially cool under cold running water.

2 Lower the egg into boiling water and cook for 12 minutes. Cool under cold running water, shell and set aside.

3 Meanwhile, to make the salad dressing, finely chop the parsley in a food processor. Alternatively, use a sharp knife or mezzaluna.

4 If you have chopped the parsley by hand, transfer it to a food processor. Add the olive oil, lemon juice and toasted walnuts to the food processor. Process for about 1–2 minutes, until smooth.

5 Adjust the consistency with about 90ml/6 tbsp water. Add the sugar and season to taste with salt and pepper.

6 Place the leeks on an attractive plate, then spoon on the sauce. Finely grate the hard-boiled egg and sprinkle it over the sauce. Garnish with the reserved parsley sprigs and serve immediately.

Cook's Tip
While raw and lightly cooked eggs increase the risk of salmonella and may be inadvisable for vulnerable people, such as the young, the elderly, pregnant women and invalids, to eat, hard-boiled eggs are quite safe.

WINTER VEGETABLE SALAD

* * *

*Mixed vegetables are flavoured
with white wine and herbs.*

INGREDIENTS

*175ml/6fl oz/³/₄ cup white wine
5ml/1 tsp olive oil
30ml/2 tbsp lemon juice
2 bay leaves
1 fresh thyme sprig
4 juniper berries
450g/1 lb leeks, trimmed and cut
into 2.5cm/1in lengths
1 small cauliflower, broken
into florets
4 celery sticks, sliced diagonally
30ml/2 tbsp chopped fresh parsley
salt and freshly ground
black pepper*

SERVES 4

1 Put the white wine, olive oil, lemon juice, bay leaves, thyme and juniper berries into a large, heavy pan and bring to the boil. Lower the heat, cover and simmer for 20 minutes.

2 Add the leeks, cauliflower and celery. Simmer very gently for 5–6 minutes, or until just tender.

3 Remove the vegetables with a slotted spoon and transfer them to a serving dish. Briskly boil the cooking liquid for 15–20 minutes, or until reduced by half. Strain through a sieve.

4 Stir the parsley into the liquid and season to taste with salt and pepper. Pour over the vegetables and leave to cool. Chill in the refrigerator for at least 1 hour before serving.

Cook's Tip

Vary the vegetables
for this salad according to
the season.

AVOCADO AND SMOKED FISH SALAD

· · ·

*Avocado and smoked fish make
a good combination.*

INGREDIENTS

*2 avocados
¹/₂ cucumber
15ml/1 tbsp lemon juice
2 firm tomatoes
1 fresh green chilli
salt and freshly ground
black pepper*

FOR THE FISH
*15g/¹/₂oz/1 tbsp butter
¹/₂ onion, thinly sliced
5ml/1 tsp mustard seeds
225g/8oz smoked mackerel, flaked
30ml/2 tbsp fresh chopped
coriander (cilantro) leaves
2 firm tomatoes, peeled
and chopped
15ml/1 tbsp lemon juice*

SERVES 4

1 For the fish, melt the butter in a frying pan, add the onion and mustard seeds and cook for about 5 minutes, until the onion is soft.

2 Add the mackerel, chopped coriander, tomatoes and lemon juice and cook over a low heat for 2–3 minutes. Remove from the heat and leave to cool.

3 To make the salad, cut the avocados in half and remove the stones (pits). Peel and slice the flesh thinly. Peel the cucumber thinly. Place together in a bowl and sprinkle with the lemon juice. Slice the tomatoes and seed them. Finely chop the chilli.

4 Place the fish mixture in the centre of a serving plate.

5 Arrange the avocados, cucumber and tomatoes decoratively around the outside. Alternatively, spoon a quarter of the fish mixture on to each of four serving plates and divide the avocados, cucumber and tomatoes equally among them. Sprinkle with the chopped chilli, season to taste with a little salt and pepper and serve.

Variation
Smoked haddock or cod can also be used in this salad, or a mixture of smoked mackerel and haddock.

TOMATO AND BREAD SALAD

• • •

This salad, which conveniently uses up stale bread, is best made with sun-ripened tomatoes.

INGREDIENTS
400g/14oz stale white bread
4 large tomatoes
1 large red onion or
6 spring onions (scallions)
a few fresh basil leaves, to garnish

FOR THE DRESSING
60ml/4 tbsp extra virgin olive oil
30ml/2 tbsp white wine vinegar
salt and freshly ground
black pepper

SERVES 4

1 Thickly slice the bread. Place in a shallow bowl, cover with cold water and set aside for 30 minutes.

2 Cut the tomatoes into chunks and place in a serving bowl. Thinly slice the onion or spring onions and add them to the tomatoes. Squeeze as much water out of the bread as possible and add it to the bowl of vegetables.

3 To make the dressing, mix the oil and vinegar. Season to taste with salt and pepper, pour over the salad and mix well. Garnish with the basil leaves. Leave to stand in a cool place for at least 2 hours before serving.

GRILLED PEPPER SALAD

• • •

Ideally, this salad should be made with a combination of red and yellow peppers for the most jewel-like, colourful effect and the sweetest flavour.

INGREDIENTS
4 large (bell) peppers, red or yellow
or a combination of both
30ml/2 tbsp capers, rinsed
18–20 black or green olives

FOR THE DRESSING
90ml/6 tbsp extra virgin olive oil
2 garlic cloves, finely chopped
30ml/2 tbsp balsamic or red
wine vinegar
salt and freshly ground
black pepper

SERVES 6

1 Place the peppers under a hot grill and turn occasionally until they are black and blistered on all sides. Remove from the heat, place in a strong plastic bag and close the top loosely. Set aside until they are cool enough to handle. Carefully peel the peppers, then cut them into quarters. Remove and discard the stems and seeds.

2 Cut the peppers into strips, and arrange them on a serving dish. Distribute the capers and olives evenly over the peppers.

3 For the dressing, mix the oil and garlic in a small bowl, crushing the garlic with a spoon to release the flavour. Mix in the vinegar and season to taste with salt and pepper. Pour over the salad, mix well and leave to stand for at least 30 minutes before serving.

FRISÉE LETTUCE SALAD WITH BACON

. . .

INGREDIENTS

50g/2oz white bread
225g/8oz frisée lettuce or
escarole leaves
75–90ml/5–6 tbsp extra virgin
olive oil
175g/6oz piece smoked bacon,
diced, or
6 thick-cut smoked bacon rashers
(strips), cut crossways into
thin strips
1 small garlic clove, finely chopped
15ml/1 tbsp red wine vinegar
10ml/2 tsp Dijon mustard
salt and freshly ground
black pepper

SERVES 4

1 Remove and discard the crusts, then cut the bread into small cubes. Tear the frisée lettuce or escarole into bitesize pieces and put into a salad bowl.

2 Heat 15ml/1 tbsp of the oil in a medium, non-stick frying pan over a medium-low heat and add the bacon. Fry gently until well browned, stirring occasionally. Remove the bacon with a slotted spoon and drain on kitchen paper.

3 Add another 30ml/2 tbsp of the oil to the pan and fry the bread cubes over a medium-high heat, turning frequently, until evenly browned. Remove the bread cubes with a slotted spoon and drain well on kitchen paper. Discard any remaining fat.

4 Stir the garlic, vinegar and mustard into the pan with the remaining oil and heat until just warm, whisking to combine. Season to taste with salt and pepper, then pour the dressing over the salad and sprinkle with the fried bacon and croûtons. Serve immediately while still warm.

ASPARAGUS AND ORANGE SALAD

A slightly unusual combination of ingredients with a simple olive oil dressing.

INGREDIENTS

225g/8oz asparagus, trimmed and
cut into 5cm/2in lengths
2 large oranges
2 well-flavoured tomatoes, cut
into eighths
50g/2oz cos or romaine
lettuce leaves
30ml/2 tbsp extra virgin olive oil
2.5ml/½ tsp sherry vinegar
salt and freshly ground
black pepper

SERVES 4

1 Cook the asparagus in lightly salted boiling water for about 3–4 minutes, until just tender. Drain and refresh under cold water, then leave on one side to cool.

2 Grate the rind from half an orange and reserve. Working over a bowl to catch the juice, peel both the oranges and cut them into segments by slicing between the membranes with a small, sharp knife. Squeeze the juice from the membrane and reserve.

3 Put the asparagus, orange segments, tomatoes and lettuce into a salad bowl.

4 Mix together the olive oil and sherry vinegar, and add 15ml/ 1 tbsp of the reserved orange juice.

5 Add 5ml/1 tsp of the grated rind. Season to taste with salt and pepper. Just before serving, pour the dressing over the salad and mix gently to coat all the ingredients.

Cook's Tip

The cooking time for the asparagus will vary depending on the thickness of the stems. Thick stems can take as long as 10 minutes.

HARD-BOILED EGGS WITH TUNA SAUCE

* * *

*A tasty tuna mayonnaise
poured over hard-boiled eggs
makes a nourishing first course
that is quick to prepare.*

INGREDIENTS
*6 extra large eggs
200g/7oz can tuna in olive oil
3 canned anchovy fillets
15ml/1 tbsp capers, drained
30ml/2 tbsp lemon juice
60ml/4 tbsp olive oil
salt and freshly ground
black pepper
capers and anchovy fillets,
to garnish*

FOR THE MAYONNAISE
*1 egg yolk
5ml/1 tsp Dijon mustard
5ml/1 tsp white wine vinegar or
lemon juice
150ml/¼ pint/⅔ cup olive oil*

SERVES 6

1 Boil the eggs for 12–14 minutes.
Cool them under cold water. Shell
the eggs carefully and set aside.

2 Make the mayonnaise by
whisking the egg yolk, mustard and
vinegar or lemon juice together.

3 Whisk in the olive oil, a few
drops at a time to begin with, until
3–4 tablespoons have been fully
incorporated. Then pour in the
remaining oil in a slow, steady
stream, whisking constantly.

4 Place the tuna with the oil from
the can, the anchovies, capers,
lemon juice and olive oil in a
blender or food processor. Process
until the mixture is smooth.

5 Fold the tuna mixture carefully
into the mayonnaise. Season to
taste with black pepper, and salt if
necessary. Cover with clear film
(plastic wrap) and chill in the
refrigerator for at least 1 hour.

6 Cut the hard-boiled eggs in half
lengthways. Arrange on a serving
platter. Spoon on the mayonnaise
and garnish with capers and
anchovy fillets. Serve chilled.

ARTICHOKE AND EGG SALAD

∘ ∘ ∘

Artichoke hearts are best when cut from fresh artichokes, but can also be bought frozen.

INGREDIENTS

4 large artichokes or 4 frozen artichoke hearts, thawed
½ lemon
4 eggs, hard-boiled
fresh parsley sprigs, to garnish

FOR THE MAYONNAISE

1 egg yolk
10ml/2 tsp Dijon mustard
15ml/1 tbsp white wine vinegar
250ml/8fl oz/1 cup olive oil
30ml/2 tbsp chopped fresh parsley
salt and freshly ground black pepper

SERVES 4

1 If using fresh artichokes, wash them. Squeeze the lemon and put the juice and the squeezed half in a bowl of cold water.

2 Prepare the artichokes one at a time. Cut off only the tip from the stem. Peel the stem with a small knife, pulling upwards towards the leaves. Pull off the small leaves around the stem and continue snapping off the upper part of the dark outer leaves until you reach the taller inner leaves. Cut the tops off the leaves with a sharp knife. Place the artichoke in the acidulated water to prevent it from discolouring. Repeat the process with the other artichokes.

3 Boil or steam fresh artichokes until just tender (when a leaf comes away quite easily when pulled). Cook frozen artichoke hearts according to the packet instructions. Remove the pan from the heat and set aside to cool.

4 To make the mayonnaise, combine the egg yolk, mustard and vinegar in a mixing bowl. Season with salt and pepper to taste. Add the oil, a few drops at a time, beating constantly with a wire whisk. When 3–4 tablespoons have been fully incorporated, add the oil in a slow, steady stream, beating constantly. When the mixture is thick and smooth, stir in the chopped parsley. Blend well. Cover and chill until needed.

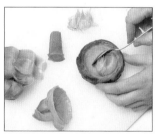

5 If using fresh artichokes, pull off the leaves. Cut the stems off level with the base. Scrape off the hairy "choke" with a knife or the side of a spoon.

6 Shell the eggs and cut them and the artichokes into wedges. Place on a serving plate, spoon the mayonnaise over the top, garnish with parsley sprigs and serve.

PANZANELLA

· · ·

Tomato juice, olive oil and wine vinegar dresses a colourful mixture of roasted peppers, anchovies and toasted ciabatta.

INGREDIENTS
225g/8oz ciabatta (about ²/3 loaf)
150ml/¹/4 pint/²/3 cup olive oil
3 red (bell) peppers
3 yellow (bell) peppers
50g/2oz can anchovy
fillets, drained
675g/1¹/2lb ripe plum tomatoes
4 garlic cloves, crushed
60ml/4 tbsp red wine vinegar
50g/2oz capers
115g/4oz/1 cup pitted black olives
salt and freshly ground
black pepper
fresh basil leaves, to garnish

SERVES 4–6

1 Preheat the oven to 200°C/ 400°F/Gas 6. Cut the ciabatta into 2cm/³/4in chunks and drizzle with 50ml/2fl oz/¹/4 cup of the oil. Grill (broil) lightly until just golden.

2 Place the peppers on a foil-lined baking sheet and bake for about 45 minutes, until the skins begin to char and blacken. Remove the peppers from the oven, place in a strong plastic bag, close the end and set aside to cool slightly.

3 Pull the skins off the peppers and cut the flesh into quarters, discarding the stalk ends and seeds. Coarsely chop the anchovies and set aside.

4 To make the tomato dressing, peel and halve the tomatoes. Scoop the seeds and pulp into a sieve set over a bowl. Using the back of a spoon, press the tomato pulp in the sieve to extract as much juice as possible. Discard the pulp and add the remaining oil, the garlic and vinegar to the juices.

5 Layer the toasted ciabatta, peppers, tomatoes, anchovies, capers and olives in a large salad bowl. Season the tomato dressing with salt and black pepper to taste and pour it over the salad. Leave to stand in a cool place for about 30 minutes. Serve garnished with plenty of fresh basil leaves.

RADICCHIO, ARTICHOKE AND WALNUT SALAD

· · ·

The distinctive, earthy taste of Jerusalem artichokes makes a lovely contrast to the sharp freshness of radicchio and lemon. Serve the salad warm or cold as an accompaniment to grilled steak or meats cooked on the barbecue.

INGREDIENTS
1 large radicchio or 150g/5oz
radicchio leaves
40g/1¹/2oz/¹/3 cup walnut pieces
45ml/3 tbsp walnut oil
500 g/1¹/4 lb Jerusalem artichokes
thinly pared rind and juice of
1 lemon
coarse sea salt and freshly ground
black pepper
fresh flat leaf parsley, to
garnish (optional)

SERVES 4

1 If using a whole radicchio, cut it into 8–10 wedges. Put the wedges or leaves in a flameproof dish. Sprinkle over the walnuts, then spoon over the oil and season to taste with salt and pepper. Grill (broil) for 2–3 minutes.

2 Peel the artichokes and cut up any large ones so that the pieces are all roughly the same size. Add the artichokes to a pan of boiling salted water with half the lemon juice and cook for 5–7 minutes, until tender. Drain well. Preheat the grill (broiler) to high.

3 Toss the artichokes into the salad with the remaining lemon juice and the pared lemon rind. Season with coarse sea salt and pepper. Grill until beginning to brown. Serve immediately garnished with torn pieces of parsley, if you like.

> *Cook's Tip*
> Look for Treviso radicchio, which has long, pointed leaves with thick white ribs. It is said to have the best flavour.

EGG, BACON AND AVOCADO SALAD

• • •

INGREDIENTS

1 large cos or romaine lettuce
8 bacon rashers (strips), fried
until crisp
2 large avocados, peeled and diced
6 hard-boiled eggs, shelled
and chopped
2 beefsteak tomatoes, peeled,
seeded and chopped
175g/6oz blue cheese, crumbled

FOR THE DRESSING
1 garlic clove, crushed
5ml/1 tsp sugar
7.5ml/1½ tsp lemon juice
25ml/1½ tbsp red wine vinegar
120ml/4fl oz/½ cup groundnut
(peanut) oil
salt and freshly ground
black pepper

SERVES 4

1 Slice the lettuce into thin strips across the leaves. Crumble the fried bacon rashers.

2 To make the dressing, combine all the ingredients in a screw-top jar, season to taste and shake well. Spread out the strips of lettuce to make a bed on a large rectangular or oval platter.

3 Arrange the diced avocados, hard-boiled eggs, tomatoes and crumbled blue cheese neatly in rows on top of the lettuce. Sprinkle the bacon on top.

4 Pour the dressing carefully and evenly all over the salad just before serving.

SPICY CORN SALAD

• • •

INGREDIENTS

30ml/2 tbsp vegetable oil
450g/1 lb drained canned
corn, or frozen corn, thawed
1 green (bell) pepper, seeded
and diced
1 small fresh red chilli, seeded
and finely diced
4 spring onions (scallions), sliced
45ml/3 tbsp chopped fresh parsley
225g/8oz cherry tomatoes, halved
salt and freshly ground
black pepper

FOR THE DRESSING
2.5ml/½ tsp sugar
30ml/2 tbsp white wine vinegar
2.5ml/½ tsp Dijon mustard
15ml/1 tbsp chopped
fresh basil
15ml/1 tbsp mayonnaise
1.5ml/¼ tsp chilli sauce

SERVES 4

1 Heat the oil in a large, heavy frying pan. Add the corn, green pepper, chilli and spring onions. Cook over a medium heat for about 5 minutes, until softened, stirring frequently.

2 Transfer the vegetables to a salad bowl. Stir in the parsley and the cherry tomatoes.

3 To make the dressing, combine all the ingredients in a small bowl and whisk together.

4 Pour the dressing over the corn mixture. Season to taste with salt and pepper. Toss well to combine, then serve immediately, while the salad is still warm.

CHORIZO IN OLIVE OIL

. . .

*Spanish chorizo sausage has a deliciously pungent taste. Frying chorizo with onions and olive oil
is one of the best ways of using it; you can also cook it on the barbecue, brushed with olive oil.*

INGREDIENTS

75ml/5 tbsp extra virgin olive oil
350g/12oz chorizo, sliced
1 large onion, thinly sliced
flat leaf parsley, coarsely chopped,
to garnish

SERVES 4

1 Heat the olive oil in a frying pan and
fry the chorizo over a high heat until
beginning to colour. Remove from the
pan with a slotted spoon.

2 Add the onion slices to the pan and
cook until golden. Return the sausage
slices to the pan to heat through for
about 1 minute.

3 Tip the mixture into a shallow
serving dish and sprinkle with the
coarsely chopped flat leaf parsley.
Serve the chorizo on its own or as
a side dish, with warm crusty bread.

Variation

Chorizo is usually available
in large supermarkets and
delicatessens, but any other
similar spicy sausage can be
used as a substitute.

BROAD BEAN, MUSHROOM AND CHORIZO SALAD

• • •

This salad can be served as a first course or as part of a buffet menu. Prepare it a day
in advance and store it in the refrigerator until needed.

INGREDIENTS

225g/8oz shelled broad (fava) beans
175g/6oz chorizo
60ml/4 tbsp extra virgin olive oil
225g/8oz brown cap
mushrooms, sliced
handful of fresh chives
salt and freshly ground
black pepper

SERVES 4

1 Cook the broad beans in a large pan
of lightly salted boiling water until just
tender. Drain and refresh under cold
running water. If the beans are large,
peel away the tough outer skins.

2 Remove the skin from the chorizo
and cut it into small chunks. Heat the
olive oil in a heavy frying pan, add the
chorizo and cook over a low heat for
2 minutes. Transfer to a bowl with
the mushrooms, mix well and set aside
to cool.

3 Chop half the chives and stir the
beans and chopped chives into the
mushroom mixture. Season to taste.
Serve the salad at room temperature,
garnished with the remaining chives.

LEEK AND GRILLED RED PEPPER SALAD WITH GOAT'S CHEESE

· · ·

The contrasting textures of silky, grilled peppers, soft cheese and slightly crisp leeks makes this salad extra-specially delicious. This would be a sophisticated first course served with plenty of fresh, crusty bread.

INGREDIENTS

4 x 1cm/¹/₂in thick slices French goat's cheese log (chèvre)
65g/2¹/₂oz/1 cup fine dry white breadcrumbs
675g/1¹/₂lb young slender leeks, trimmed
15ml/1 tbsp olive oil
2 large red (bell) peppers
few fresh thyme sprigs, chopped
vegetable oil, for shallow frying
45ml/3 tbsp chopped fresh flat leaf parsley
salt and freshly ground black pepper

FOR THE DRESSING

75ml/5 tbsp extra virgin olive oil
1 small garlic clove, finely chopped
5ml/1 tsp Dijon mustard, plain or flavoured with herbes de Provence
15ml/1 tbsp red wine vinegar

SERVES 6

1 Remove any skin from the cheese. Spread out the breadcrumbs on a plate and roll the cheese slices in them, pressing them in so that the cheese is well coated. Chill the coated cheese for 1 hour.

2 Cook the leeks in lightly salted boiling water for 3–4 minutes. Drain and cut into 7.5–10cm/3–4in lengths and toss in the olive oil and season to taste. Grill (broil) the leeks for 3–4 minutes on each side.

3 Halve and seed the peppers, then grill them, skin side uppermost, until the skin is blackened and blistered. Place them in a bowl, cover and leave to stand for about 10 minutes, so that they soften in their own steam. Remove the skin and cut the flesh into strips, then mix with the leeks and thyme, adding pepper to taste.

4 Make the dressing by shaking all the ingredients together in a screw-top jar, adding seasoning to taste. Pour the dressing over the salad and chill it for several hours. Bring the salad back to room temperature before serving.

5 When ready to serve, heat a shallow layer of vegetable oil in a non-stick frying pan and fry the goat's cheeses quickly until golden brown on each side. Drain them on kitchen paper and cool slightly, then cut into bitesize pieces. Toss the cheese and parsley into the salad and serve immediately.

ROASTED CHERRY TOMATO AND ROCKET SALAD

• • •

Little cherry tomatoes are sweet and juicy, and roasting them in the oven makes the flavour wonderfully rich and intense. Together with the pungent, fresh taste of rocket, they make an excitingly different salad.

INGREDIENTS

*225g/8oz/2 cups dried chifferini
or pipe pasta
450g/1lb ripe baby Italian plum
tomatoes, halved lengthways
75ml/5 tbsp extra virgin olive oil
2 garlic cloves, cut into thin slivers
30ml/2 tbsp balsamic vinegar
2 pieces sun-dried tomato in olive
oil, drained and chopped
large pinch of sugar
1 handful rocket (arugula), about
65g/2¹/₂oz
salt and ground black pepper*

SERVES 4

1 Preheat the oven to 190°C/375°F/ Gas 5. Meanwhile, cook the pasta in lightly salted boiling water for about 10 minutes, or according to the instructions on the packet.

2 Arrange the halved tomatoes cut side up in a roasting pan, drizzle 30ml/2 tbsp of the olive oil over them and sprinkle with the slivers of garlic. Season to taste with salt and pepper. Roast in the oven for 20 minutes, turning once.

3 Put the remaining olive oil in a large bowl with the vinegar, sun-dried tomato pieces, sugar and a little salt and pepper to taste. Stir well to mix. Drain the pasta, add it to the bowl of dressing and toss to combine. Add the roasted tomatoes and mix gently.

4 Before serving, add the rocket, toss lightly and taste for seasoning. Serve either at room temperature or chilled.

339

SALAD OF ROASTED SHALLOTS AND BUTTERNUT SQUASH WITH FETA CHEESE

• • •

This is especially good served with a grain or starchy salad, made with rice or couscous, for example. Serve plenty of good bread to mop up the juices.

INGREDIENTS

75ml/5 tbsp olive oil
15ml/1 tbsp balsamic vinegar, plus a little extra if you like
15ml/1 tbsp sweet soy sauce
350g/12oz shallots, peeled but left whole
3 fresh red chillies
1 butternut squash, peeled, seeded and cut into chunks
5ml/1 tsp finely chopped fresh thyme
15g/1/2oz flat leaf parsley
1 small garlic clove, finely chopped
75g/3oz/3/4 cup chopped walnuts
150g/5oz feta cheese
salt and freshly ground black pepper

SERVES 4–6

1 Preheat the oven to 200°C/400°F/ Gas 6. Beat the oil, vinegar and soy sauce together in a large bowl, then season with salt and pepper.

2 Toss the shallots and two of the chillies in the oil mixture and turn into a large roasting pan or an ovenproof dish. Roast, stirring once or twice, for 15 minutes.

3 Add the butternut squash and roast for a further 30–35 minutes, stirring once, until the squash is tender and browned. Remove from the oven, stir in the chopped thyme and set the vegetables aside to cool.

4 Chop the flat leaf parsley and garlic together and mix with the walnuts. Seed and finely chop the remaining chilli.

5 Stir the parsley, garlic and walnut mixture into the vegetables. Add chopped red chilli to taste and adjust the seasoning, adding a little extra balsamic vinegar if you like. Crumble the feta cheese and add to the salad. Transfer to a serving dish and serve immediately.

Cook's Tip

To peel shallots, place them in a bowl and cover with boiling water for 2 minutes. Drain and remove the skins with a knife.

LENTIL AND SPINACH SALAD WITH ONION, CUMIN AND GARLIC

This wonderful, earthy salad is great for a picnic or with food cooked on the barbecue. It improves with standing and is at its best served at room temperature rather than chilled.

INGREDIENTS
225g/5oz/1 cup Puy lentils
1 fresh bay leaf
1 celery stick
fresh thyme sprig
30ml/2 tbsp olive oil
1 onion or 3–4 shallots, finely chopped
10ml/2 tsp crushed toasted cumin seeds
400g/14oz young spinach
salt and ground black pepper
30–45ml/2–3 tbsp chopped fresh parsley, plus a few extra sprigs
toasted French bread, to serve

FOR THE DRESSING
75ml/5 tbsp extra virgin olive oil
5ml/1 tsp Dijon mustard
15–25ml/3–5 tsp red wine vinegar
1 small garlic clove, finely chopped
2.5ml/½ tsp finely grated lemon rind

SERVES 6

1 Rinse the lentils, place them in a large pan and add water to cover. Tie the bay leaf, celery and thyme into a bundle and add to the pan. Bring to the boil, reduce the heat and cook for 30–45 minutes, until just tender.

2 Meanwhile, to make the dressing, mix the olive oil, mustard, 15ml/3 tsp vinegar, the garlic and lemon rind, and season to taste with salt and pepper.

3 Drain the cooked lentils and turn them into a large bowl. Add most of the dressing and toss well so that they are well coated, then set the lentils aside, stirring occasionally. Be careful not to break up the lentils when stirring.

4 Heat the oil in a deep frying pan and cook the finely chopped onion or shallots over a low heat for 4–5 minutes, until they are beginning to soften but not brown. Add the toasted cumin seeds and cook for 1 minute.

5 Add the spinach, season to taste, cover and cook for 2 minutes. Stir, then cook again briefly until wilted.

6 Stir the spinach into the lentils and set aside to cool. Stir in the remaining dressing and chopped parsley. Adjust the seasoning, adding extra vinegar if necessary.

7 Put the salad on a serving platter and sprinkle over some parsley. Serve with toasted French bread.

TOFU AND CUCUMBER SALAD

* * *

This refreshing salad has a hot, sweet-and-sour dressing.

INGREDIENTS

1 small cucumber
115g/4oz square tofu
vegetable oil, for frying
115g/4oz/1/2 cup beansprouts
salt
celery leaves, to garnish

FOR THE DRESSING
1 small onion, grated
2 garlic cloves, crushed
5–7.5ml/1–1 1/2 tsp chilli sauce
30–45ml/2–3 tbsp dark soy sauce
15–30ml/1–2 tbsp rice
wine vinegar
10ml/2 tsp dark brown sugar

SERVES 4–6

1 Cut the cucumber into neat cubes and place on a plate. Sprinkle with salt to extract the excess liquid. Set aside, while you are preparing the remaining ingredients.

2 Cut the tofu into cubes. Heat a little oil in a pan and cook on both sides until golden brown. Drain on kitchen paper.

3 To make the dressing, put the onion, garlic and chilli sauce in a screw-top jar and shake well. Stir in the soy sauce, vinegar, sugar and salt to taste.

4 Just before serving, rinse the cucumber under cold running water. Drain and dry thoroughly. Toss the cucumber, tofu and beansprouts together in a serving bowl and pour over the dressing. Garnish with the celery leaves and serve the salad immediately.

PLANTAIN AND GREEN BANANA SALAD

· · ·

Cook the plantains and bananas in their skins. Their soft texture will then absorb the dressing.

INGREDIENTS

2 firm yellow plantains
3 green bananas
1 garlic clove, crushed
1 red onion
15–30ml/1–2 tbsp chopped fresh coriander (cilantro)
45ml/3 tbsp sunflower oil
25ml/1½ tbsp malt vinegar
salt and freshly ground black pepper

SERVES 4

1 Slit the plantains and bananas lengthways along their natural ridges, then cut in half and place in a large pan.

2 Cover the plantains and bananas with water, add a little salt and bring to the boil. Boil gently for 20 minutes, until tender, then remove from the water. When they are cool enough to handle, peel and cut into medium-size slices.

3 Put the plantain and banana slices into a large bowl and add the garlic, turning the mixture with a wooden spoon to distribute the garlic evenly.

4 Cut the onion in half and slice thinly. Add it to the bowl with the chopped coriander, oil and vinegar. Season to taste with salt and pepper. Toss together to mix, then transfer to a serving bowl.

GREEN BEAN SALAD

Beans are great served with a simple vinaigrette, but this dish is a little more elaborate.

INGREDIENTS

450g/1 lb green beans
15ml/1 tbsp olive oil
25g/1oz/2 tbsp butter
¹/₂ garlic clove, crushed
50g/2oz/1 cup fresh
white breadcrumbs
15ml/1 tbsp chopped fresh parsley
1 hard-boiled egg, shelled and
finely chopped

FOR THE DRESSING
30ml/2 tbsp olive oil
30ml/2 tbsp sunflower oil
10ml/2 tsp white wine vinegar
¹/₂ garlic clove, crushed
1.5ml/¹/₄ tsp Dijon mustard
pinch of sugar
pinch of salt

SERVES 4

1 Cook the beans in salted boiling water for 5–6 minutes, until tender. Drain, refresh under cold running water and place in a serving bowl.

2 To make the dressing, whisk the oils, vinegar garlic, mustard, sugar and salt in a jug (pitcher). Pour the dressing over the beans and toss.

3 Heat the oil and butter in a frying pan and cook the garlic, stirring, for 1 minute. Stir in the breadcrumbs and fry over a moderate heat, stirring frequently, for 3–4 minutes, until golden brown.

4 Remove the pan from the heat and stir in the chopped parsley and then the hard-boiled egg. Sprinkle the breadcrumb mixture over the green beans. Serve warm or at room temperature.

CORONATION SALAD

. . .

The salad dressing in this dish was created for the coronation dinner of Queen Elizabeth II.

INGREDIENTS
450g/1lb new potatoes
45ml/3 tbsp French Dressing
3 spring onions
(scallions), chopped
6 eggs, hard-boiled, shelled
and halved
frisée lettuce leaves
1/4 cucumber, cut into thin strips
6 large radishes, sliced
1 carton salad cress
salt and freshly ground
black pepper

FOR THE CORONATION DRESSING
30ml/2 tbsp olive oil
1 small onion, chopped
15ml/1 tbsp mild curry powder or
korma spice mix
10ml/2 tsp tomato purée (paste)
30ml/2 tbsp lemon juice
30ml/2 tbsp sherry
300ml/1/2 pint/11/4 cups
mayonnaise
150ml/1/4 pint/2/3 cup natural
(plain) yogurt

SERVES 6

1 Boil the potatoes in salted water until tender. Drain and transfer them to a large bowl.

2 Toss the potatoes in the French dressing, stir in the spring onions, season to taste and leave to cool.

3 Meanwhile, make the coronation dressing. Heat the oil in a small pan and cook the chopped onion for 3 minutes, until soft. Stir in the curry powder or spice mix and cook for 1 minute more. Remove from the heat and mix in all the other dressing ingredients.

4 Stir the dressing into the cooled potatoes, add the eggs, then cover with clear film (plastic wrap) and chill in the refrigerator. Line a serving platter with lettuce leaves and pile the salad in the centre. Sprinkle over the cucumber strips, radishes and cress.

SWEET POTATO AND CARROT SALAD

. . .

This warm salad has a sweet-and-sour flavour.

INGREDIENTS
1 medium sweet potato
2 carrots, cut into thick
diagonal slices
3 medium tomatoes
8–10 iceberg lettuce leaves
75g/3oz/¹/2 cup canned chickpeas,
drained and rinsed

FOR THE DRESSING
15ml/1 tbsp clear honey
90ml/6 tbsp natural (plain) yogurt
2.5ml/¹/2 tsp salt
5ml/1 tsp freshly ground
black pepper

FOR THE GARNISH
15ml/1 tbsp walnuts
15ml/1 tbsp sultanas
(golden raisins)
1 small onion, cut into rings

SERVES 4

1 Peel the sweet potato and cut roughly into cubes. Boil it until it is soft but not mushy, then cover the pan and set aside.

2 Boil the carrots for just a few minutes, making sure that they remain crunchy. Add the carrots to the sweet potato.

3 Drain the water from the sweet potato and carrots and place them together in a bowl.

4 Slice the tops off the tomatoes, then scoop out the seeds with a spoon and discard. Coarsely chop the flesh. Slice the lettuce into strips across the leaves.

5 Line a salad bowl with the shredded lettuce leaves. Mix together the sweet potato, carrots, chickpeas and tomatoes and place the mixture in the centre.

6 To make the dressing, mix together all the ingredients and beat well, using a fork.

7 Garnish the salad with the walnuts, sultanas and onion rings. Pour the dressing over the top just before serving, or serve it in a separate bowl with the salad.

Cook's Tip
This salad makes an excellent light lunch or an easy family supper. Serve it with a sweet mango chutney and warm naan bread.

Variation
You can substitute other canned peas or beans for the chickpeas, such as gunga peas, also known as pigeon peas, or ful medames.

POTATO SALADS

Here are two versions of a light, summery potato salad.

INGREDIENTS
900g/2lb new potatoes
5ml/1 tsp salt

FOR THE DRESSING FOR THE
WARM SALAD
30ml/2 tbsp hazelnut or walnut oil
60ml/4 tbsp sunflower oil
juice of 1 lemon
15 pistachio nuts
salt and freshly ground
black pepper
flat leaf parsley, to garnish

FOR THE DRESSING FOR THE
COLD SALAD
75ml/5 tbsp olive oil
10ml/2 tsp white wine vinegar
1 garlic clove, crushed
90ml/6 tbsp finely chopped
fresh parsley
2 large spring onions (scallions),
finely chopped
salt and freshly ground
black pepper

SERVES 4

1 Scrub the potatoes but don't peel them. Place them in a large pan, cover with cold water and bring to the boil over a medium heat. Add the salt, lower the heat and simmer for about 15 minutes, until tender. Drain the potatoes well and set aside to cool slightly.

2 For the warm salad, mix together the hazelnut or walnut oil with the sunflower oil and lemon juice and season well with salt and pepper.

3 Use a large, heavy knife to crush the pistachio nuts coarsely.

4 When the potatoes have cooled slightly, pour over the dressing and sprinkle with the chopped nuts. Serve immediately garnished with a sprig of parsley.

5 For the cold salad, cook the potatoes as above, drain and leave to cool completely.

6 Whisk together the olive oil, white wine vinegar, garlic, parsley and spring onions and season to taste with salt and pepper. Pour the dressing over the potatoes. Cover tightly and chill overnight. Allow to come to room temperature before serving.

POTATO SALAD WITH EGG AND LEMON DRESSING

This recipe draws on the contrasting flavours of egg and lemon. Chopped parsley provides a fresh green finish.

INGREDIENTS

900g/2lb new potatoes
1 medium onion, finely chopped
1 hard-boiled egg
300ml/½ pint/1¼ cups
mayonnaise
1 garlic clove, crushed
finely grated rind and juice of
1 lemon
60ml/4 tbsp chopped fresh parsley
salt and freshly ground
black pepper
fresh parsley sprig, to garnish

SERVES 4

1 Scrub or scrape the potatoes, place in a large pan, cover with cold water and bring to the boil over a medium heat. Add a pinch of salt, lower the heat and simmer for 15 minutes, until tender. Drain well and set aside to cool.

2 Cut the potatoes into large dice and season to taste with salt and pepper. Add the chopped onion.

Variation

Fresh chives make an excellent alternative to parsley.

3 Shell the hard-boiled egg and grate into a mixing bowl, then add the mayonnaise. Combine the garlic and lemon rind and juice in a small bowl and stir them carefully into the mayonnaise.

4 Fold the mayonnaise mixture gently, but thoroughly into the potatoes, then fold in the chopped parsley. Serve the potato salad warm or cold, garnished with sprigs of parsley.

SPICY POTATO SALAD

• • •

*This tasty and versatile salad is
quick to prepare.*

INGREDIENTS

900g/2lb potatoes
2 red (bell) peppers
2 celery sticks
1 shallot
2–3 spring onions (scallions)
1 fresh green chilli
1 garlic clove, crushed
10ml/2 tsp finely chopped
fresh chives, plus extra to garnish
10ml/2 tsp finely chopped
fresh basil
15ml/1 tbsp finely chopped
fresh parsley
15ml/1 tbsp single (light) cream
30ml/2 tbsp salad cream
15ml/1 tbsp mayonnaise
5ml/1 tsp prepared mild mustard
7.5ml/1½ tsp sugar
salt

SERVES 6

3 Blend the cream, salad cream,
mayonnaise, mustard and sugar in
a small bowl, stirring until the
mixture is well combined.

4 Pour the dressing over the salad
and stir gently, but thoroughly to
coat evenly. Serve, garnished with
extra chopped chives.

1 Peel the potatoes. Boil in lightly
salted water for 10–12 minutes,
until tender. Drain and cool, then
cut into cubes and place in a large
mixing bowl.

2 Halve the red peppers, cut away
and discard the core and seeds and
cut the flesh into small pieces.
Finely chop the celery, shallot and
spring onions and slice the chilli
very thinly, discarding the seeds.
Add all the vegetables to the
potatoes together with the garlic
chives, basil and parsley.

POTATO SALAD WITH GARLIC SAUSAGE

This tasty potato salad would also make a light lunch dish.

INGREDIENTS

450g/1lb small waxy potatoes
30–45ml/2–3 tbsp dry white wine
2 shallots, finely chopped
15ml/1 tbsp chopped fresh parsley
15ml/1 tbsp chopped fresh tarragon
175 g/6oz cooked garlic sausage
fresh flat leaf parsley sprig,
to garnish

FOR THE VINAIGRETTE
10ml/2 tsp Dijon mustard
15ml/1 tbsp tarragon vinegar or
white wine vinegar
75ml/5 tbsp extra virgin olive oil
salt and freshly ground
black pepper

SERVES 4

1 Scrub the potatoes. Boil in salted water for 10–12 minutes, until tender. Drain and refresh under cold running water.

2 Peel the potatoes if you like, or leave in their skins, and cut into 5mm/¼in slices. Sprinkle with the wine and shallots.

Variation

The potatoes are also delicious served on their own and perhaps accompanied by marinated herrings.

3 To make the vinaigrette, mix the mustard and vinegar in a small bowl, then whisk in the oil, 15ml/ 1 tbsp at a time. Season and pour over the potatoes.

4 Add the herbs to the potatoes and toss until well mixed.

5 Slice the garlic sausage thinly and toss with the potatoes. Season the salad with salt and pepper to taste and serve at room temperature, garnished with a sprig of parsley.

PEPPERY BEAN SALAD

• • •

INGREDIENTS
425g/15oz can red kidney beans
425g/15oz can black-eyed
beans (peas)
425g/15oz can chickpeas
¼ red (bell) pepper
¼ green (bell) pepper
6 radishes
15ml/1 tbsp chopped spring
onion (scallion)

FOR THE DRESSING
5ml/1 tsp ground cumin
15ml/1 tbsp tomato ketchup
30ml/2 tbsp extra virgin
olive oil
15ml/1 tbsp white wine vinegar
1 garlic clove, crushed
2.5ml/½ tsp hot pepper sauce

SERVES 4–6

1 Drain the red kidney beans, black-eyed beans and chickpeas and rinse under cold running water. Shake off the excess water and tip them into a large bowl.

2 Core, seed and chop the red and green peppers. Trim the radishes and slice thinly. Add the peppers, radishes and spring onion to the mixed beans.

3 Mix together the cumin, tomato ketchup, oil, vinegar and garlic in a small bowl. Add a little salt and hot pepper sauce to taste and stir again thoroughly.

4 Pour the dressing over the salad and mix gently, but thoroughly. Cover the bowl with clear film (plastic wrap) and chill the salad in the refrigerator for at least 1 hour before serving, garnished with the chopped spring onion.

SMOKED HAM AND BEAN SALAD

∘ ∘ ∘

*A substantial salad that should
be served in small quantities if
intended as an accompaniment.*

INGREDIENTS
*175g/6oz dried black-eyed
beans (peas)
1 onion
1 carrot
225g/8oz smoked ham, diced
3 medium tomatoes, peeled, seeded
and diced
salt and freshly ground
black pepper*

FOR THE DRESSING
*2 garlic cloves, crushed
45ml/3 tbsp olive oil
45ml/3 tbsp red wine vinegar
30ml/2 tbsp vegetable oil
15ml/1 tbsp lemon juice
15ml/1 tbsp chopped fresh basil
15ml/1 tbsp wholegrain mustard*

*5ml/1 tsp soy sauce
2.5 ml/½ tsp dried oregano
2.5ml/½ tsp caster
(superfine) sugar
1.5ml/¼ tsp Worcestershire sauce
2.5ml/½ tsp chilli sauce*

SERVES 8

1 Soak the beans in cold water to
cover overnight. Drain.

2 Put the beans in a large pan and
add the onion and carrot. Cover
with fresh cold water and bring
to the boil. Boil vigorously for
15 minutes, then lower the heat
and simmer for about 1 hour, until
the beans are tender.

3 Drain the beans, reserving the
onion and carrot. Transfer the
beans to a salad bowl.

4 Finely chop the onion and
carrot. Toss with the beans. Stir in
the smoked ham and tomatoes.

5 For the dressing, combine all the
ingredients in a small bowl and
whisk to mix.

6 Pour the dressing over the ham
and beans. Season to taste with
salt and pepper. Toss the salad to
combine, then serve.

WHITE BEAN AND CELERY SALAD

• • •

This simple bean salad is a
delicious alternative to the
ubiquitous potato salad.

INGREDIENTS
450g/1lb dried white beans
(haricot, cannellini, navy, butter or
lima beans)
1 litre/1³/₄ pints/4 cups
vegetable stock
3 celery sticks, cut into 1cm/
¹/₂in strips
120ml/4fl oz/¹/₂ cup
French Dressing
45ml/3 tbsp chopped fresh parsley
salt and freshly ground
black pepper

SERVES 4

1 Put the beans in a bowl, cover
with cold water and soak for at
least 4 hours. Discard the soaking
water, then place the beans in a
heavy pan. Cover with water.

2 Bring to the boil and simmer
without a lid for 1¹/₂ hours, or
until the skins are broken. Cooked
beans will squash readily between a
thumb and forefinger. Drain well.

Variation
If you are short of time, you
can substitute three 400g/14oz
cans of white beans for the
dried beans. Drain, rinse and
follow the recipe from step 3.

3 Place the cooked beans in a large
pan. Add the vegetable stock and
celery, bring to the boil, cover and
simmer for 15 minutes. Drain
thoroughly. Moisten the beans with
the French dressing and leave to
cool completely.

4 Add the chopped parsley to the
beans and mix well. Season to taste
with salt and pepper, transfer to a
salad bowl and serve.

LENTIL AND CABBAGE SALAD
. . .

This is quite a filling salad with a lovely crunchy texture.

INGREDIENTS

225g/8oz/1 cup Puy lentils
3 garlic cloves
1 bay leaf
1 small onion, peeled and studded with 2 cloves
15ml/1 tbsp olive oil
1 red onion, thinly sliced
15ml/1 tbsp fresh thyme leaves
350g/12oz cabbage, shredded
grated rind and juice of 1 lemon
15ml/1 tbsp raspberry vinegar
salt and freshly ground black pepper

SERVES 4–6

1 Rinse the lentils in cold water and place in a large pan with 1.5 litres/2½ pints/6¼ cups cold water, one of the garlic cloves, the bay leaf and clove-studded onion. Bring to the boil and cook for 10 minutes. Reduce the heat, cover the pan and simmer gently for 15–20 minutes. Drain and discard the onion, garlic and bay leaf.

2 Crush the remaining garlic cloves. Heat the oil in a large pan. Add the red onion, crushed garlic and thyme and cook, stirring occasionally, for 5 minutes, until the onion has softened.

3 Add the cabbage and cook for 3–5 minutes, until just cooked, but still crunchy.

4 Stir in the cooked lentils, lemon rind and juice and the raspberry vinegar. Season to taste with salt and pepper, transfer to a serving dish and serve warm.

BROWN BEAN SALAD

· · ·

Brown beans are available from health-food stores.

INGREDIENTS

*350g/12oz/1½ cups dried
brown beans
3 fresh thyme sprigs
2 bay leaves
1 onion, halved
4 garlic cloves, crushed
7.5ml/1½ tsp crushed cumin seeds
3 spring onions (scallions), chopped
90ml/6 tbsp chopped fresh parsley
20ml/4 tsp lemon juice
90ml/6 tbsp olive oil
3 hard-boiled eggs, shelled and
coarsely chopped
1 pickled cucumber,
coarsely chopped
salt and freshly ground
black pepper*

SERVES 6

1 Put the beans in a bowl, cover with plenty of cold water and leave to soak overnight. Drain, transfer to a pan and cover with fresh water. Bring to the boil.

2 Reduce the heat and add the thyme, bay leaves and onion. Simmer very gently for about 1 hour, until tender. Drain and discard the herbs and onion.

Cook's Tip

The cooking time for dried beans can vary considerably. They may need only 45 minutes, or a lot longer.

3 Place the beans in a large bowl. Mix together the garlic, cumin seeds, spring onions, parsley, lemon juice and olive oil in a small bowl, and add a little salt and pepper. Pour over the beans and toss the ingredients lightly together.

4 Gently stir in the hard-boiled eggs and chopped pickled cucumber. Transfer the salad to a serving dish and serve immediately.

CRACKED WHEAT SALAD

· · ·

Flavoursome, fresh herbs are essential for this salad.

INGREDIENTS
225g/8oz/1⅓ cups cracked wheat
350ml/12fl oz/1½ cups
vegetable stock
1 cinnamon stick
generous pinch of ground cumin
pinch of cayenne pepper
pinch of ground cloves
5ml/1 tsp salt
5 black olives
10 mangetouts (snow peas)
1 red and 1 yellow (bell) pepper,
roasted, peeled, seeded and diced
2 plum tomatoes, peeled, seeded
and diced
2 shallots, thinly sliced
30ml/2 tbsp each shredded fresh
basil, mint and parsley
30ml/2 tbsp coarsely
chopped walnuts
30ml/2 tbsp balsamic vinegar
120ml/4fl oz/½ cup extra virgin
olive oil
freshly ground black pepper
onion rings, to garnish

SERVES 4

1 Place the cracked wheat in a large bowl. Pour the stock into a pan and bring to the boil with the cinnamon stick, cumin, cayenne, cloves and salt.

2 Cook for 1 minute, then pour the stock, with the cinnamon stick, over the cracked wheat. Leave to stand for 30 minutes.

3 In a separate bowl, mix together the mangetouts, red and yellow peppers, tomatoes, shallots, olives, basil, mint parsley and walnuts. Add the balsamic vinegar, olive oil and a little black pepper and stir thoroughly to mix.

4 Strain the cracked wheat of any liquid and discard the cinnamon stick. Place the cracked wheat in a serving bowl, stir in the fresh vegetable and herb mixture and serve the salad, garnished with onion rings.

Fruity Brown Rice Salad

· · ·

INGREDIENTS

115g/4oz/²⁄₃ cup brown rice
*1 small red (bell) pepper, seeded
and diced*
*200g/7oz can corn
kernels, drained*
*45ml/3 tbsp sultanas
(golden raisins)*
*225g/8oz can pineapple pieces in
fruit juice*
15ml/1 tbsp light soy sauce
15ml/1 tbsp sunflower oil
15ml/1 tbsp hazelnut oil
1 garlic clove, crushed
*5ml/1 tsp finely chopped fresh
root ginger*
*salt and freshly ground
black pepper*
*4 spring onions (scallions), sliced,
to garnish*

SERVES 4–6

1 Cook the brown rice in a large pan of lightly salted boiling water for about 30 minutes, or until it is tender. Drain thoroughly and set aside to cool. Meanwhile, prepare the garnish. Slice the spring onions at an angle, as shown, then set aside until required.

2 Tip the rice into a large serving bowl and add the red pepper, corn and sultanas. Drain the pineapple pieces, reserving the juice, then add them to the rice mixture and toss lightly to mix.

3 Pour the reserved pineapple juice into a clean screw-top jar. Add the soy sauce, sunflower and hazelnut oils, garlic and root ginger. Season to taste with salt and black pepper. Close the jar tightly and shake well to combine.

4 Pour the dressing over the salad and toss well. Sprinkle the spring onions over the top and serve.

Cook's Tip
Hazelnut oil gives a wonderfully distinctive flavour to any salad dressing. Like olive oil, it contains mainly monounsaturated fats.

COUSCOUS SALAD

· · ·

This salad has a delicate flavour and is excellent with kebabs.

INGREDIENTS

275g/10oz/1²/₃ cups couscous
550ml/18fl oz/2¼ cups boiling vegetable stock
16–20 black olives
2 small courgettes (zucchini)
25 g/1oz/¼ cup flaked (sliced) almonds, toasted
60ml/4 tbsp olive oil
15ml/1 tbsp lemon juice
15ml/1 tbsp chopped fresh coriander (cilantro)
15ml/1 tbsp chopped fresh parsley
good pinch of ground cumin
good pinch of cayenne pepper
salt

SERVES 4

3 Carefully mix the courgette strips, olives and toasted almonds into the couscous.

4 Mix together the olive oil, lemon juice, herbs, spices and a pinch of salt in a small jug (pitcher) or bowl. Stir into the salad.

1 Place the couscous in a bowl and pour over the boiling stock. Stir with a fork and then set aside for 10 minutes for the stock to be absorbed. Fluff up with a fork.

2 Halve the olives, discarding the pits. Trim the courgettes and cut them into small julienne strips.

Variation

You can add a variety of other vegetables to this salad. Try peeled and chopped tomatoes or seeded red (bell) pepper cut into small julienne strips.

ORANGE AND CRACKED WHEAT SALAD

• • •

Cracked wheat makes an excellent alternative to rice or pasta as a filling side salad with a delightful texture.

INGREDIENTS

*1 small green (bell) pepper
150g/5oz/scant 1 cup cracked wheat
¼ cucumber, diced
15g/½oz/½ cup chopped fresh mint
40 g/1½oz/⅓ cup flaked (sliced) almonds, toasted
grated rind and juice of 1 lemon
2 seedless oranges, peeled
salt and freshly ground black pepper
fresh mint sprigs, to garnish*

SERVES 4

1 Using a sharp vegetable knife, carefully halve and seed the green pepper. Cut into small cubes and set aside.

2 Place the cracked wheat in a large pan and add 600ml/1 pint/ 2½ cups water. Bring to the boil, lower the heat, cover and simmer for 10–15 minutes, until tender. Alternatively, place the cracked wheat in a heatproof bowl, pour over boiling water and leave to soak for 30 minutes. Most, if not all, of the water should be absorbed; drain off any excess.

3 Toss the cracked wheat with the cucumber, green pepper, mint and toasted almonds in a serving bowl. Add the grated lemon rind and the lemon juice.

4 Working over the salad bowl to catch the juice, cut the oranges into neat segments, leaving the membrane behind. Add the segments to the cracked wheat mixture, then season to taste with salt and pepper and toss lightly. Garnish with mint sprigs and serve.

Cook's Tip

Cracked wheat is known by a number of names, the best known being bulgur wheat. It is also called burghul and pourgouri in the Middle East.

VARIATION
Cracked wheat salad with fennel and pomegranate

This version uses the added crunchiness of fennel and the sweetness of pomegranate seeds. It is a perfect choice for a summer lunch.

INGREDIENTS

*225g/8oz/1⅓ cups cracked wheat
2 fennel bulbs
1 small red chilli, seeded and finely chopped*

*1 celery stick, thinly sliced
30ml/2 tbsp olive oil
finely grated rind and juice of 2 lemons
6–8 spring onions (scallions), chopped
90ml/6 tbsp chopped fresh mint
90ml/6 tbsp chopped fresh parsley
the seeds from 1 pomegranate
salt and freshly ground black pepper
lettuce leaves, to serve*

SERVES 6

1 Place the cracked wheat in a bowl and pour over enough boiling water to cover. Leave to stand for 30 minutes. Drain through a sieve, pressing out excess water.

2 Halve the fennel bulbs and cut into very thin slices.

3 Mix all the remaining ingredients together, then stir in the cracked wheat and fennel. Season to taste with salt and pepper, cover and set aside for 30 minutes before serving with lettuce leaves.

Not just for summer, main course salads are so versatile they are

welcome all year round. This chapter includes a wonderful

range of dishes made with fish and shellfish, chicken and cheese,

nuts, noodles and, of course, salad vegetables.

MAIN COURSE
SALADS

SALADE NIÇOISE

∘ ∘ ∘

Served with good French bread, this regional classic makes a wonderful summer lunch or light supper dish.

INGREDIENTS

225g/8oz green beans
450g/1lb new potatoes, peeled and cut into 2.5cm/1in pieces
white wine vinegar and olive oil, for sprinkling
1 small cos (romaine) or round lettuce, torn into bitesize pieces
4 ripe plum tomatoes, quartered
1 small cucumber, peeled, seeded and diced
1 green or red (bell) pepper, seeded and thinly sliced
4 hard-boiled eggs, shelled and quartered
24 black olives
225g/8oz can tuna in brine, drained
50g/2oz can anchovy fillets in olive oil, drained
basil leaves, to garnish
garlic croûtons, to serve

FOR THE ANCHOVY VINAIGRETTE
20ml/4 tsp Dijon mustard
50g/2oz can anchovy fillets in olive oil, drained
1 garlic clove, crushed
60ml/4 tbsp lemon juice or white wine vinegar
120ml/4fl oz/½ cup sunflower oil
120ml/4fl oz/½ cup extra virgin olive oil
freshly ground black pepper

SERVES 4–6

1 First, make the anchovy vinaigrette. Place the mustard, anchovies and garlic in a bowl and mix together by pressing the garlic and anchovies against the sides of the bowl. Season generously with pepper. Using a small whisk, blend in the lemon juice or vinegar. Slowly whisk in the sunflower oil in a thin stream, followed by the olive oil, whisking until the dressing is smooth and creamy.

2 Alternatively, put all the ingredients except the oils in a food processor fitted with the metal blade and process to combine. With the machine running, slowly add the oils in a thin stream until the vinaigrette is thick and creamy.

3 Drop the green beans into a large pan of boiling water and boil for 3 minutes, until tender, but crisp. Transfer the beans to a colander with a slotted spoon, then rinse under cold running water to refresh. Drain well again and set aside until required.

4 Add the potatoes to the same boiling water, reduce the heat and simmer for 10–15 minutes, until just tender, then drain. Sprinkle with a little vinegar and olive oil and a spoonful of the vinaigrette.

5 Arrange the lettuce on a serving platter to make a bed, top with the tomatoes, cucumber and red or green pepper, then add the green beans and potatoes.

6 Arrange the eggs around the edge. Place the olives, tuna and anchovies on top and garnish with the basil leaves. Drizzle with the remaining vinaigrette and serve with garlic croûtons.

Cook's Tip

To make garlic croûtons, thinly slice a French loaf or cut a larger loaf, such as rustic country bread, into 2.5cm/1in cubes. Place the bread in a single layer on a baking sheet and cook in the oven, preheated to 180°C/350°F/ Gas 4, for 7–10 minutes, or until golden, turning once. Rub the toast with a garlic clove and serve hot, or leave to cool and store in an airtight container until needed.

MOROCCAN TUNA SALAD

• • •

*This salad is similar to the classic
Salade Niçoise but uses tuna or
swordfish steaks and fresh broad
beans along with the familiar
green beans.*

INGREDIENTS

*about 900g/2lb fresh tuna or
swordfish, sliced into 2cm/
³/₄in steaks
olive oil, for brushing*

FOR THE SALAD
*450g/1lb green beans
450g/1lb broad (fava) beans
1 cos or romaine lettuce
450g/1lb cherry tomatoes, halved,
unless very tiny
30ml/2 tbsp coarsely chopped
fresh coriander (cilantro)
3 hard-boiled eggs
45ml/3 tbsp olive oil
10–15ml/2–3 tsp lime or
lemon juice
¹/₂ garlic clove, crushed
175–225g/6–8oz/1¹/₂–2 cups pitted
black olives*

FOR THE MARINADE
*1 onion
2 garlic cloves
¹/₂ bunch fresh parsley
¹/₂ bunch fresh coriander (cilantro)
10ml/2 tsp paprika
45ml/3 tbsp olive oil
30ml/2 tbsp white wine vinegar
15ml/1 tbsp lime or lemon juice*

SERVES 6

1 To make the marinade, place all
the ingredients in a food processor,
add 45ml/3 tbsp water and process
for 30–40 seconds.

2 Prick the fish steaks all over with
a fork, place in a shallow dish and
pour over the marinade, turning
the fish to coat. Cover with clear
film (plastic wrap) and leave in a
cool place for 2–4 hours.

3 To prepare the salad, cook the
green beans and broad beans in
boiling salted water until tender.
Drain and refresh under cold water.
Discard the outer shells from the
broad beans and place in a large
serving bowl with the green beans.

4 Discard the outer lettuce leaves
and tear the inner leaves into
pieces. Add to the beans with the
tomatoes and coriander. Shell the
eggs and cut into eighths.

5 Mix the olive oil, lime or lemon
juice and garlic to make a dressing.

6 Preheat the grill (broiler) to high
and arrange the tuna or swordfish
steaks in a grill pan. Brush with the
marinade together with a little
extra olive oil and grill (broil) for
5–6 minutes on each side, until the
fish is tender and flakes easily.
Brush again with marinade and
more olive oil when you turn the
fish over.

7 Allow the fish to cool a little,
then break the steaks into large
pieces. Toss into the salad with the
olives and the dressing. Decorate
with the eggs and serve.

WARM FISH SALAD WITH MANGO DRESSING

° ° °

This spicy salad is best served during the summer months, preferably out of doors.

INGREDIENTS

1 French loaf
4 redfish, black bream or porgy,
each about 275g/10oz
15ml/1 tbsp vegetable oil
1 mango
1cm/1/2in piece of fresh root ginger
1 fresh red chilli, seeded and
finely chopped
30ml/2 tbsp lime juice
30ml/2 tbsp chopped
fresh coriander (cilantro)
175g/6oz young spinach leaves
150g/5oz pak choi (bok choy)
175g/6oz cherry tomatoes, halved

SERVES 4

1 Preheat the oven to 180°C/ 350°F/Gas 4. Cut the French loaf into 20cm/8in lengths. Slice lengthways, then cut into thick fingers. Place the bread on a baking sheet and place in the oven for 15 minutes to dry.

2 Preheat the grill (broiler) or light the barbecue and allow the embers to settle. Slash the fish deeply on both sides and brush them all over with the vegetable oil. Grill (broil) or cook the fish on the barbecue for 6 minutes, turning once.

3 Peel the mango and cut in half, discarding the stone (pit). Thinly slice one half of the flesh and set aside. Place the other half in a food processor. Peel the ginger, grate finely, then add to the mango with the red chilli, lime juice and chopped coriander. Process until smooth. Adjust to a pouring consistency by adding 30–45ml/ 2–3 tbsp water.

4 Wash the spinach and pak choi leaves in cold water and spin dry or pat them dry with kitchen paper, then distribute them among four serving plates. Place the fish on top of the leaves. Spoon the mango dressing over them and finish with the reserved slices of mango and the tomato halves. Serve immediately with the fingers of crispy French bread.

GRILLED SALMON AND SPRING VEGETABLE SALAD

• • •

Spring is the time to enjoy sweet, young vegetables. Serve with grilled salmon topped with sorrel and quail's eggs.

INGREDIENTS

*350g/12oz small new potatoes, scrubbed or scraped
4 quail's eggs
115g/4oz young carrots, peeled
115g/4oz baby corn cobs
115g/4oz sugar snap peas
115g/4oz fine green beans
115g/4oz young courgettes (zucchini)
115g/4oz patty-pan squash (optional)
120ml/4fl oz/½ cup French Dressing
4 salmon fillets, each about 150g/5oz, skinned
115g/4oz sorrel, stems removed
salt and freshly ground black pepper*

SERVES 4

1 Bring the potatoes to the boil in lightly salted water, lower the heat and simmer for about 15 minutes, until tender. Drain well, cover and keep warm.

2 Cover the quail's eggs with boiling water and cook for 8 minutes. Refresh under cold water, shell and cut in half.

3 Bring a pan of lightly salted water to the boil, add the carrots, corn, sugar snap peas, beans, courgettes and squash, if using, and cook for 2–3 minutes, until tender-crisp. Drain well. Place the hot vegetables and potatoes in a bowl, moisten with a little of the French Dressing and set aside to cool.

4 Brush the salmon fillets with some of the French Dressing and grill (broil) for 6 minutes, turning once.

5 Place the sorrel in a stainless-steel or enamel pan with 30ml/ 2 tbsp French Dressing. Cover and soften over a gentle heat for 2 minutes. Strain in a small sieve and cool to room temperature.

6 Divide the potato and vegetable mixture among four large serving plates, then position a piece of salmon to one side of each plate. Place a spoonful of sorrel on each piece of salmon and top with two pieces of quail's egg. Season to taste with salt and pepper and serve at room temperature.

> ### Cook's Tip
> If sorrel is unavailable, use young spinach leaves instead. Cook it gently in the same way as the sorrel.

NOODLES WITH PINEAPPLE, GINGER AND CHILLIES

· · ·

A coconut, lime and fish sauce dressing is the perfect partner to this fruity and spicy salad.

INGREDIENTS

275g/10oz dried udon noodles
½ pineapple, peeled, cored and sliced into 4 cm/1½in rings
45ml/3 tbsp light brown sugar
60ml/4 tbsp lime juice
60ml/4 tbsp coconut milk
30ml/2 tbsp Thai fish sauce
30ml/2 tbsp grated fresh root ginger
2 garlic cloves, finely chopped
1 ripe mango or 2 peaches, finely diced
freshly ground black pepper
2 spring onions (scallions), thinly sliced, 2 red chillies, seeded and finely shredded, and fresh mint leaves, to garnish

SERVES 4

1 Cook the noodles in a large pan of boiling water until tender, following the directions on the packet. Drain, refresh under cold water and drain again.

2 Place the pineapple rings in a flameproof dish, sprinkle with 30ml/2 tbsp of the sugar and grill (broil) for about 5 minutes, or until golden. Cool slightly and cut into small dice.

3 Mix the lime juice, coconut milk and fish sauce in a salad bowl. Add the remaining brown sugar with the ginger, garlic and black pepper and whisk well. Add the noodles and pineapple.

4 Add the diced mango or peaches and toss lightly to mix. Sprinkle over the sliced spring onions, shredded chillies and mint leaves before serving.

BUCKWHEAT NOODLES WITH SMOKED SALMON

· · ·

Young pea sprouts are available for only a short time. You can substitute watercress, salad cress, young leeks or your favourite green vegetable or herb in this dish.

INGREDIENTS

225g/8oz buckwheat or soba noodles
15ml/1 tbsp oyster sauce
juice of ½ lemon
30–45ml/2–3 tbsp light olive oil
115g/4oz smoked salmon, cut into fine strips
115g/4oz young pea sprouts
2 ripe tomatoes, peeled, seeded and cut into strips
15ml/1 tbsp chopped chives
freshly ground black pepper

SERVES 4

1 Cook the noodles in a large pan of boiling water until tender, following the directions on the packet. Drain, then rinse under cold running water and drain well.

> *Cook's Tip*
> Soba noodles, popular in Japan, are made from a mixture of buckwheat and wheat flour.

2 Tip the noodles into a large bowl. Add the oyster sauce and lemon juice and season with pepper to taste. Moisten the noodles with the olive oil.

3 Add the smoked salmon, pea sprouts, tomatoes and chives. Mix well and serve immediately.

SMOKED TROUT AND NOODLE SALAD

* * *

It is important to use ripe, juicy tomatoes for this fresh-tasting salad. For a special occasion, you could use smoked salmon.

INGREDIENTS
225g/8oz somen noodles
2 smoked trout, skinned and boned
2 hard-boiled eggs, shelled and coarsely chopped
30ml/2 tbsp chopped fresh chives
lime halves, to serve (optional)

FOR THE DRESSING
6 ripe plum tomatoes
2 shallots, finely chopped
30ml/2 tbsp tiny capers, rinsed
30ml/2 tbsp chopped fresh tarragon
finely grated rind and juice of ½ orange
60ml/4 tbsp extra virgin olive oil
salt and freshly ground black pepper

SERVES 4

3 Toss the noodles with the dressing, then adjust the seasoning to taste. Arrange the noodles on a large serving platter or divide among four individual plates.

4 Flake the smoked trout over the noodles, then sprinkle the eggs and chives over the top. Serve, with lime halves on the side of the plate, if you like.

1 To make the dressing, halve the tomatoes, remove the cores and cut the flesh into chunks. Place in a bowl with the shallots, capers, tarragon, orange rind and juice and olive oil. Season to taste and mix well. Leave to marinate at room temperature for 1–2 hours.

2 Cook the noodles in a pan of boiling water, according to the packet instructions. Drain, rinse in cold water and drain again.

SMOKED TROUT AND HORSERADISH SALAD

Partner crisp lettuce leaves with smoked fish, warm potatoes and a creamy dressing.

INGREDIENTS
675g/1½ lb new potatoes
4 smoked trout fillets
115g/4oz mixed lettuce leaves
4 slices dark rye bread, cut
into fingers
salt and freshly ground
black pepper

FOR THE DRESSING
60ml/4 tbsp creamed horseradish
60ml/4 tbsp groundnut (peanut) oil
15ml/1 tbsp white wine vinegar
10ml/2 tsp caraway seeds

SERVES 4

1 Scrub the potatoes. Bring to the boil in a pan of lightly salted water and simmer for about 15 minutes, until tender. Drain well.

2 Meanwhile, remove the skin from the trout fillets and lift the flesh from the bone.

Cook's Tip
In some cases, it is better to season the leaves themselves rather than the dressing when making a salad.

3 To make the dressing, place all the ingredients in a screw-top jar and shake vigorously. Season the lettuce leaves and moisten them with the dressing. Distribute among four serving plates.

4 Flake the trout fillets and cut the potatoes in half. Distribute them, together with the rye bread fingers, over the salad leaves and toss to mix. Season the salad to taste with salt and pepper and serve.

PRAWN AND ARTICHOKE SALAD

INGREDIENTS

1 garlic clove
10ml/2 tsp Dijon mustard
60ml/4 tbsp red wine vinegar
150ml/¹⁄₄ pint/²⁄₃ cup extra virgin
olive oil
45ml/3 tbsp shredded fresh basil
leaves or 30ml/2 tbsp finely
chopped fresh parsley
1 red onion, very
thinly sliced
350g/12oz peeled cooked
prawns (shrimp)
400g/14oz can artichoke hearts
¹⁄₂ iceberg lettuce
salt and freshly ground
black pepper

SERVES 4

1 Chop the garlic, then crush it to a pulp with 5ml/1 tsp salt, using the flat edge of a heavy knife blade. Mix the garlic and mustard to a paste in a small bowl.

2 Beat in the vinegar and, finally, add the olive oil, beating hard to make a thick, creamy dressing. Season with black pepper and, if necessary, additional salt.

3 Stir the basil or parsley into the dressing, followed by the sliced onion. Leave the mixture to stand for 30 minutes at room temperature, then stir in the prawns and chill for 1 hour, or until ready to serve.

4 Drain the artichoke hearts well and halve each one. Shred the lettuce finely.

5 Make a bed of lettuce on a large serving platter or four individual salad plates and spread the halved artichoke hearts over it.

6 Just before serving, pour the prawns and their marinade over the top of the salad.

GHANAIAN PRAWN SALAD

· · ·

INGREDIENTS

115g/4oz peeled cooked
prawns (shrimp)
1 garlic clove, crushed
7.5ml/1½ tsp vegetable oil
2 eggs
1 yellow plantain, halved
4 lettuce leaves
2 tomatoes
1 red (bell) pepper, seeded
1 avocado
juice of 1 lemon
1 carrot
200g/7oz can tuna or
sardines, drained
1 fresh green chilli, seeded and
finely chopped
30ml/2 tbsp chopped spring
onion (scallion)
salt and freshly ground
black pepper

SERVES 4

1 Put the prawns and garlic in a small bowl. Add a little seasoning.

2 Heat the oil in a small pan, add the prawns and cook over a low heat for a few minutes. Transfer to a plate to cool.

Variation

To vary this salad, use other types of canned fish and a mixture of interesting and colourful lettuce leaves.

3 Hard-boil the eggs, place in cold water to cool, then shell and cut into slices.

4 Boil the unpeeled plantain in a large pan of water for 15 minutes. Drain, cool, then peel and cut into thick slices.

5 Shred the lettuce and arrange on a large serving plate. Slice the tomatoes and red pepper and peel and slice the avocado, sprinkling it with a little lemon juice.

6 Cut the carrot into thin batons and arrange on top of the lettuce with the other vegetables.

7 Add the plantain, eggs, prawns and tuna or sardines. Sprinkle with the remaining lemon juice, then sprinkle the chilli and spring onion on top. Season to taste with salt and pepper and serve.

PRAWN SALAD WITH CURRY DRESSING

• • •

Curry spices add an unexpected twist to this salad. The warm flavours combine especially well with the sweet prawns and grated apple.

INGREDIENTS

1 ripe tomato
1/2 iceberg lettuce
1 small onion
1 small bunch fresh
  coriander (cilantro)
15ml/1 tbsp lemon juice
450g/1lb peeled cooked
  prawns (shrimp)
1 apple
8 whole prawns (shrimp),
8 lemon wedges and 4 fresh
coriander (cilantro) sprigs,
to garnish
salt

FOR THE CURRY DRESSING
75ml/5 tbsp mayonnaise
5ml/1 tsp mild curry paste
15ml/1 tbsp tomato ketchup

SERVES 4

1 To peel the tomato, cut a cross in the skin with a sharp knife and immerse in boiling water for about 30 seconds. Remove from the bowl with a slotted spoon and cool under cold running water. Peel off the skin. Halve the tomato, push the seeds out with your thumb and discard them. Cut the flesh into large dice.

2 Finely shred the lettuce and put in a large bowl, then finely chop the onion and coriander. Add to the bowl together with the tomato, moisten with lemon juice and season with salt.

3 To make the dressing, put the mayonnaise, curry paste and tomato ketchup in a small bowl and mix well. Add 30ml/2 tbsp water to thin the dressing and season to taste with salt.

Cook's Tip
Fresh coriander (cilantro) is inclined to wilt if it is kept out of water. Put it in a jar of water, cover with a plastic bag and place in the refrigerator. It will stay fresh for several days.

4 Add the prawns to the bowl and stir gently, but thoroughly so that all the prawns are evenly coated with the dressing.

5 Quarter and core the apple and grate coarsely directly into the prawn and dressing mixture.

6 Distribute the shredded lettuce mixture among four serving plates or bowls. Pile the prawn mixture in the centre of each and decorate each with two whole prawns, two lemon wedges and a sprig of fresh coriander. Serve immediately.

PRAWN AND MINT SALAD

• • •

Cooking raw prawns in butter adds to the flavour, making all the difference to this salad. Garnish with shaved fresh coconut for a tropical touch.

INGREDIENTS

12 large raw prawns (shrimp)
15ml/1 tbsp unsalted (sweet) butter
15ml/1 tbsp Thai fish sauce
juice of 1 lime
45ml/3 tbsp thin coconut milk
5ml/1 tsp caster (superfine) sugar
1 garlic clove, crushed
2.5cm/1in piece of fresh root ginger, peeled and grated
2 fresh red chillies, seeded and finely chopped
30ml/2 tbsp fresh mint leaves
225g/8oz light green lettuce leaves
freshly ground black pepper

SERVES 4

1 Carefully peel the prawns, removing and discarding the heads and outer shells, but leaving the tails intact.

2 Using a sharp knife, carefully remove and discard the dark-coloured vein that runs along the back of each peeled prawn.

3 Melt the butter in a large frying pan. When the melted butter is foaming add the prawns and toss over a high heat until they have just turned pink. Remove from the heat; it is important not to cook them for too long so that their tenderness is retained.

4 In a small bowl mix the fish sauce, lime juice, coconut milk, sugar, garlic, ginger and chillies. Season to taste with freshly ground black pepper.

5 Toss the warm prawns into the sauce with the mint leaves. Arrange the lettuce leaves on a serving plate and place the prawn and mint mixture in the centre.

Variation

Instead of prawns, this dish also works very well with lobster tails if you are feeling very extravagant.

Cook's Tip

If you can't find any fresh, raw prawns, you could use frozen ones. To make the most of their flavour, toss very quickly in the hot butter when they are completely thawed.

MIXED SHELLFISH SALAD

. . .

*Use fresh shellfish in season or
a mixture of fresh and frozen.*

INGREDIENTS
*350g/12oz small squid
1 small onion, cut into quarters
1 bay leaf
200g/7oz raw prawns (shrimp), in
their shells
750g/1½ lb fresh mussels,
in their shells
450g/1lb fresh small clams
175ml/6fl oz/¾ cup white wine
1 fennel bulb*

FOR THE DRESSING
*75ml/5 tbsp extra virgin olive oil
45ml/3 tbsp lemon juice
1 garlic clove, finely chopped
salt and freshly ground
black pepper*

SERVES 6–8

1 Clean the squid by first peeling off the thin skin from the body section. Rinse well.

2 Using your fingers, pull the head and tentacles away from the sac section. Remove and discard the translucent quill and any remaining insides from the sac. Sever the tentacles and head.

3 Discard the head and intestines. Remove the small, hard beak from the base of the tentacles. Rinse the tentacles and sac under cold running water. Drain.

4 Bring a large pan of water to the boil. Add the onion and bay leaf. Drop in the squid tentacles and sacs and cook for 10 minutes, or until tender. Remove with a slotted spoon and leave to cool before slicing the sacs into rings 1cm/½in wide. Cut each tentacle section into two pieces. Set aside.

5 Drop the prawns into the same boiling water and cook for about 2 minutes, until they turn pink. Remove the prawns with a slotted spoon. Peel and devein. (The cooking liquid may be strained and kept for soup.)

6 Cut the "beards" from the mussels. Scrub and rinse the mussels and clams well in several changes of cold water. Any that are open should close if given a sharp tap; if they fail to do so, discard. Place in a large pan with the wine. Cover and steam until all the shells have opened. (Discard any that do not open.) Lift the clams and mussels out of the pan.

7 Remove all the clams from their shells with a small spoon. Place in a large serving bowl. Remove all but eight of the mussels from their shells and add them to the clams in the bowl. Leave the remaining mussels in their half-shells, and set aside for the garnish.

8 Cut the green fronds of the fennel away from the bulb. Chop finely and set aside. Chop the bulb into bitesize pieces and add it to the serving bowl together with the squid and prawns.

9 To make the dressing, combine the oil, lemon juice and garlic in a bowl. Add the reserved chopped fennel fronds and season to taste salt and pepper. Pour the dressing over the salad, and toss well to mix. Garnish with the remaining mussels in their half-shells. Serve at room temperature or chill very briefly before serving.

AVOCADO, CRAB AND CORIANDER SALAD

· · ·

This sophisticated salad is full of complementary flavours.

INGREDIENTS

SERVES 4
675g/1½ lb small new potatoes
1 fresh mint sprig
900g/2 lb boiled crabs
1 frisée or butterhead lettuce
175g/6oz lamb's lettuce
1 avocado, peeled and sliced
175g/6oz cherry tomatoes
salt, freshly ground black pepper
and freshly grated nutmeg

FOR THE DRESSING
75ml/5 tbsp olive oil
15ml/1 tbsp lime juice
45ml/3 tbsp chopped fresh
coriander (cilantro)
2.5ml/½ tsp caster (superfine) sugar

SERVES 4

1 Scrape or peel the potatoes and place in a large pan. Cover with water, add a good pinch of salt and a sprig of mint. Bring to the boil and simmer for about 15 minutes, until tender. Drain the potatoes, cover and keep warm until needed.

Variation
Frozen crab meat is a good alternative to fresh and retains much of its original sweetness. You will require 275g/10oz.

2 Remove the legs and claws from each crab. Crack these open with the back of a chopping knife and remove the white meat.

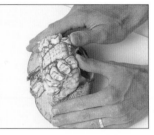

3 Turn the crab on its back and push the rear leg section away with the thumb and forefinger of each hand. Remove the flesh from inside the shell.

4 Discard the "dead men's fingers", the soft gills which the crab uses to filter impurities in its diet. These lie close together along either side of the body. Apart from these and the shell, everything else is edible, both white and dark or brown meat.

5 Split the central body section open with a knife and remove the white and dark flesh with a pick or a metal skewer.

6 To make the dressing, combine all the ingredients in a screw-top jar and shake well. Put the salad leaves in a large bowl, pour the dressing over them and toss well.

7 Distribute the leaves among four serving plates. Top with the avocado, crab, tomatoes and warm new potatoes. Season to taste with salt, pepper and freshly grated nutmeg and serve.

Cook's Tip
Young crabs offer the sweetest meat, but they are are more awkward to prepare than older, larger ones. The hen crab carries more flesh than the cock, which is considered to have a better overall flavour. The cock crab, shown here, is identified by his narrow apron flap at the rear. The hen has a broader flap, under which she carries her eggs.

THAI NOODLE SALAD

· · ·

The addition of coconut milk and sesame oil gives an unusual nutty flavour to this salad.

INGREDIENTS

350g/12oz somen noodles
1 large carrot, cut into thin strips
1 bunch asparagus, trimmed and cut into 4cm/1¹/₂in lengths
1 red (bell) pepper, seeded and cut into fine strips
115g/4oz mangetouts (snow peas), trimmed and halved
115g/4oz baby corn cobs, halved lengthways
115g/4oz beansprouts
115g/4oz can water chestnuts, drained and thinly sliced
1 lime, cut into wedges,
50g/2oz/¹/₂ cup roasted peanuts, coarsely chopped, and fresh coriander (cilantro) leaves, to garnish

FOR THE DRESSING

45ml/3 tbsp torn fresh basil
75ml/5 tbsp chopped fresh mint
250ml/8fl oz/1 cup coconut milk
30ml/2 tbsp dark sesame oil
15ml/1 tbsp grated fresh root ginger
2 garlic cloves, finely chopped
juice of 1 lime
2 spring onions (scallions), chopped
salt and cayenne pepper

SERVES 4–6

1 To make the dressing, combine all the ingredients in a bowl and mix well. Season to taste with salt and cayenne pepper.

2 Cook the noodles in a pan of boiling water, following the directions on the packet, until just tender. Drain, rinse under cold running water and drain again, then set aside until required.

3 Cook all the vegetables, except the water chestnuts, in separate pans of lightly salted boiling water until they are tender, but still crisp. Drain, plunge them immediately into cold water and drain again.

4 Toss the noodles, vegetables, water chestnuts and dressing together. Arrange on individual serving plates and garnish with the lime wedges, chopped peanuts and coriander leaves.

PRAWN NOODLE SALAD WITH FRAGRANT HERBS

A light, refreshing salad with all the tangy flavour of the sea.

INGREDIENTS

115g/4oz cellophane noodles, soaked in hot water until soft
1 small green (bell) pepper, seeded and cut into strips
½ cucumber, cut into strips
1 tomato, cut into strips
2 shallots, thinly sliced
16 peeled cooked prawns (shrimp)
salt and freshly ground black pepper
fresh coriander (cilantro) leaves, to garnish

FOR THE DRESSING

15ml/1 tbsp rice-wine vinegar
30ml/2 tbsp Thai fish sauce
30ml/2 tbsp lime juice
2.5ml/½ tsp grated fresh root ginger
1 lemon grass stalk, finely chopped
1 red chilli, seeded and thinly sliced
30ml/2 tbsp coarsely chopped fresh mint
few sprigs of tarragon, chopped
15ml/1 tbsp chopped fresh chives

SERVES 4

3 In a large bowl, combine the noodles with the green pepper strips, cucumber, tomato and shallots. Lightly season with salt and black pepper, then toss with the dressing.

1 To make the dressing, combine all the ingredients in a small bowl or jug (pitcher) and whisk well.

2 Drain the noodles, then plunge them into a pan of boiling water for 1 minute. Drain, rinse under cold running water to refresh and drain again well.

Cook's Tip

Prawns (shrimp) are available ready-cooked and often shelled. To cook prawns, boil them for 5 minutes. Leave them to cool in the cooking liquid, then gently pull off the tail shell and twist off the head.

4 Spoon the cellophane noodles on to four individual serving plates and arrange the prawns on top of them. Garnish with a few coriander leaves and serve immediately.

EGG NOODLE SALAD WITH SESAME CHICKEN

INGREDIENTS

400g/14oz fresh thin egg noodles
1 carrot, cut into long fine strips
50g/2oz mangetouts (snow peas),
trimmed, cut into fine strips
and blanched
115g/4oz/¹/₂ cup
beansprouts, blanched
30ml/2 tbsp olive oil
225g/8oz skinless, boneless chicken
breast portions, thinly sliced
30ml/2 tbsp sesame seeds, toasted
2 spring onions (scallions), thinly
sliced diagonally, and fresh
coriander (cilantro) leaves,
to garnish

FOR THE DRESSING

45ml/3 tbsp sherry vinegar
75ml/5 tbsp soy sauce
60ml/4 tbsp sesame oil
90ml/6 tbsp light olive oil
1 garlic clove, finely chopped
5ml/1 tsp grated fresh root ginger
salt and freshly ground
black pepper

SERVES 4–6

1 To make the dressing, whisk together all the ingredients in a small bowl. Season to taste.

2 Cook the noodles in a large pan of boiling water. Stir them occasionally to separate. They will take only a few minutes to cook; be careful not to overcook them. Drain the noodles, rinse under cold running water and drain well. Tip into a bowl.

3 Add the carrot, mangetouts and beansprouts to the noodles. Pour in about half the dressing, then toss the mixture well and adjust the seasoning according to taste.

4 Heat the oil in a large frying pan. Add the chicken and stir-fry for 3 minutes, or until cooked and golden. Remove from the heat. Add the sesame seeds and drizzle in some of the remaining dressing.

5 Arrange the noodle mixture on individual serving plates, making a nest on each plate. Spoon the chicken on top, dividing it equally. Sprinkle with the spring onions and coriander leaves and serve any remaining dressing separately.

CHICKEN AND PASTA SALAD

This is a delicious way to use up left-over cooked chicken.

INGREDIENTS

225g/8oz tricolour pasta twists
30ml/2 tbsp bottled pesto sauce
15ml/1 tbsp olive oil
1 beefsteak tomato
12 pitted black olives
225g/8oz green beans, cooked
350g/12oz cooked chicken, cubed
salt and freshly ground
black pepper
fresh basil, to garnish

SERVES 4

3 Peel the beefsteak tomato by cutting a cross in the skin at the top with a sharp knife and then plunging it in boiling water for about 30 seconds. The skin will now pull off easily. Cut the tomato flesh into small cubes.

4 Add the tomato and olives to the pasta. Cut the green beans into 4cm/1½in lengths. Add the beans and chicken and season to taste with salt and pepper. Toss gently, transfer to a serving platter, garnish with basil and serve.

1 Cook the pasta in plenty of lightly salted boiling water for 10–12 minutes, until *al dente*, or as directed on the packet.

2 Drain the pasta and rinse in plenty of cold running water. Put into a bowl and stir in the pesto sauce and olive oil.

HOT AND SOUR CHICKEN SALAD

• • •

This chicken salad from Vietnam is equally delicious made with prawns.
Allow 450g/1lb fresh prawn tails to serve four people.

INGREDIENTS

2 skinless, boneless chicken
breast portions
115g/4oz beansprouts
1 head Chinese leaves (Chinese
cabbage), shredded
2 medium carrots, cut into batons
1 red onion, thinly sliced
2 large gherkins, sliced

FOR THE MARINADE
1 small fresh red chilli, seeded and
finely chopped
1cm/½in piece of fresh root
ginger, chopped
1 garlic clove, crushed
15ml/1 tbsp crunchy peanut butter
30ml/2 tbsp chopped fresh
coriander (cilantro)
5ml/1 tsp sugar
2.5ml/½ tsp salt
15ml/1 tbsp rice or white
wine vinegar
60ml/4 tbsp vegetable oil
10ml/2 tsp Thai fish sauce

SERVES 4–6

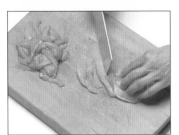

1 Slice the chicken breast portions thinly and place in a shallow bowl. Grind the chilli, ginger and garlic in a food processor or with a mortar and pestle, then add the peanut butter, chopped fresh coriander, sugar and salt.

2 Add the rice or white wine vinegar, 30ml/2 tbsp of the oil and the fish sauce to the ingredients in the food processor. Combine well. Cover the chicken with the spice mixture and marinate for at least 2–3 hours.

3 Cook the chicken in a frying pan on the hob (stovetop) or on a medium-hot barbecue for about 5 minutes, basting often and turning once. Arrange the salad ingredients on a serving dish and top with the cooked chicken.

CHICKEN SALAD WITH CORIANDER DRESSING

Serve this salad warm to make the most of the wonderful flavour of chicken basted with a marinade of coriander, sesame and mustard.

INGREDIENTS

*4 medium skinless, boneless
chicken breast portions
225g/8oz mangetouts (snow peas)
2 heads decorative lettuce such as
lollo rosso or oak leaf
3 carrots, cut into batons
175g/6oz button (white)
mushrooms, sliced
175g/6oz bacon, fried and chopped*

FOR THE CORIANDER DRESSING
*120ml/4fl oz/¹/₂ cup lemon juice
30ml/2 tbsp wholegrain mustard
250ml/8fl oz/1 cup olive oil
65ml/2¹/₂ fl oz/¹/₃ cup sesame oil
5ml/1 tsp coriander seeds, crushed
15ml/1 tbsp chopped fresh
coriander (cilantro), to garnish*

SERVES 6

1 Mix all the dressing ingredients in a bowl. Place the chicken in a dish and pour over half the dressing. Cover and marinate overnight in the refrigerator. Chill the remaining dressing.

2 Cook the mangetouts for 2 minutes in boiling water, then refresh in cold water. Tear the lettuces into small pieces and mix all the other salad ingredients and the bacon together. Arrange the salad on individual dishes.

3 Cook the chicken breast portions under the grill (broiler) or on a medium barbecue for 10–15 minutes, basting with the marinade and turning once, until cooked through. Thinly slice them on the diagonal. Divide between the bowls of salad and add some of the dressing. Combine and sprinkle some fresh coriander over each bowl.

CORN-FED CHICKEN SALAD WITH GARLIC BREAD

o o o

This salad also makes a light first course for eight people.

INGREDIENTS

1.75kg/4–4½ lb corn-fed chicken
300ml/½ pint/1¼ cups white wine and water, mixed
24 slices French bread, 5mm/¼in thick
1 garlic clove, peeled
225g/8oz green beans
115g/4oz young spinach leaves
2 celery sticks, thinly sliced
2 sun-dried tomatoes, chopped
2 spring onions (scallions), sliced
fresh chives and parsley, to garnish

FOR THE VINAIGRETTE

30ml/2 tbsp red wine vinegar
90ml/6 tbsp olive oil
15ml/1 tbsp wholegrain mustard
15ml/1 tbsp clear honey
30ml/2 tbsp chopped fresh mixed thyme, parsley and chives
10ml/2 tsp finely chopped capers
salt and freshly ground black pepper

SERVES 4

1 Preheat the oven to 190°C/ 375°F/Gas 5. Put the chicken into a casserole with the wine and water. Cook in the oven for about 1½ hours, until tender. Remove the casserole form the oven and leave the chicken to cool in the liquid. Remove the chicken and place on a chopping board. Discard the skin and bones and cut the flesh into small pieces.

2 To make the vinaigrette, put all the ingredients into a screw-top jar and shake vigorously to combine. Season to taste with a little salt and ground black pepper.

3 Toast the French bread under the grill (broiler) or in the oven until dry and golden brown, then lightly rub with the peeled garlic clove.

4 Trim the green beans, cut into 5cm/2in lengths and cook in boiling water until just tender. Drain and rinse under cold running water to refresh.

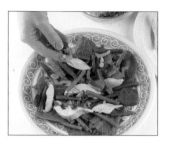

5 Wash the spinach, discarding the stalks, and tear into small pieces. Arrange on individual serving plates with the celery, green beans, sun-dried tomatoes, chicken and spring onions.

6 Spoon over the vinaigrette dressing. Arrange the toasted slices of French bread on top, garnish with fresh chives and parsley and serve immediately.

WARM CHICKEN SALAD

∘ ∘ ∘

INGREDIENTS

50g/2oz mixed salad leaves
50g/2oz baby spinach leaves
50g/2oz watercress
30ml/2 tbsp chilli sauce
30ml/2 tbsp dry sherry
15ml/1 tbsp light soy sauce
15ml/1 tbsp tomato ketchup
10ml/2 tsp olive oil
8 shallots, finely chopped
1 garlic clove, crushed
350g/12oz skinless, boneless
chicken breast portions, cut into
thin strips
1 red (bell) pepper, seeded
and sliced
175g/6oz mangetouts (snow
peas), trimmed
400g/14oz can baby corn cobs,
drained and halved
275g/10oz/scant 1½ cups brown
rice, cooked
salt and freshly ground
black pepper
fresh parsley sprig, to garnish

SERVES 6

1 If any of the salad leaves are large, tear them into smaller pieces and arrange with the spinach leaves on a serving dish. Add the watercress and toss together.

2 In a small bowl, mix together the chilli sauce, sherry, soy sauce and tomato ketchup. Set the sauce mixture aside.

3 Heat the oil in a large, non-stick frying pan or wok. Add the shallots and garlic and stir-fry over a medium heat for 1 minute.

4 Add the chicken to the pan and stir-fry for a further 3–4 minutes.

5 Add the pepper, mangetouts, baby corn cobs and rice and stir-fry for a further 2–3 minutes.

6 Pour in the chilli sauce mixture and stir-fry for 2–3 minutes, until hot and bubbling. Season to taste with salt and pepper.

7 Spoon the chicken mixture over the salad leaves, toss together to mix and serve immediately, while still warm, garnished with a sprig of fresh parsley.

Variation
Use other lean meat, such as turkey breast, beef or pork in place of the chicken.

Cook's Tip
Chilli sauce varies in strength, depending on the brand. Be careful if you are using an unfamiliar one.

SPICY CHICKEN SALAD

· · ·

INGREDIENTS

5ml/1 tsp ground cumin seeds
5ml/1 tsp paprika
5ml/1 tsp ground turmeric
1–2 garlic cloves, crushed
30ml/2 tbsp lime juice
4 skinless, boneless chicken
breast portions
225g/8oz dried rigatoni
1 red (bell) pepper, seeded
and chopped
2 celery sticks, thinly sliced
1 shallot or small onion,
finely chopped
25g/1oz/¼ cup stuffed green
olives, halved
30ml/2 tbsp clear honey
15ml/1 tbsp wholegrain mustard
15–30ml/1–2 tbsp lime juice
salt and freshly ground
black pepper
mixed salad leaves,
to serve

SERVES 6

1 Combine the cumin, paprika, turmeric, garlic and lime juice in a bowl. Season to taste with salt and pepper. Rub this mixture over the chicken portions. Lay these in a shallow dish, cover with clear film (plastic wrap) and leave in a cool place for 3 hours or overnight.

2 Preheat the oven to 200°C/ 400°F/Gas 6. Put the chicken on a rack in a single layer and bake for 20 minutes. Alternatively, grill (broil) for 8–10 minutes each side.

3 Cook the pasta in a large pan of lightly salted boiling water for 8–10 minutes, until *al dente*. Drain and rinse under cold water. Leave to drain thoroughly.

4 Put the red pepper, celery, shallot or small onion and stuffed olives into a large bowl with the pasta. Mix together.

5 Mix the honey, mustard and lime juice together in a small bowl and pour over the pasta mixture. Toss well to coat.

6 Cut the chicken portions into bitesize pieces. Arrange the mixed salad leaves on a serving dish, spoon the pasta mixture into the centre and top with the spicy chicken pieces.

CHICKEN MARYLAND SALAD

Grilled chicken, corn, bacon, banana and watercress combine in a sensational salad.

INGREDIENTS

*4 boneless free-range chicken
breast portions
oil, for brushing
225g/8oz rindless unsmoked bacon
4 corn cobs
45ml/3 tbsp soft butter (optional)
4 ripe bananas, peeled and halved
4 firm tomatoes, halved
1 escarole or butterhead lettuce
1 bunch watercress
salt and freshly ground
black pepper*

FOR THE DRESSING
*75ml/5 tbsp groundnut (peanut) oil
15ml/1 tbsp white wine vinegar
10ml/2 tsp maple syrup
10ml/2 tsp prepared mild mustard*

SERVES 4

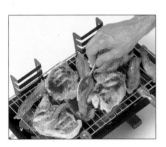

1 Season the chicken breast portions with salt and pepper, brush with oil and grill (broil) or cook on a medium-hot barbecue for 15 minutes, turning once. Grill the bacon or cook on the barbecue for 8–10 minutes, or until crisp.

2 Bring a large pan of salted water to the boil. Shuck and trim the corn cobs or leave the husks on if you like. Boil the corn cobs for 20 minutes.

3 For extra flavour, brush the corn cobs with butter and brown under the grill or on the barbecue. Grill the bananas and tomatoes or cook on the barbecue for 6–8 minutes; you can brush these with butter too if you like.

4 To make the dressing, combine the oil, wine vinegar, maple syrup and mustard with 15ml/1 tbsp water in a screw-top jar and shake well to mix.

Cook's Tip

The most commonly used mustard in salad dressings is Dijon, but you can use other varieties. Bavarian mustard is mild and fairly sweet, while American mustard is very mild.

5 Wash the lettuce and watercress leaves and spin or pat dry. Place them in a large bowl, pour over the dressing and toss well.

6 Distribute the salad leaves among four large serving plates. Slice the chicken and arrange it on top of the salad leaves together with the bacon, banana, corn cobs and tomatoes.

CHICKEN, TONGUE AND GRUYÈRE CHEESE SALAD

· · ·

The rich, sweet flavours of this salad marry well with the tart, peppery watercress. A minted lemon dressing freshens the overall effect.

INGREDIENTS

2 skinless, boneless chicken breast portions
½ chicken stock (bouillon) cube
225g/8oz ox tongue or cured ham, sliced 5 mm/¼ in thick
225g/8oz Gruyère cheese
1 lollo rosso lettuce
1 butterhead or frisée lettuce
1 bunch watercress
2 green-skinned apples, cored and sliced
3 celery sticks, sliced
60ml/4 tbsp sesame seeds, toasted
salt, freshly ground black pepper and freshly grated nutmeg

FOR THE DRESSING
75ml/5 tbsp sunflower oil
5ml/1 tsp sesame oil
45ml /3 tbsp lemon juice
10ml/2 tsp chopped fresh mint
3 drops Tabasco sauce

SERVES 4

1 Place the chicken breast portions in a shallow pan, add 300ml/ ½ pint/1¼ cups water and the stock cube and bring to the boil. Cover the pan and simmer for 15 minutes. Drain, reserving the stock for another occasion, then cool the chicken under cold running water.

2 To make the dressing, place the sunflower and sesame oils, lemon juice, chopped mint and Tabasco sauce into a screw-top jar and shake vigorously. Cut the chicken, tongue or cured ham and cheese into fine strips. Moisten with a little of the dressing and set aside until required.

3 Combine the lettuce and watercress leaves with the apple and celery. Add the dressing and toss well. Distribute among four large serving plates. Pile the chicken, tongue or ham and cheese in the centre, sprinkle with sesame seeds, season with salt, pepper and freshly grated nutmeg and serve.

CURRIED CHICKEN SALAD

INGREDIENTS
2 cooked, skinless, boneless chicken
breast portions
175g/6oz green beans
350g/12oz tricolour dried penne
150ml/¹/₄ pint/²/₃ cup natural
(plain) yogurt
5ml/1 tsp mild curry powder
1 garlic clove, crushed
1 fresh green chilli, seeded and
finely chopped
30ml/2 tbsp chopped
fresh coriander (cilantro)
4 firm ripe tomatoes, peeled,
seeded and cut into strips
salt and freshly ground
black pepper
fresh coriander (cilantro) leaves,
to garnish

SERVES 4

1 Cut the chicken into strips. Cut
the green beans into 2.5cm/
1in lengths and cook in boiling
water for 5 minutes. Drain and
rinse under cold water.

2 Cook the pasta in a pan of salted
boiling water for 8–10 minutes,
until *al dente*. Drain and rinse.

3 To make the sauce, mix the
yogurt, curry powder, garlic, chilli
and chopped coriander together in
a bowl. Stir in the chicken pieces,
cover with clear film (plastic wrap)
and leave to stand for 30 minutes.

4 Transfer the pasta to a large
serving bowl and toss with the
beans and tomatoes. Spoon over
the chicken and sauce mixture.
Garnish with the coriander leaves
and serve immediately.

CHICKEN AND MANGO SALAD WITH ORANGE RICE

• • •

This succulent, fruity salad is inspired by the exotic flavours of Indian cooking. Serve with poppadums for an authentic extra touch to a summer meal.

INGREDIENTS

*15ml/1 tbsp sunflower oil
1 onion, chopped
1 garlic clove, crushed
30ml/2 tbsp red curry paste
10ml/2 tsp apricot jam
30ml/2 tbsp chicken stock
450g/1lb cooked chicken, cut into
small pieces
150ml/¹/4 pint/²/³ cup natural
(plain) yogurt
60–75ml/4–5 tbsp mayonnaise
1 large mango, cut into
1cm/¹/2in dice
fresh flat leaf parsley sprigs,
to garnish
poppadums, to serve*

FOR THE ORANGE RICE
*175g/6oz/scant 1 cup white long
grain rice
225g/8oz/1¹/2 cups grated carrots
1 large orange, cut into segments
40g/1¹/2oz/¹/³ cup toasted flaked
(sliced) almonds*

FOR THE DRESSING
*45ml/3 tbsp olive oil
60ml/4 tbsp sunflower oil
45ml/3 tbsp lemon juice
1 garlic clove, crushed
15ml/1 tbsp chopped mixed fresh
herbs, such as tarragon, parsley
and chives
salt and ground black pepper*

SERVES 4

1 Heat the oil in a frying pan. Add the onion and garlic and cook for 3–4 minutes, until soft.

2 Stir in the curry paste, cook for about 1 minute, then lower the heat and stir in the apricot jam and stock. Mix well, add the chopped chicken and stir until the chicken is thoroughly coated in the paste. Spoon the mixture into a large bowl and leave to cool.

3 Meanwhile, boil the rice in plenty of lightly salted water until just tender. Drain, rinse under cold water and drain again. When cool, stir into the grated carrots and add the orange segments and almonds.

4 Make the dressing by whisking all the ingredients together in a bowl.

5 When the chicken mixture is cool, stir in the yogurt and mayonnaise, then add the mango, stirring it in carefully so as not to break the flesh. Chill for about 30 minutes.

6 When ready to serve, pour the dressing into the rice salad and mix well. Spoon on to a platter and mound the cold curried chicken on top. Garnish with flat leaf parsley and serve with poppadums.

Cook's Tip

To toast almonds, place them on a baking sheet in a moderate oven for 3 minutes, or dry-fry in a small pan. Turn the nuts occasionally so that they brown evenly.

CRUNCHY SALAD WITH BLACK PUDDING

• • •

Fried until crisp, slices of black pudding are extremely good in salad, particularly with crunchy bread croûtons and sweet cherry tomatoes. Serve this salad in bowls or shallow soup plates.

INGREDIENTS

250g/9oz black pudding (blood sausage), sliced
1 focaccia loaf, plain or flavoured with sun-dried tomatoes and herbs
45ml/3 tbsp olive oil
1 cos or romaine lettuce, torn into bitesize pieces
250g/9oz cherry tomatoes, halved

FOR THE DRESSING
juice of 1 lemon
90ml/6 tbsp olive oil
10ml/2 tsp French mustard
15ml/1 tbsp clear honey
30ml/2 tbsp chopped fresh herbs, such as coriander (cilantro), chives and parsley
salt and freshly ground black pepper

SERVES 4

1 Dry-fry the black pudding in a large, non-stick frying pan for 5–10 minutes, or until browned and crisp, turning occasionally. Remove the black pudding from the pan with a slotted spoon and drain on kitchen paper.

2 Cut the focaccia into chunks. Add the oil to the juices in the frying pan and cook the focaccia cubes in two batches, turning frequently, until golden on all sides. Drain on kitchen paper.

3 Mix together the focaccia, black pudding, lettuce and cherry tomatoes in a large bowl. Mix together the dressing ingredients and season to taste with salt and pepper. Pour the dressing over the salad. Mix well and serve.

PASTA SALAD WITH SALAMI AND OLIVES

· · ·

Garlic and herb dressing gives a Mediterranean flavour to a few ingredients from the pantry and refrigerator, making this an excellent salad for winter.

INGREDIENTS

225g/8oz/2 cups dried gnocchi or conchiglie
50g/2oz/¹/2 cup pitted black olives, quartered lengthways
75g/3oz thinly sliced salami, any skin removed, diced
¹/2 small red onion, finely chopped
1 large handful fresh basil leaves

FOR THE DRESSING
60ml/4tbsp extra virgin olive oil
good pinch of sugar, to taste
juice of ¹/2 lemon
5ml/1 tsp Dijon mustard
10ml/2 tsp dried oregano
1 garlic clove, crushed
salt and ground black pepper

SERVES 4

1 Cook the pasta in a pan of salted boiling water according to the packet instructions.

2 Meanwhile, make the herb dressing for the pasta. Put all the ingredients for the dressing in a large bowl with a little salt and ground black pepper to taste, and whisk well to mix.

3 Drain the pasta thoroughly, add it to the bowl of dressing and toss well to mix. Leave the dressed pasta to cool, stirring occasionally.

4 When the pasta is cold, add the remaining ingredients and toss well to mix again. Taste for seasoning, then serve immediately.

WALDORF HAM SALAD

. . .

Waldorf Salad first appeared at the Waldorf-Astoria Hotel, New York, in the 1890s. This modern-day version is something of a meal in itself.

INGREDIENTS

3 eating apples
15ml/1 tbsp lemon juice
2 slices cooked cured ham, each about 175g/6oz
2 celery sticks
150ml/¼ pint/⅔ cup mayonnaise
1 escarole or frisée lettuce
1 small radicchio, finely shredded
½ bunch watercress
45ml/3 tbsp walnut or olive oil
50g/2oz/½ cup broken walnuts, toasted
salt and freshly ground black pepper

SERVES 4

1 Peel, core, slice and finely shred the apples. Moisten with lemon juice to prevent them from turning brown. Cut the ham into 5cm/2in strips. Cut the celery sticks into similar-size pieces. Combine the apples, ham and celery in a bowl.

2 Add the mayonnaise and mix thoroughly.

3 Shred all the salad leaves finely, then moisten with oil. Distribute the leaves among four serving plates. Pile the mayonnaise mixture in the centre, sprinkle with toasted walnuts, season and serve.

CHICKEN LIVER, BACON AND TOMATO SALAD

• • •

Warm salads are especially welcome during the cooler months of the year.

INGREDIENTS

*225g/8oz young spinach,
stems removed
1 frisée lettuce
105ml/7 tbsp groundnut (peanut)
or sunflower oil
175g/6oz rindless unsmoked
bacon, cut into strips
75g/3oz day-old bread, crusts
removed and cut into short fingers
450g/1lb chicken livers
115g/4oz cherry tomatoes
salt and freshly ground
black pepper*

SERVES 4

1 Place the spinach and lettuce leaves in a salad bowl. Heat 60ml/ 4 tbsp of the groundnut or sunflower oil in a large, heavy frying pan, add the bacon strips and cook for 3–4 minutes, or until crisp and brown. Remove the bacon with a slotted spoon and drain on kitchen paper.

2 To make croûtons, fry the bread in the bacon-flavoured oil, tossing until crisp and golden. Drain on kitchen paper.

3 Heat the remaining oil in the frying pan, add the chicken livers and fry briskly for 2–3 minutes. Turn the chicken livers out over the salad leaves and add the bacon, croûtons and tomatoes. Season to taste with salt and pepper, toss and serve warm.

Variation

If you can't find any baby spinach leaves you can use lamb's lettuce. Watercress would make a deliciously peppery substitute, but you should use less of it and bulk the salad out with a milder leaf so that the watercress doesn't overwhelm the other flavours.

CURRY FRIED PORK AND RICE VERMICELLI SALAD

INGREDIENTS

225g/8oz lean pork
2 garlic cloves, finely chopped
2 slices fresh root ginger, peeled
and finely chopped
30–45ml/2–3 tbsp rice wine
45ml/3 tbsp vegetable oil
2 lemon grass stalks, finely chopped
10ml/2 tsp curry powder
175g/6oz/³/4 cup beansprouts
225g/8oz rice vermicelli, soaked in
warm water until soft, then drained
¹/2 lettuce, finely shredded
30ml/2 tbsp fresh mint leaves
lemon juice and Thai fish sauce,
to taste
salt and freshly ground
black pepper
2 spring onions (scallions),
chopped, 25g/1oz/¹/2 cup toasted
peanuts, chopped, and pork
crackling (optional) to garnish

SERVES 4

1 Cut the pork into thin strips.
Place in a shallow dish with half
the garlic and ginger. Season to
taste with salt and pepper, pour
over 30ml/2 tbsp rice wine and
marinate for at least 1 hour.

2 Heat the vegetable oil in a frying
pan or wok. Add the remaining
garlic and ginger and stir-fry over
a medium heat for a few seconds
until fragrant and golden. Stir in
the strips of pork, with the
marinade, and add the lemon grass
and curry powder.

3 Stir-fry over a high heat until
the pork is golden and cooked
through, adding more rice wine if
the mixture seems too dry.

4 Place the beansprouts in a sieve.
Blanch them by lowering the sieve
into a pan of boiling water for
1 minute, then drain and refresh
under cold running water. Drain
again. Using the same water, cook
the rice vermicelli for 3–5 minutes,
until tender. Drain and rinse under
cold running water.

5 Drain the vermicelli well and tip
into a large bowl. Add the
beansprouts, shredded lettuce and
mint leaves. Season with lemon
juice and fish sauce to taste. Toss
lightly to combine the flavours.

6 Divide the vermicelli mixture
among individual serving plates,
making a nest on each plate.
Arrange the pork mixture on top.
Garnish with spring onions,
toasted peanuts and pork
crackling, if using. Serve.

405

SWEET POTATO, EGG, PORK AND BEETROOT SALAD

This is a good way to use up leftover pork. Sweet flavours balance the bitter chicory.

INGREDIENTS
*900g/2 lb sweet potatoes
4 chicory (Belgian endive) heads
5 eggs, hard-boiled
450g/1 lb pickled young
beetroot (beets)
175g/6oz cold roast pork
salt*

FOR THE DRESSING
*75ml/5 tbsp sunflower oil
30ml/2 tbsp white wine vinegar
10ml/2 tsp Dijon mustard
5ml/1 tsp fennel seeds, crushed*

SERVE 4

1 Peel the sweet potatoes and dice into equal-size pieces.

2 Add the diced sweet potatoes to a pan of salted boiling water. Bring back to the boil, then simmer for 10–15 minutes, or until the potatoes are soft. Drain and set aside to cool.

3 To make the dressing, combine the sunflower oil, vinegar, mustard and fennel seeds in a screw-top jar and shake well.

4 Separate the chicory leaves and arrange them around the edges of four serving plates.

5 Pour two thirds of the dressing over the sweet potatoes, then stir so that all the pieces of potato are coated in the dressing. Spoon the sweet potatoes on top of the chicory leaves.

6 Shell the hard-boiled eggs. Slice the eggs and beetroot and arrange to make an attractive pattern around the sweet potato.

7 Slice the pork, then cut into strips about 4 cm/1½in wide. Place in a bowl and moisten with the rest of the dressing.

8 Pile the strips of pork into the centre of each salad. Season with salt to taste and serve.

Cook's Tip

To crush the fennel seeds, grind using a mortar and pestle. If you don't have these, use two dessertspoons instead. For extra flavour try toasting the fennel seeds before crushing.

FRANKFURTER SALAD WITH MUSTARD DRESSING

This is a last-minute salad, which you can make quickly.

INGREDIENTS

675g/1½lb small new potatoes, scrubbed or scraped
2 eggs
350g/12oz frankfurters
1 butterhead or frisée lettuce
225g/8oz young spinach leaves, stems removed
salt and freshly ground black pepper

FOR THE DRESSING

45ml/3 tbsp safflower oil
30ml/2 tbsp olive oil
15ml/1 tbsp white wine vinegar
10ml/2 tsp mustard
5ml/1 tsp caraway seeds, crushed

SERVES 4

2 Score the frankfurter skins corkscrew fashion with a small knife, then cover with boiling water and simmer for about 5 minutes to heat through. Drain well, cover and keep warm.

5 Moisten the warm potatoes and frankfurters with the remainder of the dressing and arrange them over the salad.

1 Bring the potatoes to the boil in lightly salted water and simmer for about 15 minutes, or until tender. Drain, cover and keep warm. Hard-boil the eggs for 12 minutes. Refresh in cold water, shell and cut into quarters.

3 To make the dressing, place all the ingredients in a screw-top jar and shake well.

4 Moisten the salad leaves with half of the dressing and distribute among four large serving plates.

6 Finish off the salad by topping with sections of hard-boiled egg, season to taste with salt and black pepper and serve warm.

Cook's Tip
This salad has a German slant to it and calls for a sweet-and-sour German-style mustard. American mustards have a similar quality.

SMOKED BACON AND GREEN BEAN PASTA SALAD

. . .

INGREDIENTS

*350g/12oz/3 cups dried
wholewheat pasta twists
225g/8oz green beans
8 rashers (strips) smoked bacon
350g/12oz cherry tomatoes, halved
2 bunches spring onions
(scallions), chopped
400g/14oz can chickpeas, drained
and rinsed*

FOR THE DRESSING

*90ml/6 tbsp tomato juice
30ml/2 tbsp balsamic vinegar
5ml/1 tsp ground cumin
5ml/1 tsp ground coriander
30ml/2 tbsp chopped fresh
coriander (cilantro)
salt and freshly ground
black pepper*

SERVES 4

2 Preheat the grill (broiler) and cook the bacon for 2–3 minutes on each side, until tender. Dice the bacon and add to the beans.

3 Put the tomatoes, spring onions and chickpeas in a large bowl.

4 In smaller bowl, mix together the tomato juice, vinegar, spices, fresh coriander and seasoning.

5 Pour the dressing into a large bowl. Drain the cooked pasta thoroughly and add to the tomato mixture with the green beans and bacon. Toss all the ingredients together to mix thoroughly. Adjust the seasoning, if necessary. Serve warm or cold.

1 Cook the pasta in a large pan of lightly salted boiling water for about 8–10 minutes, until *al dente*. Meanwhile, trim and halve the green beans and cook them in boiling water for about 5 minutes, until tender. Drain thoroughly, set aside and keep warm.

Cook's Tip

Always rinse drained canned beans and pulses well before using, to remove as much of the salt solution as possible. Drain again before use.

WARM PASTA SALAD WITH ASPARAGUS

. . .

Warm pasta, ham, eggs and Parmesan – a heavenly match.

INGREDIENTS

450g/1lb asparagus
450g/1lb dried tagliatelle
225g/8oz cooked cured ham, sliced
5mm/¼in thick, and cut
into fingers
2 eggs, hard-boiled, shelled
and sliced
50g/2oz piece Parmesan cheese

FOR THE DRESSING
50g/2oz cooked potato
75ml/5 tbsp olive oil
15ml/1 tbsp lemon juice
10ml/2 tsp Dijon mustard
120ml/4fl oz/½ cup
vegetable stock
salt and freshly ground
black pepper

SERVES 4

1 Bring a pan of lightly salted water to the boil. Trim and discard the tough, woody part of the asparagus stalks. Cut the asparagus in half and boil the thicker halves for 12 minutes, adding the asparagus tips after 6 minutes. Refresh under cold water until warm, then drain.

Cook's Tip

You can use either thin, green asparagus or the thicker blanched type with yellow or purple tips.

2 Finely chop 150g/5oz of the thicker asparagus pieces. Place in a food processor together with the dressing ingredients and process until smooth. Season the dressing to taste with salt and pepper.

3 Boil the pasta in a pan of salted water for 8–10 minutes, until *al dente*. Refresh under cold water.

4 Tip the pasta into a bowl and toss with the asparagus sauce. Turn out into four serving bowls. Top each pile of pasta with some of the ham, eggs and asparagus tips. Finish with shavings of Parmesan cheese and serve warm.

DEVILLED HAM AND PINEAPPLE SALAD

* * *

INGREDIENTS

*225g/8oz/2 cups dried
wholewheat penne
150ml/¹/₄ pint/²/₃ cup natural
(plain) yogurt
15ml/1 tbsp cider vinegar
5ml/1 tsp wholegrain mustard
large pinch of caster
(superfine) sugar
30ml/2 tbsp hot mango chutney
115g/4oz cooked lean ham, cubed
200g/7oz can pineapple
chunks, drained
2 celery sticks, chopped
¹/₂ green (bell) pepper, seeded
and diced
15ml/1 tbsp toasted flaked (sliced)
almonds, coarsely chopped
salt and freshly ground
black pepper
crusty bread, to serve*

SERVES 4

1 Cook the pasta in a large pan of lightly salted boiling water for 8–10 minutes, until *al dente*. Drain well and rinse thoroughly. Leave to cool.

2 To make the dressing, mix the yogurt, vinegar, mustard, sugar and mango chutney together in a large bowl. Season to taste with salt and pepper. Add the pasta and toss lightly together.

3 Transfer the pasta to a serving dish. Add the ham, pineapple, celery and green pepper.

4 Sprinkle toasted almonds over the top of the salad. Serve with crusty bread.

PEAR AND PECAN NUT SALAD

· · ∘

Toasted pecan nuts have an affinity with crisp white pears.

INGREDIENTS

75g/3oz/³/4 cup shelled pecan nuts, halved
3 crisp pears
175g/6oz young spinach, stems removed
1 escarole or butterhead lettuce
1 radicchio
30ml/2 tbsp Blue Cheese and Chive Dressing
salt and freshly ground black pepper
crusty bread, to serve

SERVES 4

1 Toast the pecan nuts under a moderate grill (broiler) to bring out their flavour.

Cook's Tip

The pecan nuts will burn very quickly under the grill (broiler), so keep constant watch over them and remove them as soon as they change colour.

2 Cut the pears into even slices, leaving the skins intact but discarding the cores.

3 Place the spinach, lettuce and radicchio leaves into a large bowl. Add the pears and toasted pecans, pour over the Blue Cheese and Chive Dressing and toss well.

4 Distribute equally among four large serving plates and season to taste with salt and pepper. Serve the salad with warm crusty bread.

GOAT'S CHEESE AND FIG SALAD

· · ·

*Fresh figs and walnuts are
perfect partners for goat's
cheese and toasted buckwheat.
The olive and nut oil dressing
contains no vinegar, depending
instead on the acidity of the
goat's cheese.*

INGREDIENTS

175g/6oz/1 cup couscous
30ml/2 tbsp toasted buckwheat
1 egg, hard-boiled
30ml/2 tbsp chopped fresh parsley
60ml/4 tbsp olive oil
45ml/3 tbsp walnut oil
115g/4oz rocket (arugula) leaves
1/2 frisée lettuce
*175g/6oz crumbly white
goat's cheese*
*50g/2oz/1/2 cup broken
walnuts, toasted*
*4 ripe figs, trimmed and almost cut
into four (leave the pieces joined at
the base)*

SERVES 4

1 Place the couscous and toasted
buckwheat in a bowl, cover with
boiling water and leave to soak for
15 minutes. Place in a sieve to
drain off any remaining water, then
spread out on a baking tray and
allow to cool.

2 Shell the hard-boiled egg and
grate finely.

3 Toss the grated egg, parsley,
couscous and buckwheat together
in a bowl. Combine the olive and
walnut oils using half to moisten
the couscous mixture.

4 Toss the salad leaves in the
remaining oil and distribute among
four large serving plates.

5 Pile the couscous mixture in the
centre of each plate and crumble
the goat's cheese over the top.
Sprinkle with toasted walnuts,
place a fig in the centre of each
plate and serve immediately.

Variation

If you find the flavour of goat's
cheese a little too strong, try
making this salad with a milder,
crumbly cheese, such as feta
or Caerphilly.

Cook's Tip

Goat's cheeses vary in strength
from the youngest, which are
soft and mild, to strongly-
flavoured, mature (sharp)
cheeses, which have a firm and
crumbly texture. The crumbly
varieties are particularly well
suited to salads.

AVOCADO, TOMATO AND MOZZARELLA SALAD

• • •

This popular salad is made from ingredients representing the colours of the Italian flag – a sunny, cheerful dish!

INGREDIENTS

175g/6oz/1½ cups dried pasta bows
6 tomatoes
225g/8oz mozzarella cheese
1 large avocado
30ml/2 tbsp chopped fresh basil
30ml/2 tbsp pine nuts, toasted
fresh basil sprig, to garnish

FOR THE DRESSING
90ml/6 tbsp olive oil
30ml/2 tbsp wine vinegar
5ml/1 tsp balsamic vinegar
5ml/1 tsp wholegrain mustard
pinch of sugar
salt and freshly ground black pepper

SERVES 4

1 Cook the pasta bows in a large pan of lightly salted boiling water for 8–10 minutes, until *al dente*. Drain well, rinse in cold water and set aside.

2 Using a sharp knife, slice the tomatoes and mozzarella cheese into thin rounds.

3 Halve the avocado, remove the stone (pit) and peel off the skin. Slice the flesh lengthways.

4 To make the dressing, put the olive oil, wine and balsamic vinegars, mustard and sugar into a small bowl and whisk until combined. Season to taste with salt and black pepper.

5 Arrange the tomato, mozzarella and avocado slices in overlapping slices around the edge of a flat serving plate.

6 Toss the pasta with half of the dressing and the chopped basil. Pile into the centre of the plate. Pour over the remaining dressing, sprinkle over the pine nuts and garnish with a sprig of fresh basil. Serve immediately.

Cook's Tip

The pale green flesh of the avocado quickly discolours once it is cut. Prepare it at the last minute and place immediately in dressing. If you do have to prepare it ahead, squeeze lemon juice over the cut side and cover with clear film (plastic wrap).

ROQUEFORT AND WALNUT PASTA SALAD

• • •

This is a simple, earthy salad, relying totally on the quality of the ingredients. There is no real substitute for the Roquefort – a blue-veined ewe's-milk cheese.

INGREDIENTS

*225g/8oz/2 cups dried pasta shapes
selection of salad leaves such as
rocket (arugula), frisée, lamb's
lettuce, baby spinach, radicchio
30ml/2 tbsp walnut oil
60ml/4 tbsp sunflower oil
30ml/2 tbsp red wine vinegar or
sherry vinegar
225g/8oz Roquefort
cheese, crumbled
115g/4oz/1 cup walnut halves
salt and freshly ground
black pepper*

SERVES 4

1 Cook the pasta in a large pan of lightly salted, boiling water for 8–10 minutes, until *al dente*. Drain well and cool. Place the salad leaves in a bowl.

2 Whisk together the walnut oil, sunflower oil and vinegar. Season to taste with salt and pepper.

3 Pile the pasta in the centre of the salad leaves, sprinkle the crumbled Roquefort over them and pour over the dressing.

4 Sprinkle the walnuts over the top. Gently toss the salad just before serving.

Cook's Tip

Toast the walnuts under a preheated grill (broiler) to add extra flavour.

418

PASTA, ASPARAGUS AND POTATO SALAD

• • •

Made with wholewheat pasta, this delicious salad is a real treat, especially when made with fresh asparagus that has just come into season.

INGREDIENTS

225g/8oz/2 cups dried wholewheat pasta shapes
60ml/4 tbsp extra virgin olive oil
350g/12oz baby new potatoes
225g/8oz asparagus
115g/4oz piece Parmesan cheese
salt and freshly ground black pepper

SERVES 4

1 Cook the pasta in a large pan of lightly salted boiling water for 8–10 minutes, until *al dente*. Drain well and toss with the olive oil while it is still warm. Season to taste with salt and pepper.

2 Scrub the potatoes and cook in boiling salted water for about 15 minutes, or until tender. Drain and toss with the pasta.

3 Trim any woody ends off the asparagus and halve the stalks if very long. Blanch in lightly salted boiling water for 6 minutes, until bright green and still crunchy. Drain well. Plunge into cold water to stop the asparagus from further cooking and leave to cool. Drain and dry on kitchen paper.

4 Gently toss the asparagus with the potatoes and pasta, adjust the seasoning to taste, if necessary, and transfer to a shallow serving bowl. Using a vegetable peeler, shave the Parmesan over the salad and serve.

COURGETTE, CARROT AND PECAN SALAD

· · ·

INGREDIENTS

2 carrots
25g/1oz/¹/₄ cup pecan nuts
4 spring onions
(scallions), sliced
50ml/2fl oz/¹/₄ cup Greek (US strained plain) yogurt
35ml/7 tsp olive oil
5ml/1 tsp lemon juice
15ml/1 tbsp chopped fresh mint
2 courgettes (zucchini)
25 g/1oz/¹/₄ cup plain (all-purpose) flour
2 pitta breads
salt and freshly ground black pepper
shredded lettuce, to serve

SERVES 2

1 Trim the carrots. Grate them coarsely into a bowl.

2 Stir in the pecans and spring onions and toss well.

3 To make the dressing, put the yogurt, 7.5ml/1½ tsp of the olive oil, the lemon juice and the mint into a bowl and whisk well. Stir into the carrot mixture and mix well. Cover with clear film (plastic wrap) and chill until required.

4 Trim the courgettes and cut them diagonally into slices. Season the flour with salt and pepper. Spread it out on a plate and turn the courgette slices in it until they are well coated.

Cook's Tip

Warm the pitta breads in the oven or under a medium grill (broiler). Do not fill the pitta breads too soon or the carrot mixture will make the bread soggy and liable to collapse.

5 Heat the remaining oil in a large, heavy frying pan. Add the coated courgette slices and cook for about 3–4 minutes, turning once, until browned. Drain the courgettes on kitchen paper.

6 Make a slit in each pitta bread to form a pocket. Fill the pittas with the carrot mixture and the courgette slices. Serve immediately on a bed of shredded lettuce.

PASTA, OLIVE AND AVOCADO SALAD

The ingredients of this salad are united by a wonderful sun-dried tomato and fresh basil dressing.

INGREDIENTS

225g/8oz/2 cups dried pasta spirals or other small pasta shapes
115g/4oz can corn, drained, or frozen corn, thawed
1/2 red (bell) pepper, seeded and diced
8 black olives, pitted and sliced
3 spring onions (scallions), chopped
2 medium avocados

FOR THE DRESSING

2 sun-dried tomato halves, loose-packed (not preserved in oil)
25ml/1 1/2 tbsp balsamic vinegar
25ml/1 1/2 tbsp red wine vinegar
1/2 garlic clove, crushed
2.5ml/1/2 tsp salt
75ml/5 tbsp olive oil
15ml/1 tbsp chopped fresh basil

SERVES 6

1 To make the dressing, drop the sun-dried tomatoes into a pan containing 2.5cm/1in boiling water and simmer for about 3 minutes, until tender. Drain thoroughly and chop finely.

2 Combine the sun-dried tomatoes, both types of vinegar, the garlic and salt in a food processor. With the motor running, add the olive oil in a steady stream. Transfer to a bowl and stir in the basil.

3 Cook the pasta in a large pan of lightly salted boiling water for 8–10 minutes, until *al dente*. Drain well. In a large bowl, combine the pasta, corn, red pepper, olives and spring onions. Pour in the dressing and toss well.

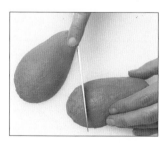

4 Just before serving, peel and stone (pit) the avocados and cut the flesh into cubes. Mix gently into the pasta, being careful not to break up the cubes, then transfer the salad to a serving dish. Serve at room temperature.

ROAST PEPPER AND MUSHROOM PASTA SALAD

• • •

Mixed peppers are combined with two kinds of mushrooms.

INGREDIENTS

1 red (bell) pepper, halved
1 yellow (bell) pepper, halved
1 green (bell) pepper, halved
350g/12oz/3 cups dried
wholewheat pasta shells or twists
30ml/2 tbsp olive oil
45ml/3 tbsp balsamic vinegar
75ml/5 tbsp tomato juice
30ml/2 tbsp chopped fresh basil
15ml/1 tbsp chopped fresh thyme
175 g/6oz/2¼ cups shiitake
mushrooms, diced
175g/6oz/2¼ cups oyster
mushrooms, sliced
400g/14oz can black-eyed beans
(peas), drained and rinsed
115g/4oz/¾ cup sultanas
(golden raisins)
2 bunches spring onions (scallions),
finely chopped
salt and freshly ground
black pepper

SERVES 6

1 Preheat the grill (broiler) to hot.
Put the peppers, cut-side down, on
a grill pan rack and place under the
grill for 10–15 minutes, until the
skins are charred. Transfer to a
bowl, cover with a clean, damp
dishtowel and set aside to cool.

2 Meanwhile, cook the pasta shells
or twists in lightly salted, boiling
water for 8–10 minutes, until *al
dente*, then drain thoroughly.

3 Mix together the oil, vinegar,
tomato juice, basil and thyme, add
to the warm pasta and toss.

4 Remove and discard the skins
from the peppers. Seed and slice
and add to the pasta.

5 Add the mushrooms, beans,
sultanas and spring onions and
season to taste with salt and
pepper. Toss the ingredients to mix
and serve warm. Alternatively,
cover and chill in the refrigerator
before serving.

MEDITERRANEAN PASTA SALAD

• • •

This is a type of Salade Niçoise made with pasta.

INGREDIENTS
225g/8oz/2 cups dried chunky pasta shapes
175g/6oz fine green beans
2 large ripe tomatoes
50g/2oz fresh basil leaves
200g/7oz can tuna in oil, drained
2 hard-boiled eggs, shelled and sliced or quartered
50 g/2oz can anchovy fillets, drained
capers and black olives, to taste

FOR THE DRESSING
90ml/6 tbsp extra virgin olive oil
30ml/2 tbsp white wine vinegar
2 garlic cloves, crushed
2.5ml/½ tsp Dijon mustard
30ml/2 tbsp chopped fresh basil
salt and freshly ground black pepper

SERVES 4

1 To make the dressing, whisk all the ingredients together in a small bowl. Season to taste with salt and pepper and set aside for the flavours to mingle while you prepare the salad.

Cook's Tip

Don't be tempted to chill this salad – the flavour will be dulled.

2 Cook the pasta in salted, boiling water for 8–10 minutes, until *al dente*. Drain well and cool.

3 Trim the green beans and blanch in lightly salted, boiling water for 3 minutes. Drain and refresh in cold water.

4 Slice the tomatoes and arrange on the base of a serving bowl. Moisten with a little dressing and cover with a quarter of the basil leaves. Then cover with the beans. Moisten with a little more dressing and cover with a third of the remaining basil.

5 Cover the vegetables with the pasta tossed in a little more dressing, half the remaining basil and the coarsely flaked tuna.

6 Arrange the eggs on top, then finally sprinkle over the anchovy fillets, capers and olives. Spoon over the remaining dressing and garnish with the remaining basil. Serve immediately.

424

The recipes in this chapter feature luxurious ingredients, exotic
combinations, spectacular presentations and sophisticated
flavours – truly dining in style. There is a special salad to suit
every occasion, from an *al fresco* dinner to a buffet party.

SPECIAL OCCASION
SALADS

GADO GADO

. . .

This classic Indonesian vegetable salad is served with a delicious hot peanut sauce.

INGREDIENTS

2 medium potatoes
175g/6oz green beans, trimmed
175g/6oz Chinese leaves (Chinese cabbage), shredded
1 iceberg lettuce
175g/6oz beansprouts
½ cucumber, cut into fingers
150g/5oz mooli (daikon), shredded
3 spring onions (scallions)
225g/8oz tofu, cut into large slices
3 hard-boiled eggs, shelled and quartered
1 small bunch fresh coriander (cilantro)
prawn (shrimp) crackers, to serve

FOR THE PEANUT SAUCE

150g/5oz/1¼ cups raw peanuts
15ml/1 tbsp vegetable oil
2 shallots or 1 small onion, finely chopped
1 garlic clove, crushed
1–2 small fresh chillies, seeded and finely chopped
1cm/½in square shrimp paste or 15ml/1 tbsp Thai fish sauce (optional)
30ml/2 tbsp tamarind sauce
120ml/4fl oz/½ cup canned coconut milk
15ml/1 tbsp clear honey

SERVES 4–6

1 Peel the potatoes. Bring to the boil in salted water and simmer for about 15 minutes, or until tender. Cook the green beans for about 3–4 minutes. Drain the potatoes and beans and refresh under cold running water.

2 To make the peanut sauce, dry-fry the peanuts in a wok, or place under a moderate grill (broiler), tossing them all the time to prevent them from burning.

3 Turn the peanuts on to a clean cloth and rub them vigorously with your hands to remove the papery skins. Place the peanuts in a food processor and process for about 2 minutes until finely crushed.

4 Heat the vegetable oil in a wok and soften the shallots or onion, garlic and chillies without letting them colour. Add the shrimp paste or fish sauce, if using, together with the tamarind sauce, coconut milk and honey.

5 Simmer briefly, add to the blended peanuts and process to form a thick sauce. Transfer to a small serving bowl and keep hot.

6 Arrange the potatoes, green beans and all the other salad ingredients on a large serving platter. Serve with the bowl of peanut sauce and prawn crackers.

Cook's Tip

Shrimp paste, also known as terasi and blachan, is widely used throughout South-east Asia. It is made from fermented shrimp, pounded to a paste with salt.

COMPOSED SALADS

∘ ∘ ∘

A composed salad makes a perfect appetizer or light main course for a special occasion. They are light and colourful and lend themselves to endless variation – and the components can often be prepared ahead for quick assembly.

Almost any combination of ingredients can be used – let your imagination and your palate guide you. Arranged attractively on a plate or in a bowl, this type of salad offers contrasting flavours, textures and colours. Raw or cooked vegetables, fresh fruits, hard-boiled hen's or quail's eggs, smoked or cooked poultry, meat, fish or shellfish can all be used, but it is important that the dressing or other kind of seasoning unites all the varied elements harmoniously.

Unlike a more basic tossed salad in which the leaves or vegetables are tossed together with a simple vinaigrette, the components of a composed salad are kept more separate and distinctive. The ingredients might be arranged in groups, sometimes on a bed of lettuce or other salad leaves, or simply arranged in circles or rows on the serving plates.

Prawn, Avocado and Citrus Salad

INGREDIENTS

15ml/1 tbsp lemon juice
15ml/1 tbsp lime juice
15ml/1 tbsp clear honey
45ml/3 tbsp olive oil
30–45ml/2–3 tbsp walnut oil
30ml/2 tbsp chopped fresh chives
450g/1lb large cooked prawns (shrimp), peeled and deveined
1 avocado, peeled, stoned (pitted) and cut into small dice
1 pink grapefruit, peeled and segmented
1 large navel orange, peeled and segmented
30ml/2 tbsp pine nuts, toasted
salt and freshly ground black pepper

SERVES 6

1 Blend the lemon and lime juices, salt and pepper and honey in a bowl. Gradually whisk in the olive oil, then the walnut oil, to make a creamy dressing. Stir in the chives.

2 Arrange the prawns with the avocado and grapefruit and orange segments on individual serving plates. Drizzle over the dressing, sprinkle with the toasted pine nuts, and serve.

Smoked Salmon Salad with Dill

INGREDIENTS

225g/8oz smoked salmon, thinly sliced
1 fennel bulb, thinly sliced
1 medium cucumber, seeded and cut into julienne strips
30ml/2 tbsp lemon juice
120ml/4fl oz/1/2 cup olive oil
30ml/2 tbsp chopped fresh dill, plus a few sprigs to garnish
freshly ground black pepper
caviar, to garnish (optional)

SERVES 4

1 Arrange the salmon slices on four serving plates and arrange the slices of fennel alongside, together with the cucumber strips.

2 Combine the lemon juice and pepper in a small bowl. Gradually whisk in the olive oil to make a creamy vinaigrette. Stir in the dill.

3 Spoon a little vinaigrette over the fennel and cucumber. Drizzle the remaining vinaigrette over the smoked salmon and garnish with sprigs of dill. Top each salad with a spoonful of caviar, if you like, before serving.

Chicory Salad with Roquefort

INGREDIENTS

30ml/2 tbsp red wine vinegar
5ml/1 tsp Dijon mustard
50ml/2oz/1/4 cup walnut oil
15–30ml/1–2 tbsp sunflower oil
2 chicory (Belgian endive) heads
1 celery heart or 4 celery sticks, cut into julienne strips
75g/3oz/3/4 cup walnut halves, lightly toasted
115g/4oz Roquefort cheese
salt and freshly ground black pepper
fresh parsley sprigs, to garnish

SERVES 4

1 Whisk together the vinegar, mustard and salt and pepper to taste in a small bowl. Slowly whisk in the oils, to make a vinaigrette.

2 Arrange the chicory on serving plates. Sprinkle over the celery and walnuts. Crumble the Roquefort on top of each salad, drizzle over a little vinaigrette, garnish and serve.

Clockwise from far right: Prawn, Avocado and Citrus Salad; Smoked Salmon Salad with Dill; and Chicory Salad with Roquefort.

WARM MONKFISH SALAD

· · ·

Monkfish has a matchless flavour and benefits from being cooked simply. Teaming it with wilted baby spinach and toasted pine nuts is inspirational.

INGREDIENTS

*2 monkfish fillets, about
350g/12oz each
25g/1oz/⅓ cup pine nuts
15ml/1 tbsp olive oil
15g/½oz/1 tbsp butter
225g/8oz baby spinach leaves,
washed and stalks removed
salt and freshly ground
black pepper*

FOR THE DRESSING
*5ml/1 tsp Dijon mustard
5ml/1 tsp sherry vinegar
60ml/4 tbsp olive oil
1 garlic clove, crushed*

SERVES 4

1 Holding the knife at a slight angle, cut each monkfish fillet into 12 diagonal slices. Season lightly with salt and pepper and set aside.

2 Dry-fry the pine nuts in a heavy frying pan, shaking it occasionally, until golden brown. Do not burn. Transfer to a plate; set aside.

Variation

Substitute a variety of salad leaves for the spinach.

3 Make the dressing by whisking all the ingredients together until smooth and creamy. Pour it into a small pan, season to taste with salt and pepper and heat gently.

4 Heat the oil and butter in a ridged griddle pan or frying pan until sizzling. Add the fish; sauté for 20–30 seconds on each side.

5 Put the spinach leaves in a bowl and pour over the warm dressing. Sprinkle with the toasted pine nuts, reserving a few, and toss together well. Divide the spinach leaves among four plates and arrange the monkfish slices on top. Sprinkle the reserved pine nuts on top and serve.

ASPARAGUS AND LANGOUSTINE SALAD

. . .

For a really extravagant treat, you could make this attractive salad with medallions of lobster. For a more economic version, use large prawns, allowing six per serving.

INGREDIENTS
16 langoustines
16 fresh asparagus spears, trimmed
2 carrots
30ml/2 tbsp olive oil
1 garlic clove, peeled
4 fresh tarragon sprigs and some chopped, to garnish

FOR THE DRESSING
30ml/2 tbsp tarragon vinegar
120ml/4fl oz/¹/₂ cup olive oil
salt and freshly ground black pepper

SERVES 4

1 Peel the langoustines and keep the shells for stock. Set aside.

2 Steam the asparagus over boiling salted water until just tender, but still a little crisp. Refresh under cold water, drain and place in a shallow dish.

3 Peel the carrots and cut into fine julienne shreds. Cook in a pan of lightly salted boiling water for about 3 minutes, until tender but still crunchy. Drain, refresh under cold water, then drain again. Place in the dish with the asparagus.

4 Make the dressing. Whisk the tarragon vinegar with the oil. Season to taste with salt and pepper. Pour over the vegetables and leave to marinate.

5 Heat the oil with the garlic in a frying pan until very hot. Add the langoustines and sauté until just heated through. Discard the garlic.

6 Cut the asparagus spears in half and arrange on four individual plates with the carrots. Drizzle over the dressing left in the dish and top each portion with four langoustine tails. Top with the tarragon sprigs and sprinkle the chopped tarragon on top. Serve immediately.

THAI SCENTED FISH SALAD

• • •

INGREDIENTS

350g/12oz fillet of red mullet, sea
bream or snapper
1 cos or romaine lettuce
½ lollo biondo lettuce
1 papaya or mango, peeled
and sliced
1 pitahaya, peeled and sliced
1 large tomato, cut into wedges
½ cucumber, peeled and cut
into strips
3 spring onions (scallions), sliced

FOR THE MARINADE
5ml/1 tsp coriander seeds
5ml/1 tsp fennel seeds
2.5ml/½ tsp cumin seeds
5ml/1 tsp caster (superfine) sugar
2.5ml/½ tsp hot chilli sauce
30ml/2 tbsp garlic oil
salt

FOR THE DRESSING
15ml/1 tbsp creamed coconut
(coconut cream)
60ml/4 tbsp groundnut (peanut) or
safflower oil
finely grated rind and juice of
1 lime
1 fresh red chilli, seeded and
finely chopped
5ml/1 tsp sugar
45ml/3 tbsp chopped fresh
coriander (cilantro)
salt

SERVES 4

1 Cut the fish into even strips and
place them on a plate or in a
shallow bowl.

2 To make the marinade, crush the
coriander, fennel and cumin seeds
together with the caster sugar. Add
the chilli sauce, garlic oil and salt
and combine.

3 Spread the marinade over the
fish, cover and leave to stand in a
cool place for at least 20 minutes –
longer if you have time.

4 To make the dressing, place the
creamed coconut and salt in a
screw-top jar with 45ml/3 tbsp
boiling water and leave to dissolve.
Add the oil, lime rind and juice,
chilli, sugar and chopped
coriander. Shake well and set aside.

5 Combine the lettuce leaves with
the papaya or mango, pitahaya,
tomato, cucumber and spring
onions. Toss with the dressing,
then distribute among four large
serving plates.

6 Heat a large, heavy non-stick
frying-pan, add the fish and cook
for 5 minutes, turning once. Place
the cooked fish on the salad and
serve immediately.

Cook's Tip

If planning ahead, you can
leave the fish in the marinade
for up to 8 hours. The dressing
can also be made in advance,
without the fresh coriander
(cilantro). Store at room
temperature and add the
coriander just before
assembling the salad.

SAN FRANCISCO SALAD

· · ·

California is a salad-maker's paradise and is renowned for the healthiness of its produce. San Francisco has become the salad capital of California.

INGREDIENTS

*900g/2 lb langoustines or scampi
(extra large shrimp)
50g/2oz bulb fennel, sliced
2 medium tomatoes, quartered
4 small tomatoes
30ml/2 tbsp olive oil, plus extra for
moistening the salad leaves
60ml/4 tbsp brandy
150ml/¼ pint/⅔ cup dry
white wine
200ml/7fl oz can lobster or
crab bisque
30ml/2 tbsp chopped
fresh tarragon
45ml/3 tbsp double (heavy) cream
225g/8oz green beans, trimmed
2 oranges
175g/6oz lamb's lettuce
115g/4oz rocket (arugula) leaves
½ frisée lettuce
salt and cayenne pepper*

SERVES 4

1 Bring a large pan of salted water to the boil, add the langoustines or scampi and simmer for 10 minutes. Refresh under cold running water.

2 Preheat the oven to 220°C/425°F/Gas 7. Twist the tails from all but four of the langoustines or scampi – reserve these to garnish the dish. Peel the outer shell from the tail meat. Put the tail peelings, carapace and claws in a heavy roasting pan with the fennel and medium tomatoes. Toss with the olive oil and roast near the top of the oven for 20 minutes to bring out the flavours.

3 Remove the roasting pan from the oven and place it over a moderate heat. Add the brandy and ignite to release the flavour of the alcohol. Add the white wine and simmer briefly.

4 Transfer the contents of the roasting pan to a food processor and reduce to a coarse purée: this will take only 10–15 seconds. Rub the purée through a fine nylon sieve into a bowl. Add the lobster or crab bisque, tarragon and cream. Season to taste with salt and a little cayenne pepper.

5 Bring a pan of salted water to the boil, add the beans and cook for 6 minutes. Drain and cool under cold running water. To segment the oranges, cut the peel from the top and bottom, and then from the sides, with a serrated knife. Loosen the segments by cutting between the membranes and the flesh with a small knife.

6 Moisten the salad leaves with olive oil and distribute among four serving plates. Fold the langoustine tails or scampi into the dressing and distribute among the plates. Add the beans, orange segments and small tomatoes. Garnish each plate with a whole langoustine or scampi and serve warm.

MILLIONAIRE'S LOBSTER SALAD

When money is no object and you're in a decadent mood, this salad is the perfect choice.

INGREDIENTS

1 medium lobster, live or cooked
1 bay leaf
1 fresh thyme sprig
675g/1½ lb new potatoes
2 ripe tomatoes
4 oranges
½ frisée lettuce
175g/6oz lamb's lettuce leaves
60ml/4 tbsp extra virgin olive oil
200g/7oz can young artichokes in brine, quartered
1 small bunch fresh tarragon, chervil or flat leaf parsley
salt

FOR THE DRESSING

30ml/2 tbsp frozen concentrated orange juice, thawed
75g/3oz/6 tbsp unsalted (sweet) butter, diced
salt and cayenne pepper

SERVES 4

1 If the lobster needs cooking, add it whole to a large pan of cold salted water with the bay leaf and thyme. Bring to the boil and simmer for 15 minutes. Cool under running water.

2 Twist off the legs and claws, and separate the tail from the body. Break the claws with a hammer and remove the meat. Cut the tail piece open, slice the meat and set aside.

3 Bring the potatoes to the boil in salted water and simmer for about 15 minutes, until tender. Drain, cover and keep warm.

4 Cut a cross in the skin of the tomatoes, cover with boiling water and leave for 30 seconds. Cool under cold running water and slip off the skins. Halve the tomatoes, discard the seeds, then cut the flesh into large dice.

5 To segment the oranges, remove the peel from the top, bottom and sides with a serrated knife. With a small paring knife, loosen the orange segments by cutting carefully between the flesh and the membranes, holding the fruit over a small bowl.

Variation

This dish is also delicious prepared in exactly the same way with crawfish, which is also known as langouste or rock lobster.

6 To make the dressing, pour the orange juice into a heatproof bowl and set it over a pan containing about 2.5cm/1in gently simmering water. Heat the juice for 1 minute, turn off the heat, then add the butter, a little at a time, whisking constantly, until the dressing reaches a coating consistency.

7 Season to taste with salt and a pinch of cayenne pepper, cover and keep warm.

8 Dress the salad leaves with olive oil, then divide among four large serving plates. Moisten the potatoes, artichokes and orange segments with olive oil and distribute among the leaves.

9 Lay the sliced lobster over the salad, spoon on the warm dressing, add the diced tomato and decorate with the fresh herbs. Serve the salad at room temperature.

GENOESE SQUID SALAD

. . .

INGREDIENTS

450g/1lb prepared squid,
cut into rings
4 garlic cloves, coarsely chopped
300ml/¹/₂ pint/1¹/₄ cups Italian
red wine
450g/1lb waxy new
potatoes, scrubbed
225g/8oz green beans, trimmed
and cut into short lengths
2–3 sun-dried tomatoes in oil,
drained and thinly
sliced lengthways
60ml/4 tbsp extra virgin olive oil
15ml/1 tbsp red wine vinegar
salt and freshly ground
black pepper

SERVES 4–6

1 Preheat the oven to 180°C/ 350°F/Gas 4. Put the squid rings in an earthenware dish with half the garlic, the wine and pepper to taste. Cover and bake for 45 minutes, or until the squid is tender.

2 Put the potatoes in a pan, cover with cold water and add a good pinch of salt. Bring to the boil, cover and simmer over a low heat for about 15 minutes, until tender. Using a slotted spoon, lift out the potatoes and set aside. Add the beans to the boiling water and cook for 3 minutes. Drain.

3 When the potatoes are cool enough to handle, slice them thickly on the diagonal and place them in a bowl with the warm beans and sun-dried tomatoes. Whisk the oil, vinegar and the remaining garlic in a jug (pitcher) and add salt and pepper to taste. Pour over the potato mixture.

4 Drain the squid and discard the liquid. Add the squid to the potato mixture and mix very gently. Arrange on individual plates and season liberally with pepper.

Cook's Tip

The French potato called Charlotte is perfect for this salad because it retains its shape when boiled. Prepared squid can be bought from supermarkets with fresh fish counters, and from fishmongers.

TUNA CARPACCIO

. . .

Fillet of beef is most often used for carpaccio, but meaty fish, such as tuna and swordfish, make a change. The secret is to slice the fish wafer thin.

INGREDIENTS

2 fresh tuna steaks, about 450g/1lb
total weight
60ml/4 tbsp extra virgin olive oil
15ml/1 tbsp balsamic vinegar
5ml/1 tsp caster (superfine) sugar
30ml/2 tbsp bottled green
peppercorns or capers, drained
salt and freshly ground
black pepper
lemon wedges and green salad,
to serve

SERVES 4

1 Remove the skin from each tuna steak and place each steak between two sheets of clear film (plastic wrap) or baking parchment. Pound with the side of a rolling pin or the flat side of a meat mallet until the steak is flattened slightly.

2 Roll up the tuna steaks as tightly as possible, then wrap tightly in clear film. Place the tuna steaks in the freezer for about 4 hours, or until firm.

3 Unwrap the tuna and cut crossways into the thinnest possible slices. Arrange the slices on four individual serving plates.

4 Whisk together the oil, vinegar, sugar and peppercorns or capers, season to taste with salt and pepper and pour over the tuna. Cover and allow to come to room temperature for 30 minutes before serving with lemon wedges and green salad.

Cook's Tip
Don't skimp the freezing, as this makes it possible to cut wafer-thin slices of tuna.

Cook's Tip
Raw fish is safe to eat as long as it is very fresh, so check with your fishmonger before purchase and make and serve the carpaccio the same day. Do not buy fish that has been frozen and thawed.

SALADE MOUCLADE

• ◦ ◦

*Mouclade is a famous dish from
La Rochelle in South-west
France. It consists of mussels in
a light curry cream sauce. Here
the flavours appear in a salad of
warm lentils and spinach.*

INGREDIENTS

*45ml/3 tbsp olive oil
1 onion, finely chopped
350g/12oz/1¹/₂ cups Puy or
green lentils
900ml/1¹/₂ pints/3³/₄ cups
vegetable stock
2 kg/4¹/₂lb fresh mussels in
their shells
75ml/5 tbsp white wine
2.5ml/¹/₂ tsp curry paste
pinch of saffron
30ml/2 tbsp double (heavy) cream
2 large carrots, peeled
4 celery sticks
900g/2lb young spinach,
stalks removed
15ml/1 tbsp garlic oil
salt and cayenne pepper*

SERVES 4

1 Heat the oil in a heavy pan and
cook the onion for 6–8 minutes,
until soft, but not coloured. Add
the lentils and vegetable stock,
bring to the boil, lower the heat
and simmer for 45 minutes, until
tender. Remove from the heat and
set aside to cool.

2 Clean the mussels thoroughly,
discarding any that are damaged.
Any that are open should close if
given a sharp tap; if they fail to do
so, discard these too.

3 Place the mussels in a large pan,
add the wine, cover and steam
over a high heat, shaking the pan
occasionally, for 12 minutes. Strain
the mussels in a colander, reserving
the cooking liquid. Discard any
that have not opened during the
cooking. Take all but four of the
mussels out of their shells.

4 Strain the mussel liquid through
a fine sieve or muslin (cheesecloth)
into a wide, shallow pan to remove
any grit or sand.

5 Add the curry paste and saffron
to the pan, then reduce the liquid
over a high heat until the pan is
almost dry. Remove from the heat,
stir in the cream, season to taste
with salt and pepper and combine
with the mussels.

6 Cut the carrot and celery into
5cm/2in batons and cook in lightly
salted boiling water for 3 minutes.
Drain well, cool and moisten with
olive oil.

7 Wash the spinach, put the wet
leaves into a large pan, cover and
steam for 30 seconds. Immerse in
cold water, then press the leaves dry
in a colander. Moisten with garlic
oil and season.

8 Spoon the lentils into the centre of
four plates. Place heaps of spinach
around the edge, with some carrot
and celery on top. Spoon over the
mussels and garnish with the
reserved mussels in their shells.

HOT COCONUT, PRAWN AND PAPAYA SALAD

• • •

Transport yourself to the Far East with this wonderful dish.

INGREDIENTS

225g/8oz raw or cooked prawn (shrimp) tails, peeled and deveined
2 ripe papayas
225g/8oz cos or romaine or iceberg lettuce leaves, Chinese leaves (Chinese cabbage) and young spinach leaves
1 firm tomato, peeled, seeded and coarsely chopped
3 spring onions (scallions), shredded
1 small bunch fresh coriander (cilantro), shredded, and 1 large chilli, sliced, to garnish

FOR THE DRESSING
15ml/1 tbsp creamed coconut (coconut cream)
90ml/6 tbsp vegetable oil
juice of 1 lime
2.5ml/½ tsp hot chilli sauce
10ml/2 tsp Thai fish sauce
5ml/1 tsp sugar

SERVES 4–6

2 If using raw prawn tails, cover with cold water in a pan, bring to the boil and simmer for no longer than 2 minutes. Drain thoroughly and set aside. If using cooked prawns, pat dry with kitchen paper.

3 Cut the papayas in half from top to bottom and remove the black seeds. Peel off the skin and cut the flesh into equal-size pieces.

4 Place the salad leaves in a bowl. Add the prawn tails, papayas, tomato and spring onions. Pour over the dressing, garnish with the coriander and chilli, and serve.

1 To make the dressing, place the creamed coconut in a screw-top jar and add 30ml/2 tbsp boiling water to soften it. Add the oil, lime juice, chilli sauce, fish sauce and sugar. Shake well to mix and set aside. Do not chill.

ROASTED CHICKEN AND WALNUT SALAD

∘ ∘ ∘

The chickens may be cooked the day before eating and the salad finished on the day itself.

INGREDIENTS
4 fresh tarragon or rosemary sprigs
2 x 1.75kg/4–4¹/₂lb chickens
65g/2¹/₂oz/5 tbsp softened butter
150ml/¹/₄ pint/²/₃ cup chicken stock
150ml/¹/₄ pint/²/₃ cup white wine
115g/4oz/1 cup walnut pieces
1 small cantaloupe melon
lettuce leaves
450g/1 lb seedless grapes or pitted cherries
salt and freshly ground black pepper

FOR THE DRESSING
30ml/2 tbsp tarragon vinegar
120ml/4fl oz/¹/₂ cup light olive oil
30ml/2 tbsp chopped fresh mixed herbs such as parsley, mint, tarragon

SERVES 8

1 Preheat the oven to 200°C/400°F/Gas 6. Put the herb sprigs inside the chickens and season with salt and pepper.

2 Spread the chickens with 50g/2oz/4 tbsp of the softened butter, place in a roasting pan and pour the stock around them. Cover loosely with foil and roast for about 1½ hours, basting twice, until browned and the juices run clear. Remove from the roasting pan and leave to cool.

3 Add the wine to the roasting pan. Bring to the boil over a medium heat and cook until syrupy. Strain and leave to cool. Heat the remaining butter in a frying pan and gently fry the walnuts until lightly browned. Scoop the melon flesh into balls or cut into cubes.

4 To make the dressing, whisk the vinegar and olive oil together with a little salt and pepper to taste. Skim off the fat from the chicken juices and add the juices to the dressing with the herbs. Adjust the seasoning to taste.

5 Cut the chicken into serving portions and arrange them on a bed of lettuce leaves. Sprinkle over the grapes or cherries and melon balls or cubes and spoon over the dressing. Sprinkle with the toasted walnuts and serve.

CHICKEN LIVER SALAD

* * *

This delicious salad may be served as a main course for a summer lunch party, or as a tasty first course served on individual plates.

INGREDIENTS

mixed salad leaves, such as frisée, oak leaf lettuce, radicchio, rocket (arugula)
1 avocado
30ml/2 tbsp lemon or lime juice
2 pink grapefruit
350g/12oz chicken livers
30ml/2 tbsp olive oil
1 garlic clove, crushed
salt and freshly ground black pepper
whole fresh chives, to garnish

FOR THE DRESSING
30ml/2 tbsp lemon juice
60ml/4 tbsp olive oil
2.5ml/1/2 tsp wholegrain mustard
2.5ml/1/2 tsp clear honey
15ml/1 tbsp chopped fresh chives
salt and freshly ground black pepper

SERVES 4

1 To make the dressing, put the lemon juice, olive oil, wholegrain mustard, honey and fresh chives into a screw-top jar, and shake vigorously. Season to taste with salt and freshly ground black pepper.

2 Arrange the mixed salad leaves attractively on a large serving plate.

3 Peel and stone (pit) the avocado, dice the flesh and mix with the lemon or lime juice to prevent it from browning. Add to the plate of mixed leaves.

4 Peel the grapefruit with a small serrated knife, removing as much of the white pith as possible. Split into segments and arrange with the salad leaves and avocado on the serving plate.

5 Pat dry the chicken livers on kitchen paper and remove any unwanted pieces.

6 Using a sharp knife, cut the larger chicken livers in half. Leave the smaller ones whole.

Cook's Tip

If using frozen chicken livers, thaw them thoroughly first.

7 Heat the oil in a large frying pan. Stir-fry the chicken livers and garlic briskly until the livers are brown all over (they should be slightly pink inside).

8 Season the chicken livers to taste with salt and black pepper, remove from the pan and drain well on kitchen paper.

9 Place the chicken livers, while still warm, on the salad leaves and spoon over the dressing. Garnish with the whole chives and serve the salad immediately.

GRILLED CHICKEN SALAD WITH LAVENDER

○ ○ ○

Lavender may seem an odd ingredient, but its delightful scent has a natural affinity with garlic, orange and other herbs.

INGREDIENTS

4 boneless, skinless chicken breast portions
900ml/1½ pints/3¾ cups light chicken stock
175g/6oz/1 cup fine polenta or cornmeal
50g/2oz/4 tbsp butter
450g/1 lb young spinach leaves
175g/6oz lamb's lettuce leaves
8 small tomatoes, halved
salt and ground black pepper
8 fresh lavender sprigs, to garnish

FOR THE LAVENDER MARINADE
6 fresh lavender flowers
10ml/2 tsp finely grated orange rind
2 garlic cloves, crushed
10ml/2 tsp clear honey
30ml/2 tbsp olive oil
10ml/2 tsp chopped fresh thyme
10ml/2 tsp chopped fresh marjoram
salt

SERVES 4

1 To make the marinade, strip the lavender flowers from their stems and combine with the orange rind, garlic, honey and a pinch of salt. Add the olive oil, thyme and marjoram. Slash the chicken deeply, spread over the mixture and leave to marinate in a cool place for at least 20 minutes.

2 To prepare the polenta, bring the chicken stock to the boil in a large, heavy pan. Add the polenta or cornmeal in a slow, steady stream, stirring constantly, until thick: this will take 2–3 minutes. Turn the cooked polenta out on to a 2.5cm/1in deep buttered tray and leave to cool.

3 Heat the grill (broiler) to a moderate temperature. If using a barbecue, let the embers settle to a steady glow. Grill (broil) the chicken breast portions for about 15 minutes, turning them once.

Cook's Tip

This lavender marinade is a delicious flavouring for salt-water fish as well as chicken. Try it spread over grilled cod, haddock, halibut, sea bass or bream.

4 Cut the cooled polenta into 2.5cm/1in cubes with a wet knife. Heat the remaining butter in a large frying pan and fry the polenta cubes until golden brown.

5 Divide the salad leaves and tomatoes among four large serving plates. Slice each chicken breast portion and lay over the salad. Place the polenta cubes among the salad and season to taste with salt and pepper. Garnish with the sprigs of lavender and serve.

DIJON CHICKEN SALAD

This attractive and classical dish is ideal to serve for a simple but tasty and elegant lunch.

INGREDIENTS

*4 skinless, boneless chicken
breast portions
mixed salad leaves such as frisée,
oakleaf lettuce and radicchio*

FOR THE MARINADE
*30ml/2 tbsp tarragon wine vinegar
5ml/1 tsp Dijon mustard
5ml/1 tsp clear honey
90ml/6 tbsp olive oil
salt and freshly ground
black pepper*

FOR THE MUSTARD DRESSING
*30ml/2 tbsp Dijon mustard
3 garlic cloves, crushed
15ml/1 tbsp grated onion
60ml/4 tbsp white wine*

SERVES 4

1 To make the marinade mix the vinegar, mustard, honey and olive oil, together in a shallow glass or earthenware dish that is large enough to hold the chicken breasts in a single layer. Season to taste with salt and pepper.

2 Add the chicken breast portions to the dish, making sure they do not overlap each other.

3 Turn the chicken over in the marinade to coat completely, cover with clear film (plastic wrap) and chill in the refrigerator overnight.

4 Preheat the oven to 190°C/ 375°F/Gas 5. Transfer the chicken and the marinade into an ovenproof dish, cover with kitchen foil and bake for about 35 minutes, or until tender. Leave the chicken to cool in the liquid.

5 To make the mustard dressing, put all the ingredients into a screw-top jar and shake vigorously.

6 Thinly slice the chicken and fan out the slices.

7 Arrange the chicken slices on a serving dish with the salad leaves. Spoon over some of the mustard dressing and serve. Serve the rest of the dressing separately in a bowl or jug (pitcher).

Cook's Tip
The dressing can be made several days in advance and stored in the refrigerator.

DUCK AND PASTA SALAD

· · ·

The acidity of fruit is a very good accompaniment to a rich meat, such as duck, as it adds a tartness that makes the meat more digestible. This luxurious salad includes apple, orange and, in the dressing, dried cherries. The rigatoni adds a welcome element of carbohydrate and makes the dish a complete meal.

INGREDIENTS

2 boneless duck breast fillets
5ml/1 tsp coriander seeds, crushed
350g/12oz dried rigatoni
1 eating apple, diced
2 oranges, segmented
salt and freshly ground
black pepper
fresh chopped coriander (cilantro)
and mint, to garnish

FOR THE DRESSING

150ml/¹/4 pint/²/3 cup orange juice
15ml/1 tbsp lemon juice
10ml/2 tsp clear honey
1 shallot, finely chopped
1 garlic clove, crushed
1 celery stick, chopped
75g/3oz/³/4 cup dried cherries
45ml/3 tbsp port
15ml/1 tbsp chopped fresh mint
30ml/2 tbsp chopped fresh coriander (cilantro)

SERVES 6

1 Preheat the grill (broiler). Remove the skin and fat from the duck breast fillets, season with salt and pepper and rub with the crushed coriander seeds.

2 Grill (broil) the duck fillets for 7–10 minutes (depending on the size). Wrap the duck fillets in foil and leave for 20 minutes.

3 Cook the pasta in a large pan of lightly salted, boiling water for 8–10 minutes, until *al dente*. Drain thoroughly and rinse under cold running water. Set the pasta aside to cool.

4 To make the dressing, put the orange juice, lemon juice, honey, shallot, garlic, celery, cherries, port, mint and fresh coriander into a small bowl. Whisk together, cover with clear film (plastic wrap) and leave to marinate for 30 minutes.

5 Unwrap the duck fillets from the foil and, using a very sharp carving knife, slice the duck very thinly. (It should still be slightly pink in the centre.)

6 Put the pasta into a large mixing bowl, add the dressing, diced apple and segments of orange. Toss well to coat the pasta.

7 Transfer the salad to a serving plate with the duck slices and garnish with the chopped coriander and mint.

DUCK SALAD WITH ORANGE SAUCE

• • •

The rich, gamey flavour of duck provides the foundation for this delicious salad.

INGREDIENTS
*1 small orange
2 boneless duck breast fillets
150ml/¼ pint/⅔ cup dry
white wine
5ml/1 tsp ground coriander seeds
2.5ml/½ tsp ground cumin or
fennel seeds
30ml/2 tbsp caster
(superfine) sugar
juice of ½ small lime or lemon
75g/3oz day-old bread,
thickly sliced
45ml/3 tbsp garlic oil
½ escarole lettuce
½ frisée lettuce
30ml/2 tbsp sunflower oil
salt and cayenne pepper
4 sprigs fresh coriander (cilantro),
to garnish*

SERVES 4

1 Halve the orange and slice thickly. Discard any seeds and place the slices in a small pan. Cover with water, bring to the boil and simmer for 5 minutes. Drain the orange slices and set aside.

2 Pierce the skin of the duck fillets diagonally with a small knife (this will help release the fat). Rub the skin with salt.

3 Place a steel or cast-iron frying pan over a steady heat and cook the fillets for 20 minutes, turning once, until they are medium-rare. Transfer to a warm plate, cover and keep warm.

4 Heat the sediment in the frying pan until it begins to darken and caramelize. Add the dry white wine and stir constantly to loosen the sediment. Add the ground coriander, cumin or fennel seeds, sugar and orange slices.

5 Boil quickly and reduce to a coating consistency. Sharpen with the lime or lemon juice and season to taste with salt and cayenne pepper. Transfer the orange sauce to a bowl, cover and keep warm.

6 Remove the crusts from the bread and cut the bread into short fingers. Heat the garlic oil in a heavy frying pan and brown the croûtons. Season with salt, then turn out on to kitchen paper.

7 Moisten the salad leaves with a little sunflower oil and distribute them equally among four large serving plates.

8 Slice the duck diagonally with a carving knife. Divide the meat into four and lift on to each salad plate. Spoon on the orange sauce, sprinkle the salad with croûtons, decorate with a sprig of fresh coriander and serve warm.

APRICOT DUCK WITH BEANSPROUT SALAD

Duck is rich in fat, so it stays beautifully moist when cooked on a barbecue,
while any excess fat drains away.

INGREDIENTS

4 duck breast fillets, with skin
1 small red onion, thinly sliced
115g/4oz/³/4 cup ready-to-eat
dried apricots
15ml/1 tbsp clear honey
5ml/1 tsp sesame oil
10ml/2 tsp ground star anise
salt and freshly ground
black pepper

FOR THE SALAD

2 spring onions (scallions)
¹/2 head Chinese leaves (Chinese
cabbage), finely shredded
150g/5oz/2 cups beansprouts
15ml/1 tbsp light soy sauce
15ml/1 tbsp groundnut (peanut) oil
5ml/1 tsp sesame oil
5ml/1 tsp clear honey

SERVES 4

1 Place the duck breast fillets, skin side down, on a chopping board or clean work surface and cut a long slit down one side of each one with a sharp kitchen knife, cutting almost through, to form a large pocket.

2 Tuck the slices of onion and the apricots inside the pocket and press the breast firmly back into shape. Secure with metal skewers.

3 Mix together the clear honey and sesame oil and brush generously over the duck, particularly the skin. Sprinkle over the star anise and season with plenty of salt and fresh black pepper.

4 To make the salad, shred the spring onions, then mix together with the shredded Chinese leaves and beansprouts in a large bowl.

5 Shake together all the salad dressing ingredients in a screw-top jar. Season to taste with salt and pepper. Toss into the salad.

6 Cook the duck under a medium-hot grill (broiler) or on a barbecue for 12–15 minutes, turning once, until golden brown on the outside.

Cook's Tip
If you prefer not to eat the beansprouts raw, they can be blanched by plunging them into boiling water for 1 minute. Drain and refresh in cold water.

SESAME DUCK AND NOODLE SALAD

• • •

This salad is a complete meal in itself and makes a wonderful summer lunch. The marinade is a marvellous blend of South-east Asian flavours.

INGREDIENTS

2 duck breast fillets
15ml/1 tbsp sunflower oil
150g/5oz sugar snap peas
2 carrots, cut into 7.5cm/3in sticks
225g/8oz medium egg noodles
6 spring onions (scallions), sliced
salt
30ml/2 tbsp fresh coriander (cilantro) leaves,
to garnish

FOR THE MARINADE
15ml/1 tbsp sesame oil
5ml/1 tsp ground coriander
5ml/1 tsp Chinese five-spice powder

FOR THE DRESSING
15ml/1 tbsp vinegar
5ml/1 tsp soft light brown sugar
5ml/1 tsp soy sauce
1 garlic clove, crushed
15ml/1 tbsp sesame seeds, toasted
45ml/3 tbsp sunflower oil
30ml/2 tbsp sesame oil
freshly ground black pepper

SERVES 4

1 Slice the duck breast fillets thinly across and place in a shallow dish. Mix together all the ingredients for the marinade, pour over the duck and turn well to coat thoroughly. Cover with clear film (plastic wrap) and leave in a cool place for about 30 minutes.

2 Heat the oil in a frying pan, add the slices of duck and stir-fry for 3–4 minutes, until cooked. Remove from the pan and set aside.

3 Bring a pan of lightly salted water to the boil. Place the sugar snap peas and carrots in a steamer that will fit on top of the pan. When the water boils, add the noodles. Place the steamer on top and steam the vegetables while cooking the noodles.

4 Set the steamed vegetables aside. Drain the noodles, refresh under cold running water and drain again. Place them in a large serving bowl.

5 To make the dressing, mix the vinegar, sugar, soy sauce, garlic and sesame seeds in a bowl. Add a generous grinding of pepper, then whisk in the oils.

6 Pour the dressing over the egg noodles and toss well to mix. Add the sugar snap peas, carrots, spring onions and duck slices and toss again to mix. Sprinkle the fresh coriander leaves over the top and serve immediately.

GRILLED SPICED QUAIL WITH MIXED LEAF AND MUSHROOM SALAD

. . .

This is a perfect supper dish for autumnal entertaining. Quail is at its best when the breast meat is removed from the carcass, so that it cooks quickly and can be served rare.

INGREDIENTS

8 quail breast portions
50g/2oz/¼ cup butter
5ml/1 tsp paprika
salt and freshly ground
black pepper

FOR THE SALAD
60ml/4 tbsp walnut oil
30ml/2 tbsp olive oil
45ml/3 tbsp balsamic vinegar
25g/1oz/2 tbsp butter
75g/3oz/generous 1 cup chanterelle
mushrooms, sliced if large
25g/1oz/3 tbsp walnut
halves, toasted
115g/4oz mixed salad leaves

SERVES 4

1 Preheat the grill (broiler). Arrange the quail portions on the grill rack, skin sides up. Dot with half the butter and sprinkle with half the paprika and a little salt.

2 Grill (broil) the quail portions for 3 minutes. Turn and dot with the remaining butter and sprinkle with the remaining paprika and a little salt. Grill for a further 3 minutes, or until cooked. Transfer to a warmed dish, cover and set aside.

3 To make the dressing, whisk the oils with the balsamic vinegar, then season to taste with salt and pepper.

Cook's Tip

Take care when toasting the walnuts as they scorch quickly. The best way to toast them is to heat a non-stick frying pan until hot. Add the walnuts and cook for 3–5 minutes, or until golden, turning them frequently.

4 Melt the butter in a frying pan. Cook the chanterelles for about 3 minutes, or until just beginning to soften. Add the walnuts and heat through. Remove from the heat.

5 Thinly slice the cooked quail portions and arrange them on four individual serving plates with the chanterelles, walnuts and mixed salad leaves. Drizzle the oil and vinegar dressing over the salad and serve warm.

Prosciutto Salad with an Avocado Fan

. . .

Avocados are amazingly versatile, but they are at their most elegant when sliced thinly and fanned on a plate.

INGREDIENTS
3 avocados
150g/5oz prosciutto
75–115g/3–4oz rocket
(arugula) leaves
24 marinated black olives, drained

For the dressing
15ml/1 tbsp balsamic vinegar
5ml/1 tsp lemon juice
5ml/1 tsp prepared English
(hot) mustard
5ml/1 tsp sugar
75ml/5 tbsp olive oil
salt and freshly ground
black pepper

SERVES 4

1 To make the dressing, combine the balsamic vinegar, lemon juice, mustard and sugar in a bowl. Gradually whisk in the olive oil, season to taste with salt and pepper and set aside.

2 Cut two of the avocados in half. Remove and discard the stones (pits) and skins, and cut the flesh into 1cm/½in thick slices. Gently toss with half the dressing. Place the prosciutto, avocado slices and rocket leaves on four serving plates. Sprinkle the olives and the remaining dressing over the top.

3 Halve, stone (pit) and peel the remaining avocado. Slice each half lengthways into eighths. Gently draw a cannelle knife across the quarters at 1cm/½in intervals to create regular stripes.

4 Using a sharp knife, make four cuts lengthways down each avocado eighth, leaving 1cm/½in intact at the end. Carefully fan out the slices and arrange one fan on the side of each plate.

MELON AND PROSCIUTTO SALAD

· · ·

Sections of cool, fragrant melon covered with thin slices of air-dried ham – a classic appetizer.

INGREDIENTS
1 large melon (cantaloupe or Charentais)
175g/6oz prosciutto, thinly sliced

FOR THE SALSA
225g/8oz strawberries
5ml/1 tsp caster (superfine) sugar
30ml/2 tbsp sunflower oil
15ml/1 tbsp orange juice
2.5ml/½ tsp finely grated orange rind
2.5ml/½ tsp grated fresh root ginger
salt and freshly ground black pepper

SERVES 4

1 Halve the melon and take the seeds out with a spoon. Cut the rind away with a paring knife, then slice the melon flesh thickly. Cover with clear film (plastic wrap) and chill until ready to serve.

2 To make the salsa, hull the strawberries and cut them into large dice. Place in a small mixing bowl with the sugar and crush lightly to release the juices. Add the sunflower oil, orange juice and rind and ginger. Season with salt and a generous twist of pepper.

3 Arrange the melon slices on a serving plate and lay the prosciutto over the top. Serve the salsa separately in a small bowl.

WILD MUSHROOM SALAD WITH PROSCIUTTO

Autumn provides a wealth of ingredients for the salad maker. Most treasured of all are wild mushrooms, found mainly in deciduous woodland. If you are not familiar with edible species, larger supermarkets and specialist delicatessens often sell a wide range.

INGREDIENTS

175g/6oz prosciutto, thickly sliced
½ oak leaf lettuce
½ frisée lettuce
15ml/1 tbsp walnut oil
40g/1½oz/3 tbsp butter
450g/1lb wild or cultivated mushrooms such as chanterelles, field blewits, oyster mushrooms, champignons de Paris, sliced
60ml/4 tbsp brandy
salt and freshly ground black pepper

FOR THE HERB PANCAKE
45ml/3 tbsp plain (all-purpose) flour
75ml/5 tbsp milk
1 egg, plus 1 egg yolk
60ml/4 tbsp grated Parmesan cheese
45ml/3 tbsp chopped fresh mixed herbs such as parsley, thyme, tarragon, marjoram, chives

SERVES 4

1 To make the pancakes, combine the flour with the milk in a jug (pitcher). Beat in the egg and egg yolk with the Parmesan and herbs. Season with salt and pepper. Place a non-stick frying pan over a steady heat. Pour in enough batter to coat the base of the pan.

2 When the batter has set, turn the pancake over and cook briefly on the other side. Turn the pancake out and leave to cool. Continue until you have used all the batter.

3 Roll the pancakes together and cut into 1cm/½in ribbons. Cut the prosciutto into ribbons and toss with the pancake ribbons.

4 Moisten the salad leaves with the walnut oil and divide among four plates. Place the pancake and prosciutto ribbons in the centre.

5 Melt the butter in a heavy frying pan. Add the mushrooms and cook for 6–8 minutes. Add the brandy and ignite with a match or taper. When the flames have subsided, spoon the mushrooms on to the salad, season to taste with salt and pepper and serve immediately while still warm.

WARM SALAD OF BAYONNE HAM AND NEW POTATOES

∘ ∘ ∘

INGREDIENTS

*225g/8oz new potatoes, halved
if large
50g/2oz green beans
115g/4oz young spinach leaves
2 spring onions (scallions), sliced
4 eggs, hard-boiled, shelled
and quartered
50g/2oz Bayonne ham, cut
into strips
juice of ½ lemon
salt and freshly ground
black pepper*

FOR THE DRESSING
*60ml/4 tbsp olive oil
5ml/1 tsp ground turmeric
5ml/1 tsp ground cumin
50g/2oz/½ cup shelled hazelnuts*

SERVES 4

1 Cook the potatoes in salted boiling water for 10–15 minutes, or until tender, then drain well. Cook the beans in salted boiling water for 2 minutes, then drain.

2 Toss the potatoes and green beans with the spinach and spring onions in a bowl.

3 Arrange the egg quarters on the salad and sprinkle the strips of ham over the top. Sprinkle with the lemon juice and season with plenty of salt and pepper.

4 Heat the dressing ingredients in a large frying pan and cook, stirring frequently, until the nuts turn golden. Pour the hot, nutty dressing over the salad and serve before the leaves wilt.

Variation

Replace the potatoes with a 400g/14oz can drained and rinsed mixed beans and peas.

PERUVIAN SALAD

. . .

This really is a spectacular-looking salad. It could be served as a side dish or would make a delicious light lunch. In Peru, white rice would be used, but brown rice adds an interesting texture and flavour.

INGREDIENTS

225g/8oz/2 cups cooked long grain brown or white rice
15ml/1 tbsp chopped fresh parsley
1 red (bell) pepper, halved and seeded
1 small onion, sliced into rings
olive oil, for sprinkling
115g/4oz green beans, halved
50g/2oz/1/2 cup baby corn cobs
4 quail's eggs, hard-boiled
25–50g/1–2oz Spanish ham, cut into thin slices (optional)
1 small avocado
lemon juice, for sprinkling
75g/3oz mixed salad leaves
15ml/1 tbsp capers
about 10 stuffed olives, halved

FOR THE DRESSING
1 garlic clove, crushed
60ml/4 tbsp olive oil
45ml/3 tbsp sunflower oil
30ml/2 tbsp lemon juice
45ml/3 tbsp natural (plain) yogurt
2.5ml/1/2 tsp mustard
2.5ml/1/2 tsp sugar
salt and freshly ground black pepper

SERVES 4

1 To make the dressing, whisk all the ingredients in a bowl with a fork until smooth.

2 Put the rice in a large salad bowl and spoon in half the dressing. Stir in the parsley and set aside.

3 Place the pepper, cut side down, in a small roasting pan. Add the onion rings. Sprinkle the onion with a little olive oil and place the pan under a hot grill (broiler) for 5–6 minutes until the pepper blackens and blisters and the onion turns golden. Stir the onion once or twice so that it cooks evenly.

4 Stir the sliced onion into the rice. Put the pepper in a plastic bag and knot the bag. When cool enough to handle, peel the pepper halves and cut the flesh into thin strips.

5 Cook the green beans in boiling water for 2 minutes, then add the corn and cook for 1–2 minutes more, until tender. Drain, refresh under cold water, then drain again. Place the vegetables in a mixing bowl and add the pepper strips, quail's eggs and ham, if using.

6 Peel the avocado, remove the stone (pit) and cut the flesh into slices or chunks. Sprinkle with the lemon juice. Put the salad leaves in a separate mixing bowl, add the avocado and mix lightly. Arrange the mixture on top of the rice.

7 Stir about 45ml/3 tbsp of the remaining dressing into the green bean and pepper mixture. Pile this on top of the avocado mixture.

8 Sprinkle the capers and stuffed olives on top and serve the salad with the remaining dressing.

BEEF AND HERBY PASTA SALAD

∘ ∘ ∘

Marinated beef is grilled and served warm with pasta salad.

INGREDIENTS
450g/1lb beef fillet
450 g/1 lb fresh tagliatelle with
sun-dried tomatoes and herbs
115g/4oz cherry tomatoes
¹/₂ cucumber

FOR THE MARINADE
15ml/1 tbsp soy sauce
15ml/1 tbsp sherry
5ml/1 tsp grated fresh root ginger
1 garlic clove, crushed

FOR THE HERB DRESSING
30ml/2 tbsp horseradish sauce
150ml/¹/₄ pint/²/₃ cup natural
(plain) yogurt
1 garlic clove, crushed
30–45ml/2–3 tbsp chopped fresh
mixed herbs such as chives,
parsley, thyme
salt and freshly ground
black pepper

SERVES 6

1 To make the marinade, mix all the ingredients together in a shallow dish. Add the beef fillet and turn to coat well. Cover with clear film (plastic wrap) and leave in a cool place for 30 minutes to allow the flavours to penetrate the meat.

2 Preheat the grill (broiler). Lift the fillet out of the marinade and pat it dry with kitchen paper. Place the fillet on a grill (broiler) rack and grill (broil) for 8 minutes on each side, basting with the marinade.

3 Transfer the fillet to a plate, cover with foil and leave to stand for 20 minutes.

4 To make the herb dressing, put all the ingredients into a bowl and mix thoroughly. Cook the pasta in a large pan of lightly salted boiling water according to the packet instructions until it is *al dente*. Drain thoroughly, rinse under cold water and leave to dry.

5 Halve the cherry tomatoes. Cut the cucumber in half lengthways, scoop out the seeds with a teaspoon and slice the flesh thinly into crescents.

6 Put the tagliatelle, tomato halves, cucumber and dressing into a mixing bowl and toss to coat. Slice the beef and arrange on individual serving plates with the pasta salad. Serve warm.

ROCKBURGER SALAD WITH SESAME CROÛTONS

This salad plays on the ingredients that make up the all-American beefburger.

INGREDIENTS

900g/2 lb lean minced (ground) beef
1 egg
1 medium onion, finely chopped
10ml/2 tsp Dijon mustard
2.5ml/1/2 tsp celery salt
115g/4oz Roquefort or other blue cheese
1 large sesame seed loaf
45ml/3 tbsp olive oil
1 small iceberg lettuce
50g/2oz rocket (arugula) leaves
120ml/4fl oz/1/2 cup French Dressing
4 ripe tomatoes, quartered
4 spring onions (scallions), sliced
freshly ground black pepper

SERVES 4

1 Place the minced beef, egg, onion, mustard, celery salt and pepper in a mixing bowl. Combine thoroughly. Divide the mixture into 16 equal portions.

2 Flatten the pieces between two sheets of plastic or waxed paper to form 13cm/5in rounds.

3 Place 15g/1/2oz of the blue cheese on eight of the burgers. Sandwich with the remaining burgers and press the edges firmly. Stack the burgers between sheets of plastic or waxed paper and chill until ready to cook.

4 To make the sesame croûtons, preheat the grill (broiler) to a moderate temperature. Remove the sesame seed crust from the loaf, then cut the crust into short fingers. Moisten with olive oil and toast evenly for 10–15 minutes.

5 Grill (broil) the burgers at the same temperature for 10 minutes, turning once.

6 Toss the salad leaves with the French Dressing, then distribute among four large serving plates. Place two rockburgers in the centre of each plate and arrange the tomatoes, spring onions and sesame croûtons around the edge.

Cook's Tip

If you can't find a sesame seed loaf, use a French stick. Cut the stick into slices of about 1cm/1/2in, brush with olive oil and place on a baking sheet. Bake in the oven on a low heat for about 15 minutes until the bread rounds are crisp and golden.

THAI BEEF SALAD

A hearty salad of beef and crunchy vegetables, laced with a tangy chilli and lime dressing.
Cooking the meat on the barbecue would give a truly delicious flavour to the salad.

INGREDIENTS

2 sirloin steaks, about
225g/8oz each
1 red onion, thinly sliced
1/2 cucumber, thinly sliced
into batons
1 lemon grass stalk, finely chopped
30ml/2 tbsp chopped spring
onions (scallions)
juice of 2 limes
15–30ml/1–2 tbsp Thai fish sauce
2–4 red chillies, thinly sliced, fresh
coriander (cilantro), Chinese
mustard cress and mint, to garnish

SERVES 4

1 Pan-fry the beef steaks or cook on the barbecue until medium-rare. Leave the steaks to rest for 10–15 minutes.

2 When the steaks have cooled slightly, slice them thinly, using a heavy knife, and put the slices into a large bowl.

3 Add the sliced onion, cucumber batons and chopped lemon grass.

4 Add the spring onions. Toss and season with lime juice and Thai fish sauce. Serve at room temperature or chilled, garnished with the chillies, coriander, mustard cress and mint.

NEW ORLEANS STEAK SALAD

∘ ∘ ∘

The New Orleans "Poor Boy" started life in the Italian Creole community, as a sandwich filled with leftover scraps. This salad, made with tender beef steak, is a variation on the sandwich.

INGREDIENTS

4 sirloin or rump (round) steaks, about 175g/6oz each
1 escarole lettuce
1 bunch watercress
4 tomatoes, quartered
4 large gherkins, sliced
4 spring onions (scallions), sliced
4 canned artichoke hearts, halved
175g/6oz button (white) mushrooms, sliced
12 green olives
120ml/4fl oz French dressing
salt and freshly ground black pepper

SERVES 4

1 Season the steaks with plenty of black pepper and cook under a preheated hot grill (broiler) or on a hot barbecue, for 4–6 minutes, turning once, until they are medium-rare. Transfer them to a plate, cover with foil and leave the steaks to rest in a warm place.

2 Combine the salad leaves with all the ingredients except the steak, and toss with the French dressing.

3 Divide the salad between four plates. Slice each steak diagonally and arrange the slices over the salad. Season with salt and fresh black pepper and serve.

The perfect end to a summer lunch, *al fresco* supper, a barbecue or picnic, fruit salad is a favourite with young and old alike. The recipes in this chapter make full use of the massive range of fruits available, from familiar to exotic and from fresh to dried.

FRUIT SALADS

FRESH FRUIT SALAD

. . .

This basic fruit salad is always welcome, especially after a rich main course. It is endlessly adaptable – when peaches and strawberries are out of season, use bananas and grapes, or any other fruit.

INGREDIENTS
2 eating apples
2 oranges
2 peaches
16–20 strawberries
30ml/2 tbsp lemon juice
15–30ml/1–2 tbsp orange flower water
icing (confectioners') sugar
a few fresh mint leaves, to decorate

SERVES 6

1 Peel and core the apples and cut into thin slices. Peel the oranges with a sharp knife, removing all the pith, and segment them, catching the juice in a bowl.

2 Plunge the peaches for 1 minute into boiling water, peel off the skin and cut the flesh into thick slices, discarding the stone (pit).

3 Hull the strawberries and halve or quarter if larger. Place all the fruit in a large serving bowl.

4 Blend together the lemon juice, orange flower water and orange juice. Taste and add a little icing sugar to sweeten. Pour the fruit juice mixture over the salad and serve decorated with mint leaves.

DRIED FRUIT SALAD

. . .

This wonderful combination of fresh and dried fruit makes an excellent dessert throughout the year. You can use frozen raspberries and blackberries during the winter months.

INGREDIENTS
115g/4oz/½ cup dried apricots
115g/4oz/½ cup dried peaches
1 pear
1 eating apple
1 orange
115g/4oz/⅔ cup mixed raspberries and blackberries
1 cinnamon stick
50g/2oz/¼ cup caster (superfine) sugar
15ml/1 tbsp clear honey
15ml/1 tbsp lemon juice

SERVES 4

1 Soak the dried apricots and peaches in water for 1–2 hours, until plump, then drain and halve or quarter. Peel and core the pear and apple and cut into cubes.

2 Peel the orange with a sharp knife, removing all the pith, and cut into wedges. Place all the fruit in a large pan with the raspberries and blackberries.

3 Add 600ml/1 pint/2½ cups water, the cinnamon stick, sugar and honey and bring to the boil. Cover and simmer very gently for 10–12 minutes, then remove the pan from the heat.

4 Stir in the lemon juice. Leave to cool, then transfer to a bowl and chill in the refrigerator for about 1–2 hours before serving.

COOL GREEN FRUIT SALAD

• • •

A sophisticated, simple fruit salad for any time of the year.

INGREDIENTS

3 Ogen or Galia melons
115g/4oz seedless green grapes
2 kiwi fruit
1 star fruit
1 green-skinned eating apple
1 lime
175ml/6fl oz/³⁄₄ cup sparkling grape juice

SERVES 6

1 Halve the melons and remove the seeds. Keeping the shells intact, scoop out the flesh with a melon baller or use a spoon, then cut into cubes. Reserve the melon shells.

2 Remove any stems from the grapes and, if they are large, cut them in half. Peel and chop the kiwi fruit. Thinly slice the star fruit. Core and thinly slice the apple and place in a mixing bowl with the melon, grapes, kiwi fruit and star fruit.

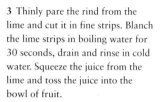

3 Thinly pare the rind from the lime and cut it in fine strips. Blanch the lime strips in boiling water for 30 seconds, drain and rinse in cold water. Squeeze the juice from the lime and toss the juice into the bowl of fruit.

4 Spoon the prepared fruit into the reserved melon shells and chill the shells in the refrigerator until required. Just before serving, spoon the sparkling grape juice over the fruit and sprinkle with the strips of lime rind.

Cook's Tip

On a hot summer's day, serve the filled melon shells nestling on a platter of crushed ice to keep them beautifully cool.

WINTER FRUIT SALAD
• • •

INGREDIENTS

225g/8oz can pineapple cubes in fruit juice
200ml/7fl oz/scant 1 cup freshly squeezed orange juice
200ml/7fl oz/scant 1 cup unsweetened apple juice
30ml/2 tbsp orange or apple liqueur
30ml/2 tbsp clear honey (optional)
2 oranges, peeled
2 green-skinned eating apples, chopped
2 pears, chopped
4 plums, stoned (pitted) and chopped
12 fresh dates, stoned (pitted) and chopped
115g/4oz/¹/₂ cup ready-to-eat dried apricots
fresh mint sprigs, to decorate

SERVES 6

1 Drain the pineapple, reserving the juice. Put the pineapple juice, orange juice, apple juice, liqueur and honey, if using, in a large serving bowl and stir.

Cook's Tip

Use other unsweetened fruit juices, such as pink grapefruit and pineapple juice, in place of the orange and apple juice.

2 Using a small sharp knife, segment the oranges, catching any juice in the bowl. Put the orange segments and pineapple in the fruit juice mixture.

3 Add the chopped apples and pears to the bowl.

4 Stir in the plums, dates and dried apricots, cover with clear film (plastic wrap) and chill in the refrigerator for several hours. Decorate with fresh mint sprigs before serving.

ITALIAN FRUIT SALAD AND ICE CREAM

In the summer in Italy, little pavement fruit stores sell small dishes of macerated soft fruits. Delectable on their own, they also make wonderful ice cream.

INGREDIENTS

900g/2lb mixed summer fruits such as strawberries, raspberries, blueberries, peaches, apricots, plums, melons
juice of 3–4 oranges
juice of 1 lemon
15ml/1 tbsp liquid pear and apple concentrate
60ml/4 tbsp whipping cream
30ml/2 tbsp orange liqueur (optional)
fresh mint sprigs, to decorate

SERVES 6

1 Prepare all the fruit according to type and then cut it into fairly small pieces.

2 Put the fruit into a serving bowl and pour over enough orange juice to cover. Add the lemon juice and chill for 2 hours.

3 Set half the macerated fruit aside to serve as it is. Process the rest in a blender or food processor to a smooth purée.

4 Gently warm the pear and apple concentrate and stir into the fruit purée. Whip the cream and fold it in, then add the liqueur, if using.

5 Churn the mixture in an ice-cream maker, following the manufacturer's instructions, or place it in a freezerproof container. Freeze until ice crystals form around the edge, then beat the mixture until smooth.

6 Repeat the process once or twice, then freeze until firm.

7 Transfer the ice cream to the refrigerator to soften slightly before serving in scoops, with the fruit, decorated with sprigs of mint.

Cook's Tip

The macerated fruit also makes a delicious drink. Purée in a blender or food processor, then press through a sieve.

WATERMELON, GINGER AND GRAPEFRUIT SALAD

This pretty, pink combination is very light and refreshing for any summer meal.

INGREDIENTS

450g/1lb/2 cups watermelon flesh
2 ruby or pink grapefruit
2 pieces preserved stem ginger and 30ml/2 tbsp of the syrup

SERVES 4

1 Remove any seeds from the watermelon and cut the flesh into bitesize chunks.

2 Using a small, sharp knife, cut away all the peel and white pith from the grapefruit. Carefully cut between the membranes and lift out the segments, catching any juice in a bowl.

Cook's Tip

Toss the fruits gently – grapefruit segments will break up easily and the appearance of the dish will be spoiled.

3 Finely chop the stem ginger and place in a serving bowl with the melon cubes and grapefruit segments, adding the reserved juice.

4 Spoon over the ginger syrup and toss the fruits lightly to mix. Cover with clear film (plastic wrap) and chill before serving.

FRESH FRUIT WITH MANGO COULIS

° ° °

This bright, flavourful sauce is easy to prepare and ideal for making a simple fruit salad seem special.

INGREDIENTS

1 large ripe mango, peeled, stoned (pitted) and chopped
rind of 1 unwaxed orange
juice of 3 oranges
caster (superfine) sugar, to taste
2 peaches
2 nectarines
1 small mango, peeled
2 plums
1 pear or ½ small melon
juice of 1 lemon
25–50g/1–2oz/heaped tbsp wild strawberries (optional)
25–50g/1–2oz/ heaped tbsp raspberries
25–50g/1–2oz/ heaped tbsp blueberries
small fresh mint sprigs, to decorate

SERVES 6

1 In a food processor fitted with a metal blade, process the large mango until smooth. Add the orange rind and juice and sugar to taste and process again until very smooth. Press through a sieve into a bowl and chill.

2 Slice and stone (pit) the peaches, nectarines, small mango and plums. Quarter the pear and remove the core or, if using, slice the melon thinly and remove the skin.

3 Place the sliced fruits on a large plate, sprinkle with the lemon juice, cover with clear film (plastic wrap) and chill in the refrigerator for up to 3 hours before serving. (Some fruits discolour if cut too far ahead of time.)

4 To serve, arrange the sliced fruits attractively on serving plates, spoon the berries on top, drizzle with a little mango coulis and decorate with mint sprigs. Serve the remaining coulis separately.

FRUITS-OF-THE-TROPICS SALAD

. . .

INGREDIENTS

1 medium pineapple
400g/14oz can guava halves
in syrup
2 medium bananas, sliced
1 large mango, peeled, stoned
(pitted) and diced
115g/4oz preserved stem ginger
and 30ml/2 tbsp of the syrup
60ml/4 tbsp thick coconut milk
10ml/2 tsp sugar
2.5ml/½ tsp grated nutmeg
2.5ml/½ tsp ground cinnamon
strips of coconut,
to decorate

SERVES 4–6

1 Peel, core and cube the pineapple, and place in a serving bowl. Drain the guavas, reserving the syrup, and chop. Add the guavas to the bowl with one of the bananas and the mango.

2 Chop the stem ginger and add to the pineapple mixture.

3 Pour the 30ml/2 tbsp of the ginger syrup and the reserved guava syrup into a blender or food processor and add the remaining banana, the coconut milk and the sugar. Process to make a smooth, creamy purée.

4 Pour the banana and coconut purée over the fruit and add a little grated nutmeg and a sprinkling of cinnamon on top. Cover with clear film (plastic wrap) and chill before serving, decorated with strips of coconut.

481

EXOTIC FRUIT SALAD

A variety of fruits, depending on what is available, can be used for this salad. Look for mandarins, star fruit, papaya, physalis and passion fruit.

INGREDIENTS

75g/3oz/scant ½ cup sugar
30ml/2 tbsp preserved stem
ginger syrup
2 pieces star anise
2.5cm/1in cinnamon stick
1 clove
juice of ½ lemon
2 fresh mint sprigs
1 mango
2 bananas
8 lychees, fresh or canned
225g/8oz/2 cups strawberries
2 pieces stem ginger, cut into sticks
1 medium pineapple

SERVES 4

3 With a long, sharp knife, cut the pineapple in half lengthways down the centre. Loosen the flesh with a small, serrated knife and remove to form two boat shapes. Cut the pineapple flesh into large chunks and place in the cooled syrup.

4 Spoon the fruit salad carefully into the pineapple halves and bring to the table on a large serving platter or board. There will be enough fruit salad left over to refill both the pineapple halves for a second serving.

1 Place the sugar in a pan and add 300ml/½ pint/1¼ cups water, the ginger syrup, spices, lemon juice and mint. Bring to the boil and simmer for 3 minutes. Strain into a large bowl.

2 Remove both the top and bottom from the mango and remove the outer skin. Stand the mango on one end and remove the flesh in two pieces either side of the flat stone (pit). Slice evenly and add to the syrup. Add the bananas, lychees, strawberries and ginger. Chill until ready to serve.

MELON AND STRAWBERRY SALAD

A beautiful and colourful fruit salad, this is equally suitable to serve as a refreshing appetizer or to round off a meal.

INGREDIENTS

1 Galia or ogen melon
1 honeydew melon
½ watermelon
225g/8oz/2 cups strawberries
15ml/1 tbsp lemon juice
15ml/1 tbsp clear honey
15ml/1 tbsp chopped fresh mint
1 fresh mint sprig (optional)

SERVES 4

1 Prepare the melons by cutting them in half and discarding the seeds. Use a melon baller to scoop out the flesh into balls or use a knife to cut it into cubes. Place these in a fruit bowl.

2 Rinse and hull the strawberries, cut in half and add to the melon balls or cubes.

Cook's Tip

Use whichever melons are available: replace Galia with cantaloupe or watermelon with Charentais, for example. Try to choose three melons with a variation in colour for an attractive effect.

---

3 Mix together the lemon juice and honey and add 15ml/1 tbsp water to make it easier to spoon over the fruit. Mix into the fruit gently.

4 Sprinkle the chopped mint over the top of the fruit. Serve the fruit salad decorated with the mint sprig, if you like.

BLUEBERRY, ORANGE AND LAVENDER SALAD

• • •

*Delicate blueberries feature in a
simple salad of sharp oranges
and sweet little meringues.*

INGREDIENTS

6 oranges
350g/12oz/3 cups blueberries
8 fresh lavender sprigs, to decorate

FOR THE MERINGUE
2 egg whites
*115g/4oz/generous ½ cup caster
(superfine) sugar*
5ml/1 tsp fresh lavender flowers

SERVES 4

1 Preheat the oven to 140°C/
275°F/Gas 1. Line a baking sheet
with six layers of newspaper and
cover with baking parchment. To
make the meringue, whisk the egg
whites in a large mixing bowl until
they hold their weight on the
whisk. Add the sugar, a little at a
time, whisking thoroughly before
each addition. Gently fold in the
lavender flowers.

2 Spoon the lavender meringue
into a piping (pastry) bag fitted
with a 5mm/¼in plain nozzle. Pipe
as many small buttons of meringue
on to the prepared baking sheet as
you can fit in. Dry the meringues
near the bottom of the oven for
1½–2 hours.

3 To segment the oranges, remove
the peel from the top, bottom and
sides with a small, sharp, serrated
knife. Loosen the segments by
cutting with a paring knife between
the flesh and the membranes,
holding the fruit over a bowl to
catch the juice.

4 Arrange the orange segments
decoratively on four plates.

5 Combine the blueberries with the
lavender meringues and pile in the
centre of each serving plate.
Decorate with sprigs of lavender
and serve immediately.

FRESH FIG, APPLE AND DATE SALAD

Sweet figs and dates combine well with crisp apples. A hint of almond unites the flavours.

INGREDIENTS

6 large eating apples
juice of ½ lemon
175g/6oz/generous 1 cup fresh dates
25g/1oz white marzipan
5ml/1 tsp orange flower water
60ml/4 tbsp natural (plain) yogurt
4 ripe green or purple figs
4 almonds, toasted

SERVES 4

1 Core the apples. Slice thinly, then cut into fine batons. Moisten with lemon juice to prevent them from turning brown.

2 Remove the stones (pits) from the dates and cut the flesh into fine strips, then combine them with the apple slices.

3 Soften the marzipan with the orange flower water and combine with the yogurt. Mix well.

4 Pile the apples and dates in the centre of four serving plates. Remove the stem from each of the figs and divide the fruit into quarters without cutting right through the base. Squeeze the base with the thumb and forefinger of both hands to open up the fig.

5 Place a fig in the centre of each fruit salad, spoon in the yogurt filling. Decorate with a toasted almond and serve.

BLACKBERRY SALAD WITH ROSE GRANITA

INGREDIENTS
*150g/5oz/²/₃ cup caster
(superfine) sugar
1 fresh red rose, petals
removed and
finely chopped
5ml/1 tsp rose water
10ml/2 tsp lemon juice
450g/1lb/2²/₃ cups blackberries
icing (confectioners') sugar,
for dusting
fresh rose petals,
to decorate*

FOR THE MERINGUE
*2 egg whites
115g/4oz/generous ½ cup caster
(superfine) sugar*

SERVES 4

1 To make the granita, bring 150ml/¹/₄ pint/²/₃ cup water to the boil in a stainless-steel or enamel pan. Add the sugar and rose petals, then simmer for 5 minutes.

2 Strain the syrup into a deep metal tray, add a further 450ml/³/₄ pint/scant 2 cups water, the rose water and lemon juice and leave to cool. Freeze the mixture for about 3 hours, or until solid.

3 Meanwhile preheat the oven to 140°C/275°F/Gas 1. Line a large baking sheet with six layers of newspaper and then cover with baking parchment.

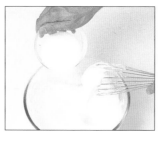

4 To make the meringue, whisk the egg whites until they hold their weight on the whisk. Add the caster sugar, a little at a time, and whisk until firm.

Cook's Tips

Blackberries are widely cultivated from late spring to autumn and are usually large, plump and sweet. The finest wild blackberries have a bitter edge and a strong depth of flavour – best appreciated with a sprinkling of sugar.

Make sure that the rose petals are free of pollution, pesticides and any other chemicals.

5 Spoon the meringue into a piping (pastry) bag fitted with a 1cm/¹/₂in plain nozzle. Pipe the meringue in lengths across the parchment-lined baking sheet. Dry the meringue near the bottom of the oven for 1¹/₂–2 hours.

6 Break the meringue into 5cm/2in lengths and place three or four pieces on each of four large serving plates. Pile the blackberries next to the meringue.

7 With a tablespoon, scrape the granita finely. Shape into ovals and place over the meringue. Dust with icing sugar, decorate with rose petals, and serve immediately.

RASPBERRIES WITH MANGO CUSTARD

· · ·

*Sharp, fresh raspberries unite
with a fragrant mango custard.*

INGREDIENTS

*1 large mango
3 egg yolks
30ml/2 tbsp caster
(superfine) sugar
10ml/2 tsp cornflour (cornstarch)
200ml/7fl oz/scant 1 cup milk
8 fresh mint sprigs, to decorate*

FOR THE RASPBERRY SAUCE
*450g/1lb/2²/₃ cups raspberries
45ml/3 tbsp caster
(superfine) sugar*

SERVES 4

1 To prepare the mango, remove
the top and bottom with a serrated
knife. Cut away the outer skin,
then remove the flesh by cutting
either side of the flat central stone
(pit). Reserve half of the mango
flesh for decoration and coarsely
chop the remainder.

Cook's Tip

Mangoes are ripe when they
yield to gentle pressure. Some
varieties show a red-gold or
yellow flush when they are
ready to eat.

2 For the custard, combine the egg
yolks, sugar, cornflour and 30ml/
2 tbsp of the milk to a smooth
paste in a small bowl.

3 Rinse out a small pan with cold
water to prevent the milk from
catching. Pour the rest of the milk
into the pan, bring to the boil and
pour it over the ingredients in the
bowl, stirring evenly.

4 Strain the mixture through a
sieve back into the pan, stir to
simmering point and cook until the
mixture has thickened.

5 Pour the custard into a food
processor, add the chopped mango
and blend until smooth. Leave the
custard to cool.

6 To make the raspberry sauce,
place 350g/12oz/2 cups of the
raspberries in a stain-resistant pan.
Add the sugar, soften over a gentle
heat and simmer for 5 minutes.
Rub the fruit through a fine nylon
sieve to remove the seeds. Set aside
to cool.

7 Spoon the raspberry sauce and
mango custard into two pools on
four serving plates. Slice the
reserved mango and fan out
or arrange in a pattern over the
raspberry sauce. Sprinkle the
remaining raspberries over the
mango custard. Decorate each
plate with two sprigs of mint
and serve immediately.

Variation

Substitute loganberries or
tayberries for the raspberries.

PINEAPPLE CRUSH WITH STRAWBERRIES AND LYCHEES

The sweet, tropical flavours of pineapple and lychees combine well with aromatic strawberries.

INGREDIENTS

2 small pineapples
450g/1lb/4 cups strawberries
400g/14oz can lychees
45ml/3 tbsp kirsch or white rum
30ml/2 tbsp icing (confectioners') sugar

SERVES 4

1 Remove the crowns from both pineapples by twisting sharply. Reserve the leaves for decoration.

2 Cut both pineapples in half diagonally using a long-bladed, serrated knife.

3 Cut around the flesh inside the skin of all the pineapple halves with a small, sharp, serrated knife, keeping the skin intact. Remove the core from the pineapple and discard. Chop the flesh. Reserve the skins.

4 Hull the strawberries and gently combine with the pineapple and lychees, taking care not to damage the fruit.

5 Mix the kirsch or rum with the icing sugar, pour over the fruit and freeze for 45 minutes.

6 Turn out the fruit into the pineapple skins, decorate with the reserved pineapple leaves and serve immediately.

Variation

Try using sapodillas instead of lychees in this recipe. Make sure that they are really ripe or they will be horrible.

Cook's Tip

A ripe pineapple will resist pressure when squeezed and will have a sweet, fragrant smell. In winter freezing conditions can cause the flesh to blacken.

MUSCAT GRAPE FRAPPÉ

● ● ●

The flavour and perfume of the Muscat grape is rarely more enticing than when captured in this sophisticated, icy-cool salad. Because of its alcohol content this dish is not suitable for young children.

INGREDIENTS

½ bottle Muscat wine, Beaumes de Venise, Frontignan or Rivesaltes
450g/1lb Muscat grapes

SERVES 4

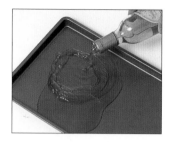

1 Pour the wine into a stainless-steel or enamel tray, add 150ml/ ¼ pint/⅔ cup water, mix well and freeze for for about 3 hours, or until the wine is completely solid.

2 Remove the seeds from the grapes with a pair of tweezers. If you have time, you can also peel the grapes. Scrape across the frozen wine with a tablespoon to make a fine ice. Combine the grapes with the ice, spoon into four shallow glasses and serve immediately.

GRAPEFRUIT SALAD WITH CAMPARI AND ORANGE

*The bitter-sweet flavour of
Campari combines especially
well with citrus fruit, such as
grapefruit and oranges. Because
of its alcohol content, this dish
is not suitable for young children.*

INGREDIENTS

*45ml/3 tbsp caster
(superfine) sugar
60ml/4 tbsp Campari
30ml/2 tbsp lemon juice
4 grapefruit
5 oranges
4 fresh mint sprigs, to decorate*

SERVES 4

1 Bring 150ml/¼ pint/⅔ cup water
to the boil in a small pan, add the
sugar and simmer until dissolved.
Transfer to a bowl; leave to cool.

2 Add the Campari and lemon
juice to the syrup and stir well to
mix. Cut the peel from the top,
bottom and sides of the grapefruit
and oranges with a serrated knife.
Segment the fruit into a bowl by
slipping a small paring knife
between the flesh and the
membranes. Combine the fruit
with the Campari syrup, cover with
clear film (plastic wrap) and chill
until ready to serve.

3 Spoon the salad into four dishes,
decorate with a sprig of fresh mint
and serve.

Cook's Tip

When buying citrus fruit,
choose brightly coloured
varieties that feel heavy for
their size.

DRESSED STRAWBERRIES

∘ ∘ ∘

INGREDIENTS

350g/12oz/2 cups raspberries or
tayberries, fresh
or frozen
45ml/3 tbsp caster
(superfine) sugar
1 passion fruit
675g/1½lb/6 cups small
fresh strawberries
8 plain finger
biscuits (cookies),
to serve

SERVES 4

4 Pass the blended fruit sauce through a fine nylon sieve to remove the seeds, pressing it through with the back of a spoon.

5 Fold the strawberries into the sauce, then spoon into four stemmed glasses. Serve with plain finger biscuits.

1 Place the raspberries or tayberries and sugar in a stain-resistant pan and soften over a gentle heat to release the juices. Simmer for 5 minutes. Leave to cool.

2 Halve the passion fruit and scoop out the seeds and juice.

3 Turn the raspberries or tayberries into a food processor or blender, add the passion fruit and process until a smooth purée forms.

494

MIXED MELON SALAD WITH WILD STRAWBERRIES

• • •

Ice-cold melon is a delicious way to end a meal. Here several varieties are combined with strongly flavoured wild or woodland strawberries.

INGREDIENTS

1 Charentais melon
1 cantaloupe melon
900g/2lb watermelon
175g/6oz/1½ cups wild
strawberries
4 fresh mint sprigs, to decorate

SERVES 4

1 Cut all the melons in half using a large knife.

2 Remove the seeds from the Charentais and cantaloupe melons with a spoon.

3 With a melon baller, take out as many balls as you can from all three melons. Combine in a large bowl, cover with clear film (plastic wrap) and chill in the refrigerator until ready to serve.

4 Add the wild strawberries to the melon balls and turn out into four stemmed glass dishes.

5 Decorate with sprigs of fresh mint and serve while still very cold and refreshing.

FRUIT KEBABS WITH MANGO AND YOGURT SAUCE

This colourful dessert is ideal for a party.

INGREDIENTS
*½ pineapple, peeled, cored
and cubed
2 kiwi fruit, peeled and cubed
150g/5oz/scant 1 cup strawberries,
hulled and cut in half lengthways
½ mango, peeled, stoned (pitted)
and cubed*

FOR THE SAUCE
*120ml/4fl oz/½ cup fresh
mango purée
120ml/4fl oz/½ cup thick natural
(plain) yogurt
5ml/1 tsp sugar
few drops of vanilla
essence (extract)
15ml/1 tbsp finely shredded fresh
mint leaves
1 fresh mint sprig, to decorate*

SERVES 4

1 To make the sauce, beat together the mango purée, natural yogurt, sugar and vanilla with an electric hand mixer.

2 Stir in the shredded mint. Cover the sauce and chill until required.

Cook's Tip
Use 1–1½ peeled and stoned (pitted) mangoes for the purée.

3 Thread the fruit on to twelve 15cm/6in wooden skewers, alternating the pineapple, kiwi fruit, strawberries and mango.

4 Transfer the mango and yogurt sauce to an attractive bowl, decorate with a mint sprig and place in the centre of a large serving platter. Surround with the kebabs and serve.

TROPICAL FRUITS IN CINNAMON SYRUP

These glistening fruits are best prepared a day in advance to allow the flavours to develop and mingle.

INGREDIENTS
*450g/1lb/2¼ cups caster
(superfine) sugar
1 cinnamon stick
1 large or 2 medium papayas
(about 675g/1½lb), peeled, seeded
and cut lengthways into thin pieces
1 large or 2 medium mangoes
(about 675 g/1½lb) peeled, stoned
(pitted) and cut lengthways into
thin pieces
1 large or 2 small star fruit (about
225g/8oz) thinly sliced*

SERVES 6

1 Sprinkle about one-third of the sugar over the base of a large, heavy pan. Add the cinnamon stick and half of the papaya, mango and star fruit pieces.

2 Sprinkle half of the remaining sugar over the fruit pieces in the pan. Add the remaining papaya, mango and star fruit and sprinkle with the remaining sugar.

3 Cover the pan and cook the fruit over medium heat for about 35–45 minutes, until the sugar dissolves completely. Gently shake the pan occasionally, but do not stir or the fruit will collapse and become soggy.

4 Uncover the pan and simmer for about 10 minutes, until the fruit becomes translucent. Remove the pan from the heat and leave to cool. Discard the cinnamon stick.

5 Transfer the fruit and syrup to a bowl, cover and chill overnight before serving.

BANANA AND MASCARPONE

• • •

*If you are a fan of cold banana
custard, you'll love this recipe.
It is an adult version of an old
favourite. No one will guess
that the secret is ready-made
custard sauce.*

INGREDIENTS

*250g/9oz/generous 1 cup
mascarpone cheese
300ml/½ pint/1¼ cups fresh
ready-made custard sauce
150ml/¼ pint/⅔ cup Greek
(US strained plain) yogurt
4 bananas
juice of 1 lime
50 g/2oz/½ cup pecan nuts,
coarsely chopped
120ml/4fl oz/½ cup maple syrup*

SERVES 4–6

1 Combine the mascarpone,
custard sauce and yogurt in a
large bowl and beat together with
a wooden spoon until smooth.
Make this mixture up to several
hours ahead, if you like. Cover
and chill, then stir before using.

2 Slice the bananas diagonally and
place in a separate bowl. Pour over
the lime juice and toss together
until the bananas are coated.

3 Divide half the custard mixture
among four to six dessert glasses
and top each portion with a
spoonful of the banana mixture.

4 Spoon the remaining custard
mixture into the glasses and top
with the rest of the bananas.
Sprinkle the nuts over the top.
Drizzle maple syrup over each
dessert and chill for 30 minutes
before serving.

BANANAS WITH LIME AND CARDAMOM

• • •

*Cardamom and bananas go
together perfectly, and this
luxurious dessert makes an
original treat.*

INGREDIENTS

*6 small bananas
50g/2oz/¼ cup butter
seeds from 4 cardamom
pods, crushed
50g/2oz/½ cup flaked
(sliced) almonds
thinly pared rind and juice
of 2 limes
50g/2oz/⅓ cup light muscovado
(brown) sugar
30ml/2 tbsp dark rum
vanilla ice cream, to serve*

SERVES 4

1 Peel and halve the bananas
lengthways. Heat half the butter in
a frying pan. Add half the bananas
and cook until the undersides are
golden. Turn carefully, using a fish
slice (metal spatula). Cook until
golden all over.

2 Once cooked, transfer the
bananas to a heatproof serving
dish. Cook the remaining bananas
in the same way.

3 Melt the remaining butter, then
add the cardamom seeds and
almonds. Cook, stirring until the
almonds are golden.

4 Stir in the lime rind and juice,
then the sugar. Cook, stirring, until
the mixture is smooth, bubbling
and slightly reduced. Stir in the
rum. Pour the sauce over the
bananas and serve immediately,
with vanilla ice cream.

Melon Trio with Ginger Biscuits

• • •

INGREDIENTS

¼ watermelon
½ honeydew melon
½ charentais melon
60ml/4 tbsp preserved stem
ginger syrup

For the biscuits (cookies)
25g/1oz/2 tbsp unsalted
(sweet) butter
25g/1oz/2 tbsp caster
(superfine) sugar
5ml/1 tsp clear honey
25g/1oz/¼ cup plain (all-
purpose) flour
25g/1oz/¼ cup luxury glacé
(candied) mixed fruit,
finely chopped
1 piece of preserved stem ginger in
syrup, drained and
finely chopped
30ml/2 tbsp flaked
(sliced) almonds

Serves 4

1 Using a spoon, remove the seeds from the melons and discard. Cut them into wedges, then slice off the rind. Cut all the flesh into chunks and mix in a bowl. Stir in the ginger syrup, cover with clear film (plastic wrap) and chill until ready to serve.

2 Meanwhile, make the biscuits. Preheat the oven to 180°C/350°F/Gas 4. Heat the butter, sugar and honey in a pan until melted. Remove from the heat and stir in the remaining ingredients.

3 Line a baking sheet with baking parchment. Space four spoonfuls of the biscuit mixture on the parchment at regular intervals, leaving plenty of room for spreading. Flatten the mixture slightly into rounds and bake for 15 minutes or until the tops are golden brown.

4 Let the biscuits cool on the baking sheet for 1 minute, then lift each one in turn, using a fish slice (metal spatula), and drape over a rolling pin to cool and harden. Repeat with the remaining ginger mixture to make eight biscuits.

5 Serve the chilled melon chunks with some of the syrup and the ginger biscuits.

Cook's Tip
For an even prettier effect, scoop the melon flesh into balls with the large end of a melon baller.

JAMAICAN FRUIT TRIFLE
<small>◦ ◦ ◦</small>

INGREDIENTS

*1 large sweet pineapple,
peeled and cored,
about 350g/12oz*
*300ml/¹/₂ pint/1¹/₄ cups double
(heavy) cream*
*200ml/7fl oz/scant 1 cup
crème fraîche*
*60ml/4 tbsp icing (confectioners')
sugar, sifted*
*10ml/2 tsp pure vanilla
essence (extract)*
30ml/2 tbsp white or coconut rum
*3 papayas, peeled, seeded
and chopped*
*3 mangoes, peeled, stoned (pitted)
and chopped*
*thinly pared rind and juice
of 1 lime*
*25g/1oz/¹/₃ cup coarsely shredded
or flaked coconut, toasted*

SERVES 8

1 Cut the pineapple into large chunks, place in a food processor or blender and process briefly until chopped. Tip into a sieve placed over a bowl and leave for about 5 minutes so that most of the juice drains from the fruit.

2 Whip the double cream to very soft peaks, then lightly, but thoroughly fold in the crème fraîche, sifted icing sugar, vanilla essence and rum.

3 Fold the drained, chopped pineapple into the cream mixture. Place the chopped papayas and mangoes in a large bowl and pour over the lime juice. Gently stir the fruit mixture to combine. Cut the pared lime rind into thin shreds and add it to the bowl.

4 Divide the fruit mixture and the pineapple cream among eight dessert plates. Decorate with the lime shreds, toasted coconut and a few small pineapple leaves, if you like, and serve immediately.

Cook's Tip

It is important to let the pineapple purée drain thoroughly, otherwise the pineapple cream will be watery. Don't throw away the drained pineapple juice – mix it with sparkling mineral water for a refreshing drink.

TROPICAL FRUIT GRATIN

. . .

This out-of-the-ordinary gratin is strictly for adults. A colourful combination of fruit is topped with a simple sabayon before being flashed under the grill.

INGREDIENTS

2 tamarillos
1/2 sweet pineapple
1 ripe mango
175g/6oz/1½ cups blackberries
120ml/4fl oz/½ cup sparkling white wine
115g/4oz/½ cup caster (superfine) sugar
6 egg yolks

SERVES 4

1 Cut each tamarillo in half lengthways and then into thick slices. Cut the rind and core from the pineapple and take spiral slices off the outside to remove the eyes. Cut the flesh into chunks. Peel the mango, cut it in half and cut the flesh away from the central stone (pit) in slices.

2 Divide all the fruit, including the blackberries, among four 14cm/ 5½in gratin dishes set on a baking sheet and set aside. Heat the wine and sugar in a pan until the sugar has dissolved. Bring to the boil and cook for 5 minutes.

3 Put the egg yolks in a heatproof bowl. Set the bowl over a pan of simmering water and whisk until pale. Gradually pour in the hot sugar syrup, whisking constantly, until the mixture has thickened. Preheat the grill (broiler).

4 Spoon the mixture over the fruit. Place the baking sheet on a low shelf under the hot grill until the topping is golden. Serve hot.

GRILLED PINEAPPLE WITH PAPAYA SAUCE

. . .

Pineapple cooked this way takes on a superb flavour and is sensational when served with the papaya sauce.

INGREDIENTS

1 sweet pineapple
melted butter, for greasing and brushing
2 pieces drained preserved stem ginger in syrup, cut into fine batons, plus 30ml/2 tbsp of the syrup from the jar
30ml/2 tbsp demerara (raw) sugar
pinch of ground cinnamon
fresh mint sprigs, to decorate

FOR THE SAUCE
1 ripe papaya, peeled and seeded
175ml/6fl oz/¾ cup apple juice

SERVES 6

1 Peel the pineapple and take spiral slices off the outside to remove the eyes. Cut it crossways into six slices, each 2.5cm/1in thick. Line a baking sheet with a sheet of foil, rolling up the sides to make a rim. Grease the foil with melted butter. Preheat the grill (broiler).

2 Arrange the pineapple slices on the lined baking sheet. Brush with butter, then top with the ginger batons, sugar and cinnamon. Drizzle over the stem ginger syrup. Grill (broil) for 5–7 minutes or until the slices are golden and lightly charred on top.

3 Meanwhile, make the sauce. Cut a few slices from the papaya and set aside, then purée the remainder with the apple juice in a blender or food processor.

4 Press the purée through a sieve placed over a bowl, then stir in any juices from cooking the pineapple.

5 Serve the pineapple slices with a little sauce drizzled around each plate. Decorate with the reserved papaya slices and the mint sprigs.

CITRUS FRUIT FLAMBÉ

. . .

*A fruit flambé is a dramatic
finale for a dinner party.*

INGREDIENTS

*4 oranges
2 ruby grapefruit
2 limes
50g/2oz/¼ cup butter
50g/2oz/⅓ cup light muscovado
(brown) sugar
45ml/3 tbsp Cointreau
fresh mint sprigs, to decorate*

FOR THE PRALINE
*oil, for greasing
115g/4oz/½ cup caster
(superfine) sugar
50g/2oz/½ cup shelled
pistachio nuts*

SERVES 4

1 First, make the pistachio praline.
Brush a baking sheet lightly with
oil. Place the caster sugar and nuts
in a small heavy pan and cook over
a low heat, gently swirling the pan
occasionally until the sugar has
completely melted.

2 Continue to cook over a fairly
low heat until the nuts start to pop
and the sugar has turned a dark
golden colour. Pour on to the oiled
baking sheet and set aside to cool.
Using a sharp knife, chop the
praline into coarse chunks.

3 Cut all the rind and pith from
the citrus fruits. Holding each fruit
in turn over a large bowl, cut
between the membranes with a
paring knife so that the segments
fall into the bowl, with any juice.

4 Heat the butter and muscovado
sugar together in a heavy frying
pan until the sugar has melted and
the mixture is golden. Strain the
orange, grapefruit and lime juices
into the pan and continue to cook,
stirring occasionally, until the juice
has reduced and is syrupy.

5 Add the fruit segments and warm
through without stirring. Pour over
the Cointreau and set it alight. As
soon as the flames die down, spoon
the fruit flambé into serving dishes.
Sprinkle some praline over each
portion and decorate with mint.

Cook's Tip
Cointreau is the best-known
brand name of an orange-
flavoured liqueur, generically
known as triple sec.

EXOTIC TROPICAL FRUIT SALAD

*Passion fruit makes a superb
dressing for any kinds of fruit,
but really brings out the flavour
of exotic varieties.*

INGREDIENTS

*1 mango
1 papaya
2 kiwi fruit
coconut or vanilla ice cream,
to serve*

FOR THE DRESSING
*3 passion fruit
thinly pared rind and juice of 1 lime
5ml/1 tsp hazelnut or walnut oil
15ml/1 tbsp clear honey*

SERVES 6

1 Peel the mango, cut it into three
slices, then cut the flesh into
chunks and place it in a large bowl.
Peel the papaya and cut it in half.
Scoop and discard out the seeds,
then chop the flesh.

Cook's Tip

A clear golden honey scented
with orange blossom or acacia
blossom would be perfect for
the dressing.

---

2 Cut both ends off each kiwi fruit,
then stand them on a board. Using
a small sharp knife, cut off the skin
from top to bottom. Cut each kiwi
fruit in half lengthways, then cut
into thick slices. Combine all the
fruit in a large bowl.

3 Make the dressing. Cut each
passion fruit in half and scoop the
seeds out into a sieve set over a
small bowl. Press the seeds well to
extract all their juices. Lightly
whisk the remaining dressing
ingredients into the passion fruit
juice, then pour the dressing over
the fruit. Mix gently to combine.
Cover and chill for 1 hour before
serving with scoops of coconut or
vanilla ice cream.

INDEX

• • •